THE PRESTES COLUMN

THE PRESTES COLUMN

An Interior History of Modern Brazil

JACOB BLANC

Duke University Press   *Durham and London*   2024

Project Editor: Ihsan Taylor
Typeset in Warnock Pro by Westchester Publishing Services

Library of Congress Cataloging-in-Publication Data
Names: Blanc, Jacob, author.
Title: The Prestes column : an interior history of modern Brazil /
Jacob Blanc.
Description: Durham : Duke University Press, 2024. | Includes
bibliographical references and index. | Contents: Rebellion and
the Backlands—The Accidental March—Bandeirantes of
Freedom—Competing Visions of the Sertão—Bandeirantes in
Bahia—Mapping a Myth—Constructing the Knight of Hope—
Political Conflict and the Spatial Legacies of Tenentismo—
Visions of the Future: Culture and Commemoration—Memory
Battles at the Turn of the Century—Memory Sites in the Interior.
Identifiers: LCCN 2023020177 (print)
LCCN 2023020178 (ebook)
ISBN 9781478030089 (paperback)
ISBN 9781478025825 (hardcover)
ISBN 9781478059080 (ebook)
ISBN 9781478091721 (ebook other)
Subjects: LCSH: Prestes, Luís Carlos, 1898–1990. | Coluna
Prestes (Revolutionary movement)—History. | Brazil— History
—1889–1930. | Brazil—Politics and government— 1922–1930. |
BISAC: HISTORY / Latin America / South America
Classification: LCC F2537 .B536 2024 (print) | LCC F2537
(ebook) | DDC 981/.05—dc23/eng/20231018
LC recordavailableathttps:// lccn.loc.gov/2023020177
LC ebook recordavailableathttps:// lccn.loc.gov/2023020178

Cover art: Newspaper images compiled from the Hemeroteca
Digital, Biblioteca Nacional do Brasil.

The author was supported by the Arts and Humanities Research
Council Fellowship no. AH/T010711/1, and this title is freely
available in an open access edition thanks to the generous support from the UKRI Open Access block grant.

As explained in the book, there are a variety of terms associated with the spaces and historical figures of Brazil's interior regions. These include:

SERTÃO: originally a reference to the unmappable expanses of Brazil's non-coastal areas, *sertão* has become a term most commonly associated with the semiarid regions of the northeastern interior.

CORONEL (plural: *coronéis*): the rural oligarchs and large landowners who held great power in the interior, often buttressed by connections to elected officials in state capitals.

JAGUNÇO: contracted fighters, often hired by coronéis.

BATALHÃO PATRIÓTICA: local militias organized by the coronéis to hunt down the Prestes Column.

CANGACEIRO (noun form as a process/historical phenomenon: *cangaço*): bandits and outlaws who roamed the interior. Brazil's most famous canga-ceiro was Lampião, who makes an appearance in chapter 4 of this book.

TENENTISMO: the umbrella term for the loose coalition of opposition groups who organized against the presidents and allied power brokers of the Old Republic. Those who belonged to this movement came to be known as *tenentes* (lieutenants).

REBELDES, REVOLTOSOS, or SEDICIOSOS: the most commonly used phrases at the time to describe the tenentes who took up arms against the government. In this book, I often translate *rebeldes*, *revoltosos*, and *sediciosos* as *rebels*.

GAÚCHO: a term for people from the southern state of Rio Grande do Sul. Of note, *gaucho* (with an unaccented *u*) refers more specifically to the rural/ranch culture of Rio Grande do Sul, often as a term for cowboys from the southern frontier.

For consistency, I choose to spell Prestes's first name as Luís Carlos, although it is sometimes spelled with a *z*—Luiz Carlos. And, although I capitalize "Prestes Column" when referring to its formal name, I use the lowercase "column" when I don't include "Prestes."

I refer to the tenente leaders by the names most commonly associated with them. For example, Miguel Costa is referred to by his full name; Lourenço Moreira Lima is referred to as Moreira Lima; and João Alberto Lins de Barros is referred to as João Alberto.

Except in noted instances when a translation is courtesy of Laiz Ferguson, all translations are my own.

ACKNOWLEDGMENTS

This book could not have been completed without extremely generous—and extremely timely—funding. In the early months of 2020, back in the "before" times, I learned that my applications for two research grants had been successful: from the National Endowment for the Humanities in the United States, and from the Arts and Humanities Research Council in the United Kingdom. Combined, the two grants released me from all teaching requirements for two years. This would have been a gift even in normal circumstances. But when the COVID-19 pandemic erupted, my prolonged research sabbatical became an almost unimaginable luxury. I had the time to concentrate on writing and to coordinate a final round of research in Brazil when the pandemic was at a relative lull. I had been working on this project since 2017, which meant that I had completed much of my research and thinking about the Prestes Column prior to COVID. But my ability to finish the book during a global pandemic is something for which I will always remain humble.

My deep gratitude goes to a long list of colleagues as well. Sarah Sarzynski and Courtney Campbell read the entire manuscript and offered detailed feedback, and our conversations over Zoom helped bring out the book's full potential. Similarly, Joel Carlos de Souza Andrade read an early version of the book, and he invited me to present my research to the História dos Sertões graduate program at the Universidade Federal do Rio Grande do Norte. Others who read chapter drafts and helped talked through my project include Marc Becker, Andrew Britt, Jerry Dávila, Kevin Donovan, John French, Todd Diacon, Chris Dunn, Jim Green, Glen Goodman, Marc Hertzman, Jeff Lesser, Frank McCann, Andre Pagliarini, Sean Purdy, Margaret Power, Joel Wolfe, Barbara Weinstein, Daryle Williams, Tony Wood, and Jacob Zumoff. And I learned a great deal from the eleven colleagues who contributed chapters on a volume I coedited with Frederico Freitas on the interior history of Brazil: Íris Kantor, Heather Roller, Judy Bieber, Fabrício Prado, Carlos Bacellar, Seth Garfield, Lúcia Sá, Antônio Luigi Negro, Sandro Dutra e Silva, Tom Rogers, and Susanna Hecht. A huge thank-you also goes to the three anonymous peer reviewers who provided detailed and truly generative comments. As always, I benefited from my Venn diagram of family academics, as my brilliant wife, Isabel Pike, and my nerd-in-crime brother, Eric Blanc, provided feedback at various stages of the book's progression. And a special word of appreciation for my dear colleague and friend Fred Freitas, with whom I have now collaborated on two projects and whose expertise has made this a better book and me a better historian.

In addition to the two large research grants from the NEH and AHRC, initial research for the project was funded by the Carnegie Trust of Scotland and the School of History, Classics, and Archaeology at the University of Edinburgh. Among my colleagues at Edinburgh, I am grateful to the feedback on grant applications from Emile Chabal, Enda Delaney, and Gordan Pentland, and I want to also thank Brian Pacey, Sue Coleman, and Asad Nazir in the Research Office for their help and patience with my applications. Edinburgh's office of Scholarly Communications, funded by a block grant from UK Research and Innovation, provided money to make this book open access. Diana Paton, Emily Brownell, Julie Gibbings, Felicity Green, and Jeremy Dell, among others, all made HCA such a great place to work. I will always cherish my time at Edinburgh.

In Brazil, my access to archival documents was facilitated by librarians and archivists such as Flávia Eduarda Suarez Baptista at the CPDOC-FGV in Rio de Janeiro, Marina Rebelo at the Arquivo Edgard Leuenroth in Campinas, Captain Celso Gonçalves at the Army's Historical Archive (AHEx), Maria José Timburibá Guimarães at the Arquivo Público Mineiro in Belo Horizonte, Claudia Barros at the Biblioteca Comunitária at the Universidade de São Carlos, and Paulo Alves at the Biblioteca de Obras Raras Átila Almeida in Campina Grande. Given that so much of my research draws on historical newspapers from across the twentieth century, an especially large thank-you goes to Brazil's National Library and its expertly maintained Hemeroteca Digital, arguably Latin America's best digital repositories of newspapers. Outside of Brazil, I am also grateful for those who aided my research at the British National Archives in London, the US National Archives in College Park, and the Special Collections library at the University of California, Los Angeles.

Two of Luís Carlos Prestes's children, Anita Prestes and Luiz Carlos Prestes Jr., were very generous with their time and insight into their father's life, and I learned a lot from our exchanges. Many others also shared their perspective, including Gilson Moura Henrique Junior, Alex Alves, Rubia Micheline Moreira Cavalcanti, Dirceu Marroquim, Micael Alvino da Silva, Patricia Orfila Barros dos Reis, Daniel Aarão Reis, and Ronald Chilcote.

At Duke University Press, it continues to be a pleasure working with Gisela Fosado and her staff, especially DUP's assistant editor Alejandra Mejía. The maps in this book were produced by Gabriel Moss, a skilled cartographer, and the parallel Portuguese-language version of this book was translated by the talented and kind Laiz Ferguson.

Something wonderous happened toward the end of writing this book: I became a father. Jonah, if you are reading this one day, I hope it brings you even a fraction of the joy that you get from your current favorite books: *Baby Koala*, *Where's Spot?*, and *The Bunny Rabbit Show!*

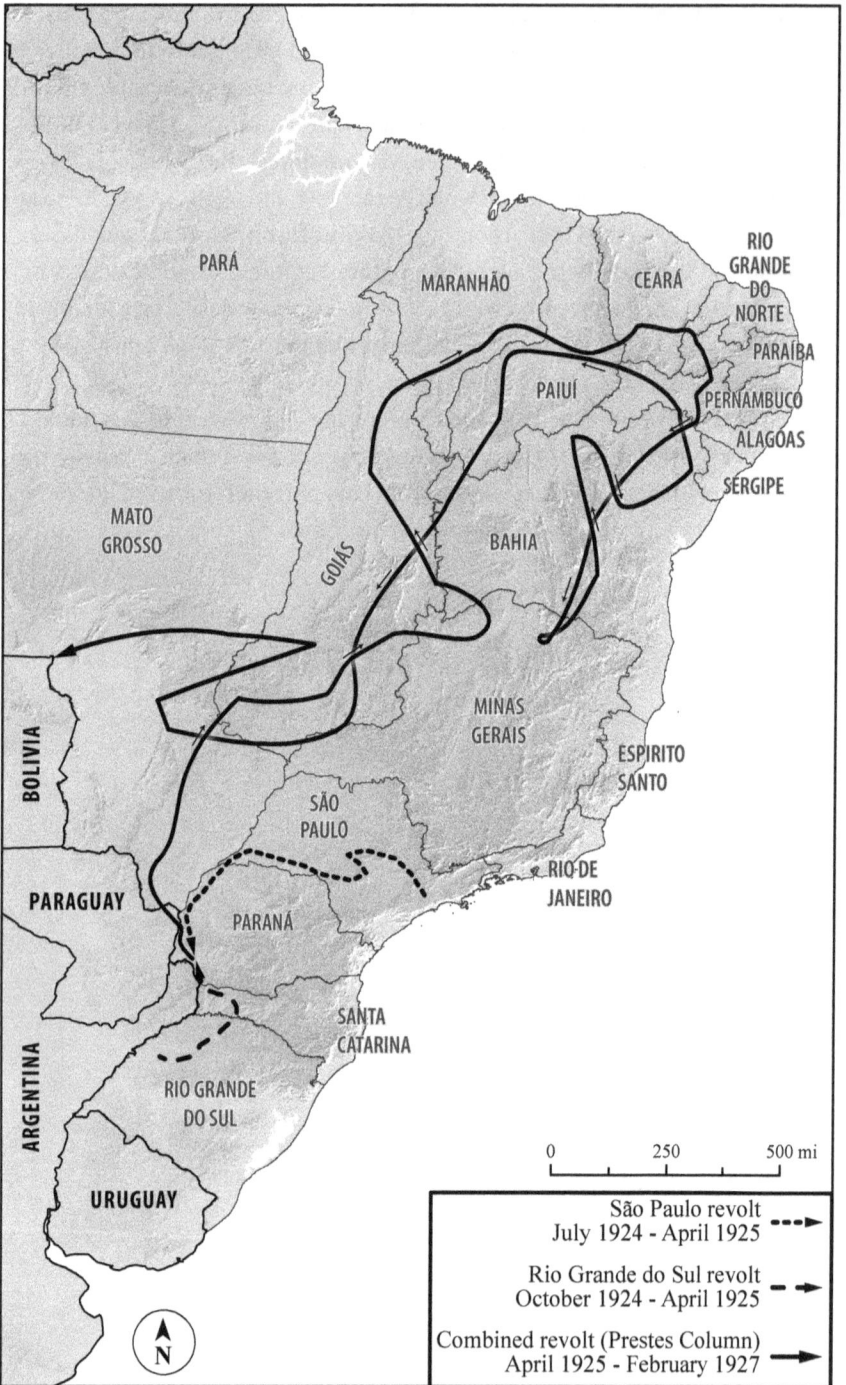

MAP I.1. Prestes Column, 1924–27. Created by Gabe Moss, made with Natural Earth.

The Prestes Column is one of the most famous events in modern Brazilian history. What started out as an unsuccessful rebellion soon morphed into a roving expedition that crisscrossed the country for almost three years. From 1924 to 1927, a group of roughly one thousand army officers and soldiers marched fifteen thousand miles through the vast interior regions of Brazil (map I.1). This is the equivalent of marching from Los Angeles to New York and back again three times. The column began as an uprising in the city of São Paulo in July 1924 that sought to overthrow President Artur Bernardes (1922–26), and it evolved into a circuitous clockwise journey across thirteen states—nearly two-thirds of the twenty states that made up the entire country at the time. Beginning in the South, the rebels (later referred to as *tenentes*, or lieutenants) then wound their way up and around the central plains and traversed the northeastern *sertão* before turning around and retracing their steps. They eventually went into exile in Bolivia in February 1927.

The Prestes Column took its name from Luís Carlos Prestes, an army captain from Rio Grande do Sul who, midway through the march, became the column's unofficial leader. In total, the column fought over 150 battles against much larger and better-supplied forces of the federal army, state troops, and local militias. The rebellion failed to achieve its original goal of toppling President Bernardes; neither were any of its reformist demands met, including the secret ballot, a balance of power among the three branches of government, and universal primary-school education. But, after fighting and evading federal and local troops for two and a half years, the rebellion came to be known as the Undefeated Column. Prestes became the leading symbol of the march across Brazil and was lauded as the Knight of Hope.

Although the tenente rebellion had not originally aimed to march across the country—it only did so when its route to Rio de Janeiro was blocked—it brought mainstream attention to far-flung regions of the country. The unplanned march into the "backlands" occurred at a pivotal moment in the formation of modern Brazil: three decades after the end of the Brazilian empire in 1889, and three years before the Revolution of 1930 that overthrew the oligarchic First Republic, the Prestes Column took place as new regional elites began to challenge the political control held by the states of São Paulo and Minas Gerais. At a moment when notions of regional power and the boundaries of nationalism grew more important, the column traced a symbolic and literal path across the nation. In doing so, it helped to set into motion the Revolution of 1930 that brought Getúlio Vargas to power. Under Vargas, and in the decades to come, many of the rebel leaders became key political figures. On the right, several former rebels served as ministers in the dictatorships under Vargas (1937–45) and the Cold War military regime (1964–85). And, on the left, some tenentes embraced radical politics—most famously, Luís Carlos Prestes, who became a Marxist and eventually assumed the leadership of the Brazilian Communist Party. In the lore of Prestes's rise as one of Latin America's most famous Communists, his march through Brazil's interior became a much-celebrated, if often-exaggerated, story of political awakening, a precursor of sorts to Che Guevara's *The Motorcycle Diaries*.

In the aftermath of the column, the rebellion was widely commemorated and romanticized. Oscar Niemeyer, Brazil's most celebrated architect, designed several monuments to it; Jorge Amado, Brazil's most celebrated writer, wrote a biography of Prestes; and, in the past century, a series of novels, poems, movies, and musical ballads have amplified the adventures of the young army officers who defied the government, braved dangerous frontiers, and, in the words of one observer, brought "the lantern of liberty to Brazil's deepest interior."[1] The Prestes Column and its leaders quickly attained a mythical status, especially among leftist leaders, writers, and scholars, as well as conservative Brazilians who wanted to stake a claim to what became an origin story for modern Brazil. However, like all legends, especially those connected to ideas of nationhood, there is a deeper story.

The column's place in the pantheon of Brazilian heroes raises two fundamental questions. Given that it failed to overthrow the government, why did the column become so famous? And, despite the fact that the rebels did almost nothing to help communities in the interior—if anything, they tended to treat locals with either indifference, contempt, or outright violence—how did the column come to symbolize an inclusionary vision of national progress? To answer these questions and to explore the broader meanings of space and nation, my book reinterprets the Prestes Column from the perspective of Brazil's interior. Whereas the prevailing narrative of and almost all scholarship on the column has focused on the highly mythologized details of the rebellion itself, I explore the meanings attached to where the column actually went: the interior.

Interior History

In Brazil, as across Latin America and elsewhere, *interior* is a complex term. In its most literal meaning, it implies a clear geographic dichotomy: the coast versus the interior. This spatial distinction has engendered a social contrast between a civilized coast and a backward interior. Moreover, the term is misleading. Whereas *the coast* has a more straightforward definition (nearness to the ocean), the interior has come to represent a general sense of not-the-coast. But, rather than a single interior, as the term implies, Brazil's interior regions represent an immense range of landscapes and communities.

The Prestes Column is an ideal case study for charting an interior history of modern Brazil, as it exemplifies how interior regions and their populations have long been seen by coastal elites as simultaneously backward (in relation to the more modern coast) and dormant, a space of untapped potential waiting to be brought into the nation. This dual narrative about the interior long predated the Prestes Column. At one end lies the stigmatized view of the interior as dangerous and uncivilized—a view that served to glorify southern and coastal Brazilians who ventured inland, whether in search of people to enslave or natural resources to extract. Yet interior spaces and populations have often been far more dynamic than the stigmas of the backlands would suggest.[2] The interior has been the cradle of some of Brazil's most important developments, including the establishment of *quilombos* (maroon societies composed of former enslaved people), the intellectual and cultural centers sparked by the Minas Gerais gold rush in the eighteenth century, the new inland capital of Brasília in the twentieth century, and the technological advances that made tropical agribusiness the center of Brazilian capitalism. The constructed duality of Brazil's interior—not only a space of barbarism but also the true locus of national authenticity—so transfixed writers and scholars that, according to the sociologist Nísia Trindade Lima, it formed the very basis of Brazilian social science and intellectual thought.[3] Within this prism of converging representations, the interior became a powerful space in which to envision and debate the country's past, present, and future.

In calling my book an "interior history" of modern Brazil, I hope to offer a new framework for scholars working on similar topics in Brazil, across Latin America, and globally. There already exist a number of historically—and historiographically—important terms used to describe interior spaces, such as *frontier, rural, border, borderland,* and *hinterland,* in addition to country-specific words, such as we will see with the term *sertão* in Brazil. My analysis of Brazil's interior offers many parallels to Greg Grandin's study of the US frontier, which Grandin describes as "a state of mind, a cultural zone, a sociological term of comparison, a type of society, an adjective, a noun, a national myth, a disciplining mechanism, an abstraction, and an aspiration."[4] In dialogue with these various ideas and categories, interior history has a wide purview: it is a way to understand an interior space as both a physical landscape comprising a wide range of topographies and populations, and also as an imaginative landscape adaptable to a range of different perspectives. Interior history can include studies about interior spaces and their inhabitants (stories set in the interior), and it can encompass the narratives and symbolisms that circulate in relation to the interior (discourses that emerge and predominate elsewhere, most often among lettered coastal society). Part of what makes the Prestes Column such a compelling example of interior history is that it combines both of the above elements: as the column zigzagged across Brazil, it drew on and aided in expanding the various meanings attached to the spaces through which the rebels traced their long march. An interior history of the Prestes Column helps explain the column's initial rise to fame and also its enduring legacy across the twentieth century.

The column's legend remained tethered to a long-standing coastal fascination with the backlands. Ever since the arrival of European colonists, Brazil's interior loomed as an enticing, if challenging, space. In 1627, the Franciscan friar Vicente do Salvador famously criticized the Portuguese for neglecting the interior of their new colony, saying that the colonists were content to remain "clinging to the coastline, like crabs."[5] The dangers, both real and imagined, of the interior were part of the reason that mainstream society lived along the coast, but it was precisely the lack of a sustained presence in the interior that made it so appealing. Over the centuries, Portuguese elites, and their Brazilian inheritors after independence in 1822, looked inland with what Mary Louise Pratt calls "imperial eyes": a coastal gaze of sorts intended to create a sense of order and make their readers feel connected to far-off lands.[6] Visions of Brazil's interior took shape in the chronicles of inland explorations such as the *bandeirante* slaving raids of the seventeenth century, the gold prospectors of the eighteenth century, the scientific expeditions of the nineteenth century, and the military campaigns at the turn of the twentieth century, most notably the Canudos War in the 1890s as chronicled by Euclides da Cunha's newspaper reports and bestselling book *Os Sertões*. Shaped by these earlier interior expeditions and given new depth by the circumstances of how the column's narrative was constructed—largely via mass-market newspapers in Rio de Janeiro—the Prestes Column greatly influenced the way mainstream audiences perceived the spaces of the interior. What has gotten lost in the established history of the column is not so much the encounter between the tenentes and the interior, but, rather, how rebels and locals alike depicted the inland march, what that implied for competing visions of the backlands, and how the enduring symbolism of the column either perpetuated or changed the prevailing views of the interior.

Given that the column marched across much of the national map—an unprecedented linkage of almost the entire country, minus the Amazon basin— it offers an especially rich case study for exploring what Tongchai Winichakul calls the "geo-body" of a nation: the territories, practices, and values that get created through spatial discourses and mapping.[7] The column covered so much national space and garnered so much media attention that it expanded public awareness of Brazil's territorial expanses, helping to shift the contours of the Brazilian geo-body. A newspaper column in January 1927, for example, written less than a month before the column crossed into exile, praised Prestes and his men for making Brazilians more acquainted with the spaces of their country: "The Prestes Column without a doubt updated our map. . . . The rebels carried weapons in their hands, and as it turns out, these weapons were actually tools for map-making."[8] Whether in the media, popular culture, or the proclamations of former tenente leaders, the spatial symbolism of the column's march served as the core of its legend. But, as historian Raymond Craib has observed in his cartographic study of Mexico, "space does not merely display itself to the world, as if it were somehow ontologically prior to the cultural and semiotic codes through which its existence is expressed.

Such myths of mimesis turn the historical into the natural, concealing its social, cultural, and political underpinnings."[9] Revealing these coded layers requires close analysis of the particular meanings that have come to define particular spaces.

In Brazil, as in most countries, the question of space is closely linked to that of nation. As exemplified by the notion of *ufanismo* (a pride in abundance of land and natural resources), Brazilian nationalism has consistently depended on the goal of opening up the interior.[10] The question of modernizing the interior forms the crux of the Prestes Column's prevailing narrative. Would-be-modernizers would invoke the column as part of a variety of campaigns across the twentieth century, ranging from government infrastructure and commercial projects to radical movements for organizing and empowering peasant communities. If one could claim to modernize the backlands, it would not only expand the nation; it would also prove the legitimacy of whichever group had done the expanding.

In the half-century after the column, two main groups, each offering a competing path for modernizing Brazil, consistently engaged the legacy of the long march: the army and the Brazilian Communist Party. For centrist and conservative Brazilians in the army, the column represented a wake-up call for mainstream society in which the tenentes saw poverty in the backlands and were inspired to bring the fruits of the nation to new regions. Oswaldo Cordeiro de Farias, a rebel commander who later served as a regional planning minister for the military dictatorship of the 1960s, said that his motivation to modernize Brazil's interior came from his experience in the Prestes Column: "For two and a half years, I lived in contact with the suffering Brazil, with its people, who had no schools, no healthcare, no roads, no police, no justice, no anything, very poor and without hope. This image of our people and their problems has never left me."[11] Brazilian leftists, on the other hand, tended to offer a refracted version of that same story, portraying the column as a tale of mutual discovery for both the rebels and the interior populations. In his biography of Prestes, the famed novelist and Communist Jorge Amado wrote that the interior "turned inside out, with its hardship on full display, discovers itself in this man, and he, Luís Carlos Prestes, discovers Brazil in its nakedness."[12] Even if retrospective and at times ahistorical, these depictions of the column's march through the Brazilian geo-body became a means to comment on interior development and, thus, the future of the nation.

It should be noted that the narrative of liberation in the backlands first emerged in force during the rebels' exile in Bolivia, when supporters recast the column in patriotic language to argue that the tenentes should receive amnesty and be allowed to return to Brazil. The newspaper, *A Manhã*, for example, wrote in 1927 that "the Prestes Column woke up the people of the interior, [freeing them] from the tyranny of local political chiefs. All corners of our immense nation are calling for the repatriation of these glorious exiles."[13] No such liberation occurred, but at a moment when the exiled rebels were seen to be languishing in an even more sinister interior of a foreign country—the eastern borderlands of Bolivia—tales of awakening became a political tool for amnesty. In the years and decades to come, long after the rebels had returned to Brazil, this language would become firmly implanted as the core of the column's dominant legend.

Although stories about the column emerged primarily among southern coastal society, interior communities also developed their own views about the rebel march. As literary scholar Zita Nunes has observed in her analysis of Blackness in the Americas, narratives like those articulated by interior communities defy simple categorization: they are neither entirely antagonistic nor assimilative toward dominant national narratives. To borrow Nunes's term, the goal is to understand the diverse and place-specific views of "resistant remainders," such as those who lived along the column's path.[14] Many in the interior considered Prestes a symbol of unity and justice, a legacy evident in the cordel poems of the Northeast, among other cultural and political products that saw the column as part of an inclusionary vision of the nation. But, in places where the column had inflicted violence, local communities have also depicted the rebels as murderous invaders; these memories are found in oral histories collected over the years by journalists and in the monuments built to those who died fighting against the column. While much of my book focuses on storytelling about the interior—a reflection of how the standard history of the column took shape—wherever possible I explore the perspectives of communities within the interior in order to properly situate the various visions of the Brazilian nation that circulated in relation to the Prestes Column.

The question of discourse, and who controlled the narrative of what supposedly took place in the interior, became one of most contested aspects of the column's history. During the rebellion, as both the column and the federal government sought to position themselves as the legitimate protectors of the Brazilian nation, the battle for public opinion often devolved into dueling accusations of "going native" in the interior. Centered on the trope of backland violence, both sides accused the other of being the real bandits, seeking, in turn, to present themselves as the true civilizing force. Although the column did not constitute a war per se, the public spotlight that followed its battles against army and militia forces is reflective of Javier Uriarte's analysis of how war in Latin America has served to incorporate interior landscapes into the nation, a process through which "deserts"—such as the Brazilian sertão, Argentinian Patagonia, or the Paraguayan countryside—are transformed from isolated, primordial voids into more legible voids ripe for modernization and consolidation into the nation.[15] As with Uriarte's case studies of late nineteenth-century fighting in various Latin American interiors, the Prestes Column's impact on perceptions of Brazil's interior reverberated most strongly at the level of discourse, with journalists, politicians, poets, and novelists holding the column aloft as a symbol of a transforming backlands.

Another tension in the column's legend is the difference between what the rebels claimed to have done (the heroic narrative of liberation in the backlands) and how their interactions with locals tended to unfold. As part of its campaign to overthrow the government, and in desperate need of reinforcements, the column called on rural Brazilians to rise up and join the rebellion. Almost none did. The lack of collaboration had several causes, including the power wielded by local oligarchs who were contracted by the federal army to fight against the column, a reluctance from townspeople to hand over what few items they had to a wandering group of outsiders, and the prejudices and violent actions of the rebels themselves. And, given that the rebels moved across the countryside as quickly as possible, rarely stopping for more than a day or two, they had neither the time—nor, on the whole, the interest—to adequately understand local cultures. Because the rebels did little to learn about the interior spaces they traversed, their default was often to reproduce the stereotypes they already held, much of which was influenced by Euclides da Cunha's writing on the Canudos War. Aside from a few instances of destroying tax records or making alliances with local leaders, the rebellion did very little that could be considered a direct act of solidarity with interior populations. More often than not, the encounters were defined either by fatigued opportunism (engaging just enough to requisition food, clothing, and weapons in order to keep the column marching forward) or violent conflict: at various points, rebel soldiers committed acts of looting, rape, and murder.

This violence left a legacy of trauma and place-specific narratives. In interviews conducted with a journalist in the 1990s, for example, elderly inhabitants spoke about the Prestes Column in terms of the cycles of drought that wreaked havoc in the sertão. Joana Gomes da Silva, ninety-one years old at the time, recalled that, in her small town in Piauí, "the rebels were worse than the drought. The fear that we had was worse than hunger;" and Maria de

Conceição da Silva, aged ninety-two, similarly said that in Ceará "the rebels were worse than the drought of [19]15 and also the one in [19]32. In a drought, we didn't have anything to eat, but we also weren't afraid."[16] Such statements indicate that people in the interior also infused the discourse of the Prestes Column with the type of backland symbolism that felt most immediate to them. By equating the column with drought, these memories show that, for people who lived along the rebel path, the realities of life in the interior were more than just tropes—for them, the column represented another element that reinforced their hardship.

Although it is often left unsaid in the column's legend, the march to the interior was not an initial objective but one that developed by circumstance. The two main catalysts of the tenentista movement were revolts in Rio de Janeiro in 1922 and São Paulo in 1924, both of which aimed to overthrow the government in the national, coastal capital of Rio de Janeiro. The rebels in 1924 only changed course and went inland when their path to Rio de Janeiro was blocked by the federal army. Once Prestes led his soldiers toward the backlands, it allowed the tenente leaders and their supporters along the coast to reframe the rebellion as a campaign to liberate the interior. Most emblematically, it was only after the column's unintended turn inland that rebel leaders began to call themselves the "bandeirantes of freedom," a twentieth-century refraction of the colonial-era explorers who carried flags (*bandeiras*) on slaving expeditions into the interior. The rebel's invocation of the bandeirantes was no coincidence, as it was precisely during this period in the mid-1920s that intellectuals and artists, mostly in São Paulo, sought to rehabilitate the image of the bandeirantes as a symbol not of violent frontier expansion, but of Brazil's democratizing spirit. This version of the bandeirantes is evident in how the column justified its unintended march into the interior. Several decades afterward, for instance, one former rebel claimed that "by opening up paths through untouched forests, where today there is now commerce, culture, and civilization, the 'Undefeated Column' paralleled the movements of the bandeiras that spread across the country in every direction."[17] The prevailing symbolism of the interior thus gave cover to the initial failures of the tenente rebellion and transformed the inland journey into an intrepid movement claiming to bring modernity to the backlands.

The column's self-ascribed status as bandeirantes of freedom operated within the constructed categories of race in twentieth-century Brazil. Because the column's leadership was made up largely of European-descendant officers from Rio Grande do Sul and São Paulo, stories about the column often presented the march as a white movement that moved triumphantly across nonwhite spaces. As it had been since the arrival of European colonizers, Brazil's interior continued to be seen as a racialized Other inhabited by Indigenous, Afro-Brazilian, and mixed-origin communities. A newspaper article from 1927, for example, celebrated the rebels for bringing "the feeling of human respect to the rude souls of our backlands, demonstrating to the savage Indian from the forests all the generosity and kindness held in the hearts of the white people from the coast."[18] Similarly, sixty years later, the journalist Edmar Morel remarked that "the column experienced two totally different Brazils. Its *gaúcho* troops were warriors, with an even temperament and accompanied by a faithful horse. . . . The *nordestinos* [on the other hand] were in poor health, malnourished, dressed in a cotton shirt and sandals made of tire rubber. . . . It was a clash of two civilizations, as if they were two different races entirely."[19]

Despite the staying power of such narratives, it is important to note that depictions of the column would parallel changing attitudes toward race and regional identity, particularly the emergent notion of Brazil as a so-called racial democracy. In his study of Pernambuco, Stanley Blake identifies the 1920s and 1930s as the moment when nordestinos "became a constituent element of Brazilian national identity, a category that was at once both racialized and devoid of racial content."[20] This shift is evident in mid-century accounts of the column. In the late 1950s, the tenente leader Miguel Costa offered a more uplifting retrospective, writing that the march "was a laboratory for understanding Brazil [in which] the coast discovered the backlands [and] learned about what happened in the interior. The locals, for their part, started to learn new words: freedom, democracy, rights." Costa not only claimed that the rebels had engaged with a full range of rural and ethnic archetypes; he also credited the column with introducing these interior groups to wider Brazilian audiences: "With the column and thanks to the column, other characters began to appear on the scene—they are the *mestizos* (mixed African and European ancestry), the *caboclos* (mixed Indigenous and European ancestry), the *nordestinos*, the *tabaréus* (simple rural folk), the *seringuerios* (rubber tappers), [and] the *garimpeiros* (miners). . . . The column discovered the truly Brazilian Brazil (*o Brasil brasileiro*)."[21] By embodying both an exclusionary and an inclusionary vision of Brazil's interior, the Prestes Column reflected the complex meanings of race in modern Brazil.

The column may never have become famous if not for the fact that it coincided with a boom in Brazil's newspaper sector. Between 1912 and 1930, the number of Brazilian periodicals more than doubled.[22] Newspapers grew in tandem with—and to satisfy the cultural and consumer demands of—an emerging middle class in urban, industrializing areas. Two decades removed from the success of Euclides da Cunha's newspaper exposés on the Canudos War, the Prestes Column offered a new interior tale to captivate Brazil's reading public. With recently installed telegraph lines stretching farther into the backlands, newspapers relayed updates of the march in real time. And, as Maite Conde has shown, print media's fascination with the backlands also extended to another innovation of the era, movies, as some of Brazil's earliest successes of national cinema were stories set in the interior.[23] The fates of the Prestes Column and Brazil's new media were tightly connected. This is best exemplified by the newspaper editor Assis Chateaubriand, who purchased his first paper in 1924, only a few months after the start of the tenente rebellion, and who made the Prestes Column one of the central stories of his early newspaper empire. As Fernando Morais observes in his biography of Chateaubriand, "For the first time, the public could read in the mainstream press something that until then had only appeared in political pamphlets: interviews in which the rebel leaders described their battles with the troops of the federal government."[24] Especially during the final phase of the rebellion, when censorship was loosened, Chateaubriand commissioned a series of multipart exposés that allowed readers to follow, over the course of days or weeks, the romanticized adventures of the heroic backland rebels. Many of these articles included grandiose maps of the march, comparing the rebels to historical personages like Alexander the Great and also mythical figures like Robin Hood and El Cid. These portrayals helped make broader ideas about nationhood accessible and entertaining for mainstream audiences.

For hundreds of years, inland regions have served as a conceptual prism between mainstream society and the spaces, both real and imagined, of Brazil's noncoastal regions. Although the constructed dichotomy between coast and interior suggests a form of mirroring—in which coastal elites gaze inland in order to see their own sense of superiority reflected back—I find that the metaphor of a prism is more appropriate. A prism refracts light and redirects it according to changes in position, angle, and perspective, allowing different wavelengths to be seen at different points. Whether rotating or still, a prism can shift perceptions from one of its various sides to another, and it can also serve as the meeting point for the various sides themselves. As historians, we can use the image of a prism to understand the refraction not of light, but of stories, and of the narratives that help construct ideas about nations and society. And, when this relates to space—and the people who inhabit it—the stories being refracted can change depending on how one chooses to perceive the spaces on the other sides. For our focus on the Prestes Column, this approach allows us to analyze the relationship between coast and interior without falling into its dichotomous trap: Why did certain groups use the Prestes Column as a way to comment on space and nation at particular moments? And how did the symbolism of the column reflect continuities as well as changes in narratives about the interior? A nuanced spatial and social analysis of the column will help reinterpret its legacy as part of the multitude of visions that existed about, and from within, the interior.

The Interior Is Everywhere

In one of the most acclaimed novels of modern Brazilian literature, *Grande Sertão: Veredas* (translated in English as *The Devil to Pay in the Backlands*), the writer and diplomat João Guimarães Rosa reflects on the nature of good and evil, and its particular permutations in Brazilian society. As embedded in the book's title, Guimarães Rosa locates his story not in a major urban center like Rio de Janeiro, São Paulo, or Salvador, but in the *sertão*—a shorthand term for the semiarid regions of the interior; in this case, Guimarães Rosa set his book in the northern backlands of Minas Gerais. There is a close historical and semiotic relationship between sertão and interior, with each deriving meaning from its status as a geographic reference to noncoastal areas. For Guimarães Rosa, the Brazilian interior encapsulated the essence of the national character. The book is written as a long monologue by a man named Riobaldo, who tells of his life as a *jagunço*, a for-hire soldier and bodyguard who would be contracted to protect the property of large landowners. Through Riobaldo's stories of the sertão, and his efforts to make sense of its social hierarchy, Guimarães Rosa posited that, rather than a peripheral space in the Brazilian nation, the sertão *was* the Brazilian nation. In one of the book's most iconic statements, Riobaldo exclaims that "the sertão is everywhere."[25]

Written in 1956, three decades after the column, *Grande Sertão* shows how the Prestes Column would become an invokable symbol not only in political myth-making but also at the cultural level. In one of Riobaldo's stories, he tells of an old man wandering around a market who ruminates out loud, to nobody in particular, "Wars and battles? It's like a game of cards; first one wins, then the other."[26] The old man goes on to talk about the Prestes Column, recalling how rebel troops stole horses from local farms. This is one of several examples of writers referencing the column as a way to insert historical events into their fictional tales about the interior.[27] Guimarães Rosa also draws our attention to the word *sertão*, arguably the most pervasive geographic and topographic term in Brazil. In its modern usage, *sertão* refers to the dry, drought-plagued backlands of the Northeast. This climatological toponym was popularized by Euclides da Cunha in his 1902 book *Os Sertões*, an account of the bloody fighting in the 1890s between the federal army and a millenarian community at Canudos in the interior of Bahia. *Os Sertões* was a cultural and political landmark that influenced generations of Brazilians, including the leaders of the Prestes Column. Yet the term emerged long before Cunha's famous book. Rex P. Nielson has shown that *sertão* originated in the sixteenth- and seventeenth-century cartography of Portuguese explorers, as a way to represent the unknown expanses of Brazil's interior lands: "The sertão paradoxically represented a space that could not be mapped. To map, that is, to locate the sertão within the rationality of the epistemological grid of European knowledge would be to endow the sertão with qualities that contradict its very definition as a sign for the unknown."[28]

As the colonial presence expanded deeper into Brazilian territory, meaning that more lands could be mapped and "known," new modifiers described the various types of interior landscapes. Carlos Bacellar writes that in the seventeenth and eighteenth centuries, one finds references to unknown sertão, uninhabited sertão, wild sertão, and unpopulated sertão. By the nineteenth century, as sertão became pervasive and thus subject to modification, the term *interior* (spelled the same in both Portuguese and English) emerged as a way to demarcate a space that was neither the coast nor the sertão; as Bacellar observes, "it was still plagued with indigenous people and thus dangerous, but it was also rich in opportunities."[29] Commercial and administrative outposts, linked to the coast and to one another by new inland road networks, helped establish an imaginative middle ground between the coast and the sertão.

The emergence of the interior is evident in the chronicles of foreign explorers, such as *Travels in the Interior of Brazil* (1812) by the British geologist John Mawe and *Voyages dans l'intérieur du Brésil* (1830) by the French botanist August de Saint-Hilaire. In these travelogues, the foreign authors use both *interior* and *sertão*, which suggests that *interior* was not simply an easier way to translate *sertão* into English or French; rather, it was distinct and pervasive, and the foreign travelers were likely influenced by how their guides and local contacts described inland spaces. The archival record confirms this trend. Beginning in the early 1820s, articles in the *Diário do Rio de Janeiro*, to name one example, consistently mentioned "the interior of the country," and, by 1829, the annals of Brazilian parliament included speeches that referenced the interior.[30] In the prism of development away from the coast, the interior came to represent a space just beyond reach—far enough away so as to still pose risks, but close enough to offer the potential of settlement or extraction. The term remained a moving target, and, as commercial activities and population centers expanded farther inland, the interior expanded as well. With the proper motivation, one could look out in seemingly any direction and find an interior on the horizon.

Over the following century, *sertão* and *interior* continued to coexist, offering slight refractions for commenting on noncoastal regions. *Sertão*, from its initial status as an unmappable unknown, came to be fixed to the Northeast—a process greatly accelerated by Euclides da Cunha's 1902 publication of *Os Sertões*.[31] As popularized by Cunha, *sertão* also provided a name for its inhabitants: the *sertanejo*, which became a catch-all term for people of the northeastern backlands. The twin phrasings of *sertão* and *sertanejos* further explains why the leaders of the Prestes Column and its supporters along the coast could draw equally on the terms *sertão*, *sertanejo*, and *interior*. (The lexicon of backland figures also included *jagunço*, the contracted fighters like Guimarães Rosa's protagonist, Riobaldo; *coronel*, the rural oligarchs who hired jagunços; and *cangaceiro*, the bandits and outlaws who roamed the interior). During the rebel march in the 1920s and its mythologizing afterward, *sertão* was most typically, though not exclusively, used to refer to the Northeast, which itself was a nascent term in the early twentieth century. *Interior*, on the other hand, could be used as a broader reference to any of the lands along its route. In a country as large as Brazil, where terminologies for noncoastal areas have been a consistent tool of nation-building, *interior* moved beyond the confines of a bounded geographic label to become a relational and imaginative category. When refracted from this perspective, almost anywhere could be an interior. We can thus return to Guimarães Rosa—if the sertão is everywhere, so, too, is the interior.

Scholarship, Sources, and Authorial Choices

The Prestes Column has inspired an extensive body of literature. According to one calculation, when combining newspaper coverage, academic articles, and books—in Portuguese and other languages—there are over five thousand pieces of writing about the column.[32] In terms of book-length projects, we can identify over sixty books written by professional scholars, journalists, and local writers. In the first category, of academic writing, the most prolific scholar is Anita Prestes, the daughter of Luís Carlos Prestes and an emeritus professor of history at the Federal University of Rio de Janeiro.[33]

Perhaps unsurprisingly, her books tend to lionize her father and perpetuate the triumphant legend of the column. But the relatively uncritical approach of Anita Prestes is also found in most scholarship.[34] Take, for example, the romanticized 1974 book from Neill Macaulay, a University of Florida professor who had famously fought alongside Fidel Castro in the Cuban Revolution and depicted the Brazilian interior as analogous to the Sierra Maestra of Cuba's revolutionary lore.[35] The second category, by far the most voluminous, includes journalistic and popular accounts.[36] While the contexts of these books, published between the 1950s and 2010s, vary widely, they recycle the same dominant narrative.[37] They recount the various battles and expeditions of the rebel excursion and, in a form of pilgrimage hagiography, often involve the writer retracing a portion or even all of the column's march.[38] A third category covers regional books about the column's passage through specific towns or states; often, local writers seek to highlight their city or region's place in the legend of the column.[39] Although my interior history of the Prestes Column represents a fundamental intervention in existing scholarship, I engage with the books in all three categories to help triangulate my archival findings and to better understand how published works have maintained the column's dominant legend.

My book is in close dialogue with a subfield in Brazilian historiography on regionalism, which examines identity-formation (both locally and in relation to the nation-state), culture, and political development in select areas. In the 1970s, a trio of US-based historians published landmark regional histories of Rio Grande do Sul, Minas Gerais, and Pernambuco.[40] Over the following decades, Brazilian scholars such as Ademir Gebara, Marco Antonio Silva, and Durval Muniz de Albuquerque Jr. helped to establish a vibrant field with a dedicated academic journal, the *Revista de História Regional*.[41] Scholarship has remained strong both within Brazil and abroad. Recently, the field has focused largely on two regions: the Northeast and São Paulo, and for good reason, as they are among the most emblematic regions of the country.[42] An interior history of the Prestes Column, a rebellion that originated in São Paulo and whose fame emerged largely from its eventual march across the Northeast, includes analysis of these two important regions. But, in tracing the Prestes Column's trek across much of Brazil's territory, I also seek to elevate the profile of lesser-studied regions (such as Paraná in the south and Maranhão in the north) and place them in relation to each other, showing how, in the prism of the column's march, the far-flung and distinct areas became seen as belonging to a singular Brazilian interior. Because the interior cannot be defined as belonging to any one region, there is much to be gained by transposing the approaches of regionalism—namely, how ideas about regional identities influenced state-building and civil society—onto a more ambiguous spatial category like interior. Given Brazil's size, it is difficult to study the history of multiple regions within a single framework. To avoid homogenizing or abstracting the interior, and in seeking to understand the convergence of regional identities, I use the Prestes Column as a mobile vector for understanding Brazil's interior as a plural, multiregional space.

Given my focus on discourse and modernity, my interior history of the Prestes Column also engages scholarship on mythology, particularly as it relates to language and the ways through which narratives become popularized.[43] In this book, I use *myth* and *legend* almost interchangeably to refer to the dominant perception of the rebel march across the interior. As an origin story for modern Brazil, where the column became a spatialized symbol for inaugurating a new era in national politics, its legend reflects the diachronic nature of modern-day mythologies: in a relatively short amount of time, the public spotlight on the column transformed *news* into *memory*, helping make the interior march into a powerful, if contested, object of collective meaning. As will be argued throughout this book, the long-standing symbolism attached to Brazil's interior served as the core element for sustaining the discursive and spatial contours of the Prestes Column's mythology.

In terms of sources, my book draws from five main components: archival documents, memoirs written by former officers in the Prestes Column, newspaper and cultural outputs, oral histories, and physical memory sites. For this project I visited archives in six Brazilian states, including major archival centers in Rio de Janeiro and São Paulo as well as smaller regional archives in the interior. I complemented these Brazilian sources with research in the National Archives of the United States and the United Kingdom, whose consular reports provided key details on the rebellion. In my reading of the archival record, I keep an eye on how the rebels, the army, and their audiences thought about and represented the interior.

The second type of source is the corpus of memoirs about the Prestes Column. I analyze which aspects of their interior experience the writers chose to include in their book, and I situate the memoirs in the periods (between the 1930s and 1950s) in which they were written. As testimony to on-the-ground experiences—whether written a few years or a few decades after the column—memoirs serve as elongated primary sources. But, given the various contexts in which they were written, and the retrospective nature of the genre, the memoirs also present several challenges. Because not all of the tenente leaders wrote memoirs, I rely on a few key texts to make broader arguments about the column, drawing above all on the memoir of Lourenço Moreira Lima, the column's official secretary. While I corroborate certain key details in the memoirs with additional historical sources (including other memoirs), this is not always possible. As with any source, memoirs have their analytical riches as well as their traps, and I seek to always be clear about how I use the memoirs; I also compare them with my archival findings. Several memoirs contain the reproduction of primary sources such as letters between rebels and the bulletins of the high command. Yet my research in various archives shows that not all of these documents were reproduced in full, selectively leaving out instances where rebel soldiers were put in front of a firing squad by their own leaders for having raped a local woman, or when troops deserted the rebellion. In dialogue with scholarship on archival silences, I analyze these examples of memoir omission to show how the partial presentation of historical documents is a form of myth-making.[44]

My third source covers public forms of commentary—namely, newspapers, novels, and poems. As John Charles Chasteen has written in his study of caudillos in Brazil's southern borderlands, "Because myths live less in archives than in newspapers, political oratory, fiction, or drama, our exploration of the topic will lead us to that sort of source material."[45] In terms of newspapers, I built a database of nearly one thousand articles spanning the twentieth century, the majority of which I consulted using the Hemeroteca Digital online repository of Brazil's National Library. Similar to my reading of archival documents, with the newspaper sources I look beyond the facts of the rebellion (e.g., troop location, number of wounded soldiers) to examine how the experience in the interior was being depicted. And, in the realm of culture, I analyze novels and poems written about the column—from positive and negative perspectives alike—as a way to trace the symbolic legacies of the march.

The fourth source is oral histories with interior populations that were collected by journalists in the late twentieth century. These interviews reveal a range of memories and multiple truths relating to the column. Although I personally visited many of the regions in which these testimonies were collected, the subjects had passed away decades before my own research; therefore, I could not confirm their details. As with my analysis of the memoirs, I treat the oral histories with a critical eye toward what their meanings conveyed both at the moment of their collection and as a symbol of larger historical trends.

My fifth source draws from the field of memory sites and monuments, as I trace memory in physical form by analyzing over a dozen memorials throughout Brazil that commemorate the rebels as well as the soldiers that pursued them. These range from large monuments and museums designed by Oscar Niemeyer to small tombstones and statues.

It is also worth explaining several of my authorial choices. In contrast to much of the literature on the column, I am concerned less with the details of the march (e.g., troop movement and battles) and more with the meanings that have been attached to those details. As such, my book is not a military history but a political and cultural history of the column and its legacy. Of the Prestes Column's 150 battles, I only mention two dozen of them. My choice to discuss a particular battle is a signal for readers about which moments of the column shaped its legend; this relates to both the heroic story (e.g., Prestes's success on the battlefield or examples when the rebels built alliances with local groups) as well as the counternarrative, such as the accidental nature of the inland march or the luck involved in several of the column's victories. My goal is to provide a general sense of how the rebellion progressed without getting bogged down in the specifics that, for nearly a century, have fascinated audiences, journalists, and scholars. In terms of people, I only give the names and biographical information of select officers who played important roles during the column and in the decades afterward—in addition to the small, but important, number of women who marched with the column. Otherwise, I prioritize stating the names of local people and their towns as a way to shift attention toward interior communities.

The interior of Brazil is an awe-inspiring and diverse series of landscapes, and it would be all too easy to go overboard with descriptions of its environment and topography. Except in small doses, I refrain from the type of lavish observations about the interior that have long been a staple of writers and explorers. I have also left out many of the smaller details readily available in the many books about the column. The large body of work on the Prestes Column has already vividly described its battles and the minutiae of daily life during the long march. Often drawing on the same rebel memoirs as their source base, most books tend to mention how the rebels spent much of their downtime (playing cards), their preferred way of using books (tearing out pages to roll cigarettes), or the fact that Prestes almost died in the Tocantins River (he was still learning how to swim). In contrast, I have chosen to elide these anecdotes and to focus instead on the meanings of the larger histories at play.

Finally, a note on maps: I include in this book eight maps that show the column's progression. These are intended to give readers a sense of chronology and also the spatial scale of Brazil. Throughout the book I also analyze historical maps depicting the column that were published in newspapers at different moments of the twentieth century. As we will see, these published maps represent what I call a *cartographic picaresque*, and I analyze them as part of the broader arc of how the Prestes Column drew from the symbolism of Brazil's interior to influence the history of space and nation in Brazil.

Book Structure

The Prestes Column took place from 1924 to 1927, but only half of my book relates to the two and a half years that the tenente rebels trekked across Brazil's interior. The other half focuses either on events prior to the column—providing the context for the spatial histories that would expand after the 1924 rebellion—or afterward, when the intertwined histories of the Prestes Column and the interior reverberated across the twentieth century. Chapter 1 foregrounds the influence of Euclides da Cunha's 1902 book, *Os Sertões*, and provides background on the tenentista movement and the history of Brazil's military in the early twentieth century, culminating in the 1924 São Paulo rebellion that would evolve into the Prestes Column. The second chapter marks the start of the five-chapter chronicle of the column, tracing the rebel march up and around Brazil and back toward exile, its interactions with locals, its communications with supporters on the coast, and the many elements through which its mythology emerged and shifted.

The final four chapters of the book then trace the legacy of the column for nearly a century. Chapter 7 shows how the legend of the column became firmly attached to the figure of Luís Carlos Prestes between the rebel exile in February 1927 and the Revolution of 1930 that resulted in Getúlio Vargas seizing power. Chapter 8 charts the spatial legacies of tenentismo during the era of Vargas, from 1930 to 1954, giving particular attention to the standoff between Prestes and Vargas as well as to the wave of memoirs written by former rebels. Chapter 9 interweaves examples of culture and commemoration between the 1940s and the 1980s. Here, I analyze poetry and novels alongside three emblematic moments related to the column—its thirtieth anniversary in 1954, its fiftieth anniversary in 1974, and Prestes's death in 1990. The tenth and final chapter follows the memory battles of the 1990s, exploring three particular cases: journalistic reports about the column, a monument to Luís Carlos Prestes, and a minor scandal that occurred when historical documents were publicized by an archive in Rio de Janeiro. The tenth chapter also shows how, on the eve of the twenty-first century, reflections on the column's passage through the "old" Brazil of the 1920s served as way to lament the changes wrought by twentieth-century efforts to modernize the interior. An epilogue then closes the book, in which I offer a first-person travelogue of my research in the Brazilian interior, and a discussion of what the memory sites symbolize for how the Prestes Column is depicted in the present day.

REBELLION AND THE BACKLANDS

A primitive animality, slowly expunged by civilization, was here being resurrected intact. The knot was being undone at last. In place of the stone hatchet and the harpoon made of bone were the sword and the rifle; but the knife was still there to recall the cutting edge of the ancient flint, and man might flourish it with nothing to fear–not even the judgment of the remote future.
—EUCLIDES DA CUNHA, *Os Sertões* (*Rebellion in the Backlands*)

The above were some of the closing lines of what became one of the most influential books ever written in Brazil: Euclides da Cunha's 1902 *Os Sertões*.[1] Originally trained as a military engineer, Cunha had been dispatched to the interior of Bahia as a war correspondent for *O Estado de São Paulo*, tasked with writing about a standoff in the late 1890s between the Brazilian army and a millenarian movement of some thirty thousand residents at a rural settlement known as Canudos. By the time Cunha arrived in 1897, three government expeditions had failed to defeat the backland defenders under Canudos's leader, the itinerant preacher Antonio Conselheiro. Cunha witnessed the fourth and final assault, through which the army finally occupied

Canudos and destroyed the village, ending with the army beheading many of the locals who had been taken prisoner. Only a handful of Canudos's nearly twenty thousand residents—including women and children—survived. Mediated largely through Cunha's wartime reports and book, the violence at Canudos profoundly impacted how Brazilians viewed their national character. As Robert Levine has written, "Readers of *Os Sertões* were shown that the new symbols of Brazilian progress—the burgeoning cities of the coast with their artifacts of material culture imported from abroad—masked the primitive and antisocial impulses still resident in the rural interior."[2] Over the course of the book, as Cunha grapples with his newfound respect for the locals as well as his disdain for the ferocious violence of government forces in their destruction of Canudos, readers are confronted with a troubling dilemma: Is the coast really more civilized than the interior?

Os Sertões offers a useful opening to a book on the Prestes Column and an interior history of modern Brazil. In many ways, the column was an inheritor of the discourses made famous by Euclides da Cunha. As we will see, the leaders of the column invoked Cunha's writing about the landscapes of the backlands, mimicked his way of describing local people, and saw themselves as continuing his legacy of bringing mainstream attention to the realities of life there. Cunha helped to popularize the twinned narratives of interior spaces and their communities. Prior to describing the battles at Canudos, for example, *Os Sertões* opens with a first chapter titled "The Land," followed by the second chapter, "The Man." This duality would become a key theme in the legend of the Prestes Column in which the rebels heroically traversed the vast spaces of the Brazilian heartland while shining a light on the true nature—and fearsome potential—of its inhabitants. As it was in Cunha's depictions of Canudos, the prevailing symbolism of the Prestes Column relied on questions of civilization, backwardness, and the spatial contours of Brazil's future.

As a nod to Euclides da Cunha, this chapter is titled "Rebellion and the Backlands," a slight refraction of *Os Sertões*'s translated English title, *Rebellion in the Backlands*. Here, my choice of *and* rather than *in* is meant to signpost an important and often overlooked element in the history of the Prestes Column: the rebels in the 1920s had never intended to take their fight into the backlands. Rather, the tenentista movement was initially organized by, and for, sectors along the coast. This chapter comprises two sections that place the links between Canudos and the Prestes Column in the broader political changes of the late nineteenth and early twentieth centuries. First, it discusses *Os Sertões* and how its depiction of the Canudos War set in motion the types of spatialized discourses that would predominate in the legend of the Prestes Column. Second, it focuses on Brazil's army—the institution from which the column would emerge—and the political movement that erupted in the 1920s from disenchanted army officers: what became known as *tenentismo*. A discussion of the army is especially important because, prior to 1930, when Getúlio Vargas initiated Brazil's first centralized political system, the army was essentially the only national institution, meaning that when Prestes led the rebels on their fifteen-thousand-mile march, it injected a sort of spatial legitimacy into the army's self-image as the country's most representative body.

Coastal Gaze at Canudos

A veritable subfield of scholarship exists on Euclides da Cunha and the impact of *Os Sertões*.[3] Thus, my objective here is neither to summarize the book nor to analyze the myriad of ways in which it shaped Brazilian social thought on questions of race, region, and modernity. Instead, I discuss a set of themes about *Os Sertões* as a way to situate the formation, some two decades later, of the Prestes Column.

To begin, Cunha and his reports attained wide notoriety within mainstream coastal society because of the advent of the same platform that would soon cultivate the legend of the tenente march across the interior: newspapers. Although smaller than the media boom of the 1920s, Brazil's newspaper sector at the turn of the twentieth century benefited from the recent expansion of telegraph lines into the country's interior—a bridging of coast and interior also enabled around this time by the construction of railroads and the advent of steamships. Cunha's dispatches from the front lines in Canudos, along with those of journalists from eight other newspapers sent to cover the final and most dramatic phase of fighting, represented some of Brazil's earliest war reporting. As Levine notes, "Highlighted by the universal fascination with stories about crazed religious fanatics, the Canudos conflict flooded the press, invading not only editorials, columns, and news dispatches, but even feature stories and humor. For the first time in Brazil, newspapers were used to create a sense of public panic."[4] This panic had been building over the course of Brazil's nearly century-long transition out of colonial rule. Although both the 1822 establishment of the Brazilian Empire (which replaced Portuguese rule) and the 1889 creation of the Brazilian Republic (a replacement for the empire) occurred bloodlessly—unlike most of Latin America, Brazil never fought a war of independence—a series of revolts from enslaved people and other oppressed groups kept Brazilian elites on edge. Not only did these rebellions make elites fearful of a Brazilian version of the Haitian Revolution but their seemingly constant occurrence across the nineteenth century also undercut the elite narrative of Brazil as a peaceful and civilized nation. After decades of smaller-scale revolts, most of which received little media or public attention, the Canudos War erupted across headlines and into the psyche of the nation. In the first decade of republican rule, newspaper coverage of the war dented mainstream society's sense of exceptionalism.

One of the aspects of Cunha's reporting that set him apart was his attention to the social backdrop of Canudos. While most of the other journalists sent to Canudos stayed embedded with the military, Cunha ventured out to conduct his own research, talking with locals and exploring the area. More than merely reporting on the gory details of the war, Cunha sought to understand why it was happening in this particular space of the Brazilian nation. As Edvaldo Pereira Lima has observed, "Bringing to the field his cultural background in positivism and social Darwinism, on the one hand, and naturalism—as applied to both science and literature—on the other, [Cunha] composed war dispatches that avoided the shallow, fact-oriented approach of his competitors and instead put the dramatic situation into a personal perspective."[5] Positivism, it should be noted, was an ideology popularized by the nineteenth-century French philosopher August Comte, who argued that society should be governed by a mathematically oriented vision of rational thought. Brazil's military academies relied heavily on positivist teachings, instructing cadets like Euclides da Cunha to see society as moving through stages of progress and civilization. With these ideas in mind, Cunha reported on the inhabitants of Canudos with an eye toward their place in a broader logic of Brazilian society.[6]

Cunha's attention to personal stories in the backlands came to represent Brazil's first example of journalistic nonfiction, which would position him as the grandfather of Brazilian literary journalism.[7] Part of what made Cunha's writing so impactful was his focus on the people who inhabited the Bahian interior—the sertanejos. His descriptions of sertanejos elevated these rural people into a nationally known archetype; he wrote about them in a manner that was simultaneously condescending and awestruck. For example, he gave the following description of a sertanejo:

He is ugly, awkward, stooped. Hercules-Quasimodo reflects in his bearing the typical unprepossessing attributes of the weak. His unsteady, slightly swaying, sinuous gait conveys the impression of loose-jointedness. His normally downtrodden mien is aggravated by a dour look which gives him an air of depressing humility. . . . Yet all this apparent weariness is an illusion. Nothing is more surprising than to see the sertanejo's listlessness disappear all of a sudden. In this weakened organism complete transformations are effected in a few seconds. All that is needed is some incident that demands the release of slumbering energies. The fellow is transfigured. He straightens up, becomes a new man, with new lines in his posture and bearing; his head held high now, above his massive shoulders; his gaze straightforward and unflinching. Through an instantaneous discharge of nervous energy, he at once corrects all the faults that come from the habitual relaxation of his organs; and the awkward rustic unexpectedly assumes the dominating aspect of a powerful, copper-hued Titan.[8]

In his typography of sertanejos, Cunha's social Darwinism mixes with his newfound respect for their innate potential. As popularized by Cunha's writing, and later evident in subsequent interior expeditions like the Prestes Column, this duality would reverberate across commentary on the interior more broadly.

The Army at a National Crossroads

Cunha's respect for the sertanejos, prejudiced as it was, also reflected the failure of Brazil's modernizing project. What made the sertanejos so surprising, in part, was that they stood out so starkly against the projected vision of the Brazilian nation, still in its buoyant infancy after the abolition of slavery in 1888 and the establishment of the First Republic in 1889. At a moment when coastal elites imagined that their new republic could parallel the development of the "civilized" nations of Europe, Cunha's dispatches from Canudos and his eventual book shocked readers and made clear that Brazil's search for modernity would have to take seriously the realities of life across its vast territorial expanses.

Part of these debates related to Brazil's army, and how the new republic would deal with internal dissent. Prior to the start of the Canudos War in 1896, the government had to contend with a series of regionalist revolts earlier in the decade, most notably the Federalist Revolution of 1893 in Rio Grande do Sul, in which *gaúchos* sought greater state autonomy in the face of the republic's centralizing project. After nearly two years of fighting, the army was able to put down the revolt in Rio Grande do Sul—though the gaúchos did march to the borders of São Paulo before being driven back to southern Brazil. And, when the war at Canudos began, Brazil's first civilian president, Prudente de Morais, dispatched the army with hopes of a quick and decisive victory. Yet it took *four* campaigns to finally defeat Conselheiro and his relatively impoverished followers. More than simply a testament to the sertanejos' resilience, the drawn-out fighting at Canudos was also a result of the army's shortcomings. Journalists on the front lines sent tales of military incompetence back to readers on the coast, making the campaign into something of an embarrassment for the government. It was bad enough that the army could not easily defeat a group of supposed backland fanatics, but the behavior of government troops challenged the view of a civilized Brazilian nation.

In one of the most infamous scenes from *Os Sertões*, Euclides da Cunha tells a story of soldiers who descend ravenously on a herd of goats. Reading this text, one begins to question whether the actual barbarians were the soldiers rather than the sertanejos. The scene takes place toward the end of the war, at a moment of supposed victory for the nation, when its self-projected image of modernity gets called into question. As recounted by Cunha:

> This was the last of the skirmishes, and it ended in a providential incident. Alarmed, it may be, by the bullets, a herd of wild goats invaded the camp, almost at the moment that the defeated sertanejos retreated. This was a fortunate diversion. The [soldiers], absolutely exhausted, now gave wild chase to the swift-footed animals, delirious with joy at the prospect of a banquet after two days of enforced fasting. And an hour later these unhappy heroes, ragged, filthy, repulsive-looking, could be seen squatting about their bonfires, tearing the half-cooked flesh as the flickering light from the coals glowed on their faces, like a band of famished cannibals at a barbarous repast.[9]

In the years and decades after the war at Canudos, this type of story lingered as a reminder of the army's role in the nation's political project—and of what could go wrong when the army failed to uphold an image of virtuous defenders of the patria.[10] Even more troubling for leaders of the First Republic was the fact that, in the early years of the twentieth century, the military became an increasing source not of order, but of unrest and calls for political change. In 1904, cadets from Rio de Janeiro's military academy joined local civilians in staging riots against compulsory vaccinations, and, six years later, navy sailors mutinied by taking over two battleships in the Guanabara Bay.[11] The latter event was particularly telling of the challenges within the military and of society more broadly as Brazil navigated the afterlives of slavery. The naval mutiny was staged by Afro-Brazilian and mixed-race sailors as a way to denounce the corporal punishment used by white officers. The so-called Revolt of the Whip revealed the discrepancy between the high-minded positivist goals of military officers and the social realities of a stratified society.

Industrialization in the cities and foreign immigration to urban and rural areas alike resulted in a massive population boom. Between 1890 and 1920, Brazil's population more than doubled from fourteen million to nearly thirty-one million.[12] Much of the wealth generated by this expansion benefited elites tied to the coffee industry and their political supporters, which formed the core of the era's *café-com-leite* power-sharing system between São Paulo and Minas Gerais. Named for the states' respective commercial prowess in coffee and dairy, this system had informally governed Brazil for most of the First Republic, alternating the presidency between candidates from São Paulo (the country's most powerful financial state) and Minas Gerais (the state with the nation's largest population). The dominance of these two states led to a power imbalance that was both regionally and class-based. Brazil's growing inequality was also pervasive within the armed forces. As seen in the 1910 Revolt of the Whip, the officer corps remained almost entirely white, while the lower ranks tended to be filled by poor Brazilians who, unlike the middle and upper classes, could not escape military service. In his study of the Brazilian army, Frank McCann explains that "because most recruits came from the lower end of the social and economic scale, they were darker and less educated than those who obtained exemptions. Mulattos and mestiços predominated in the ranks, except in the immigrant south."[13]

This assessment of the military, however brief, is important for several reasons. First, given that the Prestes Column emerged from the army, we must situate its history within that of the military, particularly the legacies of positivism and its impact on the generation of military cadets who came of age in the early decades of the twentieth century. Because the tenentista movement of the 1920s was led by the military, it could claim to be a positivist intervention in society rather than an irrational uprising such as that staged by civilian "fanatics" at Canudos in the 1890s or in the Contestado War (1912–16), a millenarian revolt in the southern borderlands of Paraná and Santa Catarina. The Prestes Column resulted from this sense of the military as a civilizing force for modernity and progress. If the army's role in the interior had previously been to suppress regional revolts, the Prestes Column would allow its supporters to further elevate the military's image as heroic agents of national progress.

And, given the contours of how the column would get mythologized—white rebels venturing into the dark heart of the country—a discussion of the army is important for understanding the circulation of racialized discourses. As seen above, most of the lower-ranking soldiers in the army were of Afro-Brazilian and mixed origins. The one exception, as noted, tended to be those from southern states like Rio Grande do Sul, a demographically more European-descendent part of the country. In many ways, the depiction of the column as being led by white Brazilians holds true, especially because its leadership was almost entirely Euro-descendent, including the commanding officers who came from the northeastern states of Ceará and Pernambuco.

The archival record offers few traces of the foot soldiers and lower-ranking rebels who composed the majority of the Prestes Column, though some photographs from the early phase of the rebellion in 1924—after the initial São Paulo revolt, but before it had incorporated Prestes's gaúcho troops—show a mixed ethnic composition among the rebel ranks (fig. 1.1). Over the following months, many of the paulista rebels would cross into exile, leaving some seven hundred soldiers from the original São Paulo uprising to join

FIGURE 1.1. Photo of rebels near Guairá, Paraná, November 1924. Only one name is given, a 4th Lieutenant "Abilio" (*seated, front*). Source: Acervo da Fundação Biblioteca Nacional, Brasil.

forces with roughly eight hundred gaúcho soldiers under Prestes. We do not know how many of the resulting rebel forces were of which ethnic background. What we do know is that, on the whole, the column was portrayed as white. This portrayal of the Prestes Column reflected the larger construction of race in Brazil. In her study of São Paulo and whiteness, Barbara Weinstein shows that the actual demographics were almost immaterial—regardless of whether or not paulistas were "white" mattered less than the fact that, against the foil of nonwhite backlands, they *became* white.[14]

Tenentismo

As noted by the historian Vavy Pacheco Borges, although the term *tenentismo* is used to describe the rebellious army movements of the 1920s, it was not coined until later.[15] At the time, it was known as different combinations of military rebel or revolutionary—*militares revolucionários, revoltosos, rebeldes*, or *revoltados*. Tenentismo as a distinct—if vaguely defined—political movement only took shape retroactively, after Vargas seized power in 1930, as politicians and subsequent generations of scholars sought to discuss the armed movement that toppled the First Republic. There have been two main schools of thought as to what exactly tenentismo was and how it came about. Maria Cecília Spina Forjaz argues that tenentismo was a product of a new urban middle class that became frustrated when its aspirations of social ascent confronted the entrenched systems of the First Republic.[16] Boris Fausto, on the other hand, suggests that tenentismo emerged because the military saw itself as the guardians of Brazil's institutions, a belief that originated in the second half of the nineteenth century. In this latter view, the elites of the First Republic, who were handed power because of the military's intervention in the late 1890s, had abdicated their responsibility to the nation and thus needed to be removed.[17] Regardless of how we conceive of the movement that came to be known as *tenentismo*, its trajectory is clear: between 1922 and 1930, dissatisfied officers within the military organized a series of armed movements to overthrow the government. In the middle years of this history (1924–27), the Prestes Column became the leading symbol of tenentismo.

The tenentista movement did not have an overarching political ideology. To the extent that it had a platform, it included reforms like the secret ballot and more balance between the three branches of government. Its purpose, essentially, was to end the café-com-leite system. Although tenentismo did not have a unifying ideology, it did emerge in opposition to a clear target:

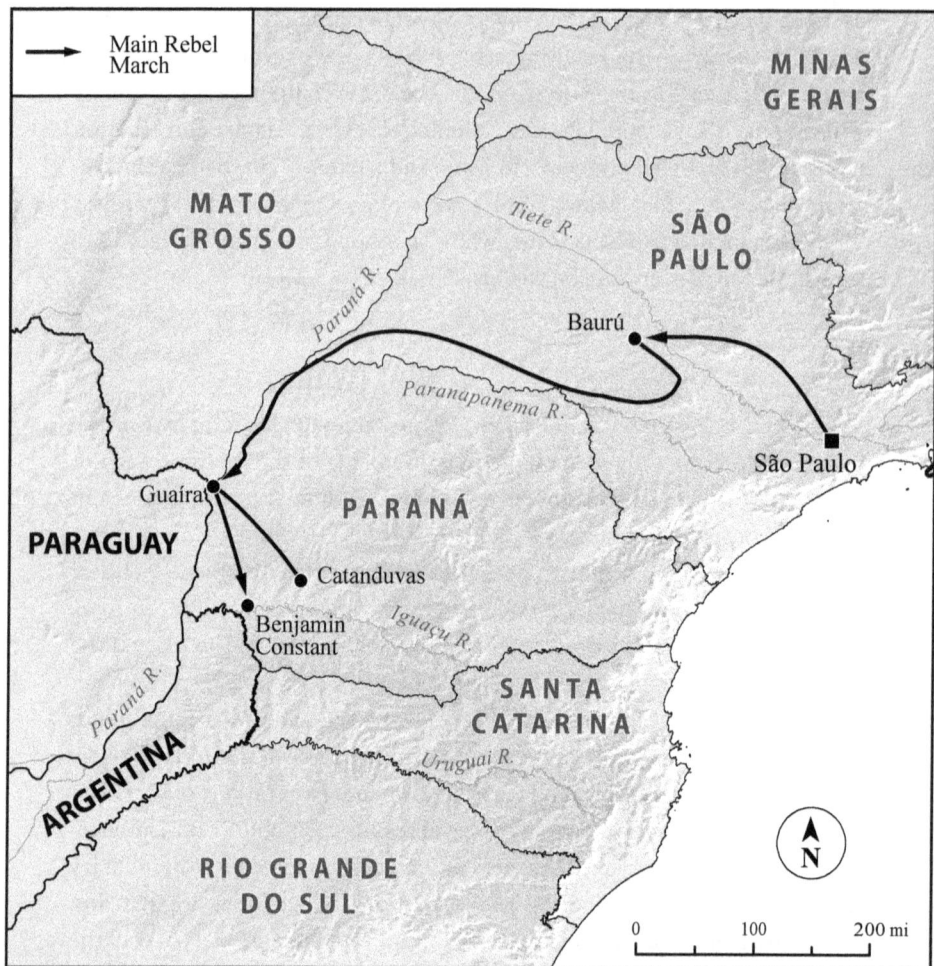

MAP 1.1. São Paulo revolt and retreat, July 1924–April 1925. Courtesy of Gabe Moss.

President Artur Bernardes, the former governor of Minas Gerais who was selected by the café-com-leite elites to run as president in 1922. The election placed the military and Bernardes in each other's crosshairs, resulting in the "false letters" scandal. Five months before the election, the Rio de Janeiro–based newspaper *Correio da Manhã* published two letters allegedly written by Bernardes in which he called Marshall Hermes da Fonseca—Brazil's most respected military leader—a scoundrel (*canalha*) and an "overblown sergeant" (*sargentão*). The letters were later shown to be forged, but they escalated tensions and led many in the military to cast doubt on the legitimacy of Bernardes's election in March 1922. The conflict continued, and, on

July 2, the new Bernardes government arrested Marshall Hermes and closed the Clube Militar, the officer fraternity of which Marshall Hermes was president. Three days later, the army staged a revolt in Rio de Janeiro, a small and unsuccessful uprising best known for ending in a gun battle along Copacabana beach. Most of the rebel soldiers who had escaped the nearby fort (the "Eighteen of Copacabana") were shot and killed. The abortive revolt etched July 5 as the origin date of tenentismo, setting into motion further events on the horizon.

Two years later, again on July 5, military rebels marked the second anniversary of the earlier uprising by staging a much larger revolt. Commanded by General Isidoro Dias Lopes—a gaúcho veteran of the Federalist Revolution of 1893–95—the coordinated action included revolts in São Paulo, Sergipe, Pará, and Amazônas. Only the uprising in São Paulo had any success, with the others being put down quickly. Despite heavy government bombing, the paulista rebels held São Paulo for nearly a month before retreating on July 28 and marching toward the Paraná borderlands. The São Paulo revolt resulted in hundreds of deaths and widespread damage to the city.[18] As the paulistas made their way west, either toward exile or to regroup for another push on Rio de Janeiro, a new front in the rebellion opened farther south in Rio Grande do Sul. And it was from within the gaúcho ranks that Luís Carlos Prestes would emerge and eventually lead the column on its march across the interior.

2

THE ACCIDENTAL MARCH

What we attempted, principally, was to arouse the masses of the interior, shaking them from the apathy in which they were living, indifferent to the fate of the nation, hopeless of any remedy for their difficulties and sufferings.—LUÍS CARLOS PRESTES, 1941

The above epigraph reflects a pillar of the Prestes Column's dominant my-thology.[1] As noted by Luís Carlos Prestes in 1941—by that point a staunch communist, and imprisoned under the Estado Novo dictatorship of Getúlio Vargas—the legend of the column depicted the rebels as having always in-tended to go into the interior. With the column's legitimacy tied to its inten-tion to liberate Brazil's impoverished rural communities, the legend of the Prestes Column evolved as one of purposeful awakening. But the column's interior march was accidental: once most of the original São Paulo rebels stopped fighting and went into exile, the column only turned north when federal troops blocked the path to Rio de Janeiro. Highlighting the accidental nature of the march is vital in order to foreground the mythologizing that, in the years and decades to come, would depict the column as a heroic quest to liberate the interior. More than just calling attention to a misleading narrative in the rebel legend, such an intervention helps to explain how the symbolism of Brazil's interior could have a profound real-world impact—in this case, shaping the route and legitimacy of a military campaign.

Rebel leaders—first in São Paulo in July and then in Rio Grande do Sul in October—never envisioned a drawn-out march, let alone one that would wind its way up and through Brazil's vast interior regions. A close reading of the initial stages of the march reveals the foundations of the narrative that would form around Prestes and the column. Prestes's rise as the head of the rebellion was enabled not only by his military skills but also by the failures of his enemies and the decision of many of his commanding officers to abandon the fight. And, although there were indeed indications that Prestes was more attuned to rural poverty than most of his fellow rebels, the actual progression of his political worldview was slower than his legend suggests. Over time, the actual intentions of Prestes and his compatriots have become subsumed by a more heroic goal projected afterward.

The Gaúcho Revolt

The rebellion in Rio Grande do Sul would come to be led by Luís Carlos Prestes, a twenty-six-year-old gaúcho army engineer who, after being trained at the Realengo Military Academy in Rio de Janeiro, had returned to his native state to oversee the construction of railroad tracks near the border with Argentina. Prestes had not participated in the original tenente revolt of 1922, but he had been sympathetic to the movement, and by 1924 he became a full conspirator. Throughout the first half of 1924, Prestes was in contact with rebel leaders such as Juarez Távora, who sought to organize a gaúcho uprising to correspond with the larger events being planned for São Paulo. Yet, partially due to Rio Grande do Sul having so recently emerged from the 1923 "Libertador" rebellion against the state government, many gaúcho leaders were hesitant to embark on another war.[2] As such, when revolts launched in São Paulo, Sergipe, Pará, and Amazônas on July 5, 1924, nothing happened in Rio Grande do Sul. Over the coming months, Prestes and other gaúcho conspirators received few updates about the revolution; the news blackout resulted largely from President Bernardes having declared a state of siege after the July 5 revolt, which included heavy censorship. But when the retreating paulista troops made their way to Foz do Iguaçu in September, they were able to feed information across the border to newspapers in Argentina and Uruguay. These reports then made their way back to the rebels in Rio Grande do Sul, along with the broadcasts of an Argentine radio station on the border.[3]

While serving as the chief engineer of the First Railroad Batallion in Santo Ângelo, Prestes corresponded with members of the revolutionary forces heading in his direction. In a letter on October 12, Juarez Távora told Prestes that the gaúcho uprisings were needed to reinvigorate the revolution. The rebels' retreat over the previous four months had left them cornered in the border regions of western Paraná, where they fought against federal army forces led by General Cândido Rondon, one of Brazil's most venerated military leaders, who had achieved prominence two decades earlier for overseeing the extension of telegraph lines into Brazil's interior and outward to Peru and Bolivia.[4] As the rebels fought against Rondon—thus creating a symbolic standoff between an earlier interior hero and an incipient one—their position along the Paraná border was a disadvantage both in terms of tactical positioning and because the close proximity to the border facilitated a steady leak of desertions. Távora suggested that "the forces of Rio Grande advance toward Ponta-Grossa, where we can celebrate, after defeating Rondon."[5] By setting the rallying point in the eastern Paraná region of Ponta Grossa—over three hundred miles from where both the gaúchos and the paulistas were currently stationed—Távora envisioned the revolution making a second charge back toward São Paulo and onward to the capital of Rio de Janeiro. The uprisings in Rio Grande do Sul did open a new front, but not in the way that Távora and other leaders had hoped. Instead of marching east, the gaúcho rebels would wind their way north and link up with the main concentration of paulistas, who themselves had been unable to break through Rondon's forces, which blocked the path to Rio de Janeiro.

Rebel commanders decided that the gaúcho revolt should begin on October 28. Forces were dispatched to four main towns: Uruguaiana, São Borja, São Luís Gonzaga, and Santo Ângelo, the latter being led by Prestes. Although he did not have the same military experience as the other leaders, Prestes proved himself an adept commander, and, in the coming days and weeks, he became the unofficial head of the new gaúcho front.

The uprising began on the night of October 28, when Prestes's forces of military and civilian recruits took over the town of Santo Ângelo. Wearing red ribbons on their hats as a marker of their rebel affiliation, the soldiers seized control of the town hall, the railroad station, the telegraph office, and the police arsenal.[6] These events would become implanted in local memory. One resident, Armando Amaral, would look back much later in his life and say that "my heart bursts when I remember my father and my brothers [that day] with red scarves around their necks. I was there, I saw Prestes, a young man, thin and short, riding a brown horse."[7] With Santo Ângelo secured, Prestes distributed a pamphlet calling on his fellow gaúchos to support the revolt, either as fighters or by donating their automobiles, carts, and horses to the cause. The uprising had mixed results: the rebels were able to secure the initial four towns (Santo Ângelo, Uruguaiana, São Borja, and São Luiz Gonzaga) but failed to expand their control to surrounding areas, most notably at Ijuí (fig. 2.1), where civilians loyal to the state governor fired on the advancing troops, killing the rebel commander.[8]

From mid-November onward, Prestes's command in São Luís Gonzaga became the base of rebel operations. Under Prestes, the rebels began to print their own newsletter, called *O Libertador* (The liberator). With its title grounded in the rebellious traditions of Rio Grande do Sul—the libertador regional conflicts—the publication also took inspiration from the São Paulo rebels. Beginning in the July uprising, the paulista rebels printed a clandestine pamphlet, *O 5 de Julho*, that, according to historian James Woodard, was "distributed furtively but with surprising regularity among the pro-rebel faithful."[9] The government considered *O 5 de Julho* to be such a threat that it offered a financial reward to anyone who could reveal its editors and printer.[10] For the gaúchos, their newspaper, *O Libertador*, sought to counter

FIGURE 2.1. Loyalist defenders of Ijuí, Rio Grande do Sul. Like the rebels they fought against, the loyalists also dressed in the traditional gaucho clothing. Courtesy of the Secretaria Municipal da Cultura, Santo Ângelo.

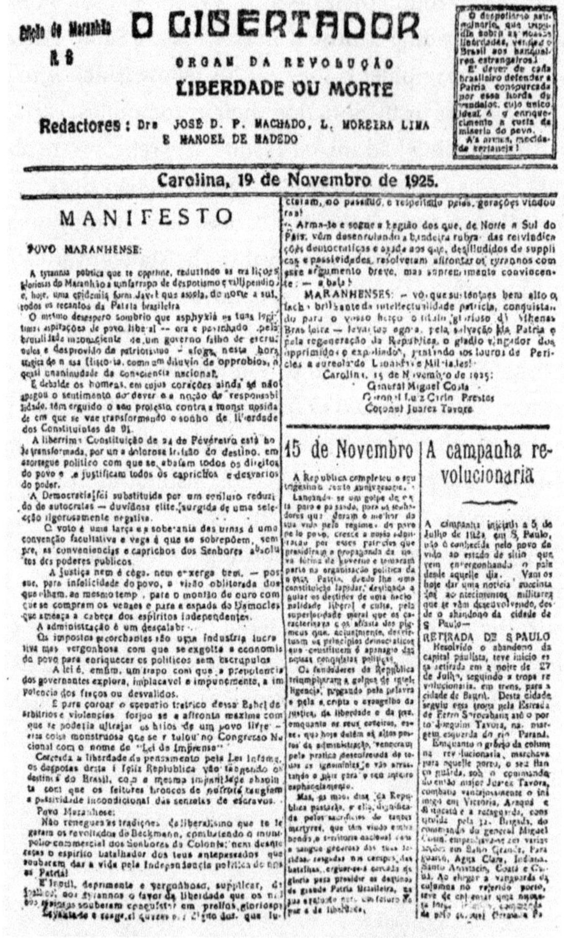

Edição do Maranhão
N. 8

O LIBERTADOR

ORGAM DA REVOLUÇÃO

LIBERDADE OU MORTE

Redactores: Drs JOSÉ D. P. MACHADO, L. MOREIRA LIMA E MANOEL DE MACEDO

Carolina, 19 de Novembro de 1925.

MANIFESTO

POVO MARANHENSE:

15 de Novembro

A campanha revolucionaria

RETIRADA DE S. PAULO

FIGURE 2.2. Cover of the eighth issue of *O Libertador*, printed in Carolina, Maranhão, on November 19, 1925. Courtesy of Museu Histórico de Carolina.

the "malevolent rumors" circulating in pro-government newspapers that depicted the rebels as murderous thieves.[11] Over the course of the entire rebellion, the tenentes would use local printing presses in various towns to publish ten issues of *O Libertador* (fig. 2.2), serving as one of the column's main platforms to inform local populations of their movements and to call for volunteers to join their fight.

After the July uprising in São Paulo, the revolution had been organized as a single force under the command of General Isidoro. But, with the new front opened in Rio Grande do Sul in late October, Isidoro anointed the gaúchos as a second division and appointed Prestes commanding officer. Prestes's promotion was not entirely a function of merit and came about only after Isidoro's original choice, General João Francisco, retreated into exile in Argentina.[12] While stationed in São Luiz Gonzaga as the new head of the gaúcho division, Prestes only authorized one major operation, a December 2 attack on the railroad town of Tupanciretã—after an eleven-hour standoff, the rebels retreated in defeat. Prolonged, stationary battles such as these would weigh heavily on Prestes, and, in the coming months, he would develop a new approach that would keep the rebellion in motion for over two years.

When Prestes and his troops returned to São Luiz Gonzaga after failing in Tupanciretã, an emissary from Isidoro instructed the gaúcho rebels to leave their native state of Rio Grande do Sul. With the paulista revolutionaries still entrenched in the western Paraná borderlands, the plan called for Prestes to lead his forces north toward the Contestado and Cima de Serra regions. Prestes's announcement of the march north was not well received by the gaúcho soldiers, many of whom deserted the revolution rather than leave behind their home state. On December 27, Prestes and his force of some two thousand soldiers headed north, but their path was blocked by fifteen thousand loyalist forces.[13] To break through what would later be called "the siege of São Luís," Prestes planned a series of strategic retreats. During the night of December 27, Prestes sent advance units to briefly engage federal troops before retreating again. The subsequent pursuit brought the federal forces closer to São Luís Gonzaga. Prestes ordered a single detachment to stay engaged with the enemy to simulate a complete retreat, while the remaining gaúcho rebels made a rapid rendezvous at São Miguel das Missões. Prestes's strategy paid off (map 2.1). In the middle of the night, all seven detachments of loyalist troops descended at once, failing to notice the rebel troops quietly marching away from São Luís Gonzaga. Before daybreak, Prestes gathered his troops and marched northeast toward the Ijuí River and, from there, onward to the northern corners of Rio Grande do Sul.[14] News of Prestes's maneuver spread through the rebel ranks and earned him widespread acclaim, including from the paulista high command. João Francisco wrote to Prestes and declared that, by "breaking the enemy's siege, dispersing him, and continuing on your desired path, that constituted one of the most brilliant operations of this campaign and it is even on par with any of the most celebrated acts of military genius carried out at any other time in history."[15] Such hyperbole would help launch and sustain Prestes's heroic status.

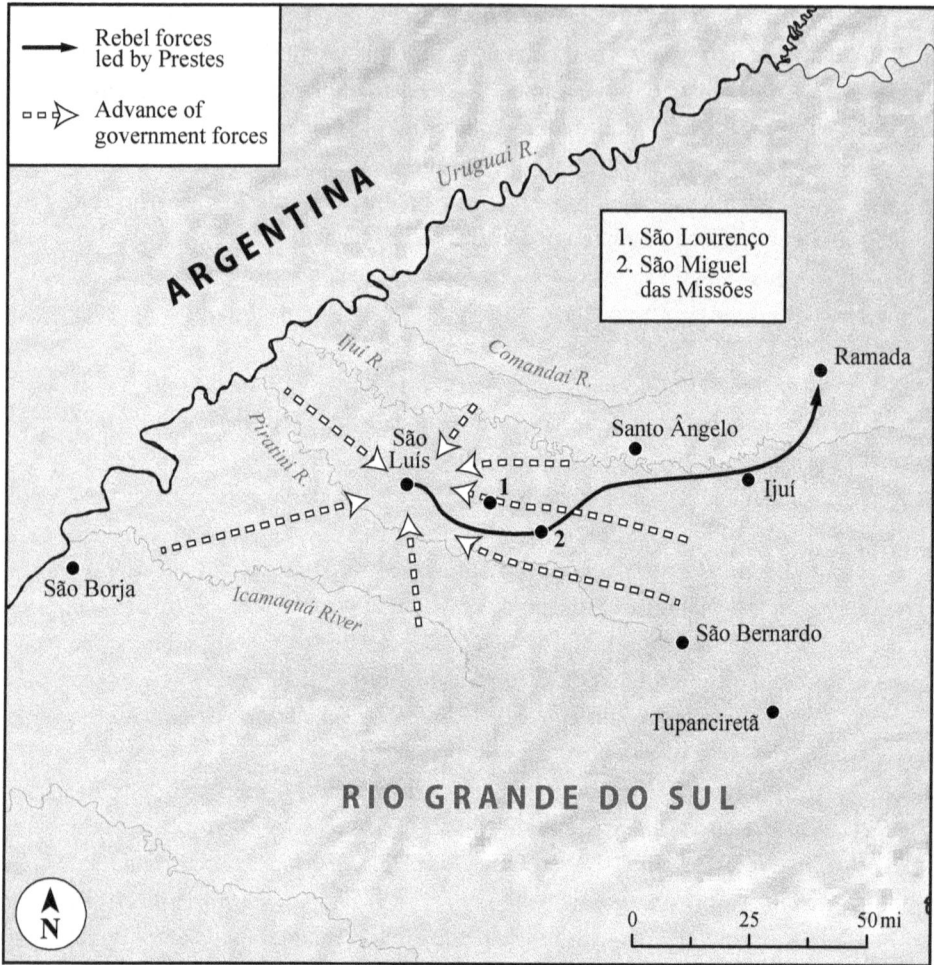

MAP 2.1. Rebel escape from the Siege of São Luís. Courtesy of Gabe Moss.

As would be the case throughout the rebellion—and even more so in the decades afterward—local narratives took shape along the column's march. One such example offers an explanation for Prestes's escape at São Luís Gonzaga. When the federal army prepared to descend on the town, a group of local housewives prayed to Saint Lourdes, offering to build a shrine in her honor if she helped to spare the town. Saint Lourdes, according to the story, answered the women's prayers and guided Prestes through the nighttime maneuver. As seen in figure 2.3, the women upheld their promise, and two years later they built a shrine to Nossa Senhora de Lourdes.

FIGURE 2.3. Inauguration of the shrine to Saint Lourdes, December 12, 1926, São Luiz Gonzaga, Rio Grande do Sul. Courtesy of the Secretaria Municipal da Cultura, Santo Ângelo.

The rebels continued north (map 2.2), and on January 9 they arrived at the Uruguay River, the border between Rio Grande do Sul and Santa Catarina. Heavy rains left the river impassable, and the rebels spent almost two weeks marching along its eastern banks, looking for a safer place to cross. The rains also meant that the terrain, already a challenging thicket of dense forests, was swollen and difficult to traverse. The plodding of the several thousand rebel horses made the ground almost impenetrably muddy.[16] Having left behind pampas fields and easy access to cattle, food now became an issue. João Alberto Lins de Barros recalled that whereas 30 men would normally eat from a single cow for their customary churrasco meal of barbecued meat, as many as 120 men now had to share the same animal.[17] And, in a letter to Prestes dated January 14, Dias Ferreira reported that his unit had to make

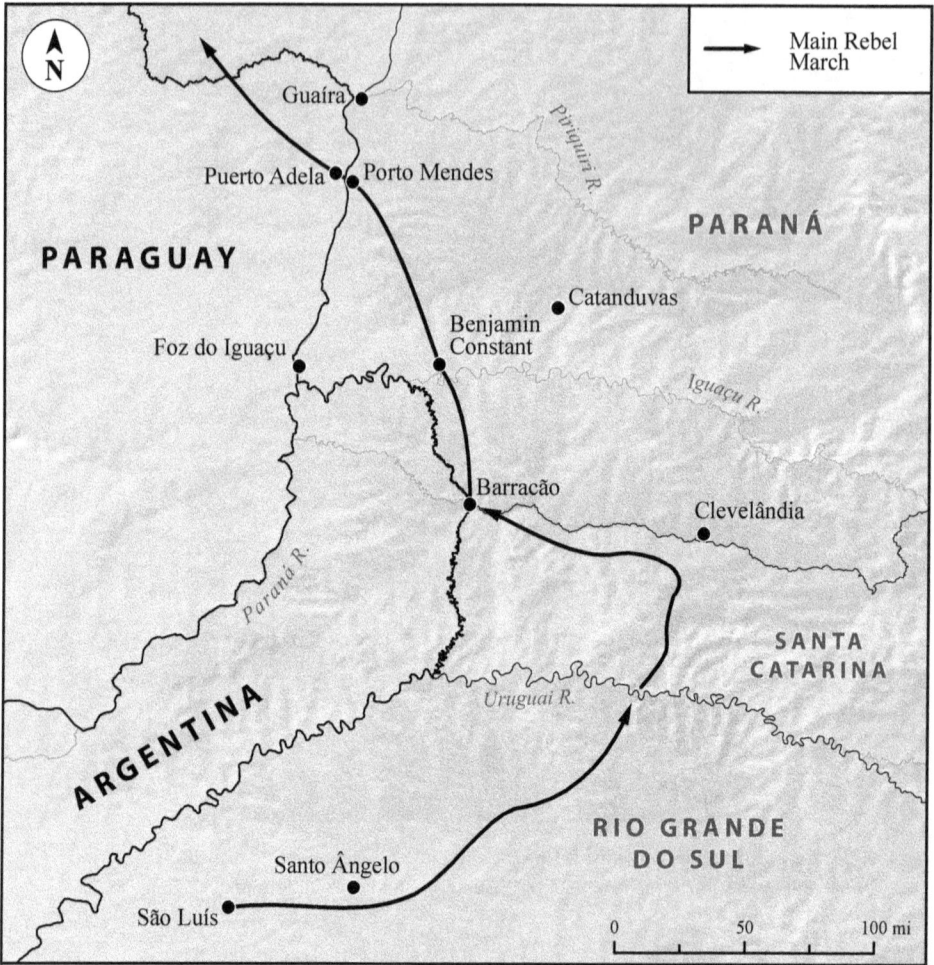

MAP 2.2. Rebel march, October 1924–April 1925. Courtesy of Gabe Moss.

one cow last several days in addition to the fact that "corn, manioc, potatoes, salt—we have nothing here."[18] Scarcity pushed the rebels to seize supplies from nearby inhabitants.

Nearly seventy years later, a local named Severino Verri remembered the column's passage through the region: "I didn't think it was right for them to take things without paying, but at the time we couldn't say anything."[19] Antônio Francisco Bortolini, who was nine years old when the column passed near his family's farm, recalled that, aside from leaving a single milk cow—so that the children would not starve to death—the rebels took almost everything else, including flour, sugar, clothes, cattle, and pigs. Even if out of necessity, this process left a mark on the rebels as well. Antenor Medeiros Pinto, a fighter who had joined Prestes in São Luiz Gonzaga, spoke with guilt about the process of stealing from his fellow gaúchos: "You know, at first we asked people for things, and they gave to us because they were afraid. They knew that if they didn't give it to us we would take it either way.... Without meaning too, we became thieves."

Leaving Rio Grande do Sul

After two weeks, the gaúchos arrived in the port town of Alto Uruguai. On the heels of an exhausting march and looking out across the water at Santa Catarina, many rebels rethought their choices. Rather than crossing into a new Brazilian state toward more fighting, almost two hundred rebels escaped into Argentina on a ferry farther downstream. The desertions at Alto Uruguai left the gaúcho rebellion with a little over one thousand soldiers.[20] As Prestes recalled, "For gaúchos, going to Santa Catarina was like emigrating [to another country]. They considered it like leaving their home."[21] When they began crossing on January 25, the only boat they found could barely hold three horses at a time—a considerable challenge, given that the rebel cavalry included almost 1,500 steeds. The soldiers built a wooden raft that sped the process along, but it still took until January 31 for the entire rebel body to enter Santa Catarina.[22]

During the river crossing, the question of women came to the fore. From the start of the gaúcho revolt in late October, the rebels had marched with a group of almost fifty women, referred to as *vivandeiras*. Yet while preparing to cross into Santa Catarina, Prestes prohibited them from continuing north. In a rare example of disobedience, Prestes's troops ferried across the river all of the women, several of whom stayed with the column for the entire course of the two-year rebellion. As will be discussed, these women played key roles as fighters, nurses, cooks, and companions. On the morning of their departure into Santa Catarina, Prestes awoke to find the vivandeiras among the rebel ranks, a number of them on horseback and ready to ride north. According to Lourenço Moreira Lima, upon seeing that his men had defied his orders to bring the women along, Prestes softened his stance, feeling "ashamed to abandon them in those desolate backlands and allowed them to continue the journey."[23]

Within Brazil's patriarchal society, the presence of women in the rebellion was a cause for alarm. As scholars such as June Edith Hahner and Cassia Roth have shown, this was a key period of women's movements in Brazil advocating for expanded employment opportunities and political rights—in this context, some observers saw the vivandeiras as evidence of broader social change.[24] The front page of the newspaper *A Capital*, for example, reported with disdain on the sightings of "many women in military clothing. They surely want to prove that they desire not only jobs in public, but, also, to take up arms."[25]

During its short passage through Santa Catarina, the column was plagued by desertions. Along with a steady stream of rebel soldiers abandoning the fight, a detachment commander named João Pedro Gay deserted the rebellion, taking many of his troops with him. The loss of Gay's unit was one of the most significant thus far; it reduced the remaining gaúcho column to some eight hundred soldiers—less than three months prior their numbers had stood at over three thousand.[26] These desertions were symptomatic of various conflicts simmering within the rebel ranks, including a pervasive lack of discipline. Prestes worried about the conduct of his troops, reporting that "more so than against our actual enemies, we have had to fight against the weakness and low morale of some of our own soldiers."[27] For gaúcho commanders, a key problem in these early phases was how to maintain order now that the initial excitement of the uprising had dissolved. Meanwhile, the leaders from São Paulo confronted much larger questions about how—and whether—to continue the revolution.

In the early months of 1925, the paulista high command faced two main challenges. First, its stronghold in western Paraná was under serious strain. Although revolutionary forces controlled the rebel headquarters of Foz do Iguaçu and the river town of Guaíra, their third holding of Catanduvas was nearly broken. From this period forward, the rebels won very few battles. Second, there was a growing tension between the "old guard" revolutionaries and a few of the younger commanders. The former was headed by General Isidoro, who advocated for disbanding the revolution, arguing that, once in exile, the rebels could better negotiate an amnesty with the Bernardes government. The latter, in contrast, rallied around Miguel Costa, the commanding officer of one of the paulista division's two brigades. Tensions grew as the revolution stretched past the half-year mark.[28] This conflict never entirely went away, as Isidoro and Costa would later fight on opposite sides during the 1932 "Constitutionalist" uprising in São Paulo.

As the senior rebel leadership faltered—whether for reasons of age, health, morale, or the lessons learned from past experience—the gaúcho rebels continued their march north, crossing from Santa Catarina into Paraná on February 7. João Alberto recalled the challenges of moving through Paraná, writing in his memoir that "[we] fought against nature. The road . . .

was getting worse and worse. It was a rarely used path, in the middle of an untouched forest—a road blocked by the trees and, at times, almost obliterated by it. We no longer had the pastures of the [Rio Grande] farmers to feed us. We were starting to run out of beef."[29] Along with a shortage of food, the rebels dealt with a lack of medical supplies that made it difficult to care for the injured soldiers. One officer wrote to Prestes from the river town of Barracão requesting medicine for his men, one of whom was suffering greatly from pulmonary tuberculosis after being shot in the lung.[30] As would be the case throughout the two-year rebellion, supplies were at a premium, and Prestes could not send much assistance to his suffering troops. A rebel commander would recall that, in moments when the column's medical stores were particularly low, some of the vivandeiras would administer "Women's Health" (Saúde da Mulher), a tonic that was meant to regulate one's menstrual cycle and was purported to help boost energy levels.[31] With a lack of supplies, Prestes remained persistent in requesting more aid from the revolutionary high command.

In one of these letters to Isidoro, Prestes coupled his request for supplies with the operational plans for what he called a "war of movement" (*guerra de movimento*). Prestes's vision, which would become adopted as the unofficial rebel strategy a few months later, was for a guerrilla-style approach of constant movement that only engaged in battle when absolutely necessary. With its emphasis on efficiency, a war of movement was a potential solution to the dwindling conditions of his troops. Of the eight hundred rebels under his command, only five hundred had weapons, and they were down to ten thousand bullets and ten automatic rifles. Prestes saw his war of movement as a way to outlast the war of position (*guerra de reserva*) that "most favors the government that has munitions factories, endless money and enough illiterate [soldiers] to throw against our guns."[32]

Along with offering the first articulation of Prestes's military strategy, this letter stands as a watershed document in the history of the Prestes Column. Here, Prestes offered one of the earliest indications of the rebellion's turn to the interior. Compounded by the increasing number of soldiers deserting or dying and accounting for the positioning of both the gaúcho and paulista troops in Paraná, Prestes realized that the original plan for a direct march on Rio de Janeiro had to be modified. He declared that with reinforcements he could march north and soon descend on Rio de Janeiro, perhaps through Minas Gerais. Prestes hoped that, with a well-supplied and quick-moving force, a detour up and around central Brazil was a viable way to then circle back down on Rio de Janeiro. Over the following months, this initial adaptation continued to change as the rebel march got pushed further from the capital.

At the end of February, Isidoro replied to Prestes, providing a frank summary of the revolution's shaky status. Writing on letterhead from the Mate Laranjeira Company in Foz do Iguaçu—the region's largest corporation, devoted to the cultivation of yerba mate tea—Isidoro explained that many soldiers and even some officers were "semi-nude and barefoot," and that their stocks had dwindled to 3,000 thousand bullets and 1,500 rifles. In terms of money, they were down to only 20 contos, meaning 20 million réis (Rs 20:000$000), the equivalent of $2.4 million in 1925 value, or 15 million USD today.[33] Despite this situation, Isidoro told Prestes that they must hold out for at least another month. As Isidoro explained, this was necessary in part for the high command and their allies in Brazil and abroad to procure more supplies; the additional time would also facilitate a possible amnesty agreement with the Bernardes government.

The campaign for amnesty was led by João Batista Luzardo, a federal deputy from Rio Grande do Sul, who had grown up in Uruguaiana on Brazil's most southwestern frontier. Luzardo was also a veteran gaúcho fighter, having participated in the Libertador rebellion of 1923. As an allied politician working in Rio de Janeiro, Luzardo organized a secret committee to pressure the federal government into negotiating with the rebels. The central demand in any peace talks remained the same: Bernardes's resignation as president. If Bernardes would step down, Isidoro was willing to order the rebels to lay down their arms.

Newspapers and the Opposition Press

While Isidoro busied himself with the logistics of the rebellion, there was also the battle for public opinion: What did the Brazilian public think of the events unfolding in western Paraná? The answer requires a brief overview of the state of newspapers in Brazil, particularly the opposition press. As mentioned earlier, the rise of tenentismo was linked to the advent of mass market newspapers in the 1920s. Previously, Brazilian newspapers tended to be somewhat niche, marketed toward the literate upper classes and focused on politics and culture. But industrialization in the early twentieth century helped to create an emerging urban middle class that, in turn, fostered a larger reading public with new consumer interests. A report from 1923 observed that "with the modernization of the press . . . media companies became infinitely more complex. . . . Newspapers became an issue more of money than of political or literary debates. . . . Winning over the public, therefore, was less a battle of ideas than a simple question of business."[34] Especially for the large daily papers in Rio de Janeiro and São Paulo, the adoption of what Nelson Werneck Sodré calls a new "business structure" encouraged several innovations.[35] The *Jornal do Brasil*, for example, hired Brazil's most popular writer of the era—at a salary of twice what the paper's editor made—to create a recurring feature called "Mistérios do Rio" that focused on crime, prostitution, and scandals of all sorts. To sell more copies, newspapers sought to meet and facilitate demand for increasingly dramatic stories.

The paragon of Brazil's emerging newspaper industry was Francisco de Assis Chateaubriand Bandeira de Melo, either known simply as Assis Chateaubriand or by his eventually ubiquitous nickname, Chatô. Chateaubriand became one of the most influential media figures in Brazilian history—often referred to as the tropical Hearst—and his rise as a media magnate coincided with the start of the tenente rebellion: he purchased his first newspaper, the Rio de Janeiro–based *O Jornal*, in September 1924, as the paulista rebels were marching toward the Paraná borderlands, and six months later he acquired a second paper, in São Paulo, the *Diário da Noite*. Along with a major influx of advertisement revenue from companies such as Antarctica Beer and General Motors, one of Chateaubriand's first changes at *O Jornal* was to consistently publish multipart serialized pieces, known in Brazil as *reportagens*.[36] The first reportagem under Chateaubriand was about the English explorer Percy Fawcett, who had disappeared while trying to discover a lost civilization in the Amazon—an early indication of both the form (serialized exposés) and the content (marches in Brazil's interior) that would soon coalesce in coverage of the Prestes Column.[37] Chateaubriand, it should be noted, had been born in Paraíba and raised in Pernambuco before moving to Rio de Janeiro at the age of twenty-five, seven years prior to purchasing his first newspaper. As a coastal elite, albeit one with personal roots in the Northeast, Chateaubriand symbolized the type of mainstream figure who used the Prestes Column to talk about the interior.

Chateaubriand, who was a staunch critic of President Bernardes, began running *O Jornal* in a climate of censorship. The martial law declared by Bernardes after the July revolt in São Paulo had been extended through the end of 1925, giving the government increased power to control public dissemination of news.[38] The Bernardes regime placed a particularly heavy hand on the *Correio da Manhã*, the main opposition paper, which was forced to stop circulating entirely between September 1924 and May 1925—a vacuum of sorts for the opposition press that further enabled the rise of Chateaubriand.[39]

The tight grip on newspapers was especially apparent in the aftermath of the gaúcho uprisings in October, as the government censored reports of the revolution's newly opened front. A US consul report from November 8—ten days after Prestes rose up at Santo Ângelo—noted the lack of public information about the events in Rio Grande do Sul: "Owing to the strict censorship the local newspapers are well controlled, and only a select few know definitely what is going on."[40] Despite the censorship in place, over the course of late 1924 and early 1925 Brazilian readers (mostly in Rio de Janeiro and São Paulo, though with some stringers in northern newspapers) could still access information about the rebellion, especially via *O Combate*, an anarcho-syndicalist São Paulo daily.[41] And, when the initial revolt evolved into the column's prolonged march across the interior, more mainstream coverage was provided by Chateaubriand's newspapers, as well as others in Rio de Janeiro such as *Gazeta de Notícias* and *A Noite*.

At the start of the rebellion, the majority of the press did not support the rebels. Newspapers such as *O Paiz*, *Correio Paulistano*, and *A Noticia* celebrated the victories won by loyalist forces, ran profiles of disillusioned rebels who had deserted, and highlighted the ragged state of the rebellion.[42] Under a headline of "Knock Out!," an article in *Gazeta de Noticias* likened the rebel passage through Santa Catarina to a boxing match in its final round, where Prestes's "disorganized" and "disheveled" forces showed that they "rose up [only] to then fall back down. . . . Soon, the ref will count to ten and nobody will get up."[43]

The Unofficial Formation of the Prestes Column

Against a media backdrop that tended to paint the rebels in a negative light, the gaúcho forces spent the months of February and March in the Contestado region of southern Paraná. Toward the end of their march through the Contestado, the rebels escaped from a particularly challenging position that, unlike the battles at São Luís Gonzaga, had little do with any brilliance from Prestes. Instead, as would happen at several moments during the next two years, the column succeeded by the grace of their enemies' failures. In the early evening of March 24, as the rebels retreated from the town of Barracão, they were advanced upon by two enemy forces: a federal army unit coming from the southwest, and a state unit from Rio Grande do Sul approaching from the east. In the lowlight of dusk, the two loyalist forces mistook each other, thinking they had found the rebels, and both sides open fired. A gun battle between the two allied units played out over four hours, killing two hundred of their own.[44] During the crossfire, the rebels evaded all confrontation, and, with the path now cleared by the loyalist blunder, Prestes marched his troops forward.

In the first weeks of April, two meetings occurred that changed the course of the rebellion. On April 3, Prestes met with Miguel Costa, the commander of the only active paulista brigade. The previous week, Catanduvas—the final stronghold of the São Paulo rebels—had fallen, and Costa now oversaw all that remained of the original paulista rebellion. Meeting in the Paraná town of Benjamin Constant, Prestes and Costa decided on a new plan to lead their troops to the central state of Mato Grosso, where they hoped to launch an offensive on Rio de Janeiro.[45] The two leaders marched with their troops north, with a stop in Foz do Iguaçu on April 12 to debrief with General Isidoro.

In his memoir, Tabajara de Oliveira recalled the uncertainty that precipitated the Foz do Iguaçu summit. Isidoro had recently returned after meeting in Argentina with representatives of Bernardes's government, and an amnesty agreement now appeared impossible. Many of the paulista rebels—having fought for over nine months—wanted to end the revolution and cross into exile. The gaúcho rebels, on the other hand, arrived in Foz do Iguaçu with what Tabajara de Oliveira described as an almost mythic aura:

> The legendary Prestes Column appeared in the Alto Paraná. At the front marched the unmatched figure of the heroic Siqueira Campos, a full beard [and] dominating gaze exuding energy. . . . . Immediately afterwards the gigantic João Alberto came forth, awkward [but] good-natured, unburdened by the responsibilities that he would take on later in life. . . . And finally, from the depths of the forest, willful, with a youthful air, framed by a big black beard, radiating confidence, Luís Carlos Prestes appeared, the most revered moral and intellectual leader of the time.[46]

In their meeting, Isidoro argued that the most viable choice was to cross as exiles into Argentina, while Prestes and Costa insisted—successfully, in the end—on the need to maintain the rebellion. Isidoro authorized the revolution to continue, though he returned to Argentina, where he would remain the nominal leader of the rebellion. Most of the paulista commanders joined Isidoro in exile, through several leaders opted to keep fighting, including a veritable who's-who of eventual political leaders in mid-twentieth-century Brazil: Oswaldo Cordeiro de Farias, Djalma Dutra, Juarez Távora, Antônio Siqueira Campos, and João Alberto Lins de Barros.[47] The forces that continued fighting became the First Revolutionary Division, under the command of

Miguel Costa. The overall division was comprised of two main detachments: the Rio Grande Detachment led by Prestes and the São Paulo Detachment led by Távora.[48] And, in an effort to maintain more systematic records of their actions, the rebels organized an internal bulletin of the high command that, for the next two years, under the direction of Lourenço Moreira Lima, would chronicle battles, promotions, punishment of disobedient soldiers, and all manner of details relating to the march.

This reorganization also marked the most important step to-date in the evolution—both mythologized and real—of what became known as the Prestes Column. Although the rebellion would not be referred to as such for another year, the leadership handed to Prestes in Foz do Iguaçu in April 1925 was the column's unofficial start. Miguel Costa remained the highest-ranking commander, yet from this point forward the rebel column would effectively become Prestes's column.

The restructured rebel division left Foz do Iguaçu with 1,500 soldiers, but those numbers dipped over the coming weeks as troops from both detachments continued to sneak across the river and abandon the revolution. These desertions were noted tersely in the rebel bulletins as well as in the pro-government media, where it was reported that deserters were arriving daily in Argentina.[49] Under a heavy downpour of rain, it took almost a week to advance north along the Paraná River.[50] Rather than cross at Guaíra and arrive directly into Mato Grosso, as initially intended, Prestes now thought that the best alternative was to cross the river thirty miles downstream at Porto Mendes and then march through Paraguay and back into Brazil.

To realize this plan, the rebels had to first contend with the Paraná River. At this bend, the Paraná was nearly five hundred meters wide with towering cliff edges. Moreira Lima remembered looking out with awe at the "steep granite banks and abrupt cliffs, reaching a height of more than one hundred meters. The speed of its currents is prodigious, creating a vast series of whirlpools, whose noise can be heard from a great distance away."[51] A lack of boats made the difficult crossing even harder. After a few days of waiting, the rebels commandeered a Paraguayan steamship on route from Asunción and spent three days ferrying their 1,500 people and 1,000 horses across the river.[52] The revolution, even if briefly, had now landed on foreign soil.

The rebel march through Paraguay required a diplomatic approach. Aware of the deep and bitter enmity between Brazil and Paraguay, column leaders delivered a lengthy statement to Paraguayan troops stationed in Puerto Adela, proclaiming that, "we are moved . . . by no intention of violence toward our brothers of the Republic of Paraguay. . . . We explicitly declare ourselves ready to respect your laws and to help you if it is necessary to defend the integrity of your sovereignty."[53] The note made its way to Asunción and was read aloud in the national parliament by the minister of foreign relations. The rebels encountered no resistance in Paraguay.

Early Exposure to Injustice

Given that many of the column leaders would later champion themselves as defenders of the downtrodden, it is notable that they did not take action when exposed to the plight of Paraguayan peasants. Eastern Paraguay was dominated by the Mate Laranjeira Company, the continent's largest supplier of yerba mate tea, and an enterprise that controlled a large swath of land and political influence across the Triple Frontier region.[54] The rebels marched along the Mate Laranjeira plantations, where they witnessed workers laboring under backbreaking conditions. In the historical record, the only evidence of any concern for the mate workers comes from the 1928 memoir of João Cabanas, who devoted several pages describing their hardships. The memoir is inflected with disdain for both the workers and their repressive employers:

> In the middle of this human flock that seemed to have emerged from ungodly places where the sun does not shine, and where there is no civilization, the famous overseers stand tall, arrogant, radiating health, and well-dressed with fine ponchos draped over their shoulders, [and] elegant silk scarves around their necks . . . these modern and bloody overseers have no soul and no conscious, [they] are brutal to the point of violence, tasked with driving their slave-like workers until they break. [All] to extract the precious [tea] leaf from the wild forests that . . . transforms into gold.[55]

Cabanas, however, abandoned the rebellion upon crossing into Paraguay, and even if rebels such as Prestes did have similar reactions, they left no record of it. In some of the column's first encounters with injustice in the countryside—a key theme in its eventual legend—the rebels did not confront the Mate Laranjeira Company. As Brazilian rebels on foreign soil, Prestes and his troops likely felt that they were in no position at that moment to take action. Along with the disjuncture between the rebels' inaction at the time and the narrative of liberation that they would later proclaim, material reasons shaped the column's decision to avoid this confrontation. In the early phases of the revolution, the company had allowed Isidoro's men to use its port and railway facilities in Paraná, and one of the company's directors was an old friend of Juarez Távora who had given him money and false papers for an earlier reconnaissance into Paraguay.[56] Moreover, once the rebels crossed back into Brazil, they made several purchases of food and supplies at Mate Laranjeira outposts, and, in one instance at least, representatives from the company donated money directly to the rebels for their passage through Mato Grosso.[57]

The rebels spent less than five days in Paraguay, marching two hundred miles through the Mbaracaju hills and across a series of smaller river crossings. The difficult terrain made it nearly impossible to march on horseback, and most soldiers proceeded entirely on foot. Moreira Lima recalled the ragged state of the column in Paraguay: "The Division looked miserable. Soldiers and officers were barefoot and almost naked, covered in filthy clothes, with long beards and straggly hair falling across their chests and shoulders."[58] Faced with these conditions, and aware of the brief window before the column was meant to cross back into Brazil, several rebel officers deserted, including Filinto Müller and João Cabanas. As preparations for the river crossing were in motion, Müller fled into exile, taking weapons and money from the rebel stocks, and Cabana deserted almost immediately after crossing into Paraguay.[59]

Feeling relieved to exit the exhausting terrain in Paraguay, the rebels crossed into Mato Grosso on May 2 with what seemed like a heightened sense of resolve. Writing during the column's first full day back in Brazil, Miguel Costa reported: "We have reentered national territory with our spirits strengthened."[60] With the column now marching north, the rebels created a new rationale for their unintended path through the interior. As we will see in the chapters to follow, the rebels' emerging discourse tapped into the longstanding symbolism of Brazil's interior as a way to legitimize their actions. These efforts were meant both for local communities—on whom the column would increasingly depend for supplies and recruits—as well as for national audiences following the march in newspapers and political speeches.

3

BANDEIRANTES OF FREEDOM

The day after the column left Paraguay and crossed back into Brazil, Miguel Costa gave a speech intended to motivate his troops. On the heels of an arduous trek across the southern states of Brazil, and finding themselves farther north than most of the rebels had ever been, Costa needed to boost morale. Ten months removed from the initial São Paulo revolt and over half a year since the gaúcho uprising, the rebel leadership sought to justify both the duration and the path of the revolution. As the column began marching toward uncertain horizons in Brazil's interior, the tenentes developed a rhetoric that reframed their direction.

While camped near a Jacarei farm on May 3, Costa addressed the troops: "The Revolution, in its new military phase, will trace a new trajectory of victory in the fight for freedom. . . . Soldiers! Never forget that you are all the bandeirantes of freedom (*bandeirantes da liberdade*) and that the greatness of Brazil depends on your courage, your strength, and your dedication."[1] This proclamation stands as the first example in the historical record of the rebels using the phrase *bandeirantes of freedom*, and its invocation here reflects the column's new orientation. At precisely the moment when the column began to turn to the northern interior, the bandeiras stood as a powerful figure to legitimize their previously unintended path.

For the next three chapters, the term *bandeirantes of freedom* will serve as a discursive and imaginative backdrop for understanding how the column, in real time, sought to redefine its march into Brazil's interior. Both the original phrase (*bandeirantes*) and the column's adaptation (*bandeirantes of freedom*) offer key insights into the sensibilities of the rebel leadership, and ultimately, into the way in which Brazil's interior served as an enduring symbol to be invoked for political gain.

In the seventeenth century, colonists from the region of São Paulo led slaving expeditions into Brazil's interior, known as *bandeiras*, from the Portuguese word for *flag*.[2] On these inland excursions—originally targeting Indigenous people and, later, runaway enslaved Africans—the bandeira would be carried as an emblem of society's venture into the backlands. Through the chronicles of their exploits, the bandeirantes helped to stigmatize Brazil's interior as a destitute space inhabited by enslaved people who had escaped their bondage, savage Indians, backwater peasants, and bandits. But, in a sign of how the interior came to embody a range of themes and aspirations, the legend of the bandeirantes also constructed the idea of a *civilização do planalto*: the notion that São Paulo's location away from the tropical coastline thus made it a more authentically Brazilian region. Within bandeirante lore, the status of a noncoastal region depended on who held the power to project meaning onto particular spaces at particular moments in time. Over the centuries, whenever groups ventured inland, whether to recapture formerly enslaved people, extract natural resources, or imagine a national future, the bandeiras stood as a testament to the image of rugged settlers in pursuit of glory and the "true" center of Brazilian nationhood.

This chapter will explore how the phrase *bandeirantes of freedom* was developed as an on-the-fly discourse to meet the changing needs of the rebellion. The use of bandeirante imagery can be understood as the tenentes needing to depict their inland march as a strategic choice. If they were seen as failed rebels forced to wander the backlands, the column would likely lose its public support—and perhaps lead to even more of its soldiers deserting. But, if seen as modern-day bandeirantes, the rebels could march through the backlands with a perceived sense of purpose and bravery as agents of the modern nation. The chosen nickname mirrored an emerging trend in the 1920s, particularly in São Paulo, when a wave of "bandeirologista" scholarship, literature, and public artwork sought to rehabilitate the image of the bandeirante.[3] Ana Lúcia Teixeira describes this push to reclaim the figure of the bandeirante as "dedicated to nothing less than the reconstruction and re-discovery of the nation."[4] The seemingly oxymoronic fusing of bandeirantes (a slaving term) and freedom embodied the contradictory core of Brazilian national identity. Long-standing notions of frontier exploration thus merged with the political expediency of the 1920s. Unlike the colonial bandeirantes for whom conquest meant the capture of interior bodies and resources, the Prestes Column began presenting itself as fighting against the injustices of life in the Brazilian interior. In the column's reframing of the bandeiras, the rebels depicted themselves not simply as frontiersmen, but as liberators.

Similar Terrain, New Path

Leaving Paraguay behind, the rebels enjoyed reentering a familiar Brazilian landscape (map 3.1). Moreira Lima wrote that Mato Grosso was a "marvelous grasslands, that unfolded like a sea of unbroken green, beneath a sky forever blue, and that spring-time climate renewed the souls of our column, after so many days of suffering."[5] João Alberto likewise recalled the passage across southern Mato Grosso as "easy. Horses and cattle were everywhere. Things were abundant again. We could again fight in the gaúcho style."[6]

The rebels marched north toward Ponta Porã, a border outpost with a single street separating it from the Paraguayan town of Pedro Juan Caballero to the west. A long-standing distrust of the federal government made the region a potential site of revolt: the US consul noted that the column's ar-rival in Mato Grosso was of "greater concern [for the Bernardes regime] than has been experienced since the retreat of the rebels from São Paulo." More-over, the consul observed that "Mato Grosso has a large class of civilians that have all the characteristics of the 'Wild West' settler—recklessness [and] fearlessness. . . . There are persistent rumors that the miners (garimpeiros) of the 'Cassanunga' district, 10,000 in number, have joined the rebels. These reports are not confirmed. But should the 'garimpeiros' . . . decide to do so, a dangerous and efficient regiment of desperate fighters would be added to the hostile forces."[7] Fearful that townspeople would join the rebel cause, the army abandoned the town.[8]

With no enemy forces to overcome, the rebel detachments of João Alberto and Siqueira Campos easily entered Ponta Porã on the morning of May 10. With no enemy in sight, Alberto's men proceeded to enjoy themselves in a manner that did not align with the image of the virtuous bandeirantes of freedom that Miguel Costa had impressed on them the previous week. João Alberto observed that, "among my men, there was great excitement at the

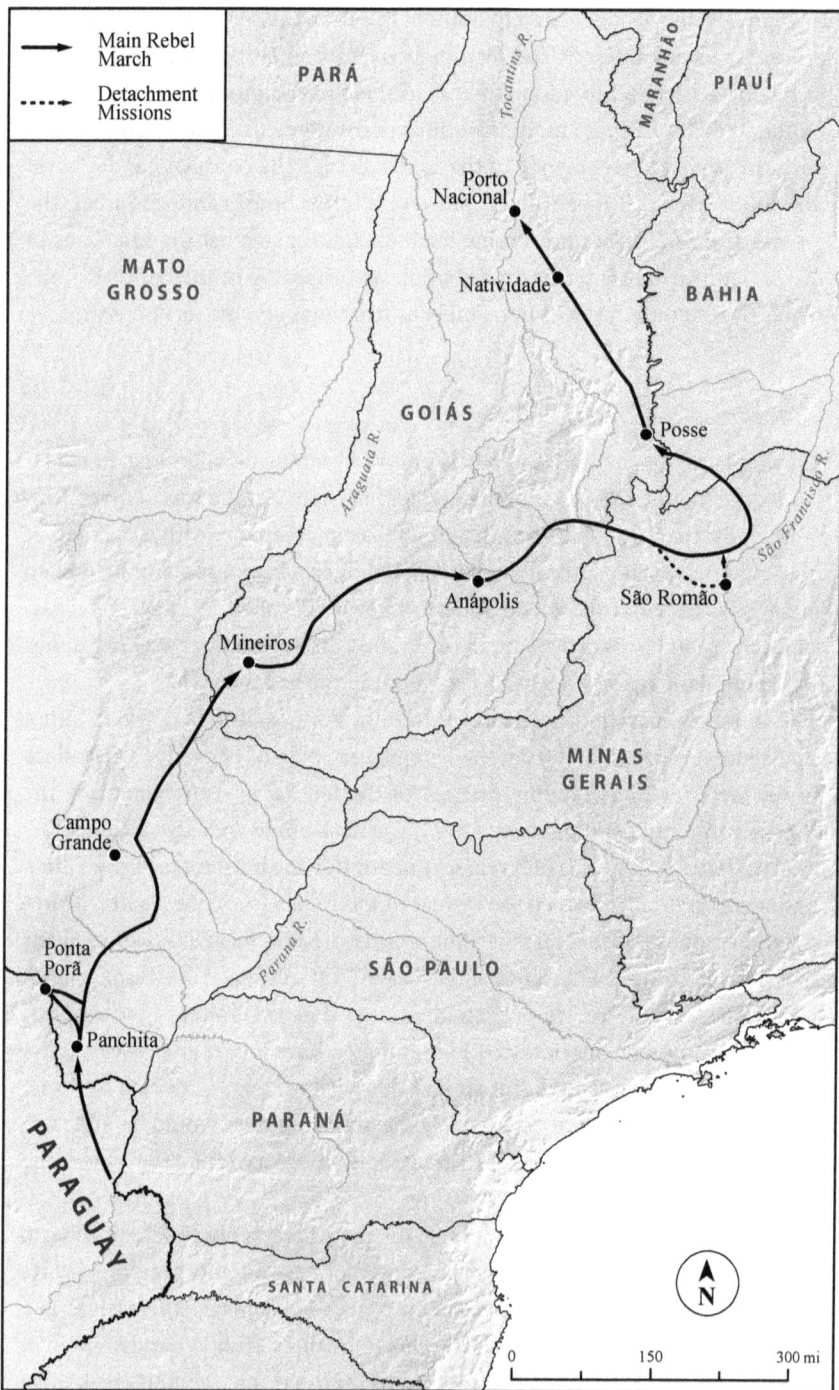

MAP 3.1. Prestes Column, May–October 1925. Courtesy of Gabe Moss.

possibility of a fun night. Since the start of the revolution at the end of October, they had forgotten what such a thing was." The rebel troops made quick haste to the *jiroquis* (small outdoor bars) that dotted the town's main avenue, and, despite having no money to pay for their beverages, the men drank heavily. It did not take long for conflict to break out. Fueled by cachaça, the rebels got involved in several fistfights that escalated into shootouts, leaving three people dead and a dozen injured. The following day, João Alberto decided to move out with his men: "I thought it would be crazy for us to stay another night."[9] Despite maintaining the plan to eventually reroute down to Rio de Janeiro, the column's path through Mato Grosso tilted evermore toward the northern hinterlands of Brazil's interior. With Brazil's *sertões* looming as an almost inevitable destination, and concerned that the soldiers' behavior could siphon off support both nationally (through newspaper reports) and locally (townspeople refusing to hand over food and supplies), column leaders made renewed efforts to present themselves as the virtuous liberators of the nation.

In late May, the column distributed a document among local populations that sought to dispel any rumors of rebel violence. The notice proclaimed: "You can remain calm as the liberating column approaches . . . because [our] soldiers are the Bandeirantes of Freedom, the men destined to commit their lives to this immortal conflict, whose motto is 'Freedom or death.'" As the bandeirantes of freedom, the document continued, the rebels were the only force capable of lifting "the nefarious shadow of Artur Bernardes" and "fighting the good fight for . . . a strong and united Brazil."[10] A draft of this proclamation, which is included in the archive of Juarez Távora, offers insight into how the bandeira myth was cultivated in real time. Although the original version was addressed "To the people of Mato Grosso," the drafted copy contains handwritten edits to replace the phrase with "To the people of Brazil." Previously, the rebels had addressed similar announcements to specific locations—for example, "To the people of São Paulo," "To the people of Santo Ângelo," and "To the people of the southern borders."[11] By directing their message to all Brazilians, the column aimed to present itself as a force of national integration, capable of uniting the historically fragmented regions of Brazil's interior. As they made their way toward the Mato Grosso-Goiás border, the rebels hoped that their projected image as bandeirantes of freedom would enable a smoother path.

As would be the case for most, but not all, phases of the column's march across Brazil, local populations often met the rebels with apprehension. The column required supplies, and, aside from occasionally seizing weapons and food from enemy forces after a battle, the majority of the rebels' material needs were met either through furtive scouting parties knows as *potreados* that would sneak onto farms and into villages, or else through "requisitions" (*requisições*) made openly on local populations. When possible, particularly in the earlier phases of the rebellion, the column issued receipts to locals for the items "requested" to serve as proof of payment that could be reimbursed by the federal government once the revolution was successful, and a new regime had been installed. For instance, on May 23, the rebels provided an itemized and priced receipt to a Mr. Lopes Pacheco, of the Barra Branca farm in Mato Grosso, who gave the column two horses and several sacks of corn, rice, and sugar.[12]

While it is not possible to know Pacheco's feelings about his "donation" to the rebels, it is important to note that peaceful interactions were not the norm. Why should hesitant communities—mostly small farmers and merchants—give their food, money, and supplies to a wandering band of unknown southerners? Hesitancy toward the rebels was aided by government propaganda, often disseminated in regional and national newspapers, depicting the rebels as marauding bandits. As seen in figure 3.1, the rebels received copies of the news, keeping them keenly aware of their own narrative. Moreira Lima recalled that "our enemies, always wicked and infamous, spread stories that we committed widespread looting and the most reprehensible attacks against peaceful people. . . . We were [thus] often met with gunfire by inhabitants of the places we passed through, as if we were the enemies."[13] As would be the case throughout the rebellion, both sides labeled the other as bandits, using the terms *bandido* and *jagunço*, the latter a reference to contracted fighters who were hired to fight on behalf of the local strongmen *coronéis*. In this shared discursive strategy, the specter of Brazil's interior shaped the way coastal forces, whether southern rebels or the federal government, perceived local conditions. Although banditry was very much a part of the interior's history, it also stood as a trope through which to delegitimize one's enemies.

In a corrosive and self-fulfilling cycle, the unwillingness of locals to part with their belongings forced the column to acquire them by force, thereby fulfilling their negative image as bandits. One farmer in Campo Limpo wrote to the column leaders during their northward march in Mato Grosso: "I will remove my family from the farm because of the frightful news [I have heard]. Because of this I ask you, my friends, to not harm them."[14] Another local, Francisco Ferreira, recalled how his town fled in advance of the column: "Our family went into the forest and hundreds of other people [from our town] also went, before the column arrived. . . . Before they arrived, we

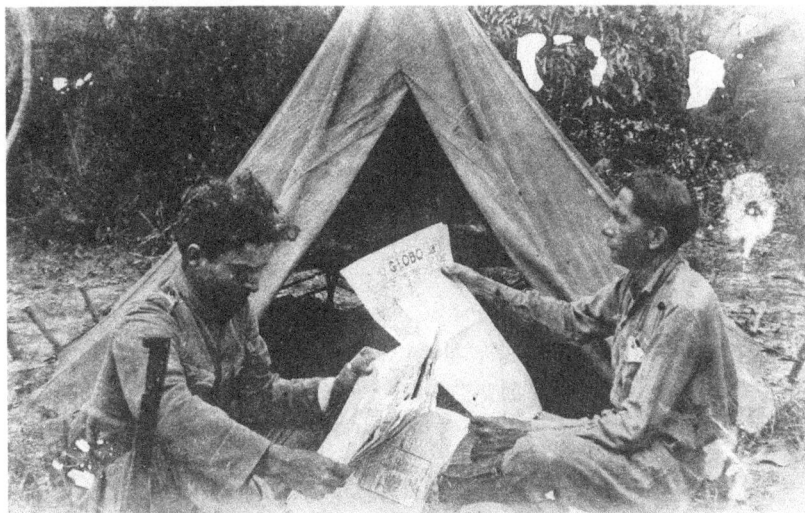

FIGURE 3.1. Lourenço Moreira Lima (*left*) and Lieutenant Fragoso read *O Globo*, likely in late 1925. CPDOC ILA photo 010.

heard news they were close. . . . So people stayed there in fear. . . . We stayed [hidden in the forest] for three days."[15] In these instances, the column's passage through the interior was not unlike the federal army's actions three decades earlier at Canudos, where the violence inflicted by coastal Brazilians might call into question who were the actual barriers to Brazil's destiny as a civilized nation.

In the initial stages of the column's march north, the rebel leadership attempted to investigate cases of violence that occurred in Mato Grosso. The first concerned the murder of two farmers during a scouting mission in late May.[16] The second took place ten days later, when a schoolteacher alleged that troops under the command of Juarez Távora looted the house on the nearby Desembarque farm.[17] In both instances, the rebel high command dispatched Moreira Lima—as the column's official scribe—to meet with witnesses and gather testimonies.

These efforts at maintaining a system of accountability did not always work. On June 4, for example, rebel soldiers staged a drunken rampage in the town of Jaraguari. Soon after their arrival, soldiers committed what Moreira Lima obliquely called "unfortunate disorder."[18] The memories of local townspeople provide far more clarity. In a 1993 interview with journalist Eliane Brum, a farmer named João Sabino Barbosa said that rebel soldiers had raped his wife.[19] The rebels' internal bulletin noted that, to avoid punishment for their actions, the offending soldiers deserted the column the following morning. Despite having announced their arrival in Mato Grosso as virtuous bandeirantes who would liberate the people from the tyranny of President Bernardes, the rebel leaders were unable to keep their soldiers disciplined enough to match the projected narrative.

As mentioned earlier, some fifty women had set off with the column— over the course of the rebellion, that number eventually dwindled to only ten.[20] The few historical sources that mention women suggest that, on the whole, their time in the column was very similar to that of the men: they marched the same distances, fought in many of the same battles, and suffered through the same hardships of a fifteen-thousand-mile march through Brazil's interior, including dying in battle, being captured by the army, and succumbing to illness. Despite this shared experience, most rebel leaders saw the women primarily as followers, not as members of the rebellion in their own right. In his memoir, Moreira Lima wrote that "the simple and naive soul of these women is formed in the sacrifices and martyrdom for the men to whom they dedicate themselves. This is the soul that makes a vivandeira."[21] Among the rebel memoirs, an exception is that of Captain João Silva—though, unfortunately for the historical recognition of the women, his memoir is arguably the least well known of the various rebel accounts. In his often overlooked chronicle, Silva lavished praise on the women: "Our beloved and brave vivandeiras were shoulder-to-shoulder with the [men]. . . . So many vivandeiras crossed the line of fire to bring back wounded soldiers, tearing off their clothing to bandage up the wounded! So many vivandeiras fell prisoner and were killed at the bloodied hands of a barbaric and cowardly enemy! Alas, our heroic and beloved vivandeiras! . . . We must give them at least some recognition in our stories, they are so deserving of it. . . . It is a shame that we do not remember all of the names of [these] heroines."[22]

Of the fifty women, we only know the names of a dozen. These women were all from Rio Grande do Sul and São Paulo, leaving it unclear whether any women joined the column after it began marching north. Most frequently, the women whose names appear in the historical record were remarked upon for either their fighting skills or their physical attributes. Of the women who fought in battle, two were known by nicknames that reflected the gendered and racial prejudices of the column. The first was a mixed-race woman known as Onça (meaning *jaguar*), and the second was called Monkey Face (Cara de Macaca), who was remarked on by Italo Landucci for dressing in leather and carrying a rifle.[23] These nicknames simultaneously acknowledged the women's contributions (e.g., showing tenacity in battle and wearing the traditional clothes of gaucho cowboys) while denigrating them at the same time. The efforts of other women were framed in similar language, often in relation to race. Tia Maria, an older Black woman who cooked for the troops, was known primarily as the Black sorceress (*a preta feiticeira*), a name that likely mimicked representations of the northeastern *cangaceiro* bandits, which often included references to a Black priestess.[24] Race could also have an inverse connotation—for example, with a nurse named Hermínia, whose bravery on the front lines was couched in a reference to her Austrian (meaning European and light-skinned) heritage.[25]

Not all rebels welcomed the presence of vivandeiras. João Alberto faulted one woman named Elza—whom he described as "a cute, blond German"—with the death of her husband, saying that he was so preoccupied setting up her tent that he did not hear an oncoming enemy attack.[26] For his part, Antônio Siqueira Campos sought to prohibit his troops from having any interaction with the women. But, in a subtle act of vivandeira resistance, the women took to mocking Siqueira Campos by calling him "Cat Eye" and "Scraggly Beard" behind his back.[27] The vivandeiras could invent nicknames, too.

For the women, their participation was a point of pride, both at the time and in the decades since. Vitalina Torres, one of the women who joined the rebellion at its inception in Santo Ângelo, marched through the very end to exile in Bolivia. In an interview in the 1990s, Torres's daughter recalled how her mother, "in a deep, manly voice, always liked to tell stories about those times, when she was almost not a woman. She had to cut her hair short and dress like a man. But when she got pregnant, she couldn't hide anymore. She always got sad when talking about my brother, who was born and died during the march."[28] Along with reflecting the gendered lens that framed her participation in the rebellion, this quotation indicates an additional challenge for women in the column: several women gave birth along the march, which meant that they had to care for themselves and their infant children in very challenging conditions. As with the son of Vitalina Torres, not all of the newborns survived. Whether in battle as fighters or in the mess tent as cooks, as well as in their roles as mothers, nurses, and partners, the women of the Prestes Column were key contributors to the rebellion.

Another Reorganization and a Surprise in Central Brazil

While camped on the Cilada farm in Mato Grosso on June 10, the rebel leadership reorganized the column. Only two months after dividing into the Paulista and Rio Grande brigades, this dual system became untenable for reasons of size (the gaúchos outnumbered the paulistas) and cohesion, as rivalries grew between the two. Now, the gaúchos and paulistas were combined within the same units. The two brigades were replaced by four detachments that mixed together all soldiers and were led, respectively, by Cordeiro de Farias, João Alberto, Siqueira Campos, and Djalma Dutra.[29] Costa remained the commanding general, but Prestes was the unquestioned, if unofficial, leader.[30]

The record-keeping at this time also offers a first example of a rebel memoir reproducing curated selections of original documents. The new command structure was codified in bulletin no. 14 of the rebel high command, which opened with a section on "Imprisonment." Here, a pair of rebels were sentenced to two weeks confinement for their role in the previously mentioned looting of the Desembarque farm. This punishment is clearly evident in the archival record.[31] In the appendix of Moreira Lima's memoir, however, where the author includes over seventy original documents, the reproduced bulletin no. 14 omitted the section on the rebel violence.[32] To Moreira Lima's credit, he at least provided a long ellipsis to indicate a missing portion, yet his reader has no way of knowing what information—nefarious or otherwise—was removed. Given that this memoir has served as the central reference for later studies of the column, these sorts of archival redaction are significant. The same omission was reproduced in a key academic work: in Anita Prestes's 1990 book on the Prestes Column, the author includes a lengthy appendix with forty reproduced primary sources, thirty-one of which were taken from published sources, including Moreira Lima's memoir, with the remaining nine coming from her own archival research. Bulletin no. 14 is one of those nine sources that she cites directly from the archive.[33] So, despite having access to the full original version (housed at the same archive that I visited three decades after she did her research, in the 1980s), Anita Prestes also chose to leave out the details of the looting and subsequent punishment. Neither Moreira Lima nor Anita Prestes erase the rebel crimes entirely, as both authors discuss some of the violence the rebels committed. Yet the curation of these reproductions stands as a form of myth protection: presenting original documents in their unoriginal form is a subtle form of creating historical silences.

Less than a week after the column's reorganization, the rebels encountered an interior population that they seemed surprised to find in the center-west state of Mato Grosso. The demographics of each region along the column's path are difficult to assess, in no small part because Brazil's 1920 census omitted questions about skin color—instead we can examine the general perceptions of the era that informed the rebel views about race and region.[34]

Compared to their eventual passage through the North and the Northeast, the rebels did not expect to encounter many Afro-descendent populations in southern and central Brazil. Yet, on their march through Mato Grosso, Siqueira Campos's detachment came across the land of the Malaquias family, who had settled on the land in 1901, barely a generation removed from the abolition of slavery. By the time the rebels arrived, the family had ten different farms in the area.[35] When the rebel unit approached, Joaquim Malaquias rallied over a dozen men to defend the farms. In his memoir, Moreira Lima offers a contradictory summary of what took place on the Malaquias farm. While acknowledging that the rebels instigated the attack—"Siqueira Campos was in charge of hitting these people, which he did with his usual energy"—Moreira Lima also writes that the rebels were victims of "an ambush" that killed two rebel soldiers.[36] This disconnect is perhaps the result of Moreira Lima's prejudice, which might not have easily allowed him to see the Malaquias as capable fighters. Moreover, Moreira Lima seemed shocked that the female head of the family (a matriarch whose name is not mentioned) took part in fending off the rebel attack. For the Malaquias family, the racial dynamics at play became an enduring source of pride. In the 1990s, Tuarpa Malaquias, Joaquim's son, would recall that "they took everything, but not a single drop of our blood was spilled by the white rebels. No Malaquias died [that day]."[37] At the Malaquias farm, a refuge of freedom built and protected by descendants of enslaved people, the column was surprised by the unexpected diversity of life in Brazil's interior regions.

Although the rebels had ventured farther north than originally intended, their location at this point in central Mato Grosso still positioned them within relative striking distance of Rio de Janeiro. But ensuing battles continued to push them east and to the north, and, in a June 15 announcement of their new leadership structure, the column referred to itself as "the 1st Division of the Liberating Army Operating in Northeastern Brazil."[38] By identifying, however briefly, as the Army of the Northeast—despite still being in the central region of Mato Grosso—the rebels seem to recognize the useful symbolism of their "liberating" march toward the backlands. As the rebels crossed into the Brazilian hinterland, and with provisions running low, the interior held the promise of bodies and supplies. Conditioned by the folklore of the bandeirantes, the backlands represented the ultimate landscape to prove—to themselves, to locals, and to audiences farther south—their self-ascribed worth as liberators.

Having steadily veered northward over the previous months, the column now embarked on its resolute march toward the sertões. As Miguel Costa observed after a battle near the border between Mato Grosso and Goiás, "we proceeded, at first daylight, on our march to the Northeast."[39] With their path now leading deeper into Brazil's interior, the rebels attempted to build an alliance with a local power broker named José Morbeck. This represented the column's first encounter with a coronel, the notorious political bosses who commanded rural militias known as patriotic battalions (*batalhões patrióticos*). Morbeck had waged a fight for many years against the state government of Mato Grosso, wanting to protect the autonomy and land claims of the local diamond miners. Prior to the column's arrival in the region, Morbeck had announced his sympathy for the rebel cause, but when Moreira Lima went to meet personally with Morbeck on June 20, it did not lead to any collaboration—as Moreira Lima reported, "Morbeck gave me some truly idiotic excuses for why he couldn't join us."[40] As they marched farther north, as we will see, the rebels came across more coronéis, all of whom rejected the column's entreaties and joined the loyalist campaign to fight against the column.

The Prestes Column left Mato Grosso and crossed into the state of Goiás on June 23. Nearly one year after the start of the São Paulo revolt, the rebellion plodded along toward an uncertain horizon. In terms of supplies, only one thousand rebel soldiers possessed a rifle, and the column no longer possessed any heavy artillery, mortars, or grenades, having shed most of these bulkier weapons during their march across Paraguay. The column began its march through Goiás at a safe distance from its pursuers. While the loyalist forces had to travel in cars and trucks over the poorly maintained and circuitous roads of southern Goiás, the rebels marched through the Serra do Baús hills. The column's vanguard unit under João Alberto arrived in the town of Mineiros on June 26, and the following day the bulk of the rebels followed suit.

At this point, Prestes was in a strong position to make a move on Rio de Janeiro. If Prestes were to take a path directly east from Mineiros, he would arrive in southern Minas Gerais, where the column would be within relative reach of Rio. There were no major natural obstacles on this potential route such as mountains or river crossings, and, although there were a series of federal and state garrisons along the way, the column had been successful so far in maneuvering around loyalist forces.[41] But a decisive defeat the following week at the Zeca Lopes farm drained the column of important supplies and pushed its path farther north. Since leaving Ponta Porã in mid-May, the rebels had gone in a steady northeasterly arc—keeping open the possibility of marching on Rio de Janeiro—but after Zeca Lopes they made an abrupt ninety-degree turn and marched due north for almost a week. The loss at

Zeca Lopes further emphasized the extremely tenuous nature of the column's supplies. Without a new cache of weapons or sufficient allies to help make use of them, the rebellion would not persist for much longer.

After their northerly march from Zeca Lopes, the column arrived in the Goías town of Rio Bonito on July 5, the one-year anniversary of the rebellion. On the outskirts of Rio Bonito, the rebels attacked family farms in search of horses, and, according to a local farmer named Manoel Zacarias, several houses were set on fire and two men killed.[42] Perhaps unaware of the rebel violence outside of town, the local priests in Rio Bonito gave the column a warm welcome. With the entire rebel force in attendance, Father José Cenabre San Roman presided over a celebratory mass in honor of July 5, and several commanding officers gave speeches. The town's second priest, Father Manuel de Macedo, even joined the rebellion, leaving with the column the next day and marching with the rebels for most of the following year. Neither the rebel memoirs nor the archival record indicates Macedo's reason for joining the rebels.[43] This was the first local leader who volunteered to fight with the column—one of only a few such examples during the entire march.

While in Rio Bonito, the column corresponded with political allies in Rio de Janeiro. Miguel Costa sent a detailed summary of the rebel's recent progression to João Batista Luzardo, the gaúcho federal deputy and the column's most outspoken ally.[44] The communication with Luzardo was a key avenue for transmitting news of the column to wider audiences. With censorship making it difficult to print certain stories, the rebels maintained a clandestine system: messengers took letters to telegraph outposts that were relayed to the central telegraph station in Rio de Janeiro, where workers sympathetic to the rebellion, in the middle of the night, retrieved the dispatch before officials arrived the next morning.[45] These reports were delivered to Luzardo, who shared them in speeches on the senate floor. Because all proceedings were published in Congress's official news organ, the *Diário Oficial da União*, Luzardo's speeches circumvented government censorship.

The rebels also wrote a lengthy proclamation about the current state of the rebellion: a de facto open letter to the Brazilian people. It is unclear whether or not this document was successfully distributed, though it shows how the column sought to portray itself at the one-year mark of the revolution. To counter the not-unfounded rumors of looting and frustration among the rebel ranks, the bulletin affirmed that "not only do our troops have magnificent morale and wellbeing, but we also are lacking for nothing." The rebels continued to present themselves as valiant bandeirantes of freedom: "We have behaved with the same norms that have always guided us, inscribing the pages of the Revolution with new and positive examples of order, valor and discipline." And, in contrast to the reality of the column's recent string of defeats, the declaration stated that, "after a march filled with victories across the vast territories of . . . Goiás, [we have] reached the heart of the country, in whose backlands we will decide the fate of [Brazil]."[46] In their bandeirante framing, the rebels continued to develop their new narrative of a purposeful inland march—now in the heart of Brazil, the column portrayed the interior as a platform for national change.

From Rio Bonito, the Prestes Column marched northeast across the central plains of Goiás. Along this route, the rebels hoped to cross into the state of Bahia, where Prestes aimed to fortify his ranks with new recruits and supplies, most notably those that General Isidoro had pledged to arrange. The plan was to dip briefly into the state of Minas Gerais to find a suitable place for crossing the São Francisco River into Bahia. During the remaining month-long journey through Goiás, the column marched relatively close to the cities of both São Paulo and Rio de Janeiro. Barely six hundred miles from the center of Brazilian politics, Prestes and his fellow officers may have felt tempted to cast a glance south, over their right shoulders, contemplating whether to change their strategy and make a direct move on the federal government. Marching this close to the Bernardes regime also posed risks: the column had to avoid the major transportation hubs that ran through central Goiás, and Prestes was careful to march his troops north of Silvânia and Pirapora, railroad towns that linked directly to São Paulo and Rio de Janeiro. Proximity to loyalist forces was far from the column's most pressing concern. If Prestes could not get more supplies, the rebels' exact location would become almost irrelevant.

The column's provisions dwindled further when a captain in Djalma Dutra's detachment persuaded a handful of his unit to abandon the rebellion. A total of six people deserted, taking with them significant stores of weapons. Dutra reported this unfortunate turn in a letter to Prestes, writing that the captain in question had "convinced my soldiers that they were wrong [to believe in the revolution] and that the benefits for loyalist soldiers were far greater."[47] Here we see some of the material underpinnings that shaped how soldiers decided their loyalties. Having fought for the past year on a combination of dedication to the rebel cause and the promise of deferred salary once the revolution was successful, switching sides must have been an appealing option. If a rebel soldier were to desert and rejoin the government army, they would not only be absolved of their current sedition but they would also start receiving their normal military salary. Without a central ideology uniting the rebels—and with the original goal of overthrowing Bernardes increasingly unlikely—soldiers had to weigh their personal reasons for fighting.

The Enduring Question of Discipline

Over the previous months, Prestes had sought to instigate more discipline by investigating accused soldiers and keeping in confinement those found guilty. But events in Goiás became so extreme that Prestes evidently felt the need to make a bold example. On August 7, the rebel high command ordered the execution by firing squad of four of their own soldiers, the first for raping a woman and the other three for deserting the rebellion, taking their rifles and supplies with them. As part of these disciplinary proceedings, the column distributed among all commanding officers a set of guidelines on how the rebels should compose themselves. Referencing the recent wave of punishments, including the execution of their own men, the note explained that "we do not have the right to fold our arms, indifferent, in the face of certain abuses, which are morally and materially compromising the fate of the Revolution." The document also outlined a series of rules: soldiers were not to disrespect women, get drunk, or shoot civilians, and only authorized commanders could enter homes and seize belongings.[48] At least for the next phase of the march, the firmness of these guidelines, accentuated by the punishment by firing squad, seems to have had its intended effect: the rebel soldiers mostly followed orders until the column's retreat across Bahia seven months later, at which point their actions spiraled into violent frustration.

The cultivation of the column's virtuous mythology took place on multiple timescales. This occurred in real time, as seen in the open letter from early July, in newspaper coverage that would soon expand across the country, and also in the rebel memoirs written afterward. The documentation of events in early August serves as this chapter's second example of memoir omission. The punishments and guidelines were stipulated in bulletin no. 16 of the rebel high command—a document that Moreira Lima, the column's official scribe, reproduced in the appendix of his memoir.[49] While Moreira Lima does include the full record of the decreed guidelines, he provides merely a glimpse into the behavior that pushed Prestes to enact the new rules. The reproduced document mentions only that column leaders ordered the dishonorable discharge of two soldiers, one for looting a local house and another for attempting to kill a civilian. The memoir removes all mention of the execution by firing squad for the four soldiers found guilty of rape and looting. Comparing the curated memoir reproduction with the original document demonstrates that Moreira Lima was willing to show a certain amount of disorder within the rebel ranks—particularly because he had to contextualize the new disciplinary rules. But completely undermining the image of the column, either through instances of rape (which shows a grave lack of morality) or desertion (which shows a lack of commitment to the cause), could have damaged the image of the rebellion. With so much of the column's legitimacy drawing from its supposed virtue in the backlands, memoirs served as platforms to disseminate these narratives from one generation to the next.

With new disciplinary rules in place, Prestes marched the column toward Bahia. The rebels had to cross the São Francisco River, the fourth largest in Brazil and the longest, which runs completely within Brazilian territory. The São Francisco stands as a fluvial border running across the western edge of Bahia, and Prestes had to choose how, and where, to attempt the river crossing. From the current position in eastern Goiás, Prestes proceeded through the northern corner of Minas Gerais and briefly south toward the São Francisco. The column left Goiás on August 11 and embarked on a ten-day journey across Minas Gerais. Prestes was determined to cross into Bahia, with its imagined promise of new recruits, supplies, and the mystic potential of fighting in Brazil's most emblematic interior. As Moreira Lima would later recall in his memoir, Bahia represented a land of rejuvenation and adventure: "We counted on being able to enlist volunteers in that state, not only because of the influence of the sectors there that were said to be revolutionary, but also because of the bellicose spirit of its population. Additionally, Bahia offered us the advantage of being a region of inexhaustible resources, where we could prolong the struggle for a long time."[50]

Bahia on the Horizon

As the rebels made their push toward Bahia, newspapers began to play an increasingly central role in both constructing and amplifying the column's public image. Censorship still remained in place, meaning that even if government censors approved a submitted article, it could take upward of a month for the news to be published.[51] This censorship often affected the major dailies in Rio de Janeiro and São Paulo more than smaller, regional papers. With less oversight from federal censors, regional newspapers provided relatively close coverage of the column as it moved into Brazil's interior. At least initially, much of this local coverage supported the column. An August 19 article in Maranhão's *Folha do Povo*, for example, reprinted in full an article from a Pernambuco paper, *Da Noite*, seeking to dispel the negative rumors about Prestes and his men: "Are they just vulgar adventurers running through the interior? No, if so they would have given up the fight by now; they have plenty of money, and could easily leave the country. . . . So why do they do it? They are driven by a higher ideal, that compels them forward, toward victory or death."[52] Yet, as we will see, local newspapers became increasingly hostile as the column ventured closer to Bahia.

The rebels followed an uncontested descent from the plateaus of Goiás through the state of Minas Gerais, and, on August 19, João Alberto's vanguard detachment arrived in São Romão, a small town on the western banks of the São Francisco River. The scouting unit found a steamship and two smaller boats, but they belonged to a battalion of state police from Bahia. Seeking to commandeer the boats, the column attempted an ambush the following morning. The rebels set up an attack point high on the forested cliffs above the river and opened fire, but the Bahians sailed out of firing range and continued down the river.[53] Despite this failure, Prestes did not yet abandon the goal of crossing the São Francisco. A few days later, Djalma Dutra's unit was sent to conduct a final reconnaissance of the area and marched thirty miles north to the city of São Francisco.[54] Again, this venture yielded no results.

Although Dutra was unable to locate any boats, his troops did find a large stockpile of cachaça in a nearby farm, and they proceeded to drink heavily. According to the rebel memoirs, such instances of drunkenness consistently plagued the column. Moreira Lima wrote that drunk soldiers often had to be tied onto to their horses to keep them from falling off.[55] When the column entered a new town, an officer would often sweep through the stores and bars to pour out any alcohol, lest the soldiers get their hands on it. Dias Ferreira observed that attempts at prohibition became so effective that rebel soldiers started breaking into pharmacies to steal bottles of Elixir do Nogueira, a medicine that supposedly tasted like the Italian liquor fernet.[56] The raiding of local pharmacies also extended to other medicines. As remembered by a local named Joaquim de Souza Cavalcanti, when the rebels came to his town of Luís Gomes, they took all of the medication used to treat syphilis: "It was a huge loss. We didn't have any more medicine for syphilis in the whole town. The rebels were all sick with it and they spread the plague everywhere."[57]

On the heels of Dutra's unsuccessful and drunken scouting mission downriver, Prestes conceded that it was not possible to cross into Bahia. Moreover, Prestes could have correctly assumed that the failed ambush would spur more troops to the eastern shores of the São Francisco. Within a week of the column's dalliance along the river, the federal army sent additional forces from state battalions in Bahia, Ceará, and Maranhão.[58] The government appeared intent on stopping the rebel march from proceeding into the Northeast. Prestes ordered the rebels northwest back into Goiás, where they hoped to swing through Maranhão and eventually back into Bahia.

It took nearly two weeks to march across Minas Gerais, since they had to proceed slowly through the São Domingos hills. On September 7, the rebels crossed back into Goiás. The V-shaped trajectory that the rebels took south toward Bahia and north again deposited them in a very different stretch of Goiás than they had left behind the previous month. Now entering the northern corners of the state, the rebels marveled at what seemed to them an isolated landscape: after a colonial-era gold rush, it looked like it had remained untouched for several centuries, evoking the uneven impacts of coastal society's excursions into the interior. João Alberto remembered that "we found ourselves in the rare moment, to calmly see the unknown Brazil and the grand remnants of its distant past. That whole region, so rich, had been plundered by the colonizers. [The ruins of] churches built of stone and prisons of strong metal showed what [the region] looked like in the 18th century."[59] Amid their self-projected march to modernize the country, these observations about "the unknown Brazil" served to justify the rebel claim of reawakening the interior and thus the nation as a whole.

The column arrived in Posse, Goiás, on September 12, the first town along its renewed march north. During a two-day rest, Prestes, Costa, and Távora wrote to General Isidoro and Deputy Luzardo. Along with summarizing the column's movements over the previous month, the letter expressed a willingness to negotiate a cease-fire with the Bernardes regime in exchange for amnesty. Through their statement, Prestes and his fellow officers wanted the Brazilian public to know that "we are not here on a mere whim of madness— nor for the ungrateful pleasure of spilling our countrymen's blood and turning the homes of our brothers into wakes—nor [are we] moved by the petty interests of personal ambition." What, then, might the rebels see as adequate conditions to end their campaign? The letter noted three demands: first, to revoke the press law (*lei da imprensa*) that sanctioned censorship; second, to adopt the secret ballot for Brazil's elections; and, third, to suspend the martial law, which President Bernardes had continuously renewed since the initial revolt of July 1924. As Prestes observed, these criteria could secure a peace that would be "honorable for the government and successful for the country."[60] As the column marched farther into Brazil's interior with decreasing supplies and tension within its own ranks, an amnesty could also bring the rebellion to a close.

After Posse, heavy rains and an increasingly arduous terrain slowed down the march. After advancing about thirty miles per day for most of the previous few months, the trek across Goiás over the next two months averaged a daily log as low as ten miles.[61] In the midst of this slow progression, the column received a letter from the Maranhão town of Arraias. Compared to most rebel correspondence, this letter was unique in that it was written at the behest of and signed exclusively by women residents of a local community.[62] While respectful toward the column—the letter was addressed to "the heroic Chiefs . . . of the glorious campaign"—the women asked the rebel leaders to "guarantee the honor, life, and property of our townspeople." By framing their letter around domestic issues such as health and hospitality, this form of political engagement from rural *nordestina* women seemed carefully crafted to remain within traditional gender norms.[63] As a justification for why Arraias would not be able to provide the column with supplies, the letter stated that the whole town was currently afflicted by a flu epidemic. This mention of contagion was likely also an attempt to dissuade the rebels from committing the abuses—sexual and otherwise—for which they were becoming notorious. And, as a further incentive to respect life and property, the Arraias women also stated that should the column peacefully visit the town, it would "enjoy a respite [for] those who have forgotten the luxuries of civilized cities in the sertões."[64]

Having seen their route change from an accidental march into a purposeful and symbolic inland route, the rebels kept their sights set northward. But, over the next phase of the march, as an initially positive time in Maranhão gave way to a contentious passage farther afield, the rebels would experience what they perceived to be entirely different interiors.

4

COMPETING VISIONS OF THE SERTÃO

Over the course of the next four months, from October 1925 through February 1926, the interior march seemed indeed to offer the oasis promised in the women's letter from Arraias. The column received more recruits in the state of Maranhão than at any other point in the rebellion, and the existence of more developed interior towns like Carolina offered the trappings of "civilization" in the backlands. But if the rebel passage through Maranhão was the high point of the column, then its continued march across the Northeast soon became the start of its low point. As it marched in a clockwise arc (map 4.1) toward Bahia—crossing through the states of Piauí, Ceará, Rio Grande do Norte, Pernambuco, and Paraíba—the column experienced increased hostility and, in response, treated local communities with increased disdain, culminating in a display of wanton violence in the Paraíba town of Piancó. Despite the column's attempts to adapt its campaign to different regional contexts and landscapes, the rebels' vision of the sertão as a welcoming haven would give way to one of violent conflict.

From Arraias, the column set its sights on Porto Nacional, Goiás, a midsized river town that could potentially serve as an important resupply point

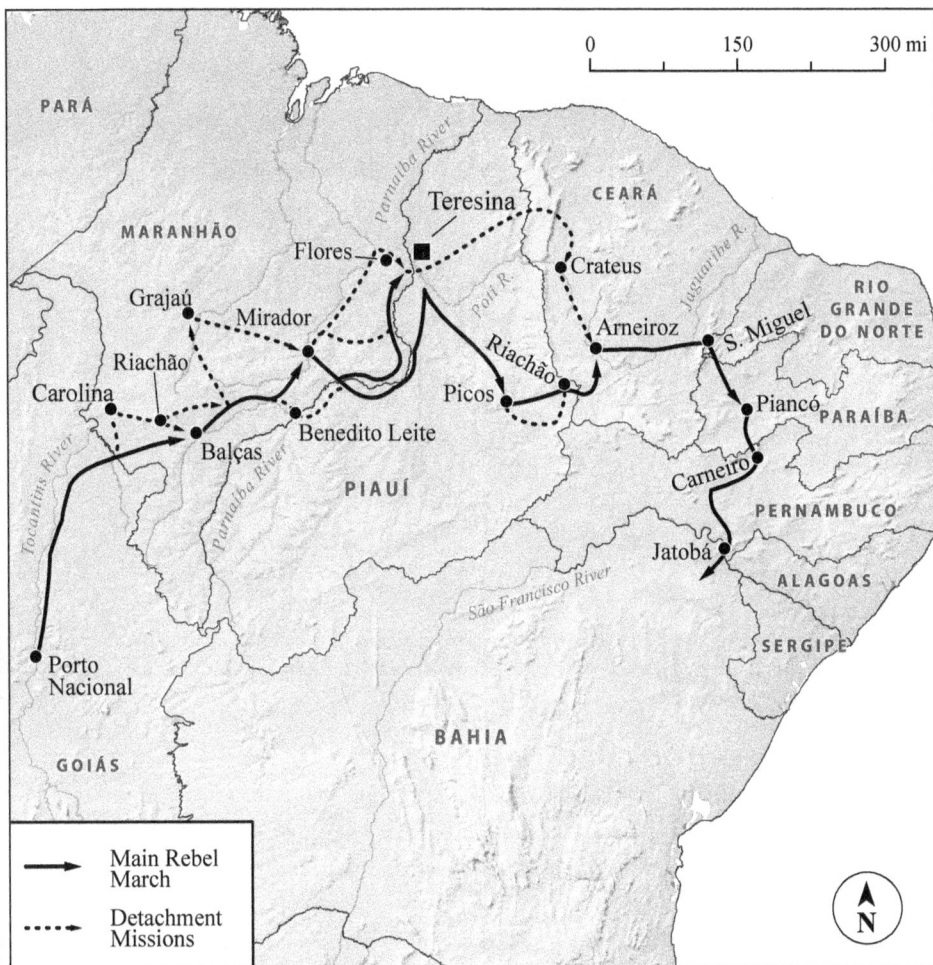

MAP 4.1. Prestes Column, October 1925–April 1926. Courtesy of Gabe Moss.

for the rebel forces. Prestes wrote two letters to be sent ahead to Porto Na-
cional. The first letter was to a local politician, state deputy João Ayres Joca,
who also published a small newspaper called *Norte de Goiaz*. Prestes asked
Ayres to notify locals of the column's arrival; in a sign of the hospitality that
Prestes and his forces would soon receive in Porto Nacional, Ayres agreed
to print the rebel bulletin in his newspaper.[1] Prestes's second letter was to
Friar José Audrin, a French missionary who ran the Dominican convent in
Porto Nacional. Seeking to reassure Audrin that the rebels would not commit any acts of violence, Prestes wrote that "we are not, as might have been
said, a horde of ruffians, from whom families must flee. . . . We are leading,

FIGURE 4.1. Rebel high command in Porto Nacional, Goiás, October 1925. Prestes is in the bottom row, third from the left, with Miguel Costa and Djalma Dutra in the two center seats. CPDOC SVM photo 010.

in this long fifteen months of struggle, a campaign that is far more righteous than our opponents have propagated."[2] Similar to Ayres's publication of the rebel bulletin, Audrin also passed on Prestes's intentions of goodwill to his congregation.

From the column's perspective, the stay in Porto Nacional proved successful and the town was very accommodating—at least at first. As various rebel units arrived between October 12 and 15, Audrin welcomed them and allowed the column leaders to establish their headquarters inside city hall.[3] According to Dias Ferreira, the rebels were "received with effusive demonstrations of sympathy and warm hospitality."[4] By October 16, the entire column had settled into Porto Nacional and Audrin invited Prestes, Costa, and Távora to personally stay in his convent (fig. 4.1), with the remaining officers and soldiers camped on various fields and farms on the outskirts of town. The column's initial days in Porto Nacional were celebratory: Audrin held Mass for the rebels several times and baptized the babies that had been born along the column's march.

Prestes took advantage of the welcoming environment to amplify the rebels' message. João Ayres Joca let the column use the *Norte de Goiaz* printing press, on which Moreira Lima oversaw the publication of the seventh issue of *O Libertador*. This particular printing press so impressed—and frustrated—Moreira Lima, that years later he recalled it as "a sacred mastodon that dated to 1860, and the type sets were so worn that the print was almost unreadable."[5] Despite the challenges of using an antiquated press, Moreira Lima published the longest issue yet of *O Libertador*. Across four pages, the bulletin included an overview of the column's recent stretch of fighting, an interview with Ayres on the state of politics in Goiás, and an open letter to the people of Brazil.[6] This public manifesto opened: "Our fellow citizens: after fifteen months of fierce struggle—marked daily by the hardships that casts a shadow on this unfortunate scene of a civil war—today we have arrived, in the heart of Brazil, along the shores of the mighty Tocantins [River]." Invoking their projected image as liberating bandeirantes in the heartland of the country, the manifesto proclaimed that "the people can be sure that the revolutionary soldiers will not roll up the flag of freedom (*a bandeira da liberdade*)" until despotism in Brazil had been overcome. And aware, as always, of the column's reputation as bandits, Prestes ordered his men to conduct several acts of local justice in Porto Nacional—the first such efforts of the rebellion. In the town's prison, the rebels freed a man who had been sentenced to thirty years in jail for a murder he claimed to have not committed, and they destroyed the stocks and chains in the prison. Prestes also directed his men to break the wooden paddles that were used in the local school as corporal punishment.[7] Prestes must have hoped that these small acts of justice would win new recruits and help to improve the column's reputation.

But after nearly a week in Porto Nacional, the column had worn out its welcome. Nearly seven decades afterward, Regina Gomes Ayres, at the age of ninety-six, remembered that, "while they played nicely in town, they [wreaked havoc] on the farms. They stole cattle and gold, they broke down doors and cracked open windows with axes. Everything was broken."[8] On October 21, Audrin wrote to the rebel leaders in hopes that they would leave, stating that he had a duty to speak out on behalf of his town, quoting, in Latin, the first Apostles: "Non possumus non loqui!" (We cannot not speak). Speaking bluntly, Audrin said that "the passage of the revolutionary column through our backlands and through our city has been a regrettable disaster that will, for years, remain irreparable. In [just] a few days, our people, mostly poor, were reduced to almost complete misery."[9] Audrin's criticism would become even more barbed with time: in a memoir he wrote twenty years later, Audrin observed that "the title of 'the Undefeated Column' is inaccurate, I prefer, if you will, the 'Column of Death.' . . . Its leaders went about releasing criminals, destroying chains, burning files and notary documents, giving off an imprudent air of their disregard for laws and authority." The same acts that the rebels had interpreted as a sign of their positive influence (e.g., freeing prisoners, "receiving" supplies from locals) were, in Audrin's view, proof of the column's destructive trek across the interior. Audrin, however, was careful not to paint all rebels as a violent monolith, noting that, of all the column leaders, "Luís Carlos Prestes was the most attentive and considerate of our sertanejos."[10] So, even among the column's detractors, Prestes stood out as an admirable figure. Prestes's empathy and his leadership skills—the basis of his eventual status as the Knight of Hope—would be tested as he marched the column farther north.

With their supplies and energy improved, if not their reputation among locals, the column left Porto Nacional on October 22, 1925. Just before departing, rebel leaders sent a letter afield to Tarquino Lopes Filho in São Luís, the state capital of Maranhão, who ran the *Folha do Povo* newspaper.[11] Although this particular letter never arrived—its messenger was arrested en route—Prestes was correct to identify Lopes Filho as a potential ally. *Folha do Povo* offered a steady voice of support for the rebel cause in the Northeast, and, with the column already marching toward the Goiás-Maranhão border, the newspaper ran an article under the headline of "Welcome!" Calling the rebels the "pioneers of liberty," the newspaper mimicked the language put forth by the column itself: "From the remote pampas of Rio Grande . . . to the sertões of Maranhão . . . come these blessed Brazilians, lifted by the sublimity of their ideas, emboldened by struggle, continuing their arduous mission of defending a country that has been shaken by the yoke of tyranny." And, reflecting the legend that was already starting to take root, the article described the Prestes Column in a mixed metaphor of mythical deities as "a colossal Titan" that soared into the Northeast "as if on a new Pegasus of legend." The pages of *Folha do Povo* offered open arms to the rebellion: "Fearless Brazilians, welcome to the lands of Maranhão!! The souls of our people vibrate in this declaration of our desires: Come here!"[12]

The "Golden Period"

The welcoming message from *Folha do Povo* was an early sign of how the column's passage through Maranhão would stand as the apex of the entire rebellion. Although the state government was strongly aligned with the Bernardes regime, there were pockets of local opposition from leaders who were eager to join forces with the column. Maranhão provided more recruits than at any other point in the whole campaign—in a little over a month, some 250 soldiers joined the rebellion in Maranhão. As Landucci wrote in his memoir, "Maranhão was the state that contributed the most in men and resources . . . that's where the column had its golden period."[13]

The Prestes Column crossed the Manoel Alves Grande River and entered Maranhão on November 11, 1925, following the banks of the Tocantins River toward the city of Carolina. During this march, the rebels were visited by members of the Xerentes Indigenous tribe—the first instance where Indigenous Brazilians made a sizable appearance along the column's route, and the only one that was chronicled afterwards in multiple rebel memoirs.[14] From the Xerentes point of view, the encounter was a positive one, particularly because the rebels had been fighting against militias who had abused Indigenous groups in the region. A member of the tribe named Sizapí was part of the visiting contingent, and in the 1990s, he told a journalist about the meeting: "I walked down there with them. [The rebels] took it out against the bad white [people], they were fierce against the whites that mistreated us. For the *índio*, the rebels didn't say anything bad, they were good."[15] The rebels, for their part, seemed impressed by the Xerentes, even if their observations were couched in racialized language. Moreira Lima was surprised to find the Xerentes more "advanced" and politically aware than he had presumed. He was taken aback, for example, that the tribe spoke about General Rondon—who had conducted extensive missions across Brazil's interior—as symptomatic of the federal government's superficial concern with Indigenous people. And when the Xerentes' chief came to speak with the column, Moreira Lima described him as both primitive and civilized: "They formed a semicircle and the *tuchaua* or chief, stepped forward and gave a speech for more than an hour, in a loud roaring voice, gesticulating widely, foaming at the corners of the mouth and stomping strongly with his feet, [he was] a gifted public speaker [well-suited] for rallies and the patriotic celebrations in our cities."[16] By calling the tuchaua a gifted orator while describing his actions in animalistic terms, Moreira Lima reflected a type of prejudiced admiration for the Xerentes, several of whom marched with the column all the way to Carolina.

If Maranhão was the golden period of rebellion, then Carolina was its most shining moment. The rebels spent eight days in Carolina, impressed by the town's wide streets and sturdy buildings, including a library and a local newspaper from which the column printed the eighth issue of *O Libertador*.[17] Upon the column's arrival on November 15, a local merchant named Diógenes Gonçalves hosted a celebration that included a series of musical performances and poetry readings. Metilene Ayres, almost sixteen years old at the time, recalled the spectacle: "Oh, there was such lovely dancing! The officers were so polite and gallant. I remember it like it was today, when I danced with the handsome one, Juarez Távora."[18] Moreira Lima was so impressed by the display of well-mannered culture that he marveled at how such "artistic development [could exist] in a place so far from the civilized milieus of the coast."[19] As in Porto Nacional, Prestes ordered his troops to destroy the tax records in Carolina. This time, the column invited the townspeople to take part in the ritual exercise of justice, which culminated in a large bonfire. While the blaze of tax documents grew, the town's orchestral band played a rendition of "Ai! Seu Mé!"—a popular opposition song of the era with lyrics that mocked President Bernardes. News of this event was announced positively in the local newspaper, *A Mocidade*.[20] And, on November 19, the townspeople and the rebels gathered to celebrate Brazil's Flag Day. To mark the occasion, Cordeiro de Farias gave a speech (fig. 4.2) in front of town hall, expressing gratitude to Carolina and expounding on the virtues of heroism and freedom.[21]

The column's stay in Carolina illustrated how the rebels perceived interior regions differently. Having enjoyed music, political debate, and good cheer in Carolina, the rebels had nothing but positive impressions of the people in that particular area of the Northeast. In his memoir, Moreira Lima described Maranhenses as "splendid soldiers [full of] bravery, resistance, natural discipline, intelligence, goodness and honor."[22] This example of admiration for interior communities was rare. Along with the supposedly civilizing markers of music and culture on display in Carolina, whether or not the rebels actually respected certain groups also depended on what—if anything—local people had contributed to the column.

If interior communities supported the rebellion, by willingly handing over supplies or even volunteering to join, such acts were held as proof of a worthy and civilized predisposition. This self-serving rationale helps to explain the comments above. Because several hundred Maranhenses joined the rebel march, they were lauded as brave, honorable soldiers. Yet, because most groups in the interior did not volunteer to fight with the column, they were dismissed as irredeemably backward. The rebel memoirs express prejudiced frustration at communities who did not support the rebels. João Alberto wrote that the lack of support "was perfectly explained by the uncivilized state of those primitive people."[23] And, in a longer assessment, Moreira Lima recalled that when the column arrived in a new town, most locals would hide in their homes or in the forests rather than join the rebel fight, a pattern that he explained as the resulting logic of the profound and inexorable ignorance of our sertanejos. . . . In the interior the people are semi-barbarous, having no clear idea of the Pátria. They are still dominated by a sense of slavery and they live in a state of terror under their *senhor* [meaning slave-master, or local lord]. . . . It is an amorphous mass that has no idea of freedom, a true herd of brutes, living a purely vegetative life. They are little more than pariahs, guided by the unthinking impulses of basic instincts. . . . The sertanejo evidently stopped on the lower rungs of civilization's ladder.[24]

The rebels' admiring views of Maranhão, on the other hand, suggests that negative perceptions of the interior were not entirely static. Instead, the material conditions of the rebellion—a pressing need for new recruits and supplies—could aid in modifying the prejudices that existed among the rebels and across Brazil more generally. The actions of local communities could influence the column's vision of the interior: while the rebels' regard for Maranhão was indeed conditioned by their need for new soldiers, the people of Maranhão earned the column's respect by volunteering to fight. Depending on the circumstances and actions of local people, stigmas could thus be adapted. The symbolism of the interior undoubtedly remained a powerful force, yet it was also subject to local agency and the changing needs of the rebels.

FIGURE 4.2. Osvaldo Cordeiro de Farias gives a speech in front of city hall, Carolina, Maranhão, November 19, 1925. CPDOC ILA photo 007–4.

The first batch of new Maranhão recruits joined under the command of Manuel Bernardino, a local leader with anti-government sympathies. Bernardino was among the most powerful figures in Maranhão's interior, and, although originally from Ceará, his long-standing battles with the state government had given him the status of a local revolutionary. For his defense of Maranhão's oppressed people, Bernardino had gained the nickname O Lenin da Mata—the Lenin of the Forest.[25] João Alberto led a delegation to meet with Bernardino, and succeeded in bringing the Lenin of the Mata—and his one hundred accompanying fighters—into the rebellion. This represented the first significant boost to the column's ranks since Paraná almost a year earlier. Bernardino and his men would march and fight alongside the Prestes Column until reaching Ceará. With Bernardino's forces now in tow, João Alberto marched east toward the town of Mirador, where he was meant to link back up with the main body of the column. Maranhão continued to bear fruit for the rebellion: during João Alberto's eastward march, he recruited a batch of fifty more local fighters under the leadership of a young Maranhense named Euclides Neiva. Between Neiva and Bernardino's soldiers, and, in addition to those that joined after Carolina, in less than two weeks the column had added 250 new soldiers, many of whom came with their own weapons.[26]

On the heels of the celebratory stay in Carolina, the addition of well-armed soldiers suggested that Maranhão was a land of mutual admiration between the rebel and local communities. In his memoir, Moreira Lima lavished praise on the generosity of Maranhenses: "As we passed through farms and small towns, families would line up along the roads to see the column come by, cheering us on and shouting words of encouragement in a calm happiness that was only interrupted by touching scenes of affection, where they would ... bring some milk or coffee to the injured and sick [soldiers]. [The people of Maranhão] were full of kindness and affection for these strangers from the most distant lands."[27] Many Maranhão towns did support the rebellion, though some of the column's supplies were taken by force. As recorded in an exchange of letters between rebel leaders, while in Riachão in late November, three members of Siqueira Campos's detachment committed a series of crimes: a soldier raped two women, one sergeant stole money and looted a farm, and another sergeant violently attacked several houses, making off with a variety of possessions.[28] Violence therefore continued even during the rebellion's so-called golden period.

By early December, the various rebel detachments were still spread across the region. While João Alberto made his way to Mirador to meet up with the bulk of the column, Djalma Dutra's unit split off east toward Benedito Leite, a town on the Parnaíba River that formed the border with Piauí. Knowing that Benedito Leite held a large concentration of loyalist forces, Prestes wanted Dutra's forces to fake an attack on Benedito Leite to attract enemy attention. With this feigned maneuver, Prestes hoped to enable the rest of the rebel body to cross safely into Piauí farther downstream. Although the plan was intended as a diversion, a fortuitous set of circumstances—namely, weather conditions and the failure of the loyalists—presented Dutra with one of the column's great victories. When Dutra's troops attacked at dusk on December 7, a thick mist lay out over the town and the adjacent river, the result of an afternoon's worth of heavy rains cutting through the summer heat. As one observer reported, "The night was covered in fog, like a thick veil.... Only the light of gunshots broke through the dense mist."[29] In the dark and cloudy battle, the loyalists assumed that the rebels were far more numerous than they actually were, though in reality Dutra's two hundred rebel soldiers confronted some one thousand loyalists, comprised of state troops from Piauí and police forces from Ceará.[30] By dawn the next morning, the loyalists abandoned the town and left behind a large cache of supplies and weapons.[31]

For the loyalists at Benedito Leite, there was another reason for having abandoned the fight: Tia Maria, the "Black sorceress" of the rebellion. According to Moreira Lima, when the column later captured some enemy soldiers, "these men looked at us with superstitious fear, saying that they knew we could not be defeated because we had under our command the Black sorceress, Tia Maria, who danced naked . . . before a battle in order to make the bodies of our men invincible to enemy bullets."[32] Barely a year into the column's march, its legend had begun to spread across the interior. The rumors about Tia Maria also reflected the racialized and gendered contours of myth-making: although the dominant narrative focused on the white men who comprised the rebel leadership, the presence of a Black woman like Tia Maria could be used to label the column as religiously and racially deviant.

The unexpected victory at Benedito Leite cleared the rebels' path into Piauí and its inland capital city of Teresina—the only northern capital at the time not situated on the coast.[33] The Prestes Column entered Piauí with over 1,100 soldiers, 900 of its own plus the 250 recent recruits. Another 160 local soldiers soon joined the fight, which propelled the column through an intense month-long march across Piauí.[34] As the column prepared to march on Teresina, Piauí's governor, Matias Olímpio de Melo, sought to turn the population against the column. In an address distributed across the state, he warned of the "rebels left over from the paulista revolt . . . a band of violence and extermination, with no discipline, no ideals, seeking only to flee from the law."[35] In the ongoing battle for public opinion—a struggle that had serious implications for how locals would react to the rebel passage—each side tried to paint the other as the true bandits.

The column's optimism in Maranhão soon dissipated. Over several days in late December, the rebels made a failed attempt to seize Teresina, resulting in numerous injuries and deaths, and the capture of Juarez Távora by enemy troops. The setback at Teresina inaugurated a new phase in the Prestes Column. Soon, the rebels marched into and across southern Ceará, and much of this period would be shaped by two emerging dynamics. First, the rebels would coordinate with political opposition leaders in major city centers toward the ultimately unsuccessful goal of leading revolts. Second, they would now come into direct and prolonged contact with several of the region's notorious coronéis. Combined, the failed attempts at broadening the rebellion and the introduction of new enemy forces suggested that the column's golden period in the interior was quickly drawing to a close.

Potential Allies on the Interior's Coast

Prestes thus far had failed to collaborate with potential urban revolutionaries. His messenger to São Luís had been arrested—complicating a potential uprising in Maranhão—and the column's plans for a similar revolt in Ceará had also been set back. In Fortaleza, Távora's own brother, Manuel do Nascimento Fernandes Távora, ran Ceará's main opposition newspaper, A Tribuna. When the column began its march through Piauí in December, a renewed state of siege forced the paper to shut down, thereby cutting off a vital platform of information and support. With rebellions unlikely in the capital cities of Maranhão and Ceará, the column shifted its energy toward a possible action in the Pernambuco capital of Recife.

A revolt in Recife was being planned by a fugitive army officer named Cleto Campelo, and, when the column entered the Parnaíba Valley, Campelo sent two representatives, Valdemar de Paula Lima and Josias Carneiro Leão, to coordinate with it. On January 5, 1926, while camped at the Cantinho farm, Lima and Leão met with Prestes and the rebel leaders, handing over a letter from Campelo and discussing the plans for an uprising in Recife. During these deliberations, Prestes embraced a set of structural aims for the rebellion—a sign that his political vision was beginning to expand beyond the reformist plank of tenentismo. Speaking on behalf of Cleto Campelo and also the Pernambuco branch of the Brazilian Communist Party (PCB), Lima wanted to secure a guarantee from Prestes that, should the uprising be successful, the eventual regime change would honor the demands of Pernambuco insurgents, including that the PCB could exist with no intervention from police—marking the first connection between the column and communism.[36] The column leaders agreed to these conditions, stating that because their revolution was guided by the "supreme ideal of complete freedom of thought," it would guarantee the free dissemination of "all social and communist ideas, along with the organization of workers parties, [and] with no vexing intervention from the police."[37] Moreover, they offered several proposals that would grant workers' rights and freedoms, including modernizing Brazil's political systems in order to protect workers against the abuses of capital, and also an agrarian program that would allow workers to own land.

Prestes's willingness to adopt redistributive policies suggests not only his own changing views but also the fact that the column desperately needed allies. Here, we see the flexible contours of coast and interior, and the qualities imbued in both: despite marching through Maranhão, Ceará, and Pernambuco—regions that are broadly classified as part of Brazil's interior—their capital cities of São Luís, Fortaleza, and Recife all lay on the Atlantic coastline. As such, their projected sense of civilization, population density, and access points to material distribution made them a sort of coastal safety valve for mounting pressure in the interior. Although the rebels had been actively seeking to recruit troops and gain supplies from backland communities, linking up with opposition groups in the northeastern capitals could provide a new outlet for keeping the rebellion alive. The collaboration with communists in Recife could thus link the column to people and political networks on the coast.

Although it is unlikely that the rebels would have known about an important event soon taking place on the northeastern coast, their gestures to regional concerns coincided with broader movements in the surrounding area. The following month, in February 1926, the first-ever "Regionalist Conference" took place in Recife.[38] With representation from six northeastern states, the conference, according to Durval Muniz de Albuquerque, sought "to protect the 'northeastern spirit' from the creeping destruction threatened by influences from Rio de Janeiro and São Paulo: cosmopolitan cities already shot through with foreign, invasive elements that weakened their true Brazilian characteristics."[39] The conference's manifesto, written by the sociologist Gilberto Freyre, called for "a new organization of Brazil" grounded in the rehabilitation of regional and traditional values, especially those of the Northeast: "This is what Brazil is all about: combination, fusion, mixing. And the Northeast [is] perhaps the main basin in which these combinations swirl."[40] The Prestes Column was therefore traversing the northeastern spaces of Brazil at precisely the moment when regional intellectual and political leaders were championing their home states as the geographic and cultural paragon for Brazil's future. It remained to be seen which movement, if either, could implement its vision—either that of Freyre and his collaborators, seeking to remake the nation in the mold of the miscegenation and cultural fusion of the Northeast, or that of the tenentes, and their stated goal of liberating the interior as a stepping stone to overthrow the federal government.[41]

Although the authorities were not yet aware of the specific plans conspiring between Prestes (fig. 4.3) and various opposition sectors in the Northeast, the column's presence in the region sparked a heightened sense of anxiety. The British consul in Pará noted that the federal government was scrambling to dispatch new waves of troops to the Northeast. The report observed that "news from the interior is scanty and contradictory and though the numbers of the insurgents are doubtless grossly exaggerated, the somewhat extensive preparations that are being taken, to deal with them, suggest that the movement is more than that of a large group of bandits exploiting an alleged political grievance as a cloak for their predatory activities."[42] In what proved to be the fleeting moments of the column's golden period, Prestes hoped that the landscapes and communities of Northeast would launch the rebels to victory. In a letter to General Isidoro, Prestes optimistically wrote: "We can affirm that we are now in the best possible situation, raising our hopes that the Revolution will soon be victorious. We are in the Northeast, where there are great sympathies for our cause."[43]

The plans for revolts in the northeastern coastal capitals did not materialize. Soon afterward, Manuel Távora was forced to flee into exile in Europe—thereby hindering the rebel activities in Fortaleza—and Cleto Campelo's mid-February uprising in Recife was quickly put down. But the efforts to reach out to a broad coalition of potential allies signaled that the column was open to expanding its political message, particularly if it helped build new alliances. There was also a false sense of expectations, where the column presumed that the recent scale of recruits from Maranhão and Paiuí would persist in Ceará, Pernambuco, and Bahia—a pattern that did not continue as the rebels ventured farther into the Northeast.

For the rebels, their arrival in Ceará in mid-January marked the start of a hostile new phase. In his memoir, João Alberto recalled that, whereas the people of the interior had previously been "welcoming and friendly," from Ceará onward local populations were "now fiercely against us. We looked on with sadness as these poor people, who would benefit from the victory of

FIGURE 4.3. Prestes (*far left*) and João Alberto Lins de Barros (*far right*) deliberate on potential strategies. Location unknown, likely early 1926. CPDOC ILA photo 008.

our revolutionary ideals, threw themselves wildly against the troops of the column. . . . The march through those forsaken lands, where we hadn't expected to find enemies, became dangerous."[44] Media coverage amplified this sense of danger. The Fortaleza-based newspaper *O Nordeste* announced in a headline: "The Invasion of [Ceará] by the Rebel Hordes." The article sought to simultaneously calm Ceará's population and delegitimize the rebel cause: "The incursion of the rebels into our state should not alarm the people or depress their spirits. . . . What they want, wherever they go, is money, [which they] extort, violently from defenseless populations. They have no military or civic aim. They are only driven by instincts to steal, and to escape the hand of the law. What the people [of Ceará] and those who feel offended by this situation, must do is react, decidedly, against this horde of uniformed evildoers."[45] The article's description of the rebels as evildoers (*malfeitores*) belonged to the wider lexicon of banditry, in which terms like bandido and jagunço were meant to stoke fear among local communities. In the evolving conflict between the column and its detractors—at both the federal and local levels—the battle for public opinion held significant weight.

The column marched east across Ceará toward the southern corner of Rio Grande do Norte. On their way, the rebels stopped on February 2 in the town of Boa Vista on the shores of the Jaguaribe River. A few miles away was the Embargo farm, birthplace of Juarez Távora. The rebel leadership decided to leave the column's entire archive to-date (e.g., correspondence, bulletins, internal reports) in the safekeeping of the Távora family.[46] As we will see in chapter 10, the publication of the Távora archive in the 1990s would spark much debate about the legacy of the interior march.

As the column made its way toward Rio Grande do Norte, newspapers expanded their anti-rebel coverage. Reporting on the rebels in Ceará, the Fortaleza-based *O Nordeste* wrote that the column "committed true acts of piracy (*piratagem*), stealing all the gold, money, animals, everything. They cleared out the shops, leaving the shelves empty. They burned fields and pastures. Their march was, really, a true plague."[47] These articles highlighted the rebellion's contradictions: How could the tenentes profess to be guided by lofty ideals and then abuse local communities? One headline criticized the column as "The Revolutionary Typhoon in Ceará," and another described the murder of a local farmer as "Yet Another Proof of Your 'Idealism!'"[48] And, when the column crossed into Rio Grande do Norte, the headline of *O Nordeste* announced that "Ceará Is Now Clean of Rebels"—insinuating that a scourge had finally been erased from the physical and moral body of the state.[49]

The column spent very little time in Rio Grande do Norte, marching fifty miles in three days, looting several towns along the way.[50] By the night of February 5, the column had crossed into Paraíba, where its main objective was to move swiftly through the Piancó Valley and into Pernambuco. Although not as short as the preceding passage through Rio Grande do Norte, the rebel march across Paraíba was also brief, covering some 220 miles in just over ten days.

As they had done upon entering most new territories, the rebels distributed a manifesto to the local populations. In the statement, the rebels invoked two Paraíba heroes from the late nineteenth century: "We unfurl the revolutionary banner on Paraíba territory, cradle of Almeida Barreto and Maciel Pinheiro, conscious that our gestures will meet with a heroic response. . . . We wish only your peace and happiness. . . . We are not bandits, . . . People of Paraíba! We count on your active support for the liberating movement."[51] The governor of Paraíba also distributed a message of his own, calling the column "the wandering remnants of an odious movement against the law and against the country. . . . They no longer attempt to gain the sympathy and support of the Brazilian people for their badly disguised intentions; on the contrary, on every side and in repeated attacks, they threaten the honor, the life, and the property of defenseless people." These dueling narratives circulated in Paraíba and across the northeastern interior.

The column's inland march continued toward the Paraíba town of Piancó, the home of Padre Aristides Ferreira da Cruz, a priest and notorious strongman who had reigned in the area for several decades.[52] The advance on Piancó sparked a mass exodus out of the town. Only a few locals stayed, including the tax collector and an old woman who worked as a baker. As we shall see, these individuals became witnesses to the violent events that took place. Padre Aristides, who had long maintained a close relationship with Paraíba's governor, received instructions to defend the town until the state militia could arrive with reinforcements. Aristides amassed thirty-two people, including himself, to hold off the rebels.[53]

The column set up camp on February 8 on the outskirts of Piancó. The following day proved to be one of the most violent and controversial moments of the entire march. Depending on the perspective of the storyteller, it was either a triumphal victory against an abusive strongman, or a vicious example of rebel atrocities. The initial details of the fighting at Piancó are relatively clear: the rebels came into the town, and Padre Aristides surrendered after a few hours of fighting. What remains controversial is what took place after the surrender, when Aristides and his followers were killed.

On the morning of February 9, a small unit under Cordeiro de Farias rode down the slopes of the nearly dry Piancó River and marched through the town. The streets—and, seemingly, all of the buildings—were empty. Only a few minutes after entering Piancó, Cordeiro's men were fired upon by loyalists taking cover in buildings. Several rebels died in this first burst of gunfire. At the sound of shooting, the remainder of Cordeiro's men rushed down through the valley and into town. The loyalists were adept fighters, moving swiftly through and behind buildings, giving the impression that there were far more than just a few dozen men. As a result, Dutra's detachment was then called in as reinforcement.[54] The combined five hundred rebels marched cautiously into the town center. With a lag in the fighting, the tax collector, Manuel Cândido, raised a white flag from his house, and a temporary truce was called while Cândido and his family took shelter in the town's prison. During this brief pause, half of the civilian fighters abandoned the fight, leaving Aristides with fourteen defenders, all of whom took cover in his house. When fighting resumed, it was sporadic, since both sides needed to save their ammunition. At one point, a soldier in Dutra's command sought to make an improvised bomb with gasoline from the mechanic's shop, but he was shot and killed before he was able to throw it through the window of

Aristides's house. Each side lost about half a dozen soldiers during the day's gun battle. The number of casualties soon doubled.

By the early afternoon, it was clear that the loyalist defenders could not hold out much longer, with barely a dozen men holed up in one house, surrounded by five hundred rebels. Aristides decided to surrender. One of the loyalists, a seventeen-year-old named João Monteiro, escaped through a back window.[55] The other thirteen men, including Aristides, were taken prisoner by the rebels.[56]

What came next is contested. The two townspeople who had not fled the city overheard what transpired between Aristides and the rebels and testified to the violence that soon unfolded. Cândido, the tax collector taking shelter with his family, and Dona Antônia César, the baker, confirmed the following exchanges. When Aristides was captured, he allegedly proclaimed: "I know that I am going to die, but I just ask the commander of these forces to grant me a small moment, to say a small prayer. . . . I am a priest and I must not die without asking God to forgive my many sins." To this, the rebels replied: "What a priest, what a nothing! Cut off his head, this man who killed our soldiers . . . and [the same fate for] all these bandits with him." Recalling the subsequent deaths of Aristides and his men, Cândido said: "Never, in my whole life, have I heard such an uproar. God forgive me for having witnessed a scene of such savagery! . . . My ears are still pained by the screams and roars of the miserable, slaughtered prisoners."[57]

The following morning when state police finally arrived in Piancó, they discovered Aristides's dead body, with his throat cut open. Notorious from the gaúcho civil wars in Rio Grande do Sul, this way of killing was intended to humiliate one's enemies—and it also showed the transposition of one interior tradition (from the southern pampas) into the spaces of the northeastern interior, where, in similar cases of violence, heads were severed and posted for public viewing. Aristides also had bruises, showing a strong blow to his face, and a stab wound in his left shoulder. The other twelve loyalists were also found dead, all with their throats cut.[58]

This violence had a lasting impact. In the immediate aftermath of the killings, newspapers in the region denounced the rebel actions. A headline in the Paraíba City-based *O Norte* announced "The Carnage at Piancó," and its article described the death of Aristides and his followers: "People who were there say that the murders took them prisoner and in cold blood and with steel blades, bled them out one by one."[59] A local newspaper in nearby Cajazeiras, *O Rebate*, devoted an entire front-page spread to the story, under the headline of "The Furies of Rebellion: Details of the Tragedy."[60] And *O Nordeste*, from neighboring Ceará, gave grisly descriptions of what allegedly took place in Piancó: "They looted, destroyed, and set fire to whatever they could. Afterwards, not content with just that, they took out personal vengeances. They arrested Padre Aristides and cut off his cheeks, where they drew blood that they made him drink. After sacrificing him in this way, they cut his neck, thus ending this savage event."[61] Regardless of whether these allegations were true, they whipped up anti-rebel sentiment throughout the region. Padre Aristides became canonized in popular lore as the Martyr of Piancó.

Although the historical record offers no tangible evidence, a subsequent story circulated in later decades, becoming a form of pro-rebel folklore that could balance the violence at Piancó. As repeated in Jorge Amado's famous 1942 book on Luís Carlos Prestes, among other retellings, the story goes that, in the aftermath of Piancó, the Paraíba police eventually captured some rebels and staged their own massacre.[62] Among the captured rebels was Tia Maria, who, for fear of her dark magic powers, was separated from the rest of the group and made to dig her own grave before having her throat slit.[63] As the historian Maria Meire de Carvalho has observed, "Tia Maria was, in the eyes of [loyalist forces], the embodiment of evil: a woman, old, Black, and rebellious. It was not an accident that she was attributed with magical powers, and those of a sorceress, not of a fairy. Because they feared this woman's magical powers, she was brutally tortured."[64] Confirming whether this was indeed how Tia Maria met her end is likely an impossible task. What is possible—and, arguably, far more analytically useful—is to see the story of her death as part of the discursive struggle to present one's enemies as the real bandit, the actual harbinger of violence in the interior. And, within the broader history of storytelling in the Northeast, the death of Tia Maria can also be read as an allegory for the column's trajectory: if her magical powers had thus far helped guide and protect the rebellion, her death marked the beginning of the column's decline.

Less than two weeks after the events at Piancó, rebel leaders received a letter from the Ceará town of Joazeiro do Norte, written by Father Cícero Romão Batista (better known as Padre Ciço). A venerated priest and local strongman in Juazeiro do Norte, Father Cícero had become a popular "miracle saint" for supposedly turning the Holy Communion into blood.[65] Father Cícero wanted to persuade the rebels to lay down their weapons, urging them to "think about the widows and orphans that . . . you are making; and the hunger and misery that accompany your every step, leaving you covered with curses from your countrymen, who do not understand the reasons for your stormy destruction through our great hinterland."[66]

Despite his gesture at peacekeeping, like many strongmen in the Northeast, Father Cícero was also organizing his own patriotic battalion to fight the rebels. As recounted by the journalist Lira Neto, when Cícero gathered together his band of local fighters, in his "dual role as political and spiritual leader, Cícero inspected the troops and blessed them."[67] In coordination with the Ceará federal deputy Floro Bartolomeu—serving as an intermediary for the federal Ministry of War—Cícero also sought to recruit Virgulino Ferreira da Silva, better known as Lampião. With a nickname meaning "lantern"— he was said to shoot his Winchester rifle so fast that it looked like a street lamp—Lampião was the most famous of the northeastern outlaws known as *cangaceiros*. With a reputation that was equal parts violent bandit and valiant folk hero, it was unclear whether Lampião would choose to fight with or against the Prestes Column. Lampião accepted Father Cícero's invitation to Joazeiro do Norte, where he was officially deputized as a captain in the army reserve. The newly commissioned "Captain" Lampião also received a stock of brand-new, army-issued Mauser rifles. Yet Lampião appeared to have no interest in fighting against the column: after receiving the weapons in Joazeiro do Norte, he and his men went on their way.[68]

For deputizing and then being robbed by the notorious backland outlaw, the Bernardes regime was mocked in the opposition press.[69] The pro-government newspapers, for their part, made no mention of Cícero's role—and that of the Ministry of War—in arming Lampião, focusing instead on the menace of a northeastern outlaw (Lampião) joining a roving southern outlaw (Prestes). *O Paiz*, for example, ran a three-part series with headlines such as "Prestes and Lampião: The Origins of a Satanic Plot."[70] In response to this anti-rebel coverage, Assis Chateaubriand, a staunch supporter of the column, wrote a front-page article for *O Jornal*: "The Minister of Justice, who is so concerned with censoring, should not allow the dishonor of this comparison. Lampião is a bandit, a vulgar thief, a wretch who murders in order to steal, a degenerate who became a cangaceiro in order to ruin goods and take the lives of his fellow men. Captain Prestes is a revolutionary. . . . [He is] brave, steadfast, and pugnacious, the likes of which Brazil has never seen."[71] And, in the end, although Prestes, Lampião, and Father Cícero never quite overlapped, the involvement of three mythic figures stood as an enduring moment in the legend of the rebellion's passage through the Northeast.

The Prestes Column left Piancó and crossed the state line into Pernambuco on February 12. During their two-week trek across the state, the rebels marched 375 miles, going southwest through the Serra Talhada mountains before turning south at the Pajeú River and through the Serra Negra hills toward

Bahia. As it had been almost half a year earlier, the São Francisco River stood as the final barrier to entering Bahia. During this trek through Pernambuco, the column fought almost incessantly against state militias, the troops of Floro Bartolomeu, and a smattering of other loyalist forces. The goal for Pernambuco remained the same: try to rendezvous with Cleto Campelo's rebels for a possible uprising in Recife and then continue toward Bahia, where the long-rumored and much-needed supplies from General Isidoro hopefully awaited. Throughout their time in Pernambuco, the rebels sought to pick up any trace of Cleto Campelo. What the rebels would not find out until a month later was that Campelo's uprising had failed. On February 18, Campelo led a small group in a revolt that started at an army barracks in Tejipió, a town just south of Recife. After moving inland for sixty miles on a commandeered train, the rebels were eventually stopped in the town of Gravatá, where Campelo was shot dead.[72] Although Prestes and his rebels marching in Pernambuco's interior were not yet aware of Campelo's demise, the failed uprising signaled that a revolt across the Northeast—an idea that just six weeks ago had provided a tantalizing, if unrealistic, hope—was now extinguished.

Prestes decided to once again make a push on Bahia. His attempt to cross the São Francisco River in August had failed, forcing a circuitous clockwise journey through the Northeast, and Prestes now hoped to find a more suitable river crossing. Loyalist leaders such as General João Gomes Ribeiro Filho—the commanding officer for the entire Northeast—and Bahia's governor, Goes Calmon, believed that the rebels could not cross the expansive river. As a result, few troops were dispatched to block the route toward the São Francisco.[73]

Marching south through the Serra Negra hills in Pernambuco, the column arrived at the São Francisco River on the morning of February 25. By the next day, the rebels had identified a suitable, if challenging, spot to cross the river—nearly two miles wide and muddied by recent rainfall.[74] The rebels abandoned all but their strongest horses, keeping only a small number to carry supply packs and transport the wounded. This meant that if the column managed to cross the river, it would either have to walk on foot in Bahia or steal large numbers of horses along the way. A scouting group eventually found a canoe that was used to bring a few rebels across, where another boat was seized to make for a small fleet.[75] On February 26, beginning at midday and continuing until nighttime, the rebels ferried back and forth across the water. Half a year after they first attempted to cross the São Francisco River, and with high expectations for what awaited them, the rebels arrived in Bahia.

5

For the tenente rebels, Bahia's interior stood as the mystical land immortalized by Euclides da Cunha in his 1902 book *Os Sertões*, the chronicle of the violent standoff in 1896–97 between federal troops and a millenarian settlement at Canudos. As described in chapter 1, Cunha had reported on the war as a journalist for *O Estado de São Paulo*, and the popularity of his articles led to the book that—similar to the coverage of the Prestes Column two decades later—depicted a clash between the coast (the federal army) and the interior (the mixed-race rural settlers). Every rebel memoir references Cunha, and it is clear that the tenentes saw themselves as continuing his legacy: they mimic Cunha's lavish descriptions of the natural landscape as well as his often-pejorative observations of sertanejos. Especially because the column's journey across Bahia was so quick, leaving them no time to interact with or learn from locals, their understanding of the region continuously defaulted to what Cunha had already predisposed them to think. Cunha's influence on coastal visions of the interior recalls Mary Louise Pratt's scholarship on the role of European colonizers who could only report back using the discourse of empire. Similar to how colonial-era explorers saw new landscapes and people through "imperial eyes," so, too, did the tenente rebels perceive Bahia through the prism of *Os Sertões*.[1] In his memoir, for example, Landucci recalled Bahia as an exotic place of danger, where the anguish described by Cunha still pervaded:

> It was the raw reality painted in such vivid colors by Euclides da Cunha. . . . Destroyed farms, villages once flourishing, now in decay, houses dotted with bullets, everything showed the belligerent spirit of relentless fanatics, giving the environment a sense of desolation and as if this tragic spectacle, unfolding before our eyes, was not enough, we felt the effects of an unspoken conspiracy of nature itself hand-in-hand with the rebellious villagers. The features of the landscape, the heavy rains, the muddy paths, the vast bogs, entangled the movement of the column.[2]

Bahia, as the quintessential Brazilian backland, embodied the rebels' image of the Northeast. It was also where General Isidoro, while living in exile, had supposedly organized for a shipment of weapons and ammunitions to be sent. As the rebels traversed the Northeast, from Goiás through Pernambuco, Bahia loomed as an almost inevitable destination, standing as both a refuge to fortify their ranks and a final symbolic interior to cross.

The column had two interlinked expectations for Bahia: to obtain new soldiers and supplies and to fulfill its self-projected image as liberators. Once the rebels had turned north and rebranded themselves as the bandeirantes of freedom, Bahia represented a potent landscape in which to prove their legitimacy by defeating the infamous coronéis. The term *coronel* originated as a military rank in the colonial militias of the eighteenth century, though over time it came to refer more broadly to strongmen in the interior.[3] With a financial base in rural activities such as sugar plantations, livestock, or mining, coronéis waged wars with each other and against state governments to gain control of municipalities and their inhabitants. As Eul-Soo Pang has written, the "coronéis subdivided the vast regions into self-ruled fiefs. Each coronel controlled a *município* or two, and a stronger one often dominated three to five."[4] Bahia was home to several of the most powerful coronéis, and it was during the column's trek across Bahia that the federal army deputized a series of them to pursue the rebels.

So, even if the column's original goal of overthrowing President Bernardes had since become a near-impossibility, perhaps they could now attempt a different sort of rebellion. Coronéis ruled in various areas of northeastern Brazil, but their concentration in Bahia—and Euclides da Cunha's description of

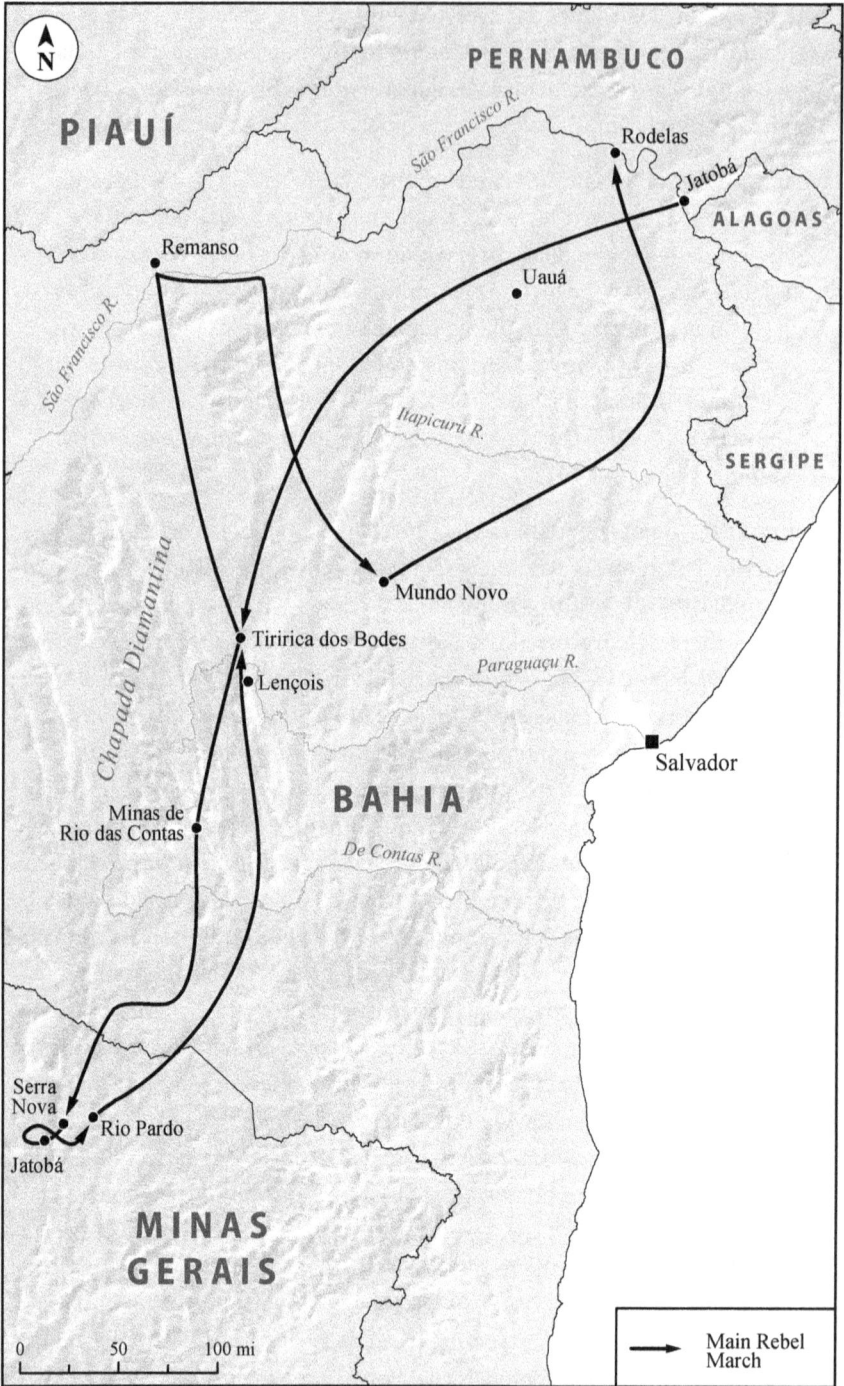

MAP 5.1. Prestes Column in Bahia, April–July 1926. Courtesy of Gabe Moss.

them—led the tenente rebels to begin framing the coronéis, not just the federal government, as "the enemy" of the Brazilian people. The rebels expected that the people of Bahia, long oppressed by strongmen coronéis, would flock to help overthrow their abusers. These expectations never materialized: communities in Bahia did not help the column fight against the coronéis, nor did they hand over food, clothing, or weapons, let alone volunteer as soldiers. As had been the case across the interior, locals in Bahia were mostly rural and poor—a situation unconducive to donating what little they had. The hesitancy of Bahians toward the column was also conditioned by the power wielded by the coronéis, propaganda distributed through local media, and the actions—and prejudices—of the rebels themselves. Unable to obtain sufficient supplies on their initial march across Bahia (map 5.1), the rebels soon turned around and began their journey to exile. In what proved to be the most intense wave of violence throughout the column's entire march, during their retreat back across the state the rebels vented their frustrations by raiding farms, burning homes, and assaulting women. These events were a far cry from the column's initial vision of liberation in the sertão.

Despite unmet expectations in Bahia, the column's myth continued to grow. When the rebels left Bahia, their recent failures appeared to have little impact on their budding national prestige as the Undefeated Column. Although true for the entirety of its march in the backlands, the column's time in Bahia—accentuated by the violence of its retreat across the state—is evocative of how the rebel mythology took root in the interior. The legend of the column became so premised on the symbolism of its passage through the backlands that, for mainstream coastal audiences at least, the details of what happened proved far less consequential.

On February 26, the column's 1,200 soldiers gathered on the northern bank of the São Francisco River, preparing to cross from Pernambuco into Bahia. With Bahia now visible on the opposite shore of the São Francisco, the rebels spent all day and into the early night ferrying back and forth across the river. Having already marched over six thousand miles, the allure of Bahia seemed to rejuvenate the rebels. Moreira Lima described the silhouette of a commanding officer as his boat cut through the rough water toward Bahia: "And in the night, a delicious Northeast night, illuminated by the crescent moon that hung in the sky like a biscuit split in two, the athletic figure of a hero stood out on the bow, with a long black beard bristling in the wind, in that moment becoming like the legendary leader of an ancient Bandeira."[5]

For the bandeirantes of freedom, Bahia marked their entrance at Brazil's ultimate interior. Landucci recalled the crossing of the São Francisco River as a "magnificent victory [that] helped cement the legend, already growing, of the column's invincibility."[6] Moreira Lima's descriptions became even more grandiose after his silhouetted bandeirantes crossed the river and began marching through Bahia: "It was as if Nature unfurled itself in blooming flowers to celebrate the arrival of the Undefeated Column."[7] The rebels' excitement dissolved over the next four months. This occurred slowly at first, during their six-week southwestward progression toward Minas Gerais, and then accelerated in a vortex of anger when they turned around and retraced their steps—taking almost twice as long to do so—back toward the same river they had previously crossed with such triumph.

Failure in the Backlands

A cause of the rebels' frustration was their inability to recruit soldiers. In a self-fulfilling cycle, the lack of new troops in Bahia kept ranks and supplies low, which led them to steal from locals, in turn dissuading people from joining the column. As had been the case throughout the rebellion, the tenentes were far outnumbered by enemy forces in Bahia. The 1,200 rebel troops who entered Bahia confronted an enemy force of almost 20,000 soldiers, including the federal army and state police (roughly 10,000 in total) as well as the coronéis that each commanded between a few hundred and several thousand men.[8] Yet size alone cannot explain the column's failure in Bahia.

The coronéis and their patriotic battalions were far more potent than the column had anticipated. Prior to their arrival in the sertão, the rebels expected that their message of liberation would be enough to topple Bahia's notorious strongmen. In his memoir, João Alberto wrote that "we imagined the great solidarity we would encounter from the oppressed populations. . . . To liberate the people of the interior from the political chiefs and despotic coronéis, men made of hardened rope and leather, seemed to us a great step for the progress of our country."[9] It is not entirely clear whether the rebels had indeed presumed that locals in Bahia would rise up to fight against the coronéis, or if these memoir recollections were projections of what later became the dominant narrative of liberation in the backlands. Either way, communities in Bahia did not join the column's fight: the coronéis proved to be the column's most formidable enemy in Bahia, adept at using clientelism, kin networks, and fear to maintain local loyalties. The system of coronelismo was a legacy of slavery, and the connections that the enslaved people (and later peons and rural workers) had to the owner or boss, who promised protection and fostered bonds with the community through rituals such as god-parentage. Even if local communities had been sympathetic to the rebel cause, they may have withheld their support because of their relationship with the coronéis. The local pursuit of the column was further bolstered by the financial support of the federal government, as the Bernardes regime delegated much of its fight against Prestes to these interior militias. Deference to the coronéis was aided by a concerted effort from pro-government sectors of Bahia to paint the column, not incorrectly, as violent invaders. This narrative was propagated widely by pro-government newspapers across the state—particularly the regional papers in the interior—and spread as well via word-of-mouth.

The prejudice of the rebels also shaped their experience in Bahia. The lack of support for the column on its first trek across the state reinforced the preconceived view of Bahians as backward. Feeling slighted by people whom they assumed would be roused by the column's message of liberation, the rebels seemed to allow the stigmas of the backlands to justify the violence of their return march. In turn, the havoc inflicted by the column dissuaded new recruits. A local resident named Domingos Rego remembered that he had been eager to join the rebellion until he witnessed the column's abusive behavior: "I was nineteen years old and I was ready to defend the rights of people. I wanted to fight for freedom. I packed my bags and waited. The rebels arrived and set fire to the house of a poor man. This was my neighbor, it took him two years to build his little plot of sugar cane and a clay still to make his cachaça. Sometimes I would lend him my ox. . . . [The rebels] burned everything . . . there was only ashes left. He died in misery."[10]

As shown in previous chapters, some tenente leaders offered unabashedly racist views to defend the low recruitment in the interior.[11] In contrast, Luís Carlos Prestes would later depict this as a political issue. Similar to the rebel memoirs written years or decades after the march, Prestes's recollections are, of course, framed by the context of when he shared his memories. In this case, his view of locals in Bahia was refracted by his eventual turn to radical politics and the communist platform that saw rural groups as potential agents of change, though without the political consciousness necessary to act upon the opportunity that the column presented. In the 1980s, near the end of his life, Prestes would explain in an interview with his daughter Anita Prestes that "very few people joined us. . . . The sertanejos understood that we were fighting against all of their enemies, meaning the federal, state, and municipal government, and also the big farmers and coronéis. . . . So yes, they saw that we were fighting against their enemies, but they had no consciousness. They thought we were just a bunch of crazies, some delusional adventurers. . . .

They didn't understand. So they didn't join us."[12] Over half a century after the journey that launched his status as the Knight of Hope, Prestes still seemed unable, or uninterested, in understanding local realities and needs on their own terms: his retrospective rationale left no room for Bahians to choose for themselves how to act and which side, if any, to support in the battles between the column and the coronéis. In addition to overlooking the agency of local communities, Prestes gave no regard to his own lack of outreach. Aside from occasional declarations for why locals should support—and resupply— the column, Prestes and the rebels never opened a sustained dialogue with townspeople. The column rarely stopped in one place for more than a few days, and, more importantly, raising the consciousness of local Brazilians was never a core mission of the march. At the time, especially during difficult stretches like that in Bahia, the goal was simply to keep moving.

On the morning of February 27, after the previous day's river crossing, the column began its incursion into Bahia. With most rebels on foot—having left almost all horses behind in Pernambuco—the column proceeded southwest toward the Chapada Diamantina Plateau. Although arid across much of its territory, Bahia is also a fluvial state, ringed on its western border by the São Francisco River, and with a series of rivers placed like steps on a ladder, flowing either west as tributaries of the São Francisco or east, from the plateaus up on high down into the Atlantic Ocean. Because the column entered Bahia during the rainy season, Prestes charted a route that sought to avoid as many river crossings as possible.[13] This effort was not always feasible, and during their time in Bahia the rebels had to traverse thirty-three different rivers, several of them more than once.[14]

For the column, Bahia's landscapes evoked the florid and frightful descriptions of the region made famous by Euclides da Cunha. It should be noted that much of the Bahian topography described by the rebels also existed elsewhere in the Northeast, including in many of the regions through which the column marched. The disproportionate attention—and pages of their memoirs—that the rebels gave to Bahia was part of the self-fulfilling legacy of *Os Sertões*: predisposed to seeing Bahia through the lens of Cunha, the rebels used his language and observations to frame their own chronicles. As a result, the legend of the backlands that Cunha helped to popularize then expanded in the subsequent spotlight generated by the Prestes Column. Dias Ferreira, for example, described Bahia's rivers as "high and with steep barren slopes . . . torrential in the rainy season, just like what the peerless Euclides da Cunha wrote about in his immortal book."[15] As it had been for Cunha, the area's vegetation was a major concern for the column. Above all, the rebels were frustrated by the caatinga, a dry, though ecologically diverse biome that dotted much of Bahia's lower-elevation regions. In *Os Sertões*, Cunha had described the caatinga: "It repulses [the traveler] with its thorns and prickly leaves, its twigs sharp as lances; and it stretches out in front of him, for mile on mile, unchanging in its desolate aspect of leafless trees, of dried and twisted boughs, a turbulent maze of vegetation standing rigidly in space or spreading out sinuously along the ground, representing, as it would seem, the agonized struggles of a tortured, writhing flora."[16] In his memoir, the rebel officer Italo Landucci offered a similar description of the column's initial march into Bahia: "We entered the insidious hinterland of Bahia through the historic area of Canudos. The caatinga, which soon surrounded us, was hostile with its strange vegetation of thorns and endless barrage of cactuses (*xiquexiques, macambiras, cabeças de frade*), a confused tangle of long spikes, curved like cat claws, which clung to you and hurt. In the caatinga we entered and in the caatinga we suffered."[17]

The tenentes were not the only ones to express fascination with Bahia's landscapes. The federal army's own report noted that, by entering northern Bahia, the Prestes Column "had arrived in the calcified and unforgiving land of rural shantytowns (*arraias*), of caatinga, and of jagunços—made famous by the genius of Euclides da Cunha."[18] It should be remembered that Cunha had been educated at some of Brazil's most elite military academies, and his depiction of the sertão thus influenced both the rebels and their pursuers.

If the column's passage through Bahia was hindered by the state's natural landscapes, it at least benefited from the ongoing failures of the army's pursuit. The long-standing issues of ineffective loyalist troops and logistical difficulties were compounded in Bahia by an emerging conflict among military leaders. General João Gomes Ribeiro Filho was the commanding officer in the Northeast, yet, when he failed to stop the rebel advance into Bahia, the minister of war, Fernando Setembrino de Carvalho, dispatched another general, Álvaro Mariante. The two generals disagreed on the best tactic to stop the column. Gomes wanted to erect a "barrier" of 250 miles where loyalist forces would stretch north to south in order to stop the rebels from marching farther into Bahia. This strategy, which Mariante mocked as theoretically possible but completely impractical, aligned with the dominant military logic of the day, particularly influenced by the French military mission that trained much of Brazil's officer corps after World War I.[19] Mariante envisioned a different approach of "hunting groups" (*grupos de caça*) to imitate the rebels with mobile and quick-moving forces.[20] Mariante's proposal won out, and the federal army began instructing its own forces to essentially copy Prestes's war of movement. In addition to the coronéis and their militias, the loyalist campaign in Bahia turned into a theater of overlapping army approaches, with two generals competing for operational power, and with several hunting groups and multiple units of army and police forces simultaneously pursuing the Prestes Column.

As the rebels began their march against a fragmented enemy, newspaper coverage fanned the anti-rebel flames already circulating throughout the Northeast. The column's first battle in Bahia took place on March 3 in the town of Várzea da Ema, where the rebels killed two locals and seized several horses and supplies. The *Correio do Bonfim* reported that these events were part of a "legion of doom" led by rebels who, "for almost two years, in a desperate fight, driven only by greed and ambition . . . have stormed from the south to the north like a cloud of dark thunder."[21] Six days later, after a much larger battle to occupy Uauá, the *Diário Oficial* quoted a farmer who said that the rebels "liquidated everything, stealing all of the animals, slaughtering cattle and other livestock. They took everything they could find in the houses, clothes, jewelry, etc. . . . They killed some people and shot many, even taking people away by the neck and making them work as guides. Now, many are dying from hunger, with nothing of their own, because the bandits pillaged everything they could."[22]

The battle at Uauá also offered a new storyline: a female rebel named Alzira who was taken prisoner became an object of fascination. The seventeen-year-old Alzira, originally from Rio Grande do Sul, was defined in the press by the fact that she "dresses like a man, with a hat, riding pants, and boots."[23] An article in the *Diário da Bahia*—a newspaper in the state's coastal capital of Salvador—described the imprisoned female rebel as "an amazon . . . [holding] a revolver in feminine hands."[24] This coverage mixed several regional tropes: with a hat, riding pants, and boots, Alzira fit the archetype of a gaucho from the southern pampas, yet the paper's portrayal of her as an Amazon also transformed her political agency into the actions of an exotic, sexualized figure—a reference perhaps to the Amazon of Brazil's interior, or to the Amazonian women warriors of Greek lore, or to a blended figure of both. Other coverage went even further with its sexualization, saying that Alzira had been in a bitter love triangle with Prestes and Miguel Costa. Under the headline of "Jealousy Spoils the Rebel Situation," the Salvador-based *Diário de Noticias* wrote that "the imprisoned rebel . . . who, by the way, is a beautiful woman . . . seems to have declared that she left the rebel camp because of Miguel Costa's unbridled jealousy of his comrade Prestes."[25] The coverage of Alzira was so widespread that General Mariante remarked on how "the newspapers of Bahia's capital and all interested parties, created a fantasy, a loud and scandalous story, of a crazy and unhappy woman, a runaway Amazon woman, a type of wandering beauty, a bewitcher and the lover of rebellious generals."[26] Mariante was particularly unhappy with these articles, as he saw them as part of Salvador's "yellow journalism, deifying the rebels, encouraging disorder . . . and exploiting scandal."[27]

These articles about Alzira indicate a regional difference within Bahia's newspaper coverage. Papers in the interior—where the column's presence was felt most directly—tended to be far more anti-rebel, but those in the coastal capital of Salvador ran stories that, even if not explicitly pro-rebel, were less antagonistic. The coverage of female rebels in Bahia soon spread nationally. Three weeks later, the Rio de Janeiro–based *Diário de Noticias* continued this gendered reporting by writing about Alzira and another female rebel named Emilia, under the headline of "A Beautiful General and a Faithful Nurse."[28] Depicted in Bahia as either murderous bandits or sexualized fighters, the tenentes had to find a way to gain the support of local communities.

Throughout the trek across Bahia, the column also needed to figure out where to go. The question of route-finding had always been key, but, compared to earlier phases of the march where the rebels had wider expanses of territory to navigate, more time to send advance scouts to map out the area, and fewer enemies in pursuit, the topography of Bahia became a serious problem. Most often, the column pressed local Bahians into service as guides. It is possible that some of these guides offered their services voluntarily, yet evidence and circumstance suggest that many had been coerced. The files of Pedro Aurélio de Góes Monteiro—General Mariante's chief of staff—contain a report that summarized the column's ability to navigate the haphazard Bahian terrain: "To orient their march, the rebels seized men from the area under threat [of harm] . . . who guided them through the local paths and shortcuts and who were discarded once they were no longer useful."[29] And a *Correio de Bonfim* article on the rebellion's first month in Bahia offered the story of Julio and Antonio Gomes Soares, two local farmers who, after their home was looted, "were made to work as guides, suffering [great] humiliation."[30]

Even with the guidance of locals who knew the landscape, the column's first push through Bahia took almost a month, tracing over three hundred miles up toward the Chapada Diamantina Plateau. This stretch was relatively conflict free, and the rebels even seized a convoy of loyalist supplies intended for the army barracks at Uauá, yielding eight wagon loads of coffee, sugar,

FIGURE 5.1. A posted
bulletin in the North-
east, from March 2,
1926, announcing the
failed Recife uprising.
Of note, the bulletin
includes a photo not of
Cleto Campelo's rebels,
but of the Prestes
Column. CPDOC PEB
photo 009.

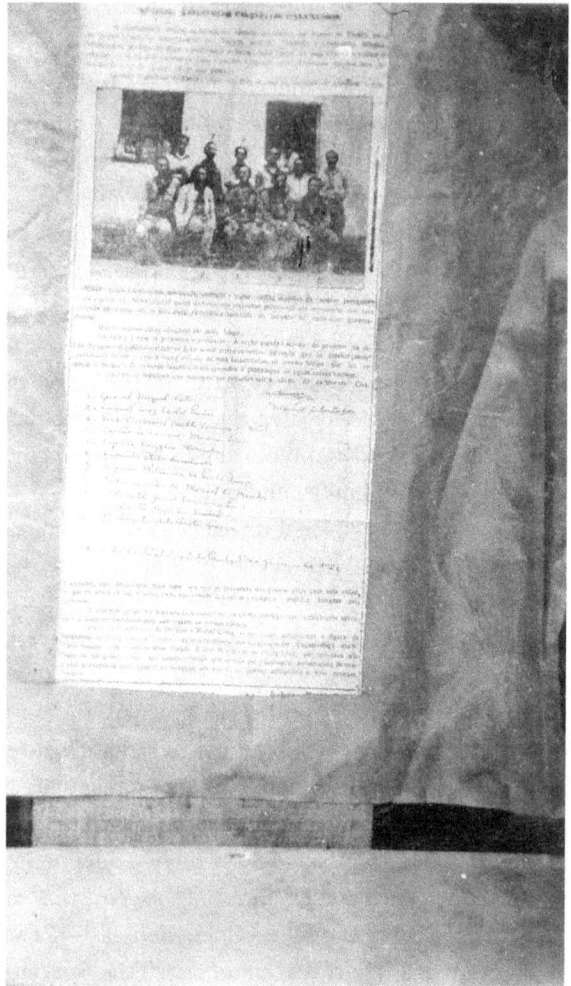

cigarettes, beans, and rice, along with large amounts of ammunition.[31] With
a renewed supply of food and weapons, and with the federal government still
scrambling to organize its pursuit, the column proceeded forward. These
positive developments were soon dampened when the rebels, while camped
near the Icó farm, read about the failed Recife uprising and death of Cleto
Campelo that had occurred a month earlier (fig. 5.1).[32] The news offered further proof that potential reinforcements from the coast might never arrive.

By going southwest through the Chapada Diamantina, the tenente leaders
had three main options. They could stick to the original plan of marching on
Rio de Janeiro to overthrow the government, though that would require an

effort well beyond their size, supplies, and energy; they could also go toward exile, returning west toward Goiás and Mato Grosso to eventually disband on foreign soil; or, the column could just keep moving, maintaining Prestes's war of movement for as long as possible. This option also kept open the possibility of receiving the supplies that Isidoro was allegedly sending to Bahia.[33] The rebels remained in contact with Isidoro, yet the long delay in communication required by sending messengers between Argentina and Brazil's Northeast complicated the logistics of where the supplies would actually be sent. Prestes, despite the risks of this final option, chose to keep his forces in motion. While waiting for potential news of where and when Isidoro's backup might arrive, the column remained along its uncertain path.

The Domain of Horácio de Matos

In mid-March, the column crossed the Bahia Central Railroad that ran between the capital city of Salvador and Juazeiro, a river port nestled in the north of the state on the banks of the São Francisco. The railroad stood as an unofficial dividing line in Bahia: along this route and to the north lay the center of the state's political and commercial power, and to the south lay the undulating plateaus and river systems that comprised much of Bahia. Among the multiple zones of Bahia's backlands, the dominating region—in terms of both topography and symbolism—was the Chapada Diamantina, the diamond plateau, extending for nearly three hundred miles across the center of Bahia. In the 1820s, diamonds were discovered in the streams running down from the towering quartzite ridges, leading to a mining boom that lasted nearly fifty years. The center of this activity was the town of Lençóis, where the Matos family unofficially ruled the plateau's mineral and political wealth.[34] By the 1920s, Horácio de Matos had become the undisputed leader of the Chapada Diamantina and was one of the most powerful chiefs in all of Brazil's interior.

The Matos clan's long-standing animosity toward the government presented a situation that might have led Horácio to be sympathetic to joining the column. Yet, in another sign of the column's disconnect from the actual politics on the ground in the Northeast, recent conflicts in Bahia had changed the Matos family's relationship with national leaders. In 1920, after many years of fighting between coronéis and the state government of Bahia, the federal government had intervened and signed a treaty directly with the coronéis, essentially ceding political autonomy in Bahia's sertão to backland oligarchs like Horácio de Matos.[35] In his book on the history of the Chapada Diamantina, Walfrído Moraes notes that Horácio had considered joining the tenente rebels, but, with his newly strengthened position—and his new con-nections to the federal government—he chose to fight against Prestes.[36] In March 1926, General Mariante officially authorized Horácio to create a pa-triotic battalion.[37]

As was the case for all of the battalions organized by the region's coronéis, in exchange for fighting against the rebels, Horácio and his troops received monthly payments and supplies from the Ministry of War. This material sup-port was often delayed or unpaid, and, although the coronéis maintained com-munication with General Mariante—via telegram, radio, and messenger—the patriotic battalions functioned as standalone armies.[38] This autonomy allowed coronéis like Horácio de Matos to rely on their local networks and influence: a US consular report said that Horácio controlled "a private armed force of some 4,000 men, all devoted to and dependent on him as a kind of feudal overlord."[39] On March 19, Horácio distributed a letter to the people of the Chapada Diamantina, announcing his fight against the rebels: "By order of General Mariante, I shall requisition animals, arms, and supplies when and whenever necessary. I request all my friends, therefore, to assist me in every way possible in the defense of the Lençóis district, which will be greatly dam-aged if allowed to fall into the hands of the rebels."[40] During the rebels' time in Bahia, and even afterward, when they retraced their steps toward exile, the patriotic battalions were the most efficient and successful loyalist forces.

Along with Horácio de Matos, other coronéis fighting against Prestes in-cluded Franklin Lins de Albuquerque, who was also from Bahia, and those from neighboring states such as José Honório Granja (from Piauí) and Abílio Wolney (from Goiás). The important role assumed by these coronéis was largely a result of the failures of the federal army and state forces. A US con-sul observed that "it is the general opinion in Bahia that Matos's troops will cause the rebels more trouble than the Federal forces, who are apparently making a studied and successful effort to avoid anything that looks like a fight."[41] Army documents suggest a chronic lack of food rations, an inability to get medical supplies to the frontlines, and an overcrowding at the few hos-pitals available.[42] Among the illnesses afflicting the loyalist troops—which can be extrapolated to cover those likely suffered by the rebels as well, though the tenentes kept far fewer notes on the matter—were malaria, ulcers, dysen-tery, syphilis and other venereal diseases, scorpion bites, and gastritis, along with broken bones and impact wounds from battle.[43] Communication was a further issue, as there were relatively few telegram stations in the Bahian in-terior, particularly in the northern area of the state.[44] General Mariante was acutely aware of these shortcomings, admitting that "the soldiers we have sent to fight [Prestes] have been absolutely incapable of doing so. . . . So far, I have only been able to use the *patriotas*, everything else has failed."[45] Yet the prominence of the patriotic battalions was equally due to their skills and knowledge, as they were the most familiar with the Bahian terrain and commanded the most respect, and fear, from local communities.

Once the Prestes Column approached the Chapada Diamantina, the patriotic battalions began an immediate pursuit. João Alberto remembered the battalions as a sort of backland specter. In what would become a consistent theme in commentary about the column, his use of the term *cangaceiro* (meaning *bandit*, such as Lampião) further reflects a slippery, if not ignorant, awareness of local categories: "The conflicts in the mountainous zone dominated by the cangaceiro Horácio de Matos increased. Our soldiers kept falling into traps prepared by an invisible enemy."[46] For three weeks, the tenentes marched over six hundred miles across the Chapada Diamantina, and they rarely went more than a day or two without a skirmish with Horácio. Because several of the battalion fighters were also members of the Matos family, the conflicts soon became personal. On April 2 at Campestre, the column fought and killed Francisco Macedo de Matos (Horácio's cousin) and José Bernardes de Matos (Horácio's nephew). Three days later, the rebels then killed Horácio's aunt, Dona Casimira, a powerful matriarch of the family who had turned her Carrapicho farm into a base of operations for the anti-rebel effort.[47] Horácio was so aggrieved by the assault on his family members that he wrote a letter to the editors of *Diário de Notícias*, a Salvador newspaper, lamenting that the rebels had "barbarically" murdered his kin.[48] And *O Sertão*, a Lençois-based newspaper owned by the Matos family, likened the rebellion to "Satan preaching Lent," denouncing the tenentes for "assaulting helpless people" while claiming to be "the brave and intrepid defenders of national valor."[49] The fighting persisted across the high plateaus of the Chapada, and, as Landucci wrote, the exhausted rebels wanted desperately to "escape from that inferno of ambushes and torments of every kind."[50] It was not until the second week of April that the column descended from the Chapada, exiting through the ravines leading down into the Brumado River valley.

With the Chapada Diamantina at their backs, the rebels continued south toward the state of Minas Gerais. Putting some distance between them and the heart of Bahia's interior came with the added benefit—both symbolic and material—of moving farther away from the sertão. In the two weeks prior to entering Minas Gerais, the column passed through numerous towns that, to their coastal eyes, did not resemble the backlands. In Minas do Rio de Contas, they were impressed that the town had a theater, a public market, and a library; in Caculé they were able to watch a film; and Condeuba was described as "rich and grand, with various paved roads and good buildings."[51] Perhaps feeling reenergized by the relative comforts of these lowland Bahia towns and likely sensing the need to build stronger bonds of support from local inhabitants, the column freed prisoners in both Minas do Rio de Contas and Condeuba—acts of vigilante justice they had not yet practiced in Bahia.

In Minas do Rio de Contas, however, two members of the column were killed in a manner that, in the eyes of the rebels, showed how the dangers of the sertão could follow them anywhere. On April 10, one of the rebel women, Albertina, was waiting with a soldier who had been seriously injured during the fighting in Piancó and had since developed tuberculosis. When the column arrived in Minas do Rio de Contas, it was decided that the soldier should stay, where he could die in peace. Albertina volunteered to wait with him in his final days, though, once the rebels moved on, a unit from Horácio's patriotic battalion swooped in and quickly killed the soldier. A militia fighter attempted to rape Albertina, and, although she fought back, she, too, was killed.[52] Moreira Lima lamented the brutal act in his memoir: "Albertina was a young woman of twenty-two years, the most beautiful of all the vivandeiras. . . . After we left the city, a patriótico came to town. A miserable man who was a lieutenant with those mercenaries tried to overpower Albertina, and, [he killed her] because she refused to satisfy his needs."[53] As the only evidence on record of a woman in the column being raped, Albertina's murder seemed particularly shocking for the rebels. In his 1942 book, Jorge Amado—with Moreira Lima's memoir and the brief description above as his main source—provided a nearly two-page description of Albertina's death.[54] Perhaps the barbarity of the act was all the more surprising given that the column had felt safe in a relatively "civilized" town.

On April 19, the column crossed into Minas Gerais, a state that shared its southern border with Rio de Janeiro. The initial goal of marching on the capital was closer than it had been since the São Paulo uprising almost two years earlier, yet the rebels spent only eleven days in Minas Gerais. After having marched 1,200 miles in fifty-two days through Bahia, the column traced a quick 150-mile loop in Minas Gerais. The incursion began with four days of southward marching that included several battles against coronel forces.[55] While camped near Jatobá on April 23, Prestes ordered the column to turn around and return northeast toward Bahia, using a maneuver that became known as the *laço húngaro* (Hungarian knot), for the shape of a hitch used by gaucho cowboys.

There are several explanations for why the column retreated after its brief excursion out of Bahia. Historian Todd Diacon explains that the federal army was better organized in Minas Gerais and used the state's more developed rail network to mount a defensive block.[56] Moreira Lima claimed that the plan was to draw loyalist forces across state lines to then allow a return to Bahia, where they held out hope that Isidoro's shipment of weapons might still materialize.[57] Turning around in Minas Gerais was also a concession that the rebellion would never achieve its goal of overthrowing the government. In his memoir, João Alberto admitted that the only remaining option was to seek exile: "We now turned our backs, forever, on our hopes of victory, and keep moving only in the fight to survive. . . . We would have to travel ten thousand kilometers in search of our own salvation."[58]

Most of the evidence about the column was produced by the tenente leaders, making it difficult to assess the views of the foot soldiers within the rebellion. One of the only archival sources that offers a window into the experience of lower-ranking rebels is a set of interrogation logs compiled by the army.[59] These prisoner files cover nearly fifty accused rebels who were captured in Bahia, Maranhão, and Pernambuco between December 1925 and April 1926. Less than half of the captured men were, in fact, rebels; the rest were mostly locals who had been forced to march with the column, often pressed into service as porters to carry supplies or as herders to take care of the animals.[60] Among the prisoners who were indeed rebels, there was a pattern of divulging information to their captors. While it is likely that they gave testimonies that could lessen their punishment, the sharing of information nonetheless reflected the fact that rebels had questionable loyalty to the rebellion. For example, two soldiers who had fought with the tenentes since Paraná divulged how the column was able to cross the São Francisco into Bahia, where it was now headed; how much ammunition remained; and the overall status of the rebellion. These interrogation logs suggest that nearly two years and eight thousand miles into their campaign, many of the rebels seemed exhausted and disenchanted. In this fraught context, the rebels left Minas Gerais and reentered Bahia.

Back to Bahia, with a Vengeance

The Prestes Column's second foray through Bahia began on April 30 and lasted sixty-four days, tracing nearly two thousand miles in a zigzag pattern across the state. Whereas the first rebel incursion in Bahia followed a somewhat linear march through the Chapada Diamantina and down into Minas

Gerais, the more disjointed second phase reflected the column's need to find a way to exit Bahia by crossing the São Francisco River. For two months, the tenentes traced an angular route across the state, intersecting three different times with the path they had taken on their initial route. On their return march, the rebels had to navigate the determination of coronéis, the apprehension of local communities, and the heavy rains that caused the spread of malaria and kept the São Francisco impassable. Because the column's first trek across Bahia had been defined by a hopeful, if misguided, vision of northeastern liberation, the retreat soon spiraled into an outburst against a region that was seen to have spurned its cause. In the crosshairs of the tenente rebellion, Bahia was in a no-win situation: by virtue of its mythologized allure, the region was targeted by the column as a site of liberation, yet, when locals did not welcome the rebels with deferential open arms, they were castigated as ungrateful and irredeemable.

In their memoirs, the rebels did not deny the violence of their retreat back through Bahia. Instead, they deflected blame onto the region and its inhabitants—a reflection of the racialized, Malthusian thought of the time, which saw the environment as having the power to turn people into savages. In this framing, any misdeeds were not the fault of the civilized liberators, but, rather, the suffocating influence of their wild and manipulative surroundings. As Landucci wrote:

> We were engaged in a struggle for survival against thousands of Bahian sertanejos. Strategic and vicious propaganda had made them believe, these simple people, that we wanted to invade their lands and destroy their homes and [they] boldly resisted the advance of the column. In this mortal landscape, where hatred seeped into every gesture, our reaction turned violent. Every day we fought, during the march, without pause. And because even the rare sources of water were guarded by these fanatics, who also hid their food, we obtained our water and food through bloody battles.[61]

When the rebels reentered Bahia, politics at the national level were changing. Presidential elections had taken place on March 1, with Washington Luís Pereira de Sousa of the Republican Party of São Paulo winning with nearly 99 percent of the vote—a tally that represented less than 10 percent of the population, given that the franchise was reserved for literate men. The near-unanimous victory of Washington Luís, as he was known, typified the era's café-com-leite power-sharing agreement between the states of São Paulo and Minas Gerais. With the government of Artur Bernardes (from Minas

Gerais) coming to end, the café-com-leite elites helped control the electoral process to put the paulista Washington Luís in power. The president-elect indicated a willingness to free some rebels who had been imprisoned after the initial 1924 revolt in São Paulo, but he opposed amnesty for the members of the Prestes Column.[62] If Washington Luís held firm on that position when he assumed office in November, it would negate one of the potential reasons for the rebellion to keep going.

In early May, with Prestes's troops making their way back into Bahia, Bernardes issued a presidential message that sought to calm the nation by presenting the rebels—not wrongly—as in a dire situation. The president emphasized that the column's ranks had been depleted through desertions, deaths, and capture. Bernardes described the rebels as "a group of bandits" who had long since given up the "confused political goals" that had originally launched the column.[63] In the coming months, debate continued to revolve around the column's actions in the interior. Supporters of the rebels, like Deputy Batista Luzardo, claimed that any excesses or looting was an unfortunate side effect of a rebellion: "At every moment in history, in all countries, there has been no revolution that has not witnessed what we are currently seeing."[64] Many of these speeches were reproduced in newspapers that were critical of Bernardes such as *O Jornal*, run by Assis Chateaubriand.[65] Supporters of the government, in contrast, cited the looting and violence in Bahia as proof that the tenentes were unpatriotic outlaws. Francisco Rocha—a federal deputy from Bahia who was the regime's main intermediary with the northeastern coronéis—became the most outspoken anti-rebel politician. Like those of Luzardo, Rocha's speeches were reprinted in newspapers, though his appeared in pro-government outlets. In one example from *O Paiz*, readers were introduced to Rocha's statement under the banner of "The Column of Death across the Brazilian Sertões: Shocking Evidence of the Barbarous Acts Committed by the Nomadic Horde of Prestes, Miguel Costa, and Other Criminals."[66]

Upon entering Bahia, Prestes charted a route that avoided the Chapada Diamantina and instead went along the plateau's western watershed, an area known as Lavras Diamantina. This path served the dual purpose of avoiding Horácio's central domain and the overflowing streams that cut down from the Chapada. Despite the advantage of a flatter terrain, the Lavras did put the column back among the caatinga vegetation they had encountered on their initial entry into Bahia. Moreira Lima wrote that "most of our troops were victimized by their thorns, especially those who had no shoes, leaving their feet bloodied."[67] Landucci described this stretch in similarly dejected tones, with the column, soldiers and officers alike, "barefooted, with beards and hair running long, presenting a scene of misery."[68]

With a combined sense of urgency (to cross the river before their enemies blocked their path) and despair (their ever-dwindling stock of supplies) the column initiated its most violent phase of the entire rebellion. In the first two weeks of May, the tenentes led assaults on half a dozen towns. On May 7, thirty people were killed in Muçugê—including soldiers and civilians—and, between May 10 and May 14, entire towns were set on fire in places like Agua de Rega, Tiririca dos Bodes, Canabrava, and Maxixe.[69] A resident of Mucugê named Ambrósio Caires provided testimony about one of these raids: "The rebels came to our house, the door was closed . . . so they slammed their rifle into it, they knocked down the door onto the floor and came in. . . . There were documents all over the table, and they said, 'The money is here,' [so a rebel] slammed his rifle on the table and knocked everything over, all of our documents for the house, taxes, everything. He didn't find [any money], but he messed up everything. He stole livestock we had behind the house, then they up and left."[70] Similar attacks took place on neighboring farms where the column seized supplies, cattle, and pack animals and murdered several farmers who had attempted to stop the looting. The rebels inflicted additional violence that had nothing to do with the material needs of the rebellion. According to testimonies collected by the army, three women were raped on the Matto Verde farm, and, in a second case of rape, soldiers also kidnapped all of the women on a nearby farm and did not return them until the following morning.

The violence also reflected the legacies of slavery and the racialized dynamics through which interior communities were considered less than human. In a 1993 interview, Manoel Lopes, ninety years old at the time, recalled that, when the column approached his town, the rebels lassoed him like a farm animal: "Ropes are made for a donkey or an ox, not for a man."[71] Another interviewee, Lindaura Rosa da Silva, aged seventy-eight, recounted how the column killed two of her neighbors in a similar manner: "The rebels destroyed everything. It was the worst thing that ever happened here. [The column] killed Manoel Cândido and João only because they said they wouldn't give their cattle to those lowlifes. They were tied up, dragged, and bled [to death like animals]."[72]

Whereas Prestes had previously tried to maintain a system of discipline whenever his troops committed such acts, the mounting rebel crimes—in addition to Prestes's own despair and uncertainty about the future—seemed too much for him to handle. The change that took root in Bahia was evident even to his enemies. In his final report on the campaign in the Northeast, General Mariante wrote that, although "Prestes had [previously] managed to maintain a certain discipline amongst these outlaw men . . . once their hope disappeared and their physical suffering increased, the bonds of obedience loosened and . . . all crimes and abuses went unpunished." In further anecdotal evidence, one farmer who had invited the rebel officers to spend the night in his home—seeking to have his farm spared from the column's violence, asked Prestes why his soldiers were acting so wrathfully. In response, according to the farmer, "Prestes became very quiet and discouraged, replying that [these acts] were turning his heart to stone and that it seemed nothing could stop his troops."[73] This burst of violence against Bahian communities was a final straw in the column's attempts to foster good relations with locals. Moreira Lima admits that, from this point onward, "the campaign took on a tragic character. In the face of broad hostility . . . the hearts [of our troops] blocked out any generosity and their souls hardened and yielded to the satisfaction of cruel vengeance."[74] For the column, the Bahian sertão thus became a space for revenge.

Violence was committed not only by the Prestes Column but also by those pursuing the rebels. In calling "the month of May [one] of the most disgraceful episodes in the history of Bahia," a US consul emphasized that "the Federal and State troops committed depredations far worse than any attributed to the rebels."[75] The violence committed by federal soldiers, like that of the column, lingered in local lore. One Bahian, Adelina Sodré Mendonça, remembered her mother telling stories about how "when the rebels came, the [government] soldiers were meant to bring the peace. [But] it was complete chaos. . . . She told me that the soldiers made things even worse than the rebels."[76] These abuses extended to the coronéis as well. Honório Granja was purported to have committed such widespread violence that he felt compelled to personally write a letter in late May to the editors of the *Diario da Bahia* attempting to deny those acts.[77] Another newspaper quoted a local merchant in Santo Antonio da Glória named Barbosa Fortes, who said that soldiers from a patriotic battalion looted their shops and killed cattle, and that, on the heels of the column, the coronéis had inflicted "a double scourge . . . on the unfortunate sertanejos of the northeast."[78]

As it was across Brazil's interior, this notion of a double scourge aptly captures the situation of many communities in Bahia. In the path of the Prestes Column, locals had to navigate an uncertain context where violence could come from both the rebels and their pursuers. The tenente trek across the state caused fear and confusion. In one letter obtained by Prestes's men, an inhabitant of Coití wrote that "we are terrified with the approach of the rebels, the last news that we received [was] that they were in the foothills, caused a real panic, families fled into the caatinga abandoning everything. This forces us to send this note asking for any information that you have. We're really scared, since we have no defense."[79] While it is true that most towns had no sustained way to fight back against either the column or the loyalists, they were not simply victims.

Caught in the middle of a violent war, locals showed creativity in their interactions with the various armed forces. This adaptability was especially noticeable when dealing with the loyalists, who were quick to assume that local Bahians had been aiding the column. Army reports indicate a pattern, wherein locals would hand over some supplies to the rebels—most likely to move them on and avoid conflict—and, when confronted by loyalist forces, they would either feign ignorance, say that the rebels had taken everything (to keep the loyalists from seizing their few remaining items), or denounce the column in order to prove that they were not rebel sympathizers. One report reflected the army's frustration: "Every town, every farmer, would shout that the rebels were threatening them . . . that in the next twenty-four or forty-eight hours they would be attacked and everything would be destroyed, etc. But, when our troops came needing [supplies], they would forget the danger, they played dumb, they didn't know anything."[80] A similar army communiqué from Bahia noted that, "after the passage of the rebel wave, these same farmers, these same leaders made an outcry about the abuses against them and said they had been victims, often saying that the amount stolen was much larger than what the rebels had actually taken."[81] Such examples suggest that, despite the "double scourge" in play, local communities found ways, however small, to navigate the various armed forces roaming their state.

These acts of resilience could not fully protect communities from violence, nor did they disrupt the larger narratives that continued to frame the people of Bahia's interior as exotic and dangerous. This was as true for the rebel and loyalist forces spreading violence in the interior as it was for news outlets reporting on the events. Under a front-page headline of "The Column of Death," an article in the Rio de Janeiro–based, pro-government *Gazeta de Noticias* included a large photo of six rebels who had been taken prisoner. As seen in figure 5.2, all six soldiers are dark skinned, fitting the stigmatized image that most Brazilians would have had of Bahia's interior communities. While there were indeed nonwhite Brazilians in the rebellion, the newspaper's choice of photo reflects a clear attempt to present the column as racially deviant. Here, the tenentes are presented not as virtuous southern gaúchos—the column's

A columna da morte

Novas aventuras do grupo sedicioso commandado pelo capitão Prestes

Em Jequitinhonha, a bravura do povo sertanejo repelle os bandoleiros

G. ... os de prisioneiros rebeldes, feito pelos voluntarios de Jequitinhonha. Da direita para a esquerda, são: Mario Augusto de Oliveira, João Martiniano da Silva, Augusto Anselmo Toledo, Pedro Paulo, Miguel de Paula Florentino e Ezequiel Dias de Oliveira.

FIGURE 5.2. Cover of *Gazeta de Noticias*, July 6, 1926.

preferred form of self-depiction—but as dangerous bandits (*bandoleiros*), whose skin color was meant to code them as northeastern. The text of the article further explains that "we offer this photograph of six comrades of Prestes [as] an opportune illustration of the fantastical tales that spread there [in Bahia], about the quality of the people who make up the column."[82] Oddly enough, despite its prejudice, the article provides some of the only personal details in the historical record of the column's foot soldiers—let alone its nonwhite soldiers. The photo's caption provides the names of all six rebels: Mario Augusto de Oliveira, João Martiniano da Silva, Augusto Anselmo Toledo, Pedro Paulo, Miguel de Paula Florentino, and Ezequiel Dias de Oliveira.

As argued throughout this book, the column's actions were conditioned by dominant coastal discourses about Brazil's interior. Often, these discourses overlapped with racialized news coverage. The column's return trek through Bahia was arguably its lowest moment: the rebels had abandoned the original goal of marching on Rio de Janeiro, their supplies were nearly extinguished, and their message of liberation had failed to rally local communities. In this context of frustration and despair, the tenentes unleashed the most violent wave of the rebellion. Moreover, when the violence was covered in local and national media, it amplified the more perverse tropes about the interior.

After its two-week burst through the Lavras Diamantina, the column arrived at the São Francisco River. At the town of Remanso, the tenentes were discouraged to find that the waters in front of them were still too high to attempt a crossing. With enemy forces navigating the impassable river, Prestes marched his troops two hundred miles east along the São Francisco, where the landscape of flooded marshes forced soldiers to wade in water up to their waists.[83] Compounded by the bouts of malaria that returned during the torrential rains, the column had to make do with almost no food, subsisting mostly on whichever small animals they could hunt. João Alberto's memoir describes an "inferno along the banks of the [São] Francisco, [we were] boxed in on one side by an aggressive and insurmountable mountain range, and, on the other, by a mighty overflowing river."[84] On May 26, the column left the river behind and went south through the Serra do Encaibro Mountains, until turning northeast at the town of Mundo Novo. For nearly all of June, the rebels then marched parallel to the Atlantic coastline.

Prestes eventually turned the column inland, near the border with Sergipe, and marched northwest. As it had been throughout Bahia, the folklore of Canudos and the writings of Euclides da Cunha influenced the rebel leaders. Moreira Lima wrote that in the week-long trek prior to arriving at the São Francisco River, the column followed the same road that federal forces in 1897 had used to advance on Canudos.[85] Although he spoke at length about sharing a path with the armies that had fought at Canudos, Moreira Lima did not acknowledge another obvious similarity: like the government thirty years prior, the Prestes Column had also failed to bend the landscapes and people of Bahia to support its campaign.

In the early days of July, the column marched nearly around the clock to reach the river before the loyalists could cut off their escape route. On July 2, the rebels broke camp just after midnight and proceeded with almost no breaks until nightfall, when they arrived on the outskirts of Rodelas, a small town on the banks of the São Francisco, thirty miles west from where they first entered Bahia.[86] Once the rebels located four small boats, Prestes wasted no time and ordered his forces to begin crossing the river in the middle of the night.[87] While waiting on the riverbank, the rebel high command also took the time to write up the details of its trek across Bahia. This bulletin included the dates and locations of battles, the places where they camped each night, and a tentative tally of desertions, imprisonments, and deaths from fighting as well as from illness such as malaria.[88] Having arrived in Bahia with 1,200 soldiers, the Column now counted some 900 among its ranks.[89] The four intense months in Bahia had made it difficult for the rebels to keep consistent records—this was only the column's second internal bulletin since leaving Pernambuco, a significantly lower output than the twenty-one reports compiled during the ten months prior to entering Bahia.[90]

With a bonfire lit on the opposite shore to guide their nocturnal crossing, the column spent the night ferrying across the São Francisco. Only at the very end of the crossing did loyalists finally appear, when Honório Granja's soldiers arrived in the early morning and shot out across the water at one of the final rebel boats as it sailed away.[91] Moreira Lima, who earlier in his memoir had so triumphantly described the rebels' bandeirante-like arrival, again invoked the same symbolism to justify their departure from the landscapes that, "three hundred years earlier, had made the Bandeiras tremble with fear during their expeditions into the unknown wild forests."[92] Rebel leaders thus framed their exit from Bahia not as a last resort of exhaustion or self-preservation but as the continuation of a long tradition of southern and coastal Brazilians surviving against the odds in a backward and dangerous space. Given the extent of violence committed by the rebels and the various difficulties they encountered, one might expect the passage through Bahia to have been omitted from the legend of the column. Yet, by attaching themselves to Euclides da Cunha and *Os Sertões*, column leaders were able to recast the column's march across the backlands.

As will be shown in chapter 6, the failure in Bahia did little to diminish the growing rebel mythology. If anything, their time in the lands of *Os Sertões* and their battles against the coronéis magnified the prevailing sense of their invincibility. Despite pockets of physical and discursive resistance from Bahians who experienced the column as violent aggressors, newspapers and politicians along the southern coast retained the power to shape the column's narrative. The legend of the Prestes Column thus served as its own form of bandeira, where coastal groups created a narrative, projected it into the interior, and framed the rebellion as a success regardless of what actually took place.

6

On July 3, 1926, the day after the rebels left Bahia, the headline of the Rio de Janeiro–based *A Noite* announced the publication of an eight-part series titled "The Prestes Column across Brazil."[1] Written by Viriato Corrêa, a respected journalist and playwright, and accompanied by an almost full-page map (fig. 6.1), the article introduced readers to the materials that would be published over the following two months: "For all of Brazil, the existence of the Prestes Column, still in full effervescence, seems as if a mystery and, at times, a miracle. It is almost beyond comprehension that a handful of men not even surpassing a thousand, can trek on foot from south to north and north to center . . . undaunted and triumphant, without being defeated." Similar to the way Euclides da Cunha's articles in the 1890s exposed Brazil's reading public to Canudos, *A Noite* hired a great writer—in this case, Viriato Corrêa—to produce an in-depth series on rebels in the backlands.

The exposé marked the unofficial start of when the column began to be referred to publicly as the Prestes Column. Of the over eight hundred newspaper articles that constituted my research, the *A Noite* series was the first to explicitly use the name that would henceforth become synonymous with the

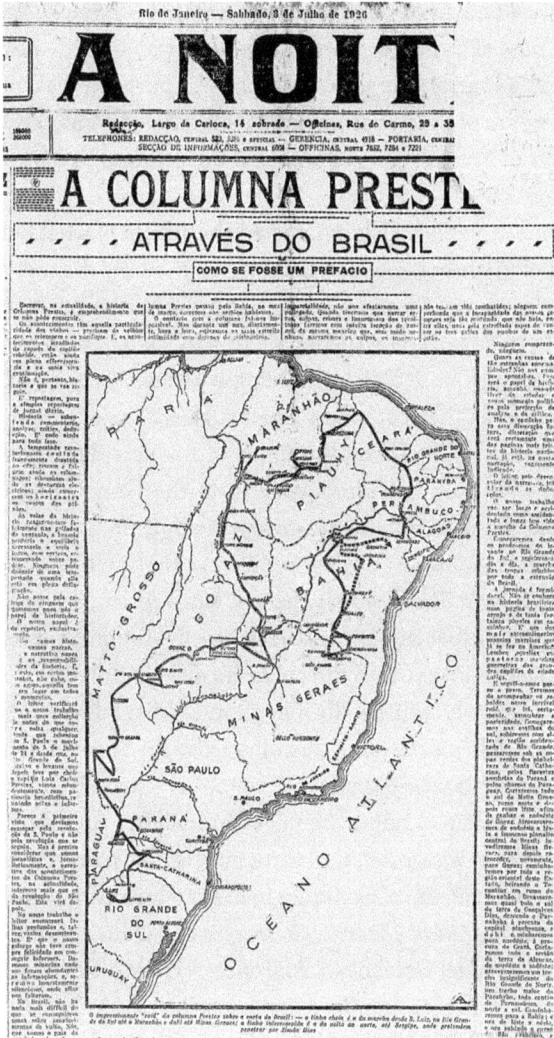

FIGURE 6.1. Cover of *A Noite*, July 3, 1926.

rebellion as a whole. Previously, in newspapers and speeches, it had mostly been called *the revolt, the column,* or *the revolution*—the tenentes, in addition to their self-ascribed title as bandeirantes of freedom, often referred to themselves as *forças revolucionárias* (revolutionary forces). Prior to the *A Noite* series, when the name *Prestes Column* had been used as such, it referred to the specific unit of soldiers commanded by Prestes. Yet, from July 1926 onward, once the rebels began their return from the Northeast, in nearly all media coverage and subsequent public discourse the rebellion became firmly attached to the image of Luís Carlos Prestes. Again echoing Cunha's coverage of Canudos, where the millenarian leader Antônio Consel-heiro served as a central story line, newspaper reports on the column helped to create the figure of Prestes as a spirited folk hero. As Viriato Corrêa wrote in his coverage of Prestes: "He is the soul of the column, which very correctly takes his name."[2]

The headline in *A Noite* also signposted the advent of what became a central platform of myth-making: newspapers, particularly the sort of serialized exposés shown above. These exposés, in turn, belonged to a wave of new developments in Brazil's newspaper sector. In his comparative history of Assis Chateaubriand and William Randolph Hearst, Jacques Alkalai Wain-berg credits 1926 as the year when Chateaubriand made some of his most enduring innovations, aided by the input of his new director of publicity, an American whom he had hired away from the Hearst-owned *New York American*. According to Wainberg, among the most important features that Chateaubriand introduced in this period were the multipart chronicles on the Prestes Column.[3] These serials, from Chateaubriand's papers as well as from others, were especially prevalent in the final months of the rebellion and throughout the first year of the column's exile in Bolivia.

Newspaper exposés additionally inaugurated what I describe in this chapter as a cartographic picaresque.[4] Drawing from the Spanish noun *picaresco* and its adjective form *pícaro* (meaning "rogue" or "knave"), *picaresque* refers to a literary genre that recounts the tales of rough but appealing heroes getting by on their own wits, often told through episodic narration of travel and discovery. From its canonical examples in Iberian literature such as the anonymously written *The Life of Lazarillo de Tormes and of His Fortunes and Adversities* (1554) and Miguel Cervantes's *Rinconete y Cortadillo* (1613), picaresque novels would include more modern instances like Mark Twain's *Adventures of Huckleberry Finn* (1884) and Thomas Mann's *The Confessions of Felix Krull* (1959). Popularized stories about the Prestes Column, whether consciously or not, created a picaresque with two protagonists: the tenente rebels, and the interior. This duality itself has two layers, given that the picaresque of the backlands related to the landscapes of the interior as well as its populations. Because the column came to represent an origin story of sorts for modern Brazil, the concept of a cartographic picaresque helps us to explore the spatial components of nationhood.

In an expanding newspaper market competing for readers and paid advertisers among an emerging middle class, most coverage included large maps of the march across the interior. The cartographic element of the column's emerging mythology celebrated the tenentes for having filled in the supposedly empty spaces of the national map. Paired with often-romanticized narratives, this visual component of myth-making—fueled as well by the financial motivation to sell copies—contributed to making the interior the conceptual and spatial core of the rebellion. At a time when many groups in Brazil hoped to embark on a new process of nation-building, maps provided a compelling way to reach the public, including illiterate people who might see newspapers being sold on the street. In most depictions of the Prestes Column, the maps were not scientific in the sense of having been produced by professional cartographers. Rather than a precise account of the column's march, newspapers used loose approximations to show the broader sweep of the interior expedition. In this sense, newspapers offered something closer to a cartographic fable, a picaresque, in which Prestes and his fellow rebels were meant to entertain and inspire the nation.

In the second half of 1926, as the column made its way back from the Northeast, the serialized newspaper exposés served as exercises to gauge how much latitude the government would give its opponents. Although Washington Luís had won the presidential election in March, he was not slated to assume office until November, and censorship remained the purview of Artur Bernardes. Less than a week after Corrêa's series first appeared, police in Rio de Janeiro confiscated issues of *A Noite*, specifically citing the material on Prestes's march through the interior. While censorship over the previous two years had not completely blocked newspapers from reporting on the rebellion, authorities took issue with the type of emboldened reports evident in Corrêa's exposé.[5] The government's attempt to restrict this coverage failed. Not only did Corrêa's series continue for almost two months—following a brief pause after the police raid—but it also became so popular that it was reprinted in *A Gazeta*, another Rio de Janeiro newspaper, as well as the Curitiba-based *O Estado do Paraná*.[6] In a likely attempt to control the narrative of the still-undefeated tenente rebellion, Bernardes intervened again: a week after the eighth and final publication of Corrêa's series, the Ministry of Justice ordered newspapers to suspend publication of all material relating to the Prestes Column.[7] Opposition newspapers seemed increasingly willing to flout the government's restrictions, and, especially once Bernardes left office, the mythology of the Prestes Column proliferated on the pages of Brazilian newspapers.

Anti-rebel media coverage also expanded during this period, denouncing the tenentes while criticizing the romanticized pro-rebel narrative itself. The São Paulo–based *A Gazeta*, which maintained a relatively neutral position on the Prestes Column, criticized the speeches of Deputy Batista Luzardo and the articles of Viriato Corrêa as a sort of one-two punch: "Every day, Mr. Batista Luzardo speaks, in Congress, about [the Column], telling of the courageous acts of its warrior forces. On the other hand, Viriato Corrêa, also writes daily, with his own take on the exact same stories as Mr. Luzardo. What this means, however strange it might be, is that the people end up getting bored with so much make-believe."[8] Similarly, an op-ed in the *Gazeta de Noticias*—a consistent supporter of the Bernardes regime—expressed annoyance at how the tall tales about the column seemed to justify its violent actions: "The march of the Prestes Column through the Brazilian 'hinterland' is becoming a tedious reality for the country, even for those who love sensationalist stories. This is about the despair of a handful of rebels who, while running away from defeat that would surely occur if they actually confronted government troops, escaped into the backlands, lashing out, looting, murdering, and destroying what was and still is within their reach."[9] As censorship lessened, newspapers would function as a primary conduit in the ongoing battle for public opinion, with each side using the other's projected image as a foil for their own. These dueling narratives became increasingly pronounced during the final phase of the column, when the rebels reversed course and began their long trek to the national border.

The Path to Exile

The rebels left Bahia and embarked on what became a seven-month, 3,700-mile return journey (map 6.1) that deposited them as exiles in Bolivia in early February 1927. The column first made a quick push through the northern states of Pernambuco and Piauí—with a brief dip back into Bahia—before spending the better part of six months circling down through the central states of Goiás and Mato Grosso. With most of the government troops still in Bahia, and before the federal army could deploy a new command unit farther south, the pursuit of the column again fell largely to patriotic battalions, particularly those of Horácio de Matos, Abílio Wolney, and Franklin Lins de Albuquerque. After two years of chasing the rebels through Brazil's interior, neither government troops nor the coronéis could stop the column as it retraced its steps and sought refuge in exile.

Having evaded enemy forces in Bahia by recrossing the São Francisco River, the column began its march toward exile on the morning of July 3, 1926. The first phase was a nine-day journey through Pernambuco. The march had an inauspicious start, when, on July 5—the two-year anniversary

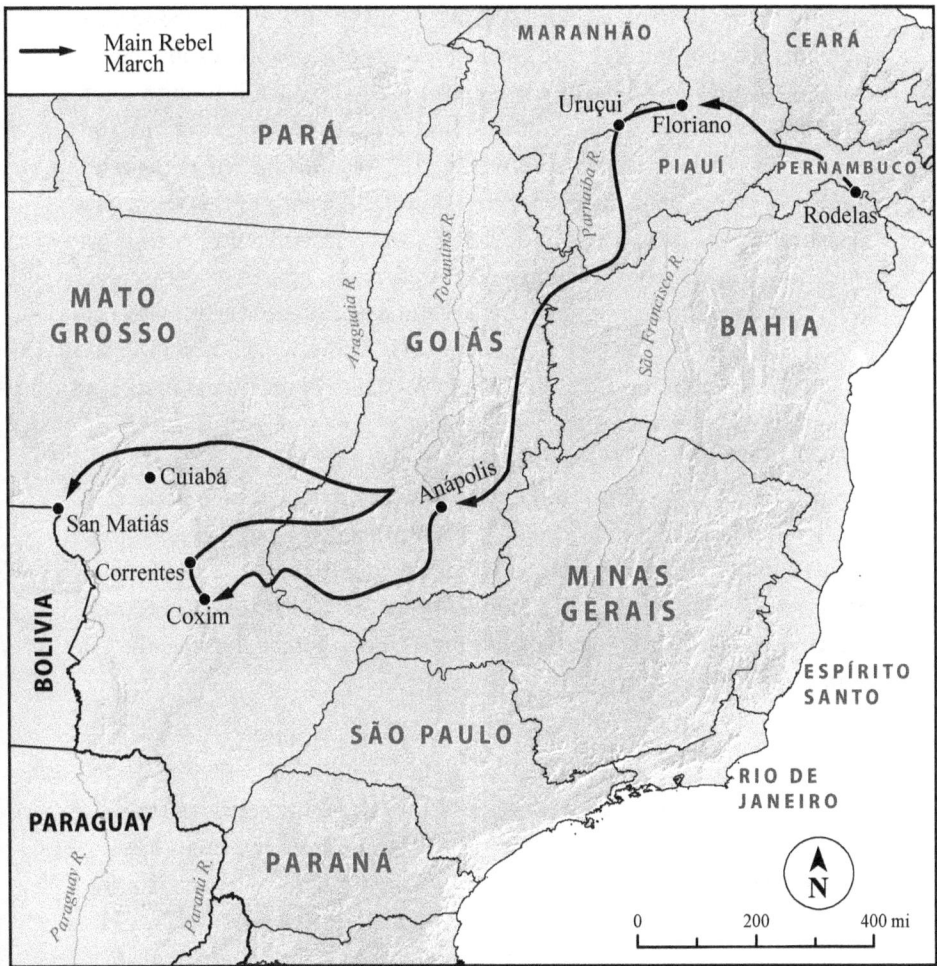

MAP 6.1. Prestes Column, July 1926–February 1927. Courtesy of Gabe Moss.

of the rebellion—Prestes ordered the expulsion of a rebel sergeant who had raped a young woman. Although the violence indicated that the abuses in Bahia had continued across state lines, Prestes's decision to expel the guilty soldier showed that he was trying to reestablish a system of discipline. The push-and-pull between the tenente leaders and their soldiers continued over the following week: on July 9, rebel troops killed a local townsperson while occupying Ouricurí, and the next day a soldier used a knife to kill a young boy in Olho d'Água. Prestes deemed the latter murder bad enough that the soldier was not only expelled from the column but also handed over to the local authorities.[10]

The Prestes Column crossed west into Piauí on July 11 near the town of Campinas, and by July 23 it had reached the city of Floriano. As on their initial stay the previous December, the rebels used Floriano's printing press to publish *O Libertador*. Although they could not have known at the time, this issue of the rebel periodical, the tenth in total, was the final one of the rebellion. In the more open media climate of late 1926, a copy of this tenth issue eventually made its way to Rio de Janeiro, where it was reproduced in national newspapers. The front page of *A Gazeta* from September 3 (a six-week delay that accounted for copies of the bulletin needing to travel by messenger from Piauí) quoted directly from *O Libertador*, which it called "the wandering organ of the Prestes Column."[11] On July 24, the column left Floriano and turned south, eventually entering the state of Goiás on August 20. In approaching the Planalto Plateau, Moreira Lima described the region as "the capital of Brazil . . . rising, symbolically, from the ground, as the impervious heart of our immense and splendid lands."[12] What the rebels intended to do at this juncture was not immediately clear, neither to Prestes and his fellow officers nor to his pursuers. In a radio call with the Ministry of War, General Mariante offered a running summary of the many potential routes the column could now take:

> What they will do in Goiás is anybody's guess. Will they try to reach the border of Mato Grosso to then go into exile in a foreign country? Will they continue their aimless trajectory wherever it is easiest and most convenient for them? Will they try to position themselves in a well-protected area in order to compel the government to try and attack them only to then flee again when threatened? . . . The only certainty is that they have now reached areas in the interior of the country that are very difficult [for us to stop them].[13]

Despite the presence of the federal army and state troops, the coronéis continued to play a central role in the pursuit of the column, and the presence of these backland strongmen received much attention in the national spotlight.[14] In the broader battle for public opinion, opponents of the government pointed to the fact that northeastern coronéis had been deputized as army commanders. In a congressional speech that the *Correio da Manhã* reproduced in full, Batista Luzardo said that the coronéis should be imprisoned for their crimes, not given a uniform to act as federal soldiers. Luzardo called it "shameful, a humiliation for the pride of the army that the government has taken the hand of people like this, [only] because they do not trust the army itself."[15] This view was echoed by other prominent media figures.

Assis Chateaubriand worried about the precedent being set by the government's collaboration with the coronéis. Reflecting a coastal conflation of diverse interior figures, Chateaubriand penned an editorial in which he referred to the coronéis as cangaceiros, the term more aptly used for backland outlaws such as Lampião: "What will happen next for Brazil, with Horácio de Matos, Abilio Wolney, all these insubordinate cangaceiros . . . who have been promoted as pillars of the Republic and defenders of order? We have now armed these sertanejo cangaceiros to the teeth."[16] Other outlets made similar statements. A front-page article in *A Gazeta* lamented that "the crimes, the thefts, the assaults became seen as tolerable acts, cloaked with official protection. After fighting against the Prestes Column, the cangaceiros [will remain] audacious, now strengthened by superior weapons and an abundance of ammunition."[17] These statements can be interpreted in two overlapping ways: the slippage between different interior categories could suggest an effort from opponents of the government to criminalize the coronéis—and, thus, the Bernardes regime that had deputized them—and it could also reflect a more pervasive mainstream ignorance, through which coastal elites lumped together everything from the interior.

In what proved to be a final coordinated effort to stop the Prestes Column, several thousand state troops from São Paulo were dispatched to the plateaus of Goiás. Whereas the previous campaign in Bahia had been led mainly by General Mariante, the action in Goiás was placed under the command of Colonel Pedro Dias de Campos, head of the São Paulo state forces. Dias de Campos's plan was to spread out loyalist forces in a 250-mile east-west line across Goiás to block the column from moving into southern Goiás and thus closer to exile.[18] This strategy was a near replica of the failed plan in Bahia, where João Gomes sought a similar human barricade. In Bahia, the column had evaded the army by marching up through the Chapada Diamantina, and in Goiás they did so by taking advantage of another topographical escape hatch: Dias de Campos had guarded the three main roadways in Goiás, yet he deployed few units to cover the region's many rivers. With the waterways of Goiás left open, Prestes avoided the paulista troops by leading his men in a series of river crossings.[19] The column continued its southward march, enjoying a relatively uneventful month-long passage across Goiás.

On October 15, the column crossed back into Mato Grosso by traversing the Correntes River. By crossing the border at Cabeceira do Capão—between the Goiás cities of Jataí and Mineiros—they retraced their steps almost exactly to where they had first left Mato Grosso back in June 1925. At this juncture, the column counted some eight hundred fighters, only six hundred of whom were deemed to be in adequate physical shape, and supplies, particularly ammunition, were running low.[20]

Having entered Mato Grosso's diamond mining district, Prestes saw the region as a potential ally for his depleted troops. The local mine workers (known as *garimpeiros*) had a long tradition of conflict with the state government, and Prestes made a bold proposal to his fellow officers: the column could be dissolved into smaller bands and dispersed throughout the mining district. This meant that, rather than escaping into exile and waiting to come back at a future date to renew the struggle, they could stay within Brazil and rebuild local support. Miguel Costa, who normally backed Prestes's decisions, vehemently opposed the idea.[21] The other rebel leaders agreed with Costa and eventually talked Prestes out of the plan. Because the tenentes opted to steer clear of the diamond districts, what they did not know was that at least some locals in Mato Grosso were open to making an alliance with the column. One such garimpeiro, Pedrito Rocha, later recalled that the column's passage was a missed opportunity: "Prestes was so stubborn! How could he think of changing this country all by himself, with a handful of men in tattered clothes and barely armed? If he had given weapons to the garimpeiros, if he had gathered a big group of soldiers, something could have changed."[22]

Prestes's proposal for staying in the mining district can be placed in the broader panorama of how his political views evolved during the march. Prestes appeared to be the tenente officer most affected by the poverty and injustice on display in Brazil's interior, and it was during this period in Mato Grosso that Prestes wrote what stands in the historical record as the first document of his path toward radicalization. Under the title of "Liberty or Death—Land Deed," Prestes handwrote a four-page pamphlet about Brazil's need for agrarian reform.[23] The document stated that "having walked amongst the Brazilian people, especially the poor, we have seen the most ferocious despotism being practiced. . . . [And] considering that public lands should be shared by the poor who need the means of subsistence. . . . [And] considering that instead of giving unused lands to small farmers, state governments have put the nation in danger by giving it freely to those who own vast latifundio [estates]. . . . We resolve to create land deeds for whichever man requests it." By calling for land redistribution and the end of the latifundio plantation system, Prestes planted the early seeds of what would later coalesce around a more radical approach—in the 1940s, for example, the Brazilian Communist Party under Prestes's leadership would make agrarian reform in the interior one of its main campaigns.[24] Rather than the reformist demands that had catalyzed the tenente movement, this pamphlet shows an incipient social critique based on what the rebels had seen, however fleetingly, during their interior march.

New Government, Same Predicament

On November 15, Washington Luís was inaugurated as Brazil's new president. The end of the Bernardes presidency sparked an even greater wave of commentary and criticism in the opposition press. As noted in a British consular report, "Censorship has been relaxed with the change of Government and the opposition papers have, without exception, seized the opportunity for attacking Dr. Bernardes and clamoring for amnesty."[25] In the early days and months of the new presidency, the question of amnesty was raised across the political spectrum. At one end of the pro-amnesty movement were outspoken supporters of the Prestes Column like Leôncio Correia, a well-known writer belonging to an influential political family from Paraná. In an op-ed for the Curitiba-based O Dia, Correia framed amnesty as a necessary step "for the harmony of the Brazilian family." More than simply wanting the tenentes to be protected in the short term against charges of sedition, Correia saw the column's "truly epic" march through the interior as proof of why Luís Carlos Prestes should be made an integral part of Brazil's future: "Overcoming the formidable obstacles of our wild and savage landscape . . . Prestes's military genius, his strategy, his vision, his courage . . . [can help us] take on the important and sacred task of elevating Brazil to the preeminence that it can and must have in America."[26]

Prestes's emerging mythology served as its own form of political capital. A column written by Mendes Fradique—the pseudonym for the doctor-turned-humorist José Madeira de Freitas—argued that the rebels deserved amnesty precisely for having explored the depths of Brazil's interior. Fradique praised Prestes as a valuable, if accidental, cartographer: "The Prestes Column without a doubt updated our map. This is perhaps the greatest contribution of the current generation of Brazilians, and even just for this, removes any culpability from those who have strayed from the legal order in their pursuit of a revolutionary ideal. Only the work of the Prestes Column deserves a broad and compassionate amnesty from the government. [Yes,] the rebels carried weapons in their hands, [but] as it turns out, these weapons were actually tools for map-making."[27] The interior had long loomed in the national imaginary as an untapped empty space, and, for commentators like Fradique, Prestes helped fill in Brazil's map and incorporate the backlands into the nation. The emptiness in this view of Brazil's interior calls to mind the observations of historian Courtney Campbell and her colleagues, who write that, "as a state, emptiness necessarily invokes what is *not* present; it is in some ways a condition of absence. It thus follows that as emptiness is a matter of perception, it is a highly subjective phenomenon, dependent to a large extent on who is doing the observing and what the subject expects to find."[28] In this case, the observing was being done by mainstream Brazilians who perceived an empty interior as a cartographic and imaginative "other," a spatialized prism to refract the civilizing march of the Prestes Column. At this moment in late 1926, supporters of the column argued that the rebels deserved amnesty, in part, for having turned the empty voids of Brazil's interior into legible spaces capable of contributing to the nation.

Although Washington Luís made a gesture of pacification the following month by releasing several political prisoners from the 1924 revolts, the new administration offered no amnesty for the rebels still in action.[29] It was not until November 8, 1930, two weeks after Getúlio Vargas successfully led the Revolution of 1930, that the Brazilian government officially absolved the rebels—those in the column as well as those involved in the various revolts since 1922.[30] With no sign of amnesty on the horizon and still reluctant to cross into exile, the column stayed in motion in Brazil.

With more coronel and state police forces moving into Mato Grosso, Prestes marched his troops back toward Goiás, where they arrived on November 19. The column spent very little time in Goiás, as Prestes traced a three-week, counterclockwise loop of five hundred miles that soon brought the rebels back into Mato Grosso on December 10.[31] This quick foray in and out of Goiás saw constant fighting. Nearly half a dozen battles took place in these three weeks. On November 20, the column passed through the town of Barra do Bugres, where, according to local newspaper reports, the rebels took 250 animals and over a million réis from farmers.[32] In response, a group of locals banded together to fight against the column, though the rebel soldiers quickly put down the resistance and killed fifteen of the town's defenders.

In late November, the column made a definitive move to exit the country. When Prestes took his troops back into Mato Grosso on December 10, the westward return left no ambiguity about their destination. As Dias Ferreira recorded in his memoir: "It was truly with the passage of the Araguaia River into Mato Grosso that the revolutionary column began to march toward exile."[33] As the rebels moved west throughout the month of December, the coronel battalions of Horácio and Franklin Lins de Albuquerque kept a close pursuit, and, although they fought the column several times, it was never enough to stop the rebels.

A Cartographic Picaresque

As would be the case for the following three years, one of the most prominent elements in the growing spotlight on the column was the mythologizing of the tenente leaders. Although the state of siege had been lifted by President Washington Luís at the end of December, it remained in place for the three states of Mato Grosso, Goiás, and Rio Grande do Sul—meaning that censorship remained in the regions with ongoing rebel activity. With freedom of the press greatly loosened in São Paulo and Rio de Janeiro, newspapers amplified their coverage. The US consul observed that, after censorship was lifted in Brazil's main cities, the opposition press unleashed "a tremendous burst of torrid language. The fugitive leaders of the revolt are exalted and any bit of news about them is repeated a dozen times with verbal alterations. Already legends are growing up about these men, and their extraordinary wanderings and escapes have placed them in the popular imagination by the side of El Cid, Robin Hood, Marion, and other heroes of troublous times."[34] The Rio de Janeiro–based *A Manhã* seemed particularly taken by the iconography of the tenentes' long march. In one article from mid-January, the paper called Prestes "a jaguar of the sertões, true and generous, he is today, with his warrior column, the column of our national pride."[35]

The grandiosity of Prestes's march across the interior engendered a series of ever-larger historical comparisons. In another article, *A Manhã* likened Prestes to Christiaan de Wet, an Afrikans general who fought in the Boer Wars of the late nineteenth century.[36] And, across a front-page spread, the *Gazeta de Noticias* declared: "Prestes, Greater than Hannibal!" with a large map comparing the tenente journey across Brazil to that of the general from ancient Carthage who, with a fleet of elephants famously in tow, had marched on Rome in the third century (fig. 6.2). In this coverage, Prestes was heralded for having travelled "three and a half times farther and twenty-eight times faster" than Hannibal, and for doing so on horseback and foot, without the benefit of "the numerous elephants that flattened the path for the Carthaginian troops."[37] Moreover, the alpine peaks of Europe and the mysterious worlds of the Mediterranean and North Africa were portrayed as if they were an easier route compared to the Brazilian backlands traversed by the tenentes.

As the most prominent hero, Prestes received the majority of attention. But his fellow officers became national figures as well. *A Manhã* gave a lionized account of the rebel high command, calling Miguel Costa intrepid and stoic: "Another type of hero [altogether]. Calm intelligence, pensive."

FIGURE 6.2. Cover of *Gazeta de Noticias*, January 19, 1927.

Siqueira Campos, for his part, was presented as unendingly brave, "the type who would march toward death . . . to fulfill a principal, for his ideals." And Juarez Távora, still imprisoned at the time, stood as "a romantic type of revolutionary."[38] Amid this cult of personality, the symbolism of the column became linked ever more closely with that of Brazil's interior. The *A Manhã* article ended its paean with a romanticized description of the path forged by the rebels across the country, providing a roll call of states as a way to trace the internal geographies of the interior: "The revolutionaries left behind the pampas of Rio Grande, crossing the dangerous lands of Paraná and Santa Catarina, tearing into the rugged jungles of Mato Grosso, taking their glorious forces into the endless fields of Goiás, invading and cutting through, in all forms, the towering plateaus of Piauí, zig-zagging among the arid sertões of Pernambuco, Ceará, Paraíba and Rio Grande do Norte and floating over enormous stretches of the jagged mountains of Bahia's interior." Paired with the visuals of maps that likened Brazil's interior to other exoticized spaces across the globe, these descriptions promulgated a story of cartographic and social wonder: readers, who themselves might never travel to the backlands, could be made to experience the thrill of backland exploration without ever leaving their homes. This narrative of inland chronicles had deep roots in Brazil. In the 1873 novella *O Índio Afonso*, for example, Bernardo Guimarães explains to his "leitoras" (female readers) that they can safely travel with him in the "soft and beautiful coach" of his story "to the depth of my remote and wild 'sertões,' without any risk of danger or exhaustion."[39] Interior stories were thus designed to sweep readers away from their (coastal) milieus and into the thrilling spaces of the backlands.

Despite the mythologizing unfolding across headlines and newspapers columns, in reality the Prestes Column had just embarked on the final and perhaps most grueling passage of its entire march. On January 10, the rebels entered the Pantanal, the massive floodplain fed by the Paraná River, a defining landscape of western Mato Grosso. The Pantanal presented a double obstacle of topography, where an initial stretch of arid forestland then gave way to the floodplains of the Paraná River. The rebels often had to hack out a path through the trees, and, in his memoir, Dias Ferreira recalled the "long and endless days that the rebel forces passed in those thick forests, suffering all sorts of anguish. Our food consisted almost entirely of hearts of palm."[40] The second phase in the Pantanal unfolded as a constant search for dry land, as the rebels had no alternative but to march straight through the floodplain. João Alberto wrote that "we no longer had a single dry piece of clothing. It was impossible! We dreamed of finding a bit of solid ground, where we could make a fire during our lunch stops, and set up some sort of camp at the end of the day."[41] With the coronel forces under Franklin Lins de Albuquerque launching several attacks, the column spent the month of January slogging its way toward the Bolivian border. Landucci described the final push toward exile as "depressingly bleak. We were reduced to about six hundred bedraggled men, without shoes and half-naked. . . . The passage [in the Pantanal] was the most difficult of our whole campaign."[42]

The hardships of the Pantanal remained out of sight for national audiences. On January, 28, *A Manhã* published an interview with an unnamed rebel officer who had supposedly passed through Rio de Janeiro. No evidence suggests that a tenente had made their way to the capital during this period, and in all likelihood the "interview" may have been an adaptation of a report sent to Batista Luzardo. Regardless of the source's provenance, the article depicted a buoyant rebel force happily marching toward exile. The interviewer for *A Manhã* asked, "How are the spirits of the troops?" to which the officer replied, "Excellent. They are all very eager and enthusiastic, persevering quite admirably. Nobody feels discouraged, nobody feels dejected."[43]

As the rebellion prepared to cross into exile, newspapers also used cartographic iconography to project a sense of triumph. As seen in figure 6.3, *A Manhã* printed two images in a lengthy article on the column: on the left, a map of the rebel march prior to its return from Bahia, and on the right, what would become a famous photograph of the rebel high command in Porto

Officialidade da columna Prestes e percurso feito pela columna atravez do Brasil, rumo ao Piauhy. Os officiaes são os seguintes: 1) tenente-coronel Djalma Dutra, commandante do 4° destacamento; 2) tenente-coronel Siqueira Campos, commandante do 3° destacamento; 3) coronel Luiz Carlos Prestes, chefe do Estado Maior da Divisão; 4) general Miguel Costa, commandante da Divisão; 5) coronel Juarez Tavora, sub-chefe do Estado Maior; 6) tenente-coronel João Alberto, commandante do 2° destacamento; 7) tenente-coronel Oswaldo Cordeiro de Farias, commandante do 1° destacamento; 8) Dr. José Pinheiro Machado, do 2° destacamento; 9) etnente João Pedro, do 1° destacamento; 10) capitão Emypdio Miranda, ajudante do 1° destacamento; 12) tenente-coronel Paulo Kruger da Cunha Cruz; 13) major Ary Salgado Freire, fiscal do 2° destacamento; 14) capitão Fritim Corréa, ajudante do 3° destacamento; 15) major Manoel Lyra, fiscal do 2° destacamento; 16) tenente Sady Valle Machado, do Estado Maior da Divisão; e 18) capitão Italo Landucci, do Estado Maior da Divisão.

FIGURE 6.3. *A Manhã*, January 1, 1927.

Nacional, Goiás (the same image shown in chapter 4). In a political context where the tenente rebels had been elevated as the guiding light of Brazil's opposition movement, newspapers did not report on how the column was actually faring in its final phase, focusing instead on the heroic details—and visual cues—of what the column could symbolize.

Yet the rebels had little cause for enthusiasm in the Pantanal. While making several challenging river crossings—including the Sepotuba, Cabaçal, and the Jauru—the rebels could not shake free of their pursuers as they approached the Bolivian border. A series of skirmishes at the end of January proved to be the final battles of the rebellion, and the exhausted column soon broke away from its enemies and prepared for exile. On the evening of February 2, Prestes and his men set up camp eight miles from the border. Thirty months since the initial São Paulo revolt and twenty-seven months since the gaúcho uprising, the rebels spent one last night sleeping on Brazilian soil. The rebels broke camp early the next morning, and by 5:30 a.m. they were marching west. A few hours later they entered Bolivia.[44]

When the Prestes Column crossed into Bolivia on February 3, 1927, it did so with a total force of only 620 soldiers.[45] Including an additional sixty-five soldiers who would enter Bolivia six weeks later, this meant that the column, which at its peak had counted almost three thousand fighters, now ended its campaign with fewer than seven hundred. And of the fifty women that had started out with the column, only ten crossed into exile, with the rest mostly having deserted, though others were captured or killed along the way.[46]

When the rebels arrived the following day in the Bolivian town of San Matiás, they went to the local army garrison to discuss the terms of their surrender. It was agreed that the column would willingly place itself under the protection of the Bolivian government. In exchange, the tenentes relinquished nearly all of their weapons, which included ninety Mauser rifles, four machine guns, two automatic rifles, and eight thousand rounds of ammunition. The rebels could only keep their pistols and Winchester rifles for hunting and personal protection.[47] A document signed by Prestes, Miguel Costa, and Major Carmona Rodó—the local Bolivian commander—outlined this agreement and stipulated that as long as the rebels behaved well and obeyed Bolivian laws, they would be treated peacefully.[48]

The opposition press celebrated the end of the column in its typically triumphant fashion. By this point, the rebel mythology had grown so much that the heroic coverage of the column's exile extended beyond its epicenter of Rio de Janeiro and São Paulo. A newspaper from the northern state of Maranhão, the *Folha do Povo*, ran a headline proclaiming that "The Revolution Marches to Its Triumphant Finish." Reflective of how the legend would flourish in the coming years, the article stated that "there is nobody, not an actual patriot, who is not proud of the esteemed efforts of Prestes and his valiant companions, in their glorious ascent toward immortality."[49]

7

CONSTRUCTING THE KNIGHT OF HOPE

The figure of Luís Carlos Prestes is, at this moment, the subject of the most curious and uncontested legends. For those who looked with hatred on the events of the past four years, [Prestes] is nothing more than a vulgar bandit; for those who bind themselves body and soul to the cause and the work of the revolution, he is a demigod.—"ENTRA PRESTES!," *Gazeta de Noticias*, 1927

These lines were published in the *Gazeta de Noticias* on February 6, 1927, three days after the Prestes Column took up exile in Bolivia. The article showed that, although a mythology had undoubtedly started to form around Prestes, a dominant narrative had yet to settle. On the one hand, he was seen by supporters as an immortal being who crisscrossed the Brazilian nation; on the other hand, in the eyes of his detractors, that same interior journey made him a violent bandit—no better than the coronéis or the cangaceiro outlaws like Lampião. The question here pertained to whether Brazil's interior was an imaginative and spatial instrument either to elevate Prestes (reflecting his coastal, civilized status) or to denigrate him (Prestes having "gone native" in the backlands). That Prestes could be made to symbolize such contrasting tropes spoke not merely to the complexities of tenentismo and the growth of Prestes's own popularity, but even more to the broader set of meanings projected onto Brazil's interior. Like Prestes at this moment in early 1927, the interior could represent both the promise of a civilizing mission and a bandit-filled space of danger. Moreover, between these two poles lay a wide range of more subtle iterations, always subject to changes in terms of who held the power to shape the boundaries of Brazilian nationhood.

For Prestes, once the column stopped its march, and the rebels excised themselves from the physical spaces of Brazil's interior, a once-incipient mythology became dominant. In the aftermath of the column crossing into Bolivia, a consistent narrative took shape: propelled by allies in the media and a growing opposition movement, Prestes's image changed from that of a vulgar bandit to a virtuous southern cowboy who had ventured into the backlands and returned as an undefeated hero. Thus emerged the legend of Luís Carlos Prestes as the Knight of Hope.

Focusing on the years between the column's exile in February 1927 and the revolution of October 1930, this chapter traces the genesis and influence of Prestes's status as the Knight of Hope. During this period, Prestes began to embrace Marxism, while, for Brazil more broadly, political conflicts deepened and culminated in Getúlio Vargas's seizure of power. Amid these national changes, Prestes became a symbol with widespread appeal for numerous political movements. By examining popular depictions of Prestes in the years immediately following the tenente march, this chapter shows how the legend of the rebellion grew out of the column's imaginative link to the interior. Because Prestes's popularity was tethered to his experience in the backlands, we can trace both the inclusionary and exclusionary elements of the stories that grew around him. As the Knight of Hope, Prestes symbolized a heroic gaúcho unifier who had brought the prospects of freedom to previously backward regions. This buoyant framing appealed to the Communist Party (who saw Prestes as key to organizing the peasantry) as well as to Vargas, whose Liberal Alliance Party wanted to capitalize on Prestes's popularity. Prestes had a back-and-forth relationship with both the Communists and the liberals, and by 1930 he had refused to join either. All the while, his status as the Knight of Hope relied on the landscapes and people of Brazil's noncoastal regions as a narrative device for his journey into the interior and back again. The power of this imagery became so entrenched in the legend of the column that, even when Prestes split from his former tenente compatriots, his romanticized connection to the backlands endured.

On the heels of their fifteen-thousand-mile march, the tenente rebels arrived in Bolivia with mixed emotions. Although they could now lay down their weapons with no fear of attack from pursuing armies or militias, their situation remained uncertain. They were tired, many were stricken by illness, and they had almost no money. While, back in Brazil, debates swirled about whether the government should offer an amnesty agreement, the rebels had to figure out what to do in exile. A majority of the tenentes made their way to Argentina, where several officers reconnected with General Isidoro to plan future rebellions. Prestes, who showed little interest in linking up with Isidoro, stayed in Bolivia with a small contingent of the rebels, including leaders like Djalma Dutra and Lourenço Moreira Lima.

Bolivia's eastern border region was a dense thicket of forest and wetlands situated 150 miles south of the headwaters of the Paraguay River. The proximity to the Paraguay's navigable waterways—the second largest river in the Plate Basin—had recently drawn the interest of commercial enterprises. The year prior to the column's arrival in exile, an English company, Bolivian Concessions Ltd., had secured permission from the Bolivian government to develop mineral extraction, agriculture, and logging across thirty million acres.[1] The company was based in La Gaiba, a small town ninety miles south of where the rebels had entered Bolivia at San Matiás. With few employment opportunities in the region, and eager to put his training as an engineer to use, Prestes traveled to La Gaiba and negotiated a contract for him and his men to work for the English company. In exchange for a modest daily salary, the rebel soldiers built a road through the forest and constructed small buildings to serve as storage silos for coffee and other crops (fig. 7.1). Prestes claimed that the money they earned was barely enough to live on, particularly as they had to constantly buy medicine to treat the malaria and dysentery that predominated in the swampy forestlands along the border.[2] To tend to the workers, Hermínia, the vivandeira nurse who had stayed with the rebellion since the initial São Paulo uprising, set up a makeshift hospital.[3]

The poverty in rural Bolivia was not unlike that in much of Brazil's interior, yet the rebels reacted to it in a different manner. In his memoir, João Alberto wrote that, "although we had crossed Brazil in every which way, traversing so many inhospitable regions, we were surprised by the isolation and poverty of [Bolivia]. The villagers were *indios* drunk on chicha (corn alcohol), they were dirty, melancholy, and rude."[4] Here, we see a nationalist refraction of the tenentes' prejudice toward interior communities. In Brazil, the racialized disdain toward interior peoples retained a certain aspirational quality, in which their backwardness could be overcome—if given a proper push by more civilized outsiders. Brazil had a coast, which meant that its backlands could still be brought into a modernizing project. But, in Bolivia, one of only two landlocked countries on the continent, and where Indigenous people made up the large majority of the population, the poverty of its backlands was seen as an innate quality of a backward country. The racialized sense of superiority held by the rebels likely conditioned their reactions to Bolivians—locals may well have been "rude" to the rebels, who, in turn, seemed to bristle at being treated as unimportant outsiders. Moreover, because the rebels were not fighting for anything in Bolivia except to make ends meet, they did not need to rely on the hospitality or fighting capabilities of local people, removing a potential gesture of respect that the column had made toward communities in the Brazilian backlands. To a dominant coastal perspective like that of the rebel leaders that was shaped by their changing material needs, not all interiors were the same.

As the rebellion came to a close, the growth of its legend accelerated. This happened for several reasons. First was the issue of timing. The loosening of censorship coincided with the end of the column, and, with newspapers now free to report on the column, readers received a surge of coverage about the recently finished march as well as the rebels' current situation. Second, exile in the Bolivian interior added further imaginative contours to the emerging mythology: although the rebels had managed to survive their two-year trek across the Brazilian backlands, their exile in eastern Bolivia represented a continued excursion into another—and even more sinister—interior. Newspapers depicted Bolivia as a dangerous place. Under the title "A Scene from Green Hell," an article in *O Jornal* (one of Assis Chateaubriand's papers) noted that the former column fighters "are being decimated by hunger and malaria in an extravagance of rustic nature, with palm fronds for beds and the semi-virgin forest looming as their cemetery."[5] In another article written by Chateaubriand himself, the "green hell" of the Bolivian borderlands highlighted the resilience of the rebels, whom Chateaubriand described as "patriots, these Brazilian soldiers, who suffer through a bitter exile and now live as pariahs in the savage forests of an inhospitable region."[6] Along with its racialized implications, the depiction of Bolivia's interior as "worse" than the Brazilian sertões functioned as a political strategy to argue for an amnesty agreement. This narrative was a patriotic appeal so that a group of Brazilians, despite their recent efforts to overthrow their own government, could at least be saved from the shame of having to suffer in a foreign interior. The

FIGURE 7.1. Exiled rebels working for Bolivian Concessions, Ltd, La Gaiba, Bolivia, 1927.
CPDOC ILA photo 011–7.

legend of heroic rebels who confronted a series of increasingly dangerous interiors served as justification for securing passage back to Brazil—and to the safe spaces of its coast.

While Prestes and a group of his men were working in eastern Bolivia, other officers such as Miguel Costa and João Alberto Lins de Barros made their way down to Argentina, and General Isidoro continued to lobby the government of Washington Luís for an amnesty agreement. Newspapers played an important role in pushing for an amnesty, and their support often invoked the symbolism of the column's march across the interior. *A Manhã*, for example, wrote that the rebels deserved amnesty because their long march through the backlands had already shown their capacity to unify the country: "They were a paragon of bravery, showing spectacular patriotic faith. . . . The Prestes Column woke up the people of the interior, [freeing them] from the tyranny of local political chiefs. All corners of our immense nation are calling for the repatriation of these glorious exiles."[7] Such examples offer important insight as to why, and when, the narrative of liberation in the backlands first gained momentum. At a moment when the rebels were depicted as suffering in a foreign interior, tales of a patriotic march through the Brazilian interior became a discursive tool in the campaign for amnesty. From its initial emergence in the political battles of the late 1920s, the legend of heroic liberators would soon predominate, becoming adaptable to different contexts across the twentieth century.

President Washington Luís never offered an amnesty agreement, but the attention lavished on Prestes constructed a cult of personality that extended far beyond the immediate conflicts at hand. Prestes's nickname as the Knight of Hope did not enter mainstream discourse until the middle of 1927. However, in the early months of the year, when it was unclear what direction, if any, the anti-government movement would take, newspapers cast an aura around him that made the column into a symbol of patriotic fortitude. At a moment when Prestes had no more battles to fight or specific messages to amplify, his exploits in Brazil's interior made him a living legend.

A central thread in this narrative concerned the actions of the rebels during their long march. As a counterpoint to the image of the column as violent invaders, newspapers depicted Prestes as a selfless and sympathetic leader. A week after he crossed into exile, the *Correio da Manhã* wrote that Prestes and his men were "knights of virtue [who] traversed the immense stretches of national territory without harming, in the cities and towns where they passed, those who gazed upon their exemplary behavior."[8] Without denying that some violence was inflicted on local communities, media coverage seemed to exonerate Prestes by elevating him as the guiding moral authority of the rebellion. One article from late February wrote that, of all the rebel commanders, Prestes was "the most humanitarian, believing they should only fight against those who actively resisted, [always] protecting the defenseless people."[9] Several articles mentioned that whenever his soldiers did stray from proper behavior, Prestes would punish them.[10] In an interview from Bolivia, Elza Schimidt, one of the women in the column, said that Prestes never drank or smoke, that he was not a womanizer, and that he always had respect for the local families along the march.[11] The figure of Prestes as fair and compassionate became so ubiquitous that journalists sought to trace its origins back to his childhood. *O Jornal* sent a reporter to interview Prestes's mother, Leocádia, who spoke about the unassuming nature of her son: "He was always very small, meek. But he loved to teach others. At school, he was so selfless, and loved tutoring his classmates. When he joined the revolution [in 1924] I didn't think he would be suited for war. He was too kind. There was no way that somebody with so much kindness could fight in a rebellion that could take the lives of his own people. To join the revolution, he must only have done that out of an immense feeling of patriotism."[12]

The same week that *O Jornal* published its interview with Prestes's mother, it also began a ten-part exposé titled "Listening to and Talking with Luís

FIGURE 7.2. La Gaiba, Bolivia, where the journalist Rafael Correia de Oliveira (*seated, far left*) interviewed Luís Carlos Prestes (*seated, center*), 1927. In the back row are Bolivians, most likely stationed at the nearby army garrison. CPDOC ILA photo 011–9.

Carlos Prestes."[13] This was not the first instance of a multipart newspaper series. As shown in chapter 6, *A Noite* had run an eight-part exposé the previous July, when the rebels began their return journey from Bahia. Compared to the earlier series that discussed the tenente journey as a whole, *O Jornal* now focused entirely on Prestes. This series was based on lengthy interviews conducted with Rafael Correia de Oliveira, one of the paper's managing editors, who, thanks in large part to his coverage of the Prestes Column, would become one of the most renown journalists of the era.[14] Correia de Oliveira's trip to Bolivia (fig. 7.2) marked the start of what became a series of pilgrimage-like journeys to meet with Prestes in which journalists as well as politicians would travel great distances to hold court with the rebel hero. In his articles, Correia de Oliveira made no effort to mask his admiration of Prestes, referring to him as "the fascinating condottieri of the revolution"—a reference to the Italian knights of the seventeenth century, and a hint at the Knight of Hope nickname that would enter mainstream discourse a few months later. In one installment, Correia de Oliveira exclaimed: "Prestes! The name of that saint, who is a brave and luminous genius, cannot even be pronounced by the wicked people who slander the honor of others. Where can one find a character more pure, a soul more generous, a conscious as clean, a mind as sharp as that of Carlos Prestes?"[15]

Along with reinforcing the heroic narrative of Prestes's personality and leadership skills, the exposés also entrenched the prismatic relationship between the figure of Prestes and that of Brazil's interior. Under the subheadline "The Lesson That Prestes Took to the Men of the Interior," Correia de Oliveira declared that

> Prestes's epic journey was more than just a great military feat. . . . He led a civilizing crusade. For the first time, our rustic people, abandoned and neglected in the tragedies of the lonely sertão, felt the pulse of a civilized soul, beating to the noble rhythm of a grand political idea. . . . Prestes's worldview, his respect for the weak, his attention to the sufferings of [the backlands], the chivalry of his military strategies, it all meant that for the first time, a new and more appealing opportunity beckoned, where a civilized man could bring sertanejos into the national community.[16]

By presenting the interior as dormant ("neglected") and backward ("rustic"), Correia de Oliveira invoked two of the core tropes of the interior. Within this framing, Luís Carlos Prestes was depicted as a pathbreaking hero whose "civilizing crusade" had allegedly awakened the sertanejos from their passive slumber, making them ready to join the modern nation. Correia de Oliveira's mention of a "grand political idea" also reflected a disconnect between the growing legend of Prestes and the actual progression of his worldview. As already discussed, the tenente rebellion did not include a specific ideology, but advocated instead a general set of reforms. And, although Prestes had begun to adopt a new social critique—evident in his deliberations with the Communists in Pernambuco and his handwritten essay on agrarian reform—these views had not yet been shared with the public. In his interviews with Correia de Oliveira, Prestes spoke about the shock he felt at witnessing poverty and desperation in Brazil's interior, but those statements could hardly be categorized as a "grand political idea." Set against the backdrop of a suffering sertão, the symbolism projected onto Prestes was outpacing his changing political sensibilities.

The exposés in March proved so successful that Assis Chateaubriand commissioned a second series. On April 1, barely a week after the final installment from Correia de Oliveira, another *O Jornal* correspondent, Luiz Amaral, left Rio de Janeiro and made his way to eastern Bolivia. As with the previous series, Amaral published a nine-part report that ran for a month beginning in late June. It even had a similar title: "Speaking with Luís Carlos Prestes."[17] A month prior to the Prestes series, however, Amaral first published an eight-part exposé about his own inland expedition to find the rebel leader in Bolivia.[18] Under the headline "A Journalistic 'Raid' of Twelve Thousand Kilometers," Amaral chronicled his journey to meet Prestes in a style that mimicked the coverage of the Prestes Column. "The dynamic journalism of today," Amaral wrote, "is demanding":

> Rather than staying put with one's pen stuck in the inkwell, to pitch ideas in the dark, it is now necessary to prepare oneself as if going on a hunting trip into the jungle, to pack quinine, long pants, a rifle and a wide-brimmed hat, and to have your body tumbled on train rides, down river rapids, in canoes and even on the back of cattle, in an exhausting trek across hundreds of kilometers just to write half a page of brand new material; to write a story collected in the source itself.[19]

The column's popularization of the interior expedition, and its prevalence in the pages of Rio de Janeiro and São Paulo's major dailies, created a media climate where newspapers became more than simply a platform for mythologizing the interior. Like the original reports from Euclides da Cunha three decades earlier, journalism about the interior functioned as its own sensationalized genre.

The celebratory tone of these articles relied on a range of underlying tropes, including gender and the Brazilian nation. As Maite Conde makes clear in her research on star culture and fandom in Brazil, media at this time "purposefully set out to cultivate a female audience," which suggests that stories about the column helped grow the legend of the rebel march by also reporting about—and appealing to—women.[20] Similar to the press coverage of the women rebels during their passage through Bahia, a gendered double-standard still predominated. As part of Amaral's "Speaking with" series, he wrote an entry on "Speaking with the Women of the Prestes Column."[21] Most of the article focused on Elza Schimidt, a nurse who had joined the column along with her husband and stayed with the rebellion all the way to Bolivia. *O Jornal* featured a picture (fig. 7.3) of Schimidt with her young son, Evandro, who was born in the final months of the march. Most photographs of the rebels (e.g., fig. 7.4) showed rugged, expressionless men with long beards and threadbare uniforms. Schimidt, on the other hand, was represented as eminently feminine: wearing a white dress and a wide-brimmed hat and holding her child, she smiles reassuringly into the camera. The picture suggested that Schimidt, and many other women in the column, were little more than ancillary, motherly figures, whereas in reality they were active participants who shared in the full ardor of the rebellion. With a growing public spotlight on the exiled rebels, the dissemination of these images helped shape who was seen as a legitimate force of change. As shown in figures 7.3 and 7.4 (both from the same *O Jornal* series), the men held guns, and the women held babies. These types of gender representations made the column into a symbol of the idealized Brazilian nation: doting white mothers and brave soldiers ready to protect the nation.

As a preview of sorts for the rebel memoirs that would predominate in later years, newspapers provided space for rebels to write about their own exploits in the interior. Juarez Távora penned a six-part series, and Lourenço Moreira Lima offered a two-part chronicle, the latter proclaiming in its subheading that, "During Our March, We Saw with Our Own Eyes That the People of Our Sertões Are an Enslaved Mass Vegetating in Extreme Misery."[22] Along with lionized coverage—an intertwined mix of inclusionary and exclusionary language—newspapers financially supported the rebels. Begun first by Assis Chateaubriand and his *O Jornal* and *Diario da Noite* and then followed by the editors of *Correio da Manhã* and *Folha do Povo*, newspapers organized donation campaigns for readers to send money to support the rebels in Bolivia. With the lifting of censorship the previous year, these campaigns reflected just how quickly public opinion had turned in favor of the rebels. Having successfully evaded government troops and local dangers across Brazil's interior, they now needed help to escape a final phase of their interior journey. Here it was the Bolivian backlands that threatened to engulf the rebels; for them, a sympathetic and mobilized readership proved essential to finally make their way back to safety in Brazil.

In total, the fundraising appeals brought in nearly fifty million réis, which supplemented the rebels' meager earnings in La Gaiba.[23] The journalists who went to interview Prestes in Bolivia played a key role in this fundraising. Luiz Amaral delivered seventeen million réis when he arrived in Bolivia, and as part of a reciprocal cycle of support and news coverage, Prestes gave the journalist two hundred pages of rebel documents and maps that would serve as the core material for subsequent newspaper exposés. Prestes also provided sixty original copies of the rebel bulletin, *O Libertador*, which newspapers raffled off for five thousand réis each. Seeking to bring the experience of the rebel's inland journey into the literal hands of eager readers, *O Jornal* proclaimed that some of the copies of *O Libertador* "are still dotted with the blood spilled by the patriots."[24] Newspapers printed running tallies of the donated funds, often listing the names of donors, the amounts they contributed,

Elza e Evandro Schimidt

and even their professions, showing that contributions came from figures as
varied as businessmen, military officers, and school teachers.[25]

Newspapers were not the only sector helping raise money. Other events
included a "pro-Prestes" festival and soccer match in the Paraná city of Curitiba, and a fundraiser by high school students in Rio de Janeiro.[26] The rebels
received such an outpouring of support that Prestes donated a portion of the
money to a hospital in Mato Grosso, helping to construct a new extension of
the hospital that was baptized the "Prestes Wing."[27] If the column had already
attained a certain level of notoriety during the final stages of its march across
the interior, once the rebels settled in exile the swirl of newspaper coverage
and growing public adoration elevated their status even higher.

Six months into the rebels' time in exile, an important discursive shift
took place. As shown in previous chapters, the rebels had been referred to
as *bandeirantes,* either in the explicit words of their leaders—using the term

FIGURE 7.4. Newspaper picture of rebel men. Source: *O Jornal*, June 30, 1927.

bandeirantes of freedom—or in the more general reference to the column as a form of modern-day bandeira expedition. This nickname implied a somewhat collective identity: as bandeirantes, the rebels stood as unnamed parts of a larger whole. But the figure of Luís Carlos Prestes soon predominated, as embodied in his nickname as the Knight of Hope—a name coined by General Isidoro, the leader of the original 1924 revolt, who took inspiration from an officer during the French Revolution known as le Chevalier de l'Espérançe.

In the aftermath of the column's exile, Isidoro began calling Prestes the Cavaleiro da Esperança.[28]

It is difficult to trace precisely how the nickname filtered into popular discourse, but by early July it was already referenced in newspapers. July 5, 1927, represented a symbolic shift from the bandeirantes to the Knight of Hope. Marking the fifth anniversary of the initial tenente uprising of 1922 and the third anniversary of the 1924 events that begat the Prestes Column, supporters of the rebellion—abroad and in Brazil—spoke about the legacy of the tenente revolution. In La Gaiba, Bolivia, Prestes's men constructed a small monument to those who died fighting for the rebellion. On a block of granite, the rebels inscribed "Glory to the Bandeirantes of Freedom, 1924–1927" (fig. 7.5). Lourenço Moreira Lima delivered a speech to mark the occasion: "Filled with emotion and pain, we inaugurate this mausoleum for the memory of the brave soldiers of the Prestes Column. . . . The revolution will continue its irrepressible march toward victory, with or without its enemy's consent, and in both peacetime and war. [On the horizon] we fix our gaze toward the triumphant march of the revolution."[29] On the same day that the rebels laid to rest the bandeirantes of freedom, newspapers in Brazil reflected on the five years of rebellion and anointed Luís Carlos Prestes as the rightful heir to the revolution's next phase. Coverage from July 5, 1927, included the first public mention of Prestes's nickname as the Knight of Hope. In a two-page spread celebrating the rebellion's progression from 1922 to 1927, *Vanguarda* devoted several sections to a discussion of Prestes. Along with crediting Isidoro for coining the nickname Knight of Hope, the paper celebrated Prestes for leading a "warrior expedition" that "throbbed with desire for a liberated Brazil."[30] July 5 served as a hinge moment, both literal and discursive, in the evolving rebellion: with the bandeirantes of freedom now symbolically buried on foreign soil, the Knight of Hope rose up as the dominant legend.

As Prestes entered the pantheon of national icons in the coming months and years, his status as the Knight of Hope became irrevocably linked to the constructed symbolism of the long march across the interior. Of the countless examples during this period, an article from the *Correio da Manhã* encompassed the dual nature of Prestes's mythology. It presented the Knight of Hope as a vector for uplift and inclusion, with Prestes as a hero who "galloped above the forests, climbed above the clouds, as he ascended into a starry infinity." Yet the article's deification of the Knight of Hope also included the following excerpt that illustrated the myth's exclusionary undertones:

FIGURE 7.5. Monument to the "Bandeirantes of Freedom," La Gaiba, Bolivia. Photograph taken sometime between July and November 1927. CPDOC ILA photo 011–8.

> [Luís Carlos Prestes] took the pulse of our savage Brazil, fraternizing with our interior populations, traveling through all the states, bringing the seeds of culture to our rural populations.... A legion of progress, this army triumphed: it brought notions of goodness and duty, and the feeling of human respect to the rude souls of our backlands, demonstrating to the savage Indian of our forests all the generosity and kindness held in the hearts of the white people from the coast.[31]

This citation highlights the interlinked contrasts of the column's mythology. Prestes was virtuous, the interior was savage. Prestes epitomized culture and modernity, the interior was backward. Prestes was white and coastal, the interior was neither.

The Radical Roots of the Knight of Hope

Decades' worth of retrospective mythologizing has drawn a direct line between Prestes's march through the interior and his embrace of radical politics. That story is not entirely untrue: what Prestes saw during the rebellion did have a genuine impact on his worldview. Not only was he taken aback by the level of poverty in the interior but he also came to see the demands of the tenente movement as insufficient to disrupt the hierarchies of power displayed by backland coronéis and their political allies. In select cases, such as his essay on agrarian reform, Prestes even expressed the need for more structural change. These sentiments suggested a budding social critique, but the actual timeline of his turn toward radical politics has often been exaggerated. In his 1942 biography of Prestes, for example, Jorge Amado celebrated the Knight of Hope for "tearing across the sertões and tearing up the deeds of lands illegally taken from small farmers by the large coronéis. . . . Before having read in books the solutions of Marx and Lenin, Prestes had already read them in the Great March. Everyday offered more than a book. He learned *Capital* in the emerald-green lands of Mato Grosso and Goiás. . . . During the Long March he . . . was a Marxist without having yet read Marx."[32]

Despite Amado's portrayal of Prestes as a Marxist in the backlands, Prestes did not actually engage with Marxism until he was living in exile. His first encounter came via Rafael Correia de Oliveira, the *O Jornal* correspondent who had traveled to Bolivia for the inaugural series of exposés. Correia de Oliveira left Prestes with a handful of books, including some on political theory, and their subsequent correspondence nudged along Prestes's radicalization. In a letter to Correia de Oliveira a few months after their time together in Bolivia, Prestes even quoted Lenin as saying that "theory can become a material force when it grips the masses."[33] Yet, in a reflection of how rudimentary his politics were at this early stage, Prestes attributed the quotation to the wrong radical: the phrase was written by Marx, not by Lenin, as Prestes had confidently stated in his letter. Despite what his legend might otherwise suggest, even as his charisma and leadership developed, Prestes's Marxist credentials remained in formation for quite some time.

In December 1927, almost a year after arriving in Bolivia, Prestes was visited by Astrojildo Pereira, the secretary-general of the Brazilian Communist Party. The PCB was still relatively new and small—it was founded in 1922 with barely seventy members, and five years later when Pereira visited Prestes in Bolivia, it had grown to only six hundred people.[34] As historian Daniel Aarão Reis writes, "The creation of the PCB went completely unnoticed by public opinion," and for several years the party was "insignificant to the point of being almost ridiculous."[35] The growing pains of building a new organization were indirectly exacerbated by the rise of tenentismo: between the first tenente revolt of 1922 and the end of the Prestes Column in 1927, the Brazilian government maintained a state of martial law for all but seven months. The repressive climate of the 1920s forced the PCB to operate in semilegality and hindered its ability to build its membership base. Toward the end of the decade, the PCB was oriented to a strategy of building a Worker and Peasant Bloc—the Bloco Operário e Camponês. As described in a 1927 statement from the PCB's central committee, the Bloco sought to build "an independent class politics [to run candidates] who would maintain permanent contact with the working class through representational sectors—unions and politicians—and public rallies."[36] Although the Bloco was envisioned to cover peasants as well as urban workers, in practice the PCB had not done much in the countryside. As Perreira himself admitted, "The 'peasant' element was little more than a word inserted into the Bloco, it was a wish."[37]

In this context, Pereira traveled to Bolivia with the explicit goal of establishing an "alliance between the Communists and the soldiers of the Prestes Column, or, in other words, between the revolutionary proletariat under the influence of the party and the . . . peasant masses under the influence of [Prestes]."[38] Pereira sought to recruit the Knight of Hope to the PCB, hoping to use Prestes's popularity to increase the party's profile and make inroads with rural sectors. After two days of discussion, Prestes declined the PCB's offer, though he was intrigued and kept the Marxist literature that Pereira had brought him, including texts from Marx, Engels, and Lenin, as well as a dozen issues of *L'Humanité*, the newspaper of the French Communist Party.[39]

Two months after his meeting with Pereira, Prestes left Bolivia and moved to Buenos Aires, where he lived for the next two and a half years, working at an import-export business that sold Brazilian products, mainly coffee.[40] Unlike in Brazil, the Argentine Communist Party was legal, and Prestes frequented its headquarters, spending time with local leaders who encouraged him to read *State and Revolution* by Lenin and volume 1 of Marx's *Capital*.[41] The Marxist texts and conversations with Party militants pushed Prestes to rethink the conditions and revolutionary potential of the Brazilian peasants he had encountered. Reflecting on his time with the column, Prestes later wrote that "during the journey through the country's undeveloped regions we received a strong psychological shock that put us in contact with the reality of Brazil. . . . Suffering from a chauvinist arrogance that gave us a false idea of life in our country, we were surprised by the backwardness and misery in which the people lived."[42] Over the course of their march, Prestes further explained, the rebels had to update "their incorrect views about workers [in the interior], whom we had seen, to be fully honest, as inferior beings who were meek and submissive."

A Symbol of Unity

Back in Brazil, Prestes's radicalization was not yet publicly known. And, with the presidential election of March 1930 looming ahead, his new status as the Knight of Hope made him a highly desirable figure. Throughout 1928 and 1929, Prestes was seen as a potential unifier. In April 1928, the *Diário Nacional* ran a full-page cover article (fig. 7.6) that included a map of the column's march—so large that it edged into the adjacent text—alongside commentary about how his time in the interior had guided his political goals: "The tasks of the armed struggle did not prevent the officers of the Column from making a detailed study of a series of problems of national interest."[43] In this depiction, complete with visual cues of Prestes's cartographic adventures, the Knight of Hope stood tall as a symbol of unity.

While much of this coverage existed in the newspapers of Rio de Janeiro and São Paulo, Prestes received similar praise from elsewhere in the country. The Ceará paper *A Cultura*, for instance, wrote that "Prestes is the mirror reflecting all of the light for our future. . . . Prestes is a god who consoles all those who suffer and all those in feel in their hearts, the genuine pulsing emotions of patriotism!"[44] It did not take long for this acclaim to trickle into the realm of politics. There were calls for Prestes to run for president, he received write-in votes for local elections, and a wide range of politicians invoked his exploits in the interior as a means to amplify their own candidacies.[45] When the Democratic Party (Partido Democrático) campaigned in Pernambuco as part of the 1928 state elections, it sought to position itself as the inheritor of the Prestes Column. The *democráticos*, as they were known, proclaimed that their party "embodies the continuation of the work started by the Prestes Column's march across Brazil's sertões. We will be its accomplice. The closing of its historical cycle, [we will bring the interior] to the edge of the Brazilian coast."[46] This type of framing used the column as a proxy for both temporal and spatial change: by "closing" the cycle of the interior's isolation, politicians could refract the symbolism of Prestes to envision a more modern Brazil.

The imaginative joining of coast and interior—a prism's rotation that brought the two regions into closer alignment—also took place in southern Brazil. When Affonso de Camargo announced his candidacy for state president of Paraná in April 1929, *A Manhã* framed it as part of an emerging national profile for politicians from supposedly "modest states," writing that "modern politics are going from the periphery to the center. . . . The Prestes Column, along with its many glories, was a great dispenser of

FIGURE 7.6. Cover of *Diário Nacional*, April 19, 1928.

the national geography, because it illuminated the dark names of the back-lands."[47] Whether in Pernambuco in the North or in Paraná in the South (two coastal states that were better known for their symbolic backlands), the column symbolized the fusion of coast and interior. As such, it became a stand in for the promise of a new nation.

As politicians and journalists amplified the interlaced myths of Prestes and the interior, two of Brazil's most influential writers of the era—with opposite political views—published novels based on the Prestes Column. In early 1929, Graça Aranha, one of the fathers of Brazilian modernist literature, published *A viagem maravilhosa* (The marvelous journey). In what proved to be Aranha's last book before his death two years later, *A viagem maravilhosa* tells the story of a young woman named Thereza who escapes a loveless marriage and travels to the far-flung corners of the country. Aranha's book includes several references to the real-life Prestes Column. At one point, a character named Manuel says that "everyone is expecting a lot from Prestes and his soldiers. They are spreading the revolution. . . . The whole country is excitedly watching the bravery of these warriors."[48] Although *A viagem maravilhosa* did not receive anywhere near the critical acclaim of Aranha's earlier works, it reflected Prestes's growing status in national culture, particularly among those who looked to him as a symbol of change.[49]

At the same time, Prestes was held aloft by reactionary sectors who warned that the tenentes would lead the country to ruin. One example was a novel by Ariosto Palombo, a conservative journalist and editor of the *O Paiz* newspaper, under the pseudonym João de Minas.[50] The author embedded his anti-rebel stance in the title, *Jantando um defunto: A mais horripilante e verdadeira descripção dos crimes da revolução* (Dining on the dead: The most horrifying and true description of the crimes of the revolution). *Jantando um defunto* follows a fictionalized loyalist unit as it pursues the Prestes Column across Mato Grosso and Goiás, graphically detailing cases of violence—which the author states are "based on real events"—committed by the rebels, including burying and burning people alive.[51] So, although the hero cult of Prestes had far outpaced the view of him as bandit, examples like *Jantando um defunto* showed the continuation of negative associations between him and the interior. Whether drawing on the narrative of myth (Prestes as backland liberator) or countermyth (Prestes as backland savage), the interior became a powerful and flexible trope in political commentary.

Prestes's symbolism began to enter more mundane spheres as well. If the two novels released in early 1929 suggested the column's arrival in high culture, we can also trace its development within popular culture—particularly, as previously mentioned, aimed at women readers and consumers. Discussion of the Prestes Column had become so common that it was employed as a marketing tool for a wide range of commercial products. One advertisement for a wood-burning stove played on the literal meaning of Prestes ("on the verge of") to promote the virtues of its smokestack (or column), with a maid named Ignacia excitedly telling her boss that the Prestes Column has arrived: "A columna, Prestes, chegou!!!!"[52] Other examples made tongue-in-cheek references to the supposed grandiosity of the column's trek across Brazil. After asking consumers, "What is the greatest wonder of the world?," an advertisement for a cold medicine listed off twelve items, including the march of the Prestes Column.[53] "It is none of those things," the ad replied, proclaiming instead that "the greatest wonder of the world only costs 3,500 réis and cures all flus and colds, can be found in pharmacies, and goes by the name of Xarope de Guaco." Moreover, the tenente journey into the interior and back offered a lesson in how to liberate oneself from the presumed "dirtiness" of noncoastal spaces. A fashion columnist writing in *O Jornal* about having returned to Rio de Janeiro after a month of travel observed that a visit to the Doret salon was just the ticket to "reapply my civilized airs and shed my Prestes Column-like appearance."[54]

As images of the Prestes Column proliferated in the late 1920s, the presidential election of 1930 offered a sobering point on the horizon. After the previous two elections in 1922 and 1926 had aggravated the country's political tensions, and with the violence still fresh from the most recent rebellion, most sectors hoped to avoid further conflict with the next presidential succession. In a country that remained deeply divided, the Knight of Hope remained an attractive figure. With the 1930 elections inching closer, Prestes's political currency continued to derive from the symbolism of his march. An April 1929 article in *A Manhã* declared that "the platform of Luis Carlos Prestes, traced in blood, across the geographic map of Brazil, is the only one the people can trust, after so much dishonesty and ridicule. So any politicians who right now want to win over the hearts of the people, will have to speak to them about Prestes and in the name of Prestes."[55] Figure 7.7 illustrates this symbolism: in what became a famous poster of the era, Prestes's face stretches across the entire country. With his gaze staring out from the interior of the national territory, he covers so much of the map that "Brazil" is forced to the edges. In his bearded, stoic glory, Prestes becomes almost bigger than the country itself.

Two groups in particular sought to bring the Knight of Hope into their fold: the Communists in the PCB, and what would become the Liberal Alliance (Aliança Liberal) led by Getúlio Vargas. Since the PCB's first recruitment pitch to Prestes two years earlier, the changing policies of the Communist International had greatly complicated an alliance with Prestes. In July 1928, only a few months after Pereira had visited Prestes in Bolivia, Moscow hosted the Sixth World Congress of the Communist International, a watershed gathering that initiated the Third Period. The Congress overturned the previous united front approach of collaborating with non-communist revolutionary groups—such as the Prestes Column—and replaced it with a more confrontational program of class warfare. The Comintern directed the delegates from across Latin America to reorient their campaigns toward a platform of "agrarian and anti-imperialist" revolution. Five months after the Moscow summit, the PCB held its Third Party Congress, and, seeking to align with Moscow's emphasis on agrarian revolution, Brazil's communist leaders reaffirmed a commitment to engaging the peasantry. The final report of the PCB Congress observed that, "for the first time in the history

FIGURE 7.7. Poster of Luís Carlos Prestes, 1929.

of the Party . . . peasants and the agrarian problem were taken seriously. . . . The Third Congress did not resolve [the problem], nor did it give a definitive solution, nor could it have; but, crucially, the question was put on the table, in its full magnitude."[56] At a time when Luís Carlos Prestes was, rightfully or not, seen as someone who could unite rural Brazilians, the PCB considered the Knight of Hope a potential solution to its so-called agrarian problem.

The Comintern's Third Period left the PCB in a delicate position. The emphasis on an agrarian and anti-imperialist revolution called for a vigorous campaign in the countryside, yet the policy of class warfare now complicated an alliance with the person that the PCB saw as its key to such an approach. Although Prestes had begun to embrace Marxism, he had not yet joined the Communist Party. Moreover, he remained a potent symbol of the reformist tenente rebellion—precisely the sort of non-communist group from which the Comintern now sought to distance itself. At this juncture, the PCB decided that Prestes's potential as a leader of the peasantry outweighed the risks of collaborating with the former head of what it considered a petit-bourgeois movement. In June 1929, the PCB invited Prestes to run as the party's candidate for the 1930 presidential elections. While in Buenos Aires for the First Conference of Latin American Communist Parties, Paulo de Lacerda—the PCB's new leader—and Leôncio Basbaum met with Prestes and pitched the idea of a presidential run. As Basbaum recalled, "Our hope was to recruit Prestes and use his national and popular prestige to win over the masses."[57] While claiming to agree with much of the PCB platform, Prestes rejected the offer, saying, "I cannot accept [the candidacy] because I am still loyal to the tenentes. Only after speaking with them can I take a position."[58]

At this time, Prestes was also being courted by Getúlio Vargas, the governor of Rio Grande do Sul, who was running for president in the 1930 elections. Over the following decades, the standoff between Vargas and Prestes would devolve into one of the defining features of Brazilian politics, yet, in the late 1920s, an alliance between the two gaúchos still seemed plausible. Vargas sought to recruit Prestes for the Liberal Alliance, a party that united political elites in Rio Grande do Sul, Minas Gerais, and Paraíba, along with a scattering of opposition leaders in Rio de Janeiro and São Paulo. Far from a cohesive bloc, the Liberal Alliance put forth what Daryle Williams calls "a reformist platform [that] drew its strength from disgruntled regional elites and a heterogeneous coalition of reform-minded military officers, urban liberals, and industrialists."[59] Underscoring the contentious status of the alliance was the fact that a prominent member was Artur Bernardes, the president whom the tenentes had sought to overthrow for most of the decade.

At Vargas's invitation, Prestes returned secretly to Brazil to meet in Porto Alegre, first in September 1929—three months after he had met with the PCB leaders—and then again in January 1930. Vargas wanted the Knight of Hope to endorse him for president.[60] At both meetings, Prestes declined to back Vargas. But their discussions kept a potential partnership on the table, and Vargas gave Prestes a fake passport and pledged to send money to Buenos Aires to help organize an armed rebellion in the event that he lost the election. Vargas's inclination proved prescient, and, on March 1, 1930, he lost the presidency by nearly twenty percentage points to the state president of São Paulo, Júlio Prestes (no relation to Luís Carlos). After losing what he claimed was a rigged election, Vargas began preparing an armed uprising and again sought out the Knight of Hope, this time offering Prestes the role of military chief of the revolution. As he had before, Prestes rejected Vargas. In a reflection of the newly shifting alliances, Vargas then offered the position to Góes Monteiro, the chief of staff during the army's pursuit of the column in Bahia. As he moved increasingly toward radical politics, Prestes saw Vargas as an insufficient vehicle for change and felt, moreover, that Vargas only wanted to "lean on the prestige of the column in order to increase his power."[61]

In the aftermath of the 1930 elections, and having turned down the entreaties of both the PCB and the Liberal Alliance, it was uncertain which position Prestes would take. In this climate of political instability, Prestes remained an attractive force. A *Correio da Manhã* article the week after Vargas's presidential defeat wrote that "Luís Carlos Prestes is a symbol. In light of the legend that has formed around him . . . he is the embodiment, perhaps, of the only hope capable of leading Brazil to better days."[62] Despite Prestes's symbolic power, during his two years in exile he had made few direct contributions to Brazilian politics, and there was a risk that his influence could diminish if he stayed on the sidelines too long.

The May Manifesto

Still refusing to join either the PCB or Vargas, Prestes opted for his own path by releasing what became known as the May Manifesto. Short of fully embracing a communist orientation, which came the following year, the May Manifesto was a direct rebuke of Vargas's Liberal Alliance. Prestes published his manifesto using the same medium that had helped create his legend: newspapers. On the May 29 front cover of the *Diário da Noite*—a Rio de Janeiro daily founded the previous year by Assis Chateaubriand, as the carioca twin to his São Paulo paper of the same name—Prestes's manifesto was printed in full, introduced with a short essay under the title "Captain Luís Carlos Prestes Defines His Current Views." Although Prestes lifted a few phrases from official Comintern policy—most notably an emphasis on the "agrarian and anti-imperialist revolution"—the manifesto did not mention the Communist Party. Its opening lines were addressed "to the suffering proletariat of our cities, to the workers oppressed by plantations and ranches, [and] to the wretched masses of our backlands." Calling on workers and peasants to rise up, Prestes outlined his vision for an "agrarian and anti-imperialist Revolution . . . [fighting] for the complete liberation of our agricultural workers, of all forms of exploitation, feudal and colonial; for the seizure, nationalization and redistribution of lands, for handing the land back to those who work it."[63] Prestes's manifesto charted a clean break from the tenentes by articulating a program based strongly on the rural injustices he had seen in the interior.

The May Manifesto was disparaged not only by the tenentes and their sympathetic allies in the press but also by the Brazilian Communist Party. The conflict over how to interpret it presaged the battle for public opinion that would play out over the following two decades. Once Vargas seized power in the Revolution of 1930, and particularly after Prestes officially joined the Communist Party while living in Moscow, a contest between the once-potential-allies took shape over who was the rightful heir to the legacy of the Prestes Column. As the origin story of both Prestes and the tenente rebellion that culminated in Vargas's 1930 victory, the march through Brazil's backlands endured as a contested symbol of political legitimacy.

Liberal detractors were careful to criticize Prestes without criticizing the actions that had originally brought him to prominence. In essence, these were efforts to purge the newly radical figure of Prestes from his symbolism as the Knight of Hope. A front-page editorial in the *Diário Carioca* declared that, while the newspaper had previously supported Prestes—"the flag-bearer of the movement . . . the young soldier who crossed Brazil from one extreme to the other"—it must now withdraw its backing in light of his "strange" new manifesto.[64] In the fallout of the manifesto, thirty-five former tenentes signed an open letter distancing themselves from what the Knight of Hope had become, and General Isidoro issued a public denouncement of "Prestes's bolshevik tendencies."[65] Asdrubal Gwyer de Azevedo, who had been imprisoned for his role in the 1924 revolt, mocked what he referred to as Prestes's "communist manifesto" and lamented that the Knight of Hope had monopolized the national spotlight: "Sure, Luís Carlos Prestes was the main leader of the movement. [But] soon enough the 'Revolution' turned into 'the Prestes Column.'"[66]

The most consistent criticism came from Juarez Távora. A few weeks after the manifesto was published, Távora wrote an open letter against Prestes that ran on the cover of the *Diário Carioca*.[67] Over the following months, Távora then engaged Prestes directly in a series of back-and-forth correspondence. In one of his letters, Távora focused on the manifesto's call for agrarian reform and empowerment of workers, stating, "I disagree that it's necessary to confiscate latifundios that were honestly acquired; sure, confiscate those that were illegally taken—and there are plenty of those. . . . But you don't just go around taking [land]."[68] Although lost to the historical record, Prestes appears to have answered Távora, as evidenced by the subsequent replies in Távora's personal files. Távora told his one-time companion: "You allowed yourself to see [in my letters] insults and hypocrisies, where there only was, and is, my noble effort to save your good name and that of all us revolutionaries. . . . I am simply trying to remind myself how broken our notions of justice are, even when dispensed by the types of men that we sometimes follow and admire as if they were demigods."[69] It is telling that, in his reaction to the May Manifesto, Távora invoked the same image used in the 1927 article that opened this chapter: Prestes as a demigod. As the symbolism of the Knight of Hope emanated outward during the intervening three years, tenentes like Távora resented the spotlight cast on their former leader.

For Brazil's communists, on the other hand, Prestes's manifesto did not go far enough. The central issue was that Prestes did not see the working class as leading the revolution. Less than two weeks after the manifesto's release, the PCB's leader Octávio Brandão issued a statement declaring that "the document and its author are not communists."[70] Throughout the following months, the PCB continued to call Prestes "petit bourgeois."[71] And, in a September interview with the *Diário de Noticias*, Brandão said that Prestes put too much importance on personality and character—the precise traits that had made the Knight of Hope such an appealing national symbol. In a reflection of the PCB's seesaw approach to Prestes, Brandão stated: "Prestes approached it all wrong. To bring about a revolutionary front, you need more than 'sincerity' and 'honesty.' . . . The working classes will never be freed by Knights of Hope."[72]

The Revolution of 1930 and the New Phase of Tenentismo

In the five months following Prestes's manifesto, a series of political and military conflicts culminated in Vargas's seizure of power on October 24. Vargas had already been working behind the scenes in the event of a contested election, though events only accelerated after July 26, when João Pessoa—the state president of Paraíba who had been Vargas's running mate—was killed. The murder resulted from a love affair gone wrong, rather than a political assassination, but it lit a spark within opposition forces. For the next two months, leaders connected to the Liberal Alliance mobilized in their respective states, and a nationwide revolt broke out late in the afternoon of October 3. The uprisings began in the three states where the Liberal Alliance was strongest: Rio Grande do Sul, Paraíba, and Minas Gerais. The rebels seized control of the first two states within twenty-four hours, and Minas Gerais fell after five days of fighting. In his call to arms, Vargas deployed the same type of spatially based nationalist discourse that had recently been amplified through the Knight of Hope. The day after the revolt began, the rebels distributed a manifesto in which Vargas declared: "We are at the beginning of a new revolution to reclaim liberty, to restore the purity of the republican regime, to rebuild our nation. This is a broad movement, with the people and soldiers working together, from the brave North forgotten by the government all the way to the extreme South."[73] Within a matter of weeks, the movement had indeed spread across the country, with all factions then converging on Rio de Janeiro. The revolution had come, but it was not connected to Luís Carlos Prestes.

Several officers of the Prestes Column played key roles in the revolt of October 1930. In the South, João Alberto led the attack on loyalist garrisons in Porto Alegre, helping to secure the capital city of Rio Grande do Sul on the revolt's pivotal first day. Miguel Costa commanded one of the three rebel columns that, starting from Rio Grande do Sul, made quick work across Santa Catarina and Paraná before pivoting east toward São Paulo. In the North, Juarez Távora oversaw all rebel forces, a selection that reflected not only his local roots—Távora came from a powerful family in Ceará—but also his evolving link to the Prestes Column. In light of his very public criticism of Prestes's May Manifesto, Távora had distanced himself from the Knight of Hope while still positioning himself as an inheritor of the column's legacy. This gave him an aura of authority to command Vargas's movement in the northern states, where he soon earned the nickname "Viceroy of the North." With the figure of Prestes currently shaded with controversy, space emerged for other leaders to fill that symbolic role. A British consular officer wrote that when Távora "performed his initial feat of arms at Pernambuco, the effect on the rest of the north was electrical. He became the idol of the people; his . . . [ideas] were eagerly swallowed by the credulous masses; and he scarcely had to fire another shot."[74] As the Viceroy of the North, Távora exemplified the heroic tenente sent to liberate the backlands and unite the country.

Along with amplifying a symbolic attachment to Brazil's interior, the Prestes Column paved the way for the Revolution of 1930 because its leading icon—the Knight of Hope—was a gaúcho. The column had been far from homogenous. Its main leaders, to say nothing of the scattering of locals who joined, came not only from the southern and central states of Rio Grande do Sul and São Paulo but also from Ceará and Pernambuco in the North. Although the revolt of 1924 had emerged in São Paulo, once the rebellion crossed into exile, Prestes's deification as the Knight of Hope changed the regional optics of the movement. With national visibility and appeal,

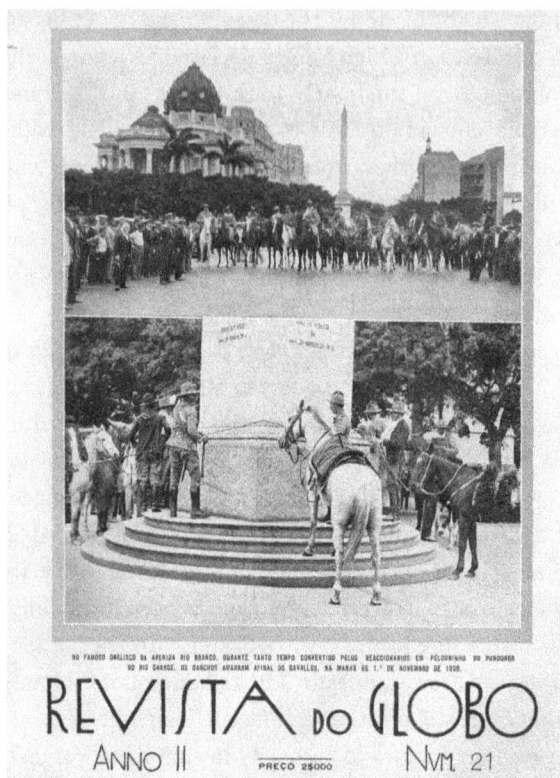

FIGURE 7.8. Rebel soldiers hitch their horses to the obelisk in Rio Branco plaza, Rio de Janeiro. *Revista do Globo*, November 1, 1930.

the mythic Knight of Hope helped enable the rise of another gaúcho, Getúlio Vargas.

Vargas's forces seized control of Rio de Janeiro on October 24, 1930, and announced the creation of a new provisional government. A few days later, Vargas entered Rio de Janeiro clad in a military uniform, a red bandanna, and a broad-brimmed gaúcho hat.[75] In a symbolic, staged photo that ended up on the front page of the *Revista do Globo* (fig. 7.8), Vargas's men, after traveling by train to the city, rode through downtown on horseback and hitched their steeds to the obelisk in the Rio Branco plaza. Such performances drew upon the popularity of the Prestes Column even without the support of Prestes himself. With these displays of pampas culture, Vargas's arrival presaged a new era: the paulista and mineira oligarchies of the Old Republic had now been replaced. Claiming to have reawakened and united the vast corners of the country, the gaúchos had arrived in the Brazilian capital.

The Prestes Column was by no means the sole reason for Vargas's rise to power. In the conclusion of his landmark book on Brazilian history, *Raízes do Brasil*, Sérgio Buarque de Holanda argued that the 1930 Revolution was the apex of a long campaign to revoke the vestiges of the old colonial system. Writing in 1936, prior to the Vargas regime's authoritarian turn, Holanda observed that "the great Brazilian revolution cannot be defined by a precise moment; rather, it is a lengthy process that has lasted for at least three quarters of a century. Its culminating moments are patterned like diverse peaks in a mountain chain."[76] Subsequent generations of scholars showed the diverse factors that conditioned the events of 1930, including changes within the military as an institution, the rise of new regional elites as viable national leaders, the global impact of the 1929 stock market crash, and a general dissatisfaction with the political systems of the First Republic, especially the dominant position of São Paulo.[77] Yet the connection—both symbolic and political—between the Prestes Column and the success of Vargas was strong enough that, in the aftermath of the Revolution of 1930, Vargas and his allies maneuvered to disassociate Prestes from his mythologized connection to the column. The legend of the Prestes Column thus endured even if its most prominent figure was temporarily cast into the background.

The day after Vargas's troops took Rio de Janeiro, a special edition of the *Diário Carioca* printed a picture of the Prestes Column on its front page. Under the headline "The Brave Warriors of an Epic Adventure," the image showed column leaders during their passage through Porto Nacional, Goiás, in October 1925; as previously shown in chapters 3 and 6, the rebel leadership was seated in front of the town's convent, where they were staying as guests of Father Audrin.[78] In a delicate approach to a figure who had become persona non grata, the paper mentioned Prestes only when listing the names of all eighteen people included in the picture. In contrast, Juarez Távora, Miguel Costa, João Alberto, and Cordeiro de Farias—four tenentes who featured prominently in the recent October revolution—received explicit adoration. The same photo, with the exact same caption, was also printed in the *Correio da Manhã*.[79] The coming weeks and months saw a triumphant narrative play on loop, with proponents proclaiming that the revolution had united the country. In his November 3 speech upon assuming the head of the provisional government, Vargas opened with an appeal to an inclusionary national identity: "The revolutionary movement, whose victory began on October 3rd in the south, center, and north of the country and triumphed on the 24th in this capital, was the strongest affirmation we have ever seen of our existence as a nationality."[80]

What this emerging nationalism represented, both regionally and racially, and how it hoped to overcome the problems that had plagued Brazil were exemplified in an essay by Assis Chateaubriand. In *O Jornal*, Chateaubriand wrote that the "historic revolution" would fuse together the best elements from Brazil's coastal and interior regions: "From 1925 to 1926, Brazil lived between two revolutionary fires: the sertão and the coast. The Prestes Column set fire to the sertão, inciting it against the caciques of the coast. The supreme chief of the coast [Getúlio Vargas] then, with ice in his veins, overcame the regional powers [to lead] a white revolution."[81] Here, Chateaubriand used language that was traditionally attached to the interior to refer to Brazil as a whole: by calling Vargas's enemies "the caciques of the coast," he repurposed the trope of backland chiefs to criticize the old guard powerbrokers of Brazil. Like the newspaper examples cited earlier in this chapter, Chateaubriand's invocation of a white coast offered a visual metaphor that would have been familiar to readers. By placing the sertão and the coast in symbolic unison—with the former being subsumed into the latter—these statements sought to trace a new symbol of national unity that could be projected across the entire map of Brazil.

As an imaginative bridge between the long march of the Prestes Column and the events of 1930, the Knight of Hope was a discursive platform for amplifying the mythologies of Brazil's interior. Between 1927 and 1930, what changed was not so much the themes associated with the interior, but, rather, the claim from political actors along the coast—politicians and media elites like Chateaubriand—to have finally brought the backlands into the nation. The interior was now rhetorically included within the national imaginary, and its populations, supposedly roused from their dormant complacency, were presented as potential participants in the Brazilian polity. As ever, the uplifting veneer of this discourse contained romanticized and racialized undertones. These patterns are exemplified in a battle hymn commemorating the Revolution of 1930, written two weeks after Vargas completed the gaúcho journey from the southern pampas all the way to the presidential palace. At this nexus of geography and mythology we see the enduring symbolism of the interior:

By seas, rivers, jungles, mountains! . . .
Blond hair on the head of those who have won!

. . .

From the revolt the first alarms
From this sky under the clear blue

Echoing, they sprang to arms
The brave of the southern pampas.
North to south, south to north, east to west
Everything vibrates with intense emotion.
The avalanche of light you brought
Glorifies and redeems the Nation.[82]

This battle hymn includes fairly predictable imagery of a victorious military campaign—several of its lines even resemble the Brazilian national anthem that had been written under the recently overthrown First Republic. But it also offers several important insights into the intersection of space and nation at this moment in Brazilian history. The double meaning of the hymn's phrasing of *louro* (meaning "laurels for the victors," but also "blond hair") was a nod to the dominant notion of ideal citizenry, and the geographic roll call—north to south, south to north, east to west—was a form of cartographic nationalism meant to differentiate Vargas's movement from the First Republic's concentration of power in only two states. Even if the gesture to a spatially diffuse Brazilian nation existed far more at the level of discourse than policy, its continuity between the tenente rebellion and the new Vargas regime hinted at the changes to come.

8

POLITICAL CONFLICT AND THE
SPATIAL LEGACIES OF TENENTISMO

Lourenço Moreira Lima had intended to publish his memoir about the Prestes Column in 1928. As the official scribe of the tenentes' long march across Brazil, Moreira Lima was singularly positioned to write the definitive account of the column. Demand for content about the topic was robust: along with the steady stream of exposés and serialized reporting in newspapers, former rebels had also begun publishing their own firsthand chronicles, all of which had focused on the initial São Paulo uprising. By 1927, participants of the paulista revolt had written over a dozen books.[1] Following this first burst of memoirs about July 1924, four more publications further chronicled a wider series of events related to the Prestes Column, including a book from João Cabanas—who had deserted the revolution in May 1925—and another that Juarez Távora had written primarily while imprisoned in 1926.[2] A memoir from Moreira Lima would be the most thorough account to date. Not only was he the member of the rebel high command tasked with keeping close records of the entire march, but also, compared to the initial memoirists, he had marched with the column until the very end.

Moreira Lima finished writing the first half of his memoir on July 5, 1928, the one-year anniversary of when he had given his "bandeirantes of freedom" speech in La Gaiba, Bolivia. Ten days later, he sneaked back into Brazil and worked on the book while living in Rio Grande do Sul.[3] By the end of the year, it seemed as though the book was set to be published. In November 1928, *A Manhã* gave an advance review, noting that the book totaled over four hundred pages and included maps, photographs, and reproductions of original documents. The article stated that Moreira Lima's account constituted "the most interesting work of all the publications about the revolution."[4]

Despite what *A Manhã* suggested, the book was not forthcoming. Although the memoir received occasional news coverage, the turbulent politics of the late 1920s kept pushing back its publication.[5] When Moreira Lima joined the rebellion being planned by Getúlio Vargas, the book was delayed even longer; it was not until November 1930, the month after Vargas assumed power, that Moreira Lima finished its second half. The memoir was then published in early 1931 under the title *Marchas e combates: A columna invicta e a revolução de Outubro* (Marches and battles: The undefeated column and the revolution of October). Moreira Lima's memoir became the most enduring chronicle of the Prestes Column. Jorge Amado based his biography of Prestes largely on the memoir and likened it to John Reed's account of the Russian Revolution, the historian Nelson Werneck Sodré compared it to Euclides da Cunha's *Os Sertões*, and the journalist Edmar Morel called it the "the Bible" of the Prestes Column.[6] Over the course of the twentieth century, the book became popular not just in mainstream coastal society, but in interior regions as well. When journalists in the 1990s retraced the column's steps, several locals mentioned Moreira Lima's memoir by referring to it simply as "the diary"—shorthand that reflects its ubiquity across the country.[7] All scholars writing about the column, myself included, have drawn heavily on the memoir.

For understanding the historical memory of the column's march through the interior, the importance of Moreira Lima's memoir goes beyond its wide readership. It can additionally be seen as both a vector and a reflection of the spatial legacies of tenentismo. In the era of Vargas—who was in power from 1930 to 1945, and again from 1951 to 1954—books played a vital role in the evolving mythology of Prestes, the column, and of tenentismo more broadly. Because this period was defined in no small measure by the standoff between Prestes and Vargas, invocations of the column had to be made with care. Despite becoming public enemy number one under Vargas, Prestes could not be written entirely out of the public narrative. His exploits in the interior had provided a symbolic core of the tenentista movement, and the fusing of space and nation continued under Vargas, when the memory battles over how to represent the column became a proxy contest over who had the legitimacy to define the legacy of tenentismo.

This chapter traces the symbolism of the Prestes Column between 1930 (when Vargas seized power) and 1954 (when he committed suicide). As a way to weave together the trajectories of former tenente leaders during the turbulent Vargas era, giving particular attention to key events in Prestes's life and his politics, this chapter draws on memoirs and books about the column, analyzing their contents (how the writers described the rebel passage through the interior) as well as the contexts of their publication. For instance, each subsequent edition of Moreira Lima's memoir, in 1934 and 1945, included a new preface that used the history of the column to criticize the Vargas regime, and, aside from Jorge Amado's biography of Prestes—written as part of an international campaign to help free Prestes from jail—none of the memoirs were published during the nine years (1936–45) that Prestes was imprisoned by Vargas. Instead, they only came out at moments when Prestes's role in society was relatively less contentious, such as before the 1935 Communist revolt or after 1945, once Vargas's grip on power had loosened.

In a sign of the column's enduring symbolic appeal, memoirs were written by tenente leaders (Moreira Lima, João Alberto Lins de Barros, and Italo Landucci) as well as by military officers who had fought against the rebels, such as Bertoldo Klinger (the main pursuer of the column in 1925) and Setembrino de Carvalho, the minister of war during most of the rebellion. Regardless of where the political pendulum was swinging at a given moment of a book's publication, visions of the interior served as a form of political currency in all of the memoirs. Whether seeking to empower the people of the interior (the chosen strategy of Prestes, the Communist Party, and other progressive sectors) or Vargas's expansion of the state's presence in the interior, the landscapes and people of the backlands gained new salience in mainstream efforts to lead the country.

Vargas in Power and the Specter of Brazil's Interior

Barely a few months after the Revolution of 1930, Moreira Lima's memoir staked a strong claim to define the legacy of the Prestes Column. As previously cited in chapter 3, the book's preface offered an early indication of how Moreira Lima would present the interior: "The sertão, in these pages, reveal themselves in their wild beauty, contrasting the splendid landscape with the deplorable mental state of its people."[8] Styling himself in the tradition of *Os Sertões*, Moreira Lima's dualistic description of the backlands runs throughout the book, where the splendor of the natural surroundings is constantly juxtaposed against the presumed backwardness of interior communities. Keen to share his close observations of Brazil's topography, Moreira Lima offered a seemingly endless array of spatial images. In one example, he proclaimed that the column "crossed hundreds of roaring rivers. It climbed endless mountains. It broke through impenetrable forests. It tore across wild canyons of *caatinga*. It crossed unimaginable stretches of wetlands. It galloped across the pampas of Rio Grande do Sul, the high plateaus of Minas Gerais and Bahia, and the wild expanses of the Northeast."[9] In this framing, the tenente rebels came to intimately know the vast regions of the Brazilian nation. Compared to his descriptions of the natural environment—which were considered markers of a great and proud nation—Moreira Lima tended to present the people of the interior as obstacles to Brazil's future development. To again quote one of the memoir's most representative lines: "In the interior the people are semi-barbarous . . . an amorphous mass that has no idea of freedom, a true herd of brutes, living a purely vegetative life. They are little more than pariahs, guided by the unthinking impulses of basic instincts. . . . The sertanejo evidently stopped on the lower rungs of civilization's ladder."[10]

The Revolution of 1930 changed the calculus of what these representations could achieve. Whereas earlier invocations of this narrative were an expression of *why* the tenentes deserved to rule (e.g., their claim to have unified the nation), now that they were actually in power, the question shifted to *how* they would rule. Revealing a political sensibility that would extend across the political spectrum in the coming decades, Moreira Lima ended his book with a series of policy prescriptions that highlighted the problems of Brazil's rural and interior populations. With Vargas in power, such pronouncements were also indictments of the previous government, as the tenentistas sought to associate the backwardness of the interior with the recently deposed First Republic. In the final section of his memoir about the Prestes Column, Moreira Lima outlined how the new government could develop the country. Before itemizing political demands such as the secret ballot and judicial reform, he first mentioned peasant farmers and the need to bring "tens of thousands of schools" to new regions of the country, stretching across "the Amazon basin, the sertões of the Northeast, the mountainous regions, the Pantanal of Mato Grosso, and the gaúcho plains."[11] To be sure, campaigns for rural modernization were also driven by factors unrelated to the Prestes Column. Yet the column's influence on the trajectory of tenentismo meant that concerns for the interior often maintained a symbolic anchor in the legacy of the long march. In the closing lines of his memoir, Moreira Lima called on the Vargas government to "better represent our beautiful territory and speak more to our soul, in this memorable phase of our history, when we feel our hearts beat with joy for the victory of freedom, of which the Prestes Column was the unshakable and undefeated leader, in its immortal march, through the sertões."[12] As the space on which the Prestes Column had traced its "immortal march," the interior was also seen as a landscape capable of helping Brazil fulfill its destiny.

The period between 1930 and 1954 witnessed sustained efforts, in the realm of policy as well as discourse, to modernize the backlands and better incorporate the interior into the nation-state. In her classic study of political imaginaries in the 1930s, Eliana de Freitas Dutra argues that the rivalry between Vargas and Prestes can in many ways be understood as a competition over who had the legitimacy to protect the land—or, more specifically, as Dutra writes, the soil: "With its connection to both extremes of cradle and grave, life and death, a bond of destiny hovers above which, as we can see, forms a core part of nationalist and patriotic feelings that . . . [results] in the worship of the soil."[13] Although labor laws and legal protections did not cover salaried rural laborers such as sugarcane workers until the 1960s, Vargas made some of Brazil's first gestures toward reforming the countryside. In his inaugural speech as head of the provisional government, barely a week after his forces seized power, Vargas included in his list of national priorities "the promotion, through nonviolent means, of a gradual end to the latifundio, bolstering small-holders through the direct transfer of land plots to agricultural workers."[14] As part of his new government, Vargas authorized the creation of unions, for both urban and rural workers, to provide members with legal protections, training, and social welfare assistance.[15] While urban workers held an outsized role in the growth and demographics of these unions, the inclusion of rural groups showed that Vargas was willing to antagonize—even if only discursively—elites in the countryside. Organizing agricultural workers into corporatist, state-supported labor unions was a far different task than addressing the broader social and political isolation of Brazil's interior. However, as we will see, after Vargas consolidated power in the 1937 Estado Novo dictatorship, he oversaw several initiatives as part of the "March to the West" that expanded the state's physical and imaginative presence in the hinterlands. A concern for the future of these areas was another way to differentiate the new regime from the First Republic and bolster the legitimacy of the Revolution of 1930.

Half a year into Vargas's regime, the celebrations of July 5 were a test of how much credence, if any, the government would lend to the rebel march across the interior. As shown in previous chapters, July 5 had functioned as a commemorative symbol for advancing the tenentista cause. Yet Prestes's split the previous year had complicated matters, and July 5 under the new regime now witnessed a balancing act, where Vargas and his allies sought to pay tribute to the column but not to Prestes himself. In almost all instances, Prestes was excised from the commemorations. Similar to what happened after Vargas's victory in late October 1930, celebrations for July 5 mentioned the column but omitted the name of Luís Carlos Prestes.[16] Not all commentary shied away from the Knight of Hope, however. As part of the July 5 celebration in Rio de Janeiro, the poet Rosalina Coelho Lisboa delivered a speech in which she not only mentioned Prestes explicitly but also framed her vision for Brazil's future as a continuation of the fight for freedom that he had brought across the country. Coelho Lisboa exclaimed that a guiding light continued to "come from the forests, still echoing the march of the column under the command of Luís Carlos Prestes, from Maranhão to the Uruguay [River], from the Atlantic [Ocean] to Bolivia, fighting an enemy a hundred times more powerful, and fighting hunger, sickness, and harsh climates. . . . It comes from the hundreds of nameless Brazilians, whose slaughtered bodies mark, across the heart of Brazil, the approaching summit of revolution!"[17] Coelho Lisboa's willingness to openly embrace Prestes reflected her own politics: a celebrated writer and frequent delegate to international women's conferences, she would soon become a prominent member of the right-wing, fascist-inspired Integralist movement. It was generally the more confrontational figures—the Integralists on the right, as well as communists like Jorge Amado on the left—who refused to ignore Prestes. In the years to come, invocations of Prestes served as indirect criticism of the Vargas regime.

The Knight of Hope and the Polarization of Brazilian Politics

As Prestes's name continued to loom as a central, if divisive, specter in the years after the 1930 Revolution, Prestes himself further radicalized. This process accelerated when he was again forced to move countries. After running afoul of Argentina's newly installed military government, Prestes moved to Montevideo, Uruguay, where he found work as a foreman for a plumbing construction company.[18] From Montevideo, Prestes followed the news of Vargas's success in October 1930. Two weeks after seizing power, Vargas issued an official amnesty law that absolved all rebels from the previous decade.[19] Many of Prestes's former companions embraced the new political opening and took on important roles in the Vargas regime: João Alberto Lins de Barros became the *interventor* of São Paulo (a governor appointed by the federal government), Miguel Costa was named the head of São Paulo's Força Pública (the state police force), Osvaldo Cordeiro de Farias was assigned to the Ministry of War, and Juarez Távora would later serve as the secretary of agriculture. Prestes, on the other hand, remained in exile in Montevideo, where he worked closely with the Uruguayan Communist Party.[20] Influenced by Communist leaders in Montevideo and eager to gain the approval of the Comintern and the PCB, Prestes wrote another manifesto. In March 1931, he provided a full-throated denunciation of his previous politics, including his original role as a tenente.[21] Although the PCB remained skeptical of Prestes for several more years, the new manifesto was seen favorably by the Comintern.

In the middle of 1931, Prestes was invited to live in the Soviet Union, and in late September he sailed from Montevideo to Le Havre, France. His mother and sisters, whom he arranged to have join him, traveled separately to Hamburg. Once the family reunited in Berlin, they continued to Moscow, where they arrived in November.[22] Prestes worked first as an engineer in a government ministry that oversaw large industrial projects and later became a communications officer in the Comintern's International Agrarian Institute, where he wrote articles—in Portuguese or French, which were then translated to Russian—on topics such as land reform. In October 1934, Moscow hosted the Third Conference of Latin American Communist Parties. At the summit, the PCB's secretary-general, Antônio Maciel Bonfim, persuaded the Comintern's Executive Committee (ECCI) that conditions in Brazil were ripe for an insurrection. The Comintern decided that Prestes should return to Brazil to help organize an armed revolt against Vargas and, to safeguard Prestes's journey back to Brazil, assigned him a bodyguard: a German militant named Olga Benário. Twenty-six years old when she met Prestes—ten years her senior—Benário had been a leader in the Communist Youth International, with experience organizing cadres in Germany, Great Britain, France, and the Soviet Union. Benário and Prestes were introduced only a few days before departing for Brazil, traveling incognito as Portuguese newlyweds on their honeymoon.

Famously, while pretending to be a couple, Prestes and Benário fell in love. The two left Moscow on December 29, 1934, and, with fake documents in hand, they made a four-month journey across Europe, to the United States, and down to South America. They secretly arrived in Rio de Janeiro on April 17, 1935.[23] After eight years in exile, the Knight of Hope had returned.

During Prestes's three years in the Soviet Union, the Vargas regime had to contend with growing internal friction. The contested legacies of tenentismo were exemplified in the proceedings of the October 3rd Club (Clube 3 de Outubro)—named after the date in 1930 when Vargas launched his full-scale revolt. The club had originally been founded in February 1931, only a few months after Vargas seized power, and its first president, Góis Monteiro, saw the group as a platform for creating a tenentista base to support Vargas's revolution. The historian John W. F. Dulles writes that, in the early period under Vargas, the October 3rd Club was "the nation's strongest political force."[24] It did not take long for a schism to form between the club's moderate and more radical sectors. A year into its existence, Góes Monteiro resigned as president, and the radical tenente Pedro Ernesto took over. A doctor and public health advocate who had joined the Revolution of 1930 as a civilian leader, Ernesto exemplified the wing of tenentismo that, while not explicitly supportive of Prestes's embrace of communism, nonetheless promoted a more radical vision. Under Ernesto's leadership, the club began advocating for farther-reaching reform. In February 1932, it released a "revolutionary program" that emphasized, among other items, the need to address Brazil's agrarian problems by giving rural workers the same rights as those in urban sectors, and for profit-sharing between landowners and peasants. More broadly, it sought to frame the countryside as a social space to be treated with respect, declaring that "he who works the land is worthy to benefit from its proceeds."[25]

The increasingly radical demands of the October 3rd Club contributed to triggering a political crisis. Because the tenentes saw a strong central government as key to implementing their desired reforms, they argued that Vargas should continue to rule by provisional authority, rather than call for new elections. In contrast, several groups called for Brazil to be "reconstitutionalized." This included liberal leaders aligned with Vargas in states like Rio Grande do Sul who saw elections as a way to gain influence in the federal government and, as a result, maintain a certain level of regional autonomy. As a bellwether of the looming national crisis, a second—more reactionary—brand of constitutionalists came from leaders in São Paulo who strongly opposed Vargas. For this latter group, the proposals from the October 3rd Club were particularly alarming, as they would significantly cut into the profits and political power of São Paulo's agricultural elites.

The political rivalries during Vargas's first two years in power came to a head in July 1932, when a counterrevolution erupted in São Paulo. This became known as the Constitutionalist Revolution, a civil war of sorts that left as many as two thousand dead.[26] After three months of fighting, federal forces put down the rebellion. Among its wide repercussions, the 1932 São Paulo revolt fundamentally shifted the balance of power within Vargas's governing coalition. Previously, he had allowed the various branches of tenentismo to coexist despite their antagonisms; as Thomas Skidmore observes, "Vargas's Machiavellian political style encouraged each of these groups to press their claims."[27] Yet, because Vargas had to lean heavily on the military to suppress the São Paulo rebels, the more conservative sectors of Vargas's regime emerged emboldened. Moreover, in the aftermath of the 1932 revolt, Vargas maneuvered to cement the stability of his own government by strategically appeasing the country's diverging regional and political movements. To the liberal constitutionalists, he pledged elections and a new constitution. To the São Paulo rebels, he offered a full amnesty for their uprising and ordered the Bank of Brazil to take on their wartime debts. And to the tenentes—however disparate the movement had become—Vargas made sure that the Constitution of 1934, which was passed in July of that year, included several of their long-standing demands such as free elections, an impartial judiciary, and federal commitments to economic development and social welfare.

The same year that Vargas brokered the 1934 Constitution, Moreira Lima's memoir was reissued. While not quite a second edition per se, the 1934 reprint was published by the Civic Legion of July 5 (Legião Cívica 5 de Julho). Although initially aligned with Vargas, the Civic Legion soon took on the characteristics of what Adalberto Coutinho de Araújo Neto calls "tenente socialism," advocating a wide range of reforms that included the end of the latifundia system, the unionization of all workers, a national land tax, and a parliamentary form of government.[28] When the Civic Legion's initial support of Vargas dissolved, it became the target of government repression. In July 1934, its headquarters were invaded—at the behest of Góes Monteiro, the newly appointed minister of war—and the group was forced to disband. It was in this context, then, that the Civil Legion reprinted Moreira Lima's memoir as an overtly political act. Notably, the book contained a new prologue that used the column's mythology as a way to attack the Vargas regime:

> The Civic Legion of July 5 . . . promotes the dissemination of this true odyssey of bravery, blood, martyrdom, and glory, which was the life of the [column], through the cities and sertões of Brazil. In the current

moment, when loose politics blow from one sector to another on misguided currents of ambition and ego, we believe there is no better service we can provide to the revolution than to remind everyone what those moments meant to fight for an ideal. . . . To the living who still seek to share in the work, the sufferings, and the glory of that time, we know that—today as it was then—Brazil, the real Brazil, the Brazil that suffered the miseries imposed on it by political hacks, still vibrates with the same ideals.[29]

The year after the reissue of Moreira Lima's memoir, it was thrust into the unfolding standoff between Vargas and his opponents. Vargas's efforts to silence his critics culminated in the National Security Law of April 4, 1935, a sweeping set of policies aimed to maintain the political and social order. Barely ten days after passage of the new law, one of the most consistent anti-Vargas newspapers, *O Radical*, began reproducing Moreira Lima's memoir about the Prestes Column. There was a long history of serialized exposés of the column, with several newspapers having run eight- or nine-part series in the late 1920s. At this moment in 1935, *O Radical* turned the memoir into an unprecedented form of exposé. Beginning in April, *O Radical* reprinted Moreira Lima's entire book over the course of six months. This amounted to 138 separate articles.[30] Other than a short section from the book's first chapter—where Moreira Lima discussed bolshevism—*O Radical* reprinted the memoir word for word. Rarely did more than a few days go by without an excerpt from the memoir. At one point four months into the series, *O Radical* even apologized to readers after several days had elapsed without an article: "Due to the absolute lack of space, we had to withhold today's publication of the History of the Prestes Column, which we will print tomorrow."[31]

The reprinting of Moreira Lima's memoir tethered the history of the Prestes Column to the evolving political crisis of the mid-1930s. As shown in figure 8.1, the headlines and articles about current politics unfolded alongside the mythologized events of the column's march across the interior. Day by day, above the memoir installments, the headlines of *O Radical* traced the accelerating news that witnessed the return of Luís Carlos Prestes from exile and his ultimately unsuccessful attempt to overthrow Vargas in November 1935. During the preceding six months, as *O Radical* escalated its opposition to Vargas, Moreira Lima's memoir condensed the past and present of rebellion in Brazil. By merging the two main platforms of the column's mythology—newspapers and memoirs—*O Radical* weaponized the legacy of the Prestes Column.

FIGURE 8.1. Cover of *O Radical*, April 18, 1935.

The Aliança Nacional Libertadora

During the six months that *O Radical* serialized Moreira Lima's memoir, one of its main stories—as was the case with newspapers across Brazil—was the rise and fall of the Aliança Nacional Libertadora (ANL, the National Liberating Alliance). The ANL, as noted by historian John French, was an "exhilarating if short lived revolutionary adventure . . . [that] promised the imminent replacement of the established order with a 'popular government' that would oppose fascism, imperialism, and the large landowners."[32] Officially launched on March 23, 1935, a month before Prestes and Olga Benário entered Brazil, and four months earlier than the Comintern's Popular Front policy that would authorize precisely this type of campaign, the ANL brought together a large swath of Brazil's radical currents, as the anti-Vargas wing of the tenentes made common cause with socialists, Trotskyists, anarchists, and communists. Between March (when the ANL was launched) and July (when it was banned by the government), the ANL captivated both public attention and the ire of Vargas. Daniel Aarão Reis writes that the four-month existence of the ANL "was the first—and last—time in history that all of the [Brazilian] left joined under the same banner."[33] Within a short period, the ANL counted over 1,500 chapters and 100,000 members, with 50,000 in Rio de Janeiro alone.

From its inception, the ANL relied heavily on the symbolism of Prestes. During the ANL's founding meeting at the João Caetano theatre in Rio de Janeiro, the organization selected Prestes as its honorary president.[34] So, despite not yet having returned to Brazil, Prestes was already a leading ANL figure. As branches of the ANL proliferated in the coming months, the influence of Prestes grew, in tandem. At several rallies in May and June, ceremonies were held to honor the Prestes Column, with ANL leaders presenting and raising a flag that had supposedly traveled with the tenentes during their march across the interior.[35] A flyer for one such rally proclaimed "Long Live the National Liberating Alliance! Long Live Luís Carlos Prestes!"[36] The infusion of Prestes's symbolism into the ANL had a knock-on effect for many of the participating militant groups, most notably the Brazilian Communist Party, whose growing membership in recent years had extended into the military as well. As recalled in the memoir of Gregório Bezerra, a Pernambucan sergeant and PCB member who became a luminary northeastern communist in the 1940s and 1950s, "Prestes continued to be, in the minds of the Brazilian people, the knight of their hopes, and his inclusion in the PCB ranks was a major contribution to the strengthening and development of the Party in all sectors, especially in the [army] barracks."[37]

On July 5, the most potent day within tenente lore, Prestes released a manifesto that was disseminated widely in newspapers and read on his behalf at the ANL commemoration. Seeking to bridge the ANL's current fight to the longer history of tenentismo, Prestes declared that, "today, we the aliancistas throughout Brazil, again raise up high the flag of the 'Eighteen of [Copacabana],' the flag of Catanduvas, the flag that fluttered in 1925 at the gates of Teresina, from the south to the north, across all of Brazil."[38] Having established its roots in the tenente battles of the previous decade, Prestes's manifesto then shifted gears and outlined an unflinchingly radical stance. The ANL had not yet adopted an official platform—let alone a discourse—of armed insurrection, but Prestes now declared that "this is a situation of war and everyone must take their post. . . . Brazilians: All of you who are united by misery, by suffering and by humiliation across the country. . . . You have nothing to lose and the immense riches of Brazil to win." Emboldened by the reception he received upon his return to Brazil, Prestes sought to capitalize on the ANL's meteoric rise to fulfill the communist vision that he had embraced during his years in exile.

In an ironic twist that showed how far Prestes had moved away from the mainstream during his time in exile, one of his earliest boosters, the newspaper editor Assis Chateaubriand, now became a staunch critic. A fervent anti-communist, Chateaubriand called Prestes the "Knight of the Moon," mocking him as a clueless radical whose pie-in-the-sky ideas threatened the nation.[39] In the same way that Chateaubriand had originally used the imagery of Brazil's interior to help cultivate the column's legend, he now made similar gestures to the backlands as a way to delegitimize Prestes. Referencing the recent manifesto and its emphatic statements, Chateaubriand declared that Prestes had ceased to be a "captain of the forest" and had morphed into "a sentry lost in the middle of a jungle of exclamation points."[40]

On the heels of four months of unprecedented mobilization, Prestes's manifesto had an immediate consequence. Although Prestes had hoped it would catapult the ANL into a new phase, it gave Vargas the perfect excuse to shut down the movement.[41] Less than a week after the manifesto's release, Vargas declared the ANL an illegal organization, and police raided its headquarters and arrested several leaders. Technically, the ANL was only suspended for six months, but in practice it was finished.[42] While labor unions, especially those in the greater São Paulo region, continued to stage strikes throughout August and September, the ANL dissolved even faster than it had taken shape.[43] As the ANL dwindled in numbers and influence, Prestes remained a lightning rod. For his supporters, he offered hope of a direct confrontation with the Vargas regime. After the ANL was banned, its remaining members drew mostly from two camps that still shared Prestes's vision for an armed insurrection: the revolutionary wing of the PCB and the remaining radicals within the tenentes. For his detractors, on the other hand, the looming presence of Prestes was ongoing proof that the ANL was little more than a Soviet puppet.

In late September, it was widely reported that *Pravda*, the official newspaper of the Comintern, had run a lengthy article on Prestes. The coverage in Brazil included a full reproduction (fig. 8.2) of the article in its original Cyrillic.[44] The news pertained to proceedings from the Comintern's Seventh World Congress, which had taken place in Moscow in July and August. Motivated by the rising specter of fascism across Europe, the Seventh Congress discarded the previous program of class warfare in favor of a new "popular front" through which communist parties could build coalitions to advance their revolutionary goals. As a sign of Prestes's rising profile, he was elected, in absentia, to the Comintern's Executive Committee. As Prestes continued to live and organize clandestinely in Rio de Janeiro, these articles suggested that

FIGURE 8.2. Profile on Luís Carlos Prestes from the Soviet newspaper *Pravda*, upon his election to the Comintern's Executive Committee, reproduced in the *Diário Carioca*, September 21, 1935, 3.

he was plotting a PCB-guided war against the current regime. As it turned out, these reports were accurate.

An uprising began on November 23, 1935, starting in the northeastern army garrisons of Natal and Recife—the latter led almost single-handedly by Gregório Bezerra, the Pernambucan sergeant and PCB militant.[45] Four days after Bezerra led the northeastern barracks revolt, Prestes initiated an uprising in Rio de Janeiro.[46] By that point, Vargas's forces had plenty of time to prepare for such a move. The military correctly anticipated that the revolt in Rio de Janeiro would be launched by rebels in the Third Infantry Regiment stationed at Praia Vermelha—in a sign of the PCB's limited reach, its revolt took place among its members in the military, rather than the working class. Cordeiro de Farias, who had been one of Prestes's detachment commanders during the long march across the interior, led the government's counterattack, and the uprising was quelled by the early afternoon.[47] The insurrection had failed.

If Prestes's manifesto in July had given Vargas a pretext to shutter the ANL, the revolt in November allowed him to go even further. With proof in hand of an actual Communist plot, Vargas moved decisively to shore up his own power and repress his opponents.[48] Over the coming months, the government tightened the National Security Law, passed a series of constitutional amendments that gave the executive branch greater emergency powers, and arrested thousands of people, keeping many of them imprisoned aboard an ancient ship docked off the coast of Rio de Janeiro. Prominent leaders were among those arrested, including several members of Congress. Most of the PCB leadership was also detained. Prestes and Olga Benário eluded capture and stayed on the lam for almost half a year.

As the Vargas regime rounded up suspected dissidents in the final months of 1935 and into the new year, Prestes and Benário remained in hiding. Unable to flee the country, Prestes and Benário stayed put, holed up for months in a safehouse in a suburb of Rio de Janeiro. By this point, the pair's militant partnership had transformed into a romantic one. It was in the early months of 1936, while hiding from the Vargas regime, that Benário became pregnant.[49] Given that their daughter, Anita, was born on November 27, the math suggests that she was conceived during what proved to be the final days of freedom for Prestes and Benário. At dawn on March 5, 1936, police surrounded the house and arrested them both. They were taken to the central police station and, after a brief interrogation, were separated. They never saw each other again.

The arrest captivated public attention. Along with fascination about the mystery woman accompanying Prestes—Benário was dismissively referred to as his "secretary"—media coverage focused on what Prestes said during his initial detainment.[50] Interrogated by Vargas's security forces, Prestes refused to discuss his actions as a communist, saying that "I can only make declarations about the Prestes Column."[51] In this moment of duress, Prestes's strategy was to invoke his own national mythology. In a knowing wink at Vargas, Prestes's mention of the column was an effort to both protect himself and remind the public that his legendary march through the interior had helped bring the current regime to power. Supporters of Prestes tapped into this same narrative. Given the current targeting of radical militants during these tense days, it is important to note that some of the most vocal support for Prestes came not from the far left, but rather from the far right. Within a week of Prestes's arrest, Plínio Salgado—the leader of the fascist-leaning Integralists, who had previously clashed with ANL supporters in the streets on several occasions—publicly declared that "the march of the column that he led represented, at a tragic moment, a symbolic serpent of fire, working its way across the lifeless body of the nation, as if to awaken it from apathy. It symbolized our restlessness [and] our despair, because we, the restless souls, had not found the correct path."[52] Because that path had facilitated the rise of Vargas, its legacy remained politically volatile. During his imprisonment and subsequent trial, Prestes continued to antagonize Vargas by keeping a spotlight on their previous interactions. When pressed for information about how the revolt was financed, Prestes denied that any money had come from Moscow, saying instead that it was funded by the money that Vargas himself had given Prestes back in the late 1920s when the two secretly met in Porto Alegre.[53]

Determined to make an example of Prestes, Vargas ordered the deportation of Olga Benário. In September 1936, the Vargas regime sent Benário, some seven months pregnant, back to Nazi Germany. Given that Benário was Jewish, her deportation has become one of the most infamous events in Vargas's history, and it also hinted at his tendency toward fascism, both in terms of the coup that he would soon stage as well as his flirtation with joining the Axis powers only a few years later. Upon arrival in Germany, Benário was detained in a women's prison in Berlin, where her daughter, Anita, was born. A year later, the young child was released to the custody of Prestes's mother, Leocádia, who had moved from Moscow to Paris to lead a campaign to free her daughter-in-law and granddaughter. In the end, only the child was given her freedom. Benário remained imprisoned and was shipped to a series of Nazi concentration camps. She was killed in the gas chambers of Bernburg in 1942.[54]

Holding Prestes aloft as proof of a Communist plot, Vargas proceeded to concentrate even more power for himself. While also maneuvering against his right-wing detractors—most notably Plínio Salgado, who sought to run in the 1937 presidential elections—Vargas's political posturing enabled and rationalized his increasing grip on power. During the year-long trial of Prestes and the other militants accused of staging the 1935 revolt, Vargas replaced several state officials with his own loyalists and strengthened the authority of the military.[55] In the midst of these machinations, Prestes was found guilty of sedition and sentenced to nearly seventeen years in prison.[56] With most of Vargas's opponents now neutralized, he proceeded to circumvent the elections being planned for early 1938. On November 10, 1937, Vargas staged a coup, albeit a bloodless one. He sent troops to surround Congress and issued a new constitution that bestowed upon him almost total executive power.

Expanding the Nation

Vargas's Estado Novo (New State) regime was a hybrid form of populist dictatorship that ran from 1937 to 1945. As an authoritarian state, it mimicked European-style fascism where a strong military helped maintain a centralized, nonelectoral government. The Estado Novo aimed to do away with Brazil's long-standing regional conflicts, and, less than a month after his coup, Vargas staged a public burning of the traditional state flags—a symbolic performance of his centralized government.[57] Repression was a common tool to meet these goals, with the police of Rio de Janeiro playing a central role in tamping down any perceived dissent. Torture became especially notorious under the command of Rio's police chief, Filinto Müller—the former tenente who had abandoned the Prestes Column in 1925.[58] Yet the Estado Novo also functioned as a technocratic, reform-minded administration. Vargas invested heavily in social programs related to education and economic development, and he built a strong social welfare net for workers, mostly in the urban sectors, though with new protections for agricultural laborers as well.[59]

Another tenet of the Estado Novo was the March to the West (Marcha para o Oeste), a series of infrastructure and commercial endeavors that sought to develop the supposedly "empty" center-west and Amazonian regions.[60] Whereas the first-wave tenentes claimed to have exposed the absence of the state in the country's interior, the Vargas government was now moving to establish a tangible presence. Former members of the Prestes Column led key initiatives, most notably João Alberto Lins de Barros, who oversaw the Fundação Brasil Central, a sprawling operation in the early 1940s that created several new cities in Goiás and Mato Grosso, along with constructing a new railroad line, highways, communication networks, and commercial outposts.[61] The work of João Alberto and the Fundação Brasil Central was indicative of the broader goals envisioned by Vargas. As historian Joel Wolfe writes, the March to the West "appealed to long-held ideas about Brazil's future resting with the successful development of the interior."[62]

Along with denoting the geographic scope of this state-directed development, marching to the west represented a geopolitical aspiration for Brazil to approach the global status of more developed, "Western" nations. This type of territorial expansion, to "fill in" Brazil's empty map, also had financial underpinnings. As Raymond Craib has written about Mexico, spatial aspirations were directed not only at the citizens that a project was meant to modernize but also "to foreign investors eager to see an image *representative* of the political stability and spatial predictability necessary for profitable investment."[63] In his assessment of Vargas's discursive framing of the March to the West, Almir Lenharo observes that Vargas tied the question of national identity to the "interiorization" of the country—as Vargas stated in a 1939 speech, "We march toward unity, we march toward the center [of Brazil]."[64] Vargas's perception of coast and interior—and his efforts to bridge the two—invoked much of the same symbolism that animated the legend of the Prestes Column. In the context of his standoff with Luís Carlos Prestes, we can also understand the March to the West as Vargas's effort, explicit or not, to *out-Prestes* Prestes. Whereas Prestes had become the mythic hero who led the column's march across the interior, thereby amplifying the deeply rooted desire among coastal elites to modernize the backlands, Vargas now raised the stakes of what the Brazilian state could accomplish in terms of national integration and development.

From the 1930s onward, Brazilian governments framed their approach to the backlands as a contrast to what, in their eyes, had kept the country from fulfilling its potential. If coastal society dating back to the colonial period had largely neglected the interior, the Brazilian state now aimed to dominate it. The shift from neglect to domination, of which the Prestes Column was one of several catalysts, inspired a renewed wave of thought about interior spaces. Although written in the early 1930s, it was only after 1938, in the throes of the Estado Novo, that Mário Travassos's book *Projeção continental do Brasil* became a pioneering work on Brazilian geopolitics and expansionism.[65] An army colonel in the late 1920s, Travassos had taken part in the pursuit of the Prestes Column during its passage through Bahia in 1926—in fact, he conducted many of the prisoner interrogations of suspected rebels analyzed in chapter 5. The policies and discourses of Vargas's March to the West resonated in Travassos's vision for expanding the Brazilian "heartland" not merely deeper into its own national territory, but even farther still, across Bolivia and out toward the Pacific Ocean.[66] For Travassos, Brazil's interior was indistinguishable from the interior of South America as a whole.

Similarly, in 1940, the journalist and literary critic Cassiano Ricardo wrote an influential book whose translated title is *March to the West: The influence of the Bandeiras in the social and political formation of Brazil.*[67] Much like how the leaders of the Prestes Column had given themselves the nickname "bandeirantes of freedom," Vargas's March to the West, in Ricardo's assessment, helped reimagine the colonial-era bandeirantes as the ultimate form of progress that spread democracy and racial harmony. By arguing that the occupation of Brazil's interior was fundamental to the development of a national identity, Ricardo offered a Brazilian version of Frederick Jackson Turner's frontier thesis, which had famously traced the westward movement of the North American frontier as the paragon of an authentic democratic national character.[68] Similar to Turner's idea of the US frontier as an elastic concept adaptable to different phases of national development, so, too, did Ricardo argue that mainstream views of the interior could change, depending on how different groups used the idea to justify expansion.[69] Therefore, at both the material and ideological levels, the March to the West allowed Vargas to propel the government's presence in the interior in ways unmatched even by the legendary Knight of Hope.

An Expansion of Stories

As Vargas's policies stretched outward across the country, Luís Carlos Prestes— who a decade earlier had trekked across many of the regions now touched by the March to the West—languished in jail. During the nine years he spent incarcerated, Prestes was allowed few visitors. Though he maintained a steady stream of correspondence with PCB leaders, contacts, and his family, the Vargas regime barred many journalists from seeing the Knight of Hope.[70] As a result, the publicity and national spotlight previously lavished on Prestes dimmed considerably under the censorship of the Estado Novo. Outside of Brazil, however, campaigns to liberate Prestes proliferated more freely. In a notable example of Prestes being allowed to correspond with a journalist, he gave an interview to the Argentine newspaper *La Nación*. In the same quotation previously shown at the start of chapter 2, he offered a retrospective rationale of the Prestes Column's objective, saying that "what we attempted, principally, was to arouse the masses of the interior, shaking them from the apathy in which they were living, indifferent to the fate of the nation, hopeless of any remedy for their difficulties and sufferings."[71] This discourse of backland awakening was pivotal for the campaign to free Prestes.

One of the strongest elements of the pro-Prestes movement came from Jorge Amado, the Brazilian writer and fellow PCB member living in exile in Argentina. In 1942, the PCB elected Prestes as the secretary-general of the party—a position he would keep until 1980—thus raising the stakes to have their leader released from prison. At the urging of the PCB, Amado wrote a biography of Prestes that sought to win public sympathy for Prestes's cause and put pressure on the Vargas regime. To avoid the Estado Novo censors, the book was published in Spanish in Buenos Aires in May 1942. It carried the title of *Vida de Luiz Carlos Prestes: El Caballero de la Esperanza* (The Life of Luís Carlos Prestes: The Knight of Hope).[72]

The book was an instant sensation. The first print run of thirty thousand copies sold out within a few months and became one of the best-selling books across Latin America in the early 1940s. Copies were also smuggled into Brazil, where they were passed secretly between readers. A Portuguese-language version came out in 1945—when Vargas was on the brink of losing power—and was eventually translated into over twenty languages.[73] The book would be banned in 1964 after the military seized power and only come back into circulation in 1979, once the regime began to acquiesce to the prospects of democratization.

In his efforts to make the strongest possible case to free Prestes, Amado dug deep into Prestes's connection to Brazil's interior. Although framed as a biography, the book focused almost exclusively on the Prestes Column, which Amado presented as the crucible of Prestes's radicalization as well as proof of the Brazilian people's love for the Knight of Hope. Of the innumerable examples that reflect this at-times ahistorical mythologizing, the following excerpt described the people of the interior flocking to Prestes and the supposed changes that took place for all involved:

> The sertanejos . . . did not have a hint of confidence for their futures. Those rivers, my friends, so full of water, so big and dotted with cascades, they are fed by the tears of an unhappy sertão. Tears and blood of the forest lands, and the sertanejo rivers. No hope for the future, only the misfortune of this unsolvable situation. But suddenly, the sertanejo drops his sickle, his ax, his chains of slavery. Your scythe is a rifle now, a machine gun is your plow, in front of the column comes the Knight of Hope. He crosses the backlands like the winds of a storm churning the waters and bringing to the surface the debris hidden deep in the oceans. [The interior], turned inside out, with festering wounds

needing to be healed, discovers itself in this man, and he, Luís Carlos Prestes, discovers Brazil in its nakedness.[74]

Throughout Amado's book, Prestes and Brazil's interior are entwined in a tale of political awakening. As part of the interior's long-standing symbolism as a dormant landscape, Amado showed how the column's march through the backlands roused Prestes from his own form of petit-bourgeois passivity. Along with praising Prestes for outmaneuvering federal armies and local militias, Amado noted his domination of the interior landscapes: "He defeated hunger, countless diseases, exotic fevers. He defeated the mountains, the rivers, the jungles, the impassable forests. He defeated the hopelessness of the sertão."[75] As a communist in the 1940s, Amado saw peasants as an untapped resource of political change, whose potential required the intervention of outside leaders. In his discussion of Prestes's march from the late 1920s—though with clear implications for future interactions as well—Amado claimed that without Prestes, the people of the interior could not escape their "infinite misery."[76]

Amado's book embodied the symbolic ripple effect of the Prestes Column and Brazil's interior. For Prestes supporters who wanted to see their comrade freed from jail, the Knight of Hope was depicted as more than just a political prisoner: he was a national hero who had confronted the truths of the Brazilian nation, had seen its problems firsthand, and was thus uniquely positioned to lead the country to a brighter future. At the very least, the understanding went, the glory of Prestes's past actions should be enough to keep him out of prison. Moreover, from a more explicitly radical approach, his leadership in rural and interior spaces was a call to arms for the next phases of revolution. As with most of the storytelling surrounding Prestes over the previous two decades, ideas about the interior could be directed for specific political purposes. Accelerated by Amado's global fame, his book helped to launch the intertwined history of Prestes and the interior into unprecedented spheres across Latin America and beyond.

The growing attention to Prestes's imprisonment did not immediately bring about his freedom. In a sign of how linked his fate was with that of Vargas, Prestes remained in jail until 1945, when the Estado Novo regime began to collapse. Among the multitude of factors that pushed Vargas from office was Brazil's role in World War II. While Vargas could proudly point to having directed Latin America's only contingent to fight in Europe, as well as a mass program of industrialization and economic development during the wartime effort, Brazil's support of the Allied powers shined an unavoidable spotlight on a core contradiction of the Estado Novo: Brazilian soldiers had fought and died to stop the advance of fascism in Europe, yet at home they were governed by a dictatorship. In the aftermath of World War II, Vargas was forced to gradually release his grip on power. On April 18, he issued an amnesty law for all political prisoners. That same day, Luís Carlos Prestes was released after nearly nine years behind bars. The front page of *O Globo* summarized the scene as Prestes exited prison: "The crowd saw him, overran the security barrier and raised a cheer to the 'Knight of Hope.'"[77] The newspaper further reported that, as the crowd swelled around him, Prestes was greeted by a man, described pejoratively as "a typical northeastern half-breed (*caboclo*)" who sought to get his attention by yelling: "I was in the column!"

A Final Wave of Memoirs

Three months after Prestes's release from jail, as Vargas held out during what became his final few months in power, the legend of the column was revived again. In July, Lourenço Moreira Lima's memoir was republished as an official second edition of the book.[78] Moreira Lima had died in jail on September 5, 1940; the immediate cause was tuberculosis, though it was brought upon by the squalor he confronted as a political prisoner under the Vargas regime. As a martyr figure with strong links to the legend of the Prestes Column, Moreira Lima was elevated as a symbol of anti-Vargas resistance. The book's publisher, Editora Brasiliense, introduced the new version with a statement that read: "We launch this definitive edition . . . as an homage to all the heroes of the tenentista era, especially its grand leader Luís Carlos Prestes, and also as an homage to Lourenço Moreira Lima, captain in the column, its historian, always loyal, who died [at the hands of] the monstrous [Estado Novo]."[79] The new edition also included two prefaces, one from Jorge Amado and another from Caio Prado Junior, a prominent historian and member of the Brazilian Communist Party. Compared to its original version, the 1945 edition contained one major difference: it entirely removed Moreira Lima's section on the Revolution of 1930. Whereas the Vargas regime had, in the aftermath of assuming power, sought to extricate Prestes from the history of tenentismo, we see the opposite here—supporters of Prestes offered a history of tenentismo that cut out Vargas.

A few months later, Vargas was removed from more than just the pages of a memoir. In late October, Vargas's own Ministry of War intervened and forced him to step down, eight years after he began the Estado Novo. The budding momentum for political liberalization brought new options for the Brazilian Left, including the legalization of the PCB for the first time in several decades. With his party now legal, Prestes ran a successful campaign for senator of Rio de Janeiro—the only time in Prestes's life that he held public office. Jorge Amado himself was elected to Congress in the state of São Paulo. Under Prestes's leadership, the PCB grew rapidly, and in 1947 it received nearly half a million votes in national elections. Although the newly elected president, Gaspar Dutra, soon reinstated the ban on the PCB, once again pushing it underground, Prestes had attained a new level of influence that allowed his own status and, by extension, that of the column, to spread more widely across mainstream society.

This period saw the final burst of memoir writing. Spurred by the success of Moreira Lima's book, and with Vargas no longer in power, new memoirs were written not only by former rebels but also by loyalist military officers that had fought against the column. This wave of memoirs began with the 1947 book by Italo Landucci, an army captain who had originally joined the tenentes as the head of the Italian Brigade of immigrant fighters in the São Paulo revolt of 1924. Two years later, a book was written by Bertoldo Klinger, who had led the federal army's pursuit of the column in Mato Grosso. In 1950, a posthumous memoir was published on behalf of Setembrino de Carvalho, the minister of war under President Bernardes.[80] A few years later, a final memoir was published in 1954 by the rebel commander João Alberto Lins de Barros. Likely influenced by his prominent role under the Vargas regime, João Alberto's memoir received the most newspaper coverage, including a review by the influential scholar Gilberto Freyre, who, despite applauding the memoir as an important historical document, dismissed it as proof that the tenente movement had suffered from a lack of cohesive ideology.[81]

As evident in my earlier chapters, where I quote extensively from these works, the books replicated certain tropes and narratives about Brazil's interior. In all of the memoirs, the landscapes were naturally beautiful, though endlessly hellish, the people were naive and uncivilized, and a great triumph—for both the rebels and the federal armies in pursuit—was the ability of the civilized forces from the coast to venture inland, confront these dangers, and return safely again. The authors offered lengthy descriptions of the backlands (the places as well as the people) as a means to prove their legitimacy, both as on-the-ground witnesses to the rebellion in the late 1920s and as political figures in the newly open climate of the 1940s and 1950s.

As this last wave of memoirs circulated in Brazil, Prestes and Vargas embarked on a final—and perhaps unexpected—stage in their rivalry. Back in March 1945, a month before he was released from prison, and with Brazilian

FIGURE 8.3. Getúlio Vargas (*left*) and Luís Carlos Prestes (*second from right*) share the stage at a rally for Cirilo Júnior's 1947 campaign for vice-governor of São Paulo. Courtesy Agência Folhapress.

soldiers still fighting overseas in World War II, Prestes released a document in which he stated that, in order to defeat the Nazis and thus support the Soviet Union, an Allied power, all of Brazil had to support Vargas.[82] As part of the Comintern's popular-front approach of the time, Prestes expressed a willingness to work with seemingly antithetical groups, even those that had done personal harm to him and his family. Moreover, as the head of the PCB, Prestes seized on the opportunity to present himself as an unflinchingly committed member of the Communist Party. As Marco Aurélio Santana asks: "What sort of man would defend a political line that entailed reconciliation with the leader who had been responsible for sending his pregnant wife to her death, and for whom he had 'the most justifiable hate'? In the subordination of personal feelings to political duty, Prestes once again gave an example to be followed and celebrated."[83] This position ushered in a public rapprochement with Vargas. In a move that would have seemed impossible a decade prior, the two men (fig. 8.3) campaigned side-by-side in subsequent elections. With national prominence bolstered by their respective attachments to Brazil's interior, Prestes and Vargas entered into a brief détente, their visions for the future seemingly more aligned than at any point in the previous three decades.

Prestes's open return to political life proved short lived. After the Dutra government outlawed the Brazilian Communist Party in 1947, Prestes had his mandate as senator canceled, and he was forced to go into hiding, though he and the party nonetheless remained active in subsequent decades. With Prestes underground, Vargas did the opposite and maneuvered a return to office. Two decades after first seizing power, Vargas won the 1950 presidential election by a comfortable margin. But a series of personal and political crises in 1954 ended with him taking his own life on August 24, 1954. In the final lines of his suicide letter, which was read over the radio and distributed across the country, Vargas wrote: "Serenely, I take the first step on the road to eternity and I leave life to enter history."[84] Vargas's self-martyring closed the end of his rule in Brazil and, by extension, his living rivalry with Luís Carlos Prestes.

Vargas and Prestes had waged a nearly three-decade contest. Along with their more overt political and personal conflicts, their standoff included a competition to claim and define Brazil's undeveloped, rural, and interior regions—areas that the column had traversed, and that Vargas had sought to modernize. After his death in 1954, Vargas himself was no longer able to shape the legacies of tenentismo that had brought him to power. Prestes, on the other hand, remained an active figure in Brazilian politics, and his impact on the political and spatial development of Brazil remained influential throughout the second half of the twentieth century.

9

VISIONS OF THE FUTURE
Culture and Commemoration

As it had been since the late 1920s, the Prestes Column remained a potent—
and pliant—symbol for commenting on Brazil's present as well as its future.
Premised on notions of the interior as both backward (an affliction to be
overcome) and untapped (capable of contributing to the nation), invocations of the column became a way for people across Brazil and abroad to
express their hopes and grievances. Having seen in previous chapters how
this manifested in the political realm, this chapter interweaves examples of
culture and commemoration from the 1940s through the early 1990s. Here,
I model my analysis on the work of the cultural theorist Stuart Hall, who
argues that representations in popular culture can have a tangible effect on
reality, shaping public opinion by upholding or disputing what is considered
to be true.[1] By examining cultural production (namely, poems and novels)
along with three emblematic moments of commemoration (most often disseminated through print media), I trace the continuities and ruptures in the
interior history of the column. Beginning in the 1940s, when a global solidarity campaign sought to win Luís Carlos Prestes's release from jail, and continuing through his death in 1990, representations of the column reflected

the overlapping visions projected onto the interior by a wide range of artists and commentators.

The cultural works discussed in this chapter provide a regionally contingent set of perspectives. Artists from outside the interior—those from the Brazilian coast as well as from other countries—tended to celebrate the column as a sign of a changing Brazil, where enlightened rebels had awakened a promising, if still underdeveloped, backlands. This buoyant framing remained the predominant narrative of the Prestes Column, disseminated in the newspapers and publishing houses of coastal society. Art from within Brazil's interior regions, on the other hand, reflected a more complex legacy. For writers who shared the heroic view of the column, their work highlighted not only the valor of Prestes and the rebels but also the contributions of communities in the interior. And, for artists who called attention to the violence inflicted by the Prestes Column, cultural forms like *cordel* poems expressed localized views that ran counter to the romanticized legend. The triumphant and violent legacies alike served as platforms for interior writers to comment on the present state of their regions: either a positive attachment that showcased the agency of local people, or a negative view of the way the rebels had exacerbated the hardships of life in the interior. By examining cultural production across Brazil and globally, this chapter shows how narratives formed both about the backlands and from within it as well.

As a way to provide contextual signposts across a period of almost five decades, this chapter intersperses three commemorations related to the Prestes Column: its thirtieth anniversary in 1954, its fiftieth anniversary in 1974, and Prestes's death in 1990. Notably, all of the major events for these commemorations took place in Rio de Janeiro and São Paulo, far from the emblematic spaces along the column's march. Each commemoration reflected a changing period in Brazil. In 1954, at the dawn of the post-Vargas era, radical groups openly celebrated the column in order to champion their vision of an empowered rural sector led by vanguard leaders such as Prestes. In 1974, in the middle of a violent military dictatorship, the tenente rebels were described in a Cold War lexicon that referred to them as "liberals" rather than "revolutionaries," all while linking the interior expedition of the 1920s to the military regime's development projects of the 1970s. In 1990, Prestes's death in the early years of Brazil's new democratic regime allowed a resurgent left to again hold the Knight of Hope aloft as a signal of unity and progressive power. Across the three moments, the interior—a legacy of the past and a concern in the present—remained an adaptable symbol of Brazil's future.

Campaigns from Foreign Coasts

The first sustained wave of artistic production about the Prestes Column emerged in the early 1940s. Similar to Jorge Amado's biography of Luís Carlos Prestes discussed in the previous chapter, the cultural outputs of this period sought to galvanize support for the Knight of Hope, who was imprisoned under the Estado Novo dictatorship. As with Amado's book, which was published while the author lived in exile, these works were mostly produced outside of Brazil. I focus here on two key examples, from the Argentine writer Alfredo Varela and the Chilean poet Pablo Neruda. In both, the Brazilian interior is reimagined as a continental interior stretching across the Americas. Moreover, because Varela and Neruda were fellow members of the Communist Party, their writings showed how authors throughout the region helped make Prestes a transnational communist icon.

In 1943, the year after Jorge Amado wrote his biography of Prestes, Alfredo Varela published his first novel, *El río oscuro* (*The Dark River*). The book, which became one of the most renowned novels of the period, was translated into fifteen languages and adapted into a successful film.[2] *El río oscuro* was set in the northern borderlands of Argentina and followed a community of *mensús*—workers on yerba mate tea plantations. In the late 1930s, the Argentine Communist Party had sent Varela to the Missiones region, where he spent time with Marcos Kanner, the radical union leader of the mensú workers. Varela's exposure to the exploitation and political struggles of the mensús formed the basis for his novel, which fictionalizes their efforts to win better working conditions. The book reaches its crescendo when Luís Carlos Prestes comes to the Argentine backlands and leads the workers to victory. This, of course, never happened. The Prestes Column did not go to Argentina, and, as shown in chapter 2, when the rebels passed through tea plantations in Paraguay and Mato Grosso, they collaborated not with the workers—as in Varela's novel—but with the Mate Laranjeiras Company, receiving supplies and money from the type of corporation demonized in *El río oscuro*. Varela discards these facts and taps instead into the symbolism of Prestes as the Knight of Hope.

In Varela's novel, Prestes is the spark that finally ignites the impoverished workers. The trope of a dormant interior was not merely a Brazilian construction; it echoed throughout the region. A native of Buenos Aires, Varela grew up amid a coastal, *porteño* worldview that saw the country's interior provinces as backward—his communist ideology, moreover, shaped his depiction of peasant workers as underdeveloped political agents. As the Argentine scholar Cristina Mateu has observed, "In *El río oscuro*, the social consciousness of the mensús . . . [only] begins to awaken when Brazilian exiles from the Prestes revolution arrive at the yerba plantations and, with their actions and words of solidarity, they instigate a response."[3] In one of the final chapters of Varela's book, the fictionalized Prestes appears on the horizon and guides the mensús in an uprising that destroys equipment, burns tax and debt records, and unleashes the power of a previously latent people:

> Under the gaze of Prestes, the old logbooks and records were broken, where the "credit" of the mensús never balanced out the "owed," along with the deceitful scales. The anger of the workers overthrew the company's foundations, upended the administration, undid the chains and the stocks and the other instruments of torture. And then they set fire to the big bundles of yerba. Vigorous and angry, the flames rose thunderously as if washing away all the pent-up humiliation. The mensú rebels could barely believe that justice, finally, was served.[4]

As a brief aside, it is important to note that, similar to Varela's novel about Prestes in the Argentine backland, one of Brazil's literary masterpieces would also blend historical facts about the column with fictional storytelling. In 1962, the gaúcho writer Érico Veríssimo published *O arquipélago*, the final installment of his trilogy, *O tempo e o vento* (*Time and the Wind*). The trilogy weaves an epic, multigenerational tale of two families in Rio Grande do Sul from the 1700s through the 1950s. In *O arquipélago*, the protagonists, brothers named Rodrigo and Toríbio, join the Prestes Column, the details of which Veríssimo combines with events from the 1923 civil war in Rio Grande do Sul—a metafictional strategy also intended to help readers draw parallels to contemporary conflicts in Brazil.[5] As argued by José Augusto de Souza, Veríssimo uses the brothers' march across Brazil as a way to "contrast primitivism and civilization . . . [and] give a snapshot of a gaucho worldview at a pivotal era in Brazilian history."[6] Veríssimo's work helped to fortify many of the same symbols underpinning the legend of the Knight of Hope, where the adventures of gaucho horsemen served as platforms to expand the boundaries—both imaginative and geographic—of modernity in Brazil.

Along with the literary efforts of Communist Party members like Alfredo Varela and Jorge Amado, the movement to win Prestes's freedom had been led in no small part by his mother, Leocádia. When her son was arrested in Brazil in 1936, she moved from Moscow to Paris to better coordinate a solidarity movement, but, when World War II began, she relocated to Mexico, bringing along her young granddaughter, Anita. In Mexico, Leocádia continued the campaign to free her son, though she died in 1943. In honor of her death, and as a way to bring attention to Prestes's ongoing imprisonment, Pablo Neruda, the famed Chilean poet and communist, wrote a poem in 1943 titled "Dura elegia" (Hard elegy). While living in Mexico City, Neruda visited Leocádia's tombstone and recited his poem, praising her for raising a son whose importance stretched across the Americas:

> Senõra, hiciste grande, más grande, a nuestra América.
> Le diste un río puro, de colosales aguas:
> le diste un árbol alto de infinitas raíces:
> un hijo tuyo digno de su patria profunda.
> Todos lo hemos querido junto a estas orgullosas
> flores que cubrirán la tierra en que reposes,
> todos hemos querido que viniera del fondo
> de América, a través de la selva y del páramo,
> para que así tocara tu frente fatigadaso
> su noble mano llena de larueles y adioses.
> . . . .
> Sombras de América, héroes coronados de furia,
> de nieve, sangre, océano, tempestad y palomos,
> aquí: venid al hueco que esta madre en sus ojos
> guardaba para el claro capitán que esperamos:
> héroes vivos y muertos de nuestra gran bandera:
> O'Higgins, Juárez, Cárdenas, Recabarren, Bolívar,
> Marti, Miranda, Artigas, Sucre, Hidalgo, Morelos,
> Belgrano, San Martin, Lincoln, Carrera, todos,
> Venid, llenad el hueco de vuestro gran Hermano
> y que Luis Carlos Prestes sienta en su celda el aire,
> las alas torrenciales de los padres de América.
> . . . .
> Pero como una brasa e centella y fulgores
> a través de las barras de hierro calcinado
> La luz del corazón de Prestes sobresale.
> Como en las grandes minas del Brasil la esmeralda,
> como en los grandes rios del Brasil la corriente,
> y como en nuestros bosques de índole poderosa
> sobresale una estatua de estrellas y follaje,
> un árbol de las tierras sedientas del Brasil.

Señora, you made our America bigger, much bigger.
You gave it a pure river, of colossal waters:
you gave it a towering tree with endless roots:
A son of yours worthy of his profound homeland.
We have all loved him with these proud
Flowers that will cover the land in which you lay,
we have all wanted him to emerge from the depths
of America, across the jungles and the plains,
so that it would reach your tired brow
Your noble hand full of so-longs and goodbyes.
. . . .

Shadows of America, heroes crowned with fury,
Of snow, blood, ocean, storm and doves,
Here: come to the void that this mother in her eyes
saved for the clear-eyed captain we await:
heroes living and dead of our great flag:
O'Higgins, Juárez, Cárdenas, Recabarren, Bolívar,
Marti, Miranda, Artigas, Sucre, Hidalgo, Morelos,
Belgrano, San Martin, Lincoln, Carrera, all,
Come, fill the void of our great Brother
So that Luis Carlos Prestes in his cell feels the air,
The thundering wings of the fathers of America.
. . . .

But like an ember's sparkle and glow
across the bars of scorched iron
The light of Prestes's heart shines forth.
As in the great mines of Brazil the emerald,
As in the great rivers of Brazil the current,
And as in our forests of powerful nature
Stands out a statue of stars and foliage,
A tree of the thirsting lands of Brazil.[7]

Neruda's poem places Prestes squarely within the pantheon of national heroes throughout the Western Hemisphere, calling upon the ghosts of legends past to lead a new movement to liberate their compatriot. Neruda depicts Prestes as the inheritor of a long legacy of American leaders capable of unleashing the revolutionary potential of rural and interior spaces. The poem draws on the topographical symbolism of revolution across the Americas. Similar to the battles of liberating figures like Bernardo O'Higgins in

Chile, Abraham Lincoln in the United States, Miguel Hidalgo in Mexico, and Simon Bolívar in northern South America, Neruda links the grandeur of Prestes to his presence in Brazil's wilderness. For Neruda, Prestes *was* the interior: he credits Leocádia with having birthed a colossal river, a towering tree, an iconic landscape that cannot be contained. Neruda embeds Prestes in the Brazilian topography, as if Prestes were the earth itself, the soil that nourishes the rivers and forest. For Neruda, this earthen, rooted Prestes represents the core of the nation, albeit with a radical tint—the red hues of the "ember's sparkle and glow" (*brasa de centella y fulgores*) can also be read as communist symbolism. The legend of Prestes thus emanated outward from the heart of Brazil across the Americas, envisioning the backlands as a hemispheric interior ready to help catalyze a new era of revolution and progress.

This view contrasts with the hemispheric representations we saw in chapter 7, when supporters of amnesty used the column's exile in the "green hell" of Bolivia's interior to argue that the rebels deserved to return to Brazil. If appeals in 1927 had invoked ideas of space and nation in an effort to return Prestes to the Brazilian coast, Neruda's poem in 1943 deployed a refracted set of tropes to argue that Prestes be released from the coast—he was imprisoned in Rio de Janeiro—and set free across the continent. As a fused symbol of hope and landscape, Prestes stood tall as "a statue of stars and foliage." When Prestes finally gained his freedom in 1945, his legacy as the Knight of Hope became even more attached to a forward-looking vision of change.

Commemoration 1: Prestes as a Radical Icon

Prior to 1954, every major commemoration of the column had taken place on July 5, the date of the first two tenente uprisings in Rio de Janeiro in 1922 and São Paulo in 1924. But the thirtieth anniversary in 1954 happened instead on October 29, the date when Prestes led the uprising in Rio Grande do Sul. The recent suicide of Getúlio Vargas meant that Prestes could now be more openly celebrated. Even with Vargas gone, however, political repression still continued—Prestes had gone into hiding when the PCB was outlawed in 1947—and the commemorations of 1954 doubled as criticism of the current government. For supporters of Prestes, the column's thirtieth anniversary was a call for the Knight of Hope to rise again.

Figures 9.1 and 9.2 were printed in *Imprensa Popular*, a radical Rio de Janeiro newspaper. The first image ran on the newspaper's cover, and the second was the full-length front spread of its nine-page supplement for the thirtieth anniversary. In both images, Prestes stands as a stoic hero, his head slightly

FIGURE 9.1. Image commemorating the thirtieth anniversary of the Prestes Column in *Imprensa Popular*, October 31, 1954.

uptilted, gazing out toward the horizon, framed by the arid landscapes of Brazil's interior, with palm trees, cactuses (fig. 9.1), and bare timbers (fig. 9.2) offering minimal variation in an otherwise bleak tableau. The huddled, almost featureless figures in both images juxtapose the mythic qualities of Prestes. Both depictions blend the stigmas of the backlands with a hopeful promise of better days. On the left, Prestes is drawn not as he would have been during the march, but, rather, as he looked in 1954: clean shaven and dressed in a suit and tie, the Knight of Hope has now left the interior and brought his campaign for justice into the modern battleground of Brazilian politics. On the right, the more classic depiction of the gaucho horseman—calmly mounted and wearing his hat and knotted bandana—looks upon a rising sun. Thirty years on from his epic march across Brazil, Prestes is shown as a living legend, always ready to chart a new path. *Imprensa Popular*'s commemorative issue included dozens of articles that tethered hope for the future to the constructed legacy of the column. Essay titles included "Prestes, Symbol of Honor"; "Prestes Is Now the Idol of the Brazilian People"; and "The March

FIGURE 9.2. Image commemorating the thirtieth anniversary of the Prestes Column in *Imprensa Popular*, October 31, 1954.

of the Column Will Never Leave the Heart of Brazil." The newspaper also ran a poem by Martins Fontes titled "O camarada lendário" (The legendary comrade), which speculated on the whereabouts of Prestes:

> Luiz Carlos Prestes onde está? Mas onde?
> Está onde anuncia a nova aurora!
> Pelo planeta, pelo espaço afora:
> Em que estria, em que mundo ele se esconde?
> Quem sabe onde está, por mais que sonde?

Dizem uns que é na Rússia que ele mora:
E outros que no Uruguai reside agora.
Porém, ninguém ao certo nos responde!
Em toda a parte, está na nossa terra!
E, se paira afastado, é que o aterra. . . .
Seu refúgio nós todos conhecemos.
Onde ele vive todos nós sabemos:
No coração dos brasileiros puros!

Luís Carlos Prestes where is he? But where?
He's where the new dawn will rise!
Across the planet, up in space on high:
On which star, on what world does he hide?
Can nobody know, can no search abide?
He lives in Russia some imply:
And others think he's now in Uruguay,
Though nobody answers firsthand!
He is everywhere across our land!
And, if he floats away, he will come back. . . .
His safe haven is known.
Where he lives is homegrown:
In the heart of all pure Brazilians![8]

The meanings imbued in the images and texts of *Imprensa Popular* echoed across a series of public events in Rio de Janeiro and São Paulo. For the Brazilian Communist Party, the thirtieth anniversary was an opportunity to link the exploits of the column in the 1920s to the context of the 1950s. Over the previous decade, the PCB had undergone several back-and-forth changes, oscillating between calls for reform and calls for revolutionary upheaval. In a sign of looming challenges to his leadership, Prestes's not-infrequent push for more confrontational strategies was often met with internal opposition.[9] By the middle of the 1950s, as noted by Ronald Chilcote, the PCB adopted a "strategy of gradual reform . . . [that] reflected the abandonment of revolutionary demands," and the party now embraced participation in elections and renewed alliances with groups such as trade unions.[10]

The PCB's celebrations of the thirtieth anniversary of the Prestes Column reflected the broadening scope of the party in the mid-1950s. The PCB hosted a commemorative event in Rio de Janeiro that celebrated the tenente rebels for having brought "the lantern of liberty to Brazil's deepest interior."

The event's program linked the legacy of Prestes to the PCB's reemerging alliance-based platform:

> Under the direction of the Brazilian Communist Party, the Party of Prestes, our people are keeping alive the flame of the struggle for freedom, broadening and enriching the fighting tradition [started by] the column. The PCB's Program of National Salvation is the compass that guides to victory the growing struggle of our people. The urban proletariat joins together with the millions of peasants who groan under the yoke of the latifundio. . . . Through their struggles in the cities and in the fields, Brazilians now march towards the formation of a democratic front of national liberation, which will bring about the peace, the progress and the happiness of our people.[11]

In its official newspaper, *Voz Operária*, the PCB printed a commemorative issue for the thirtieth anniversary. The eleven-page spread included iconography of Prestes's heroic leadership as well as the column's journey across the interior (figs. 9.3 and 9.4). On the left, Prestes is drawn in a suit and tie—just as he had been in *Imprensa Popular*, though now with his signature beard from the rebel march. The illustration shows two rural workers cheering on the passing rebels. The picture of a well-dressed Prestes set against a foreground of an awakened backlands represented the hope of bringing the coast and the interior together, emblematic of the PCB's vision for uniting the country around a worker and peasant alliance. On the right, *Voz Operária* traced the column's extensive route across Brazil—a map of the past that hinted at where the party wanted to expand its presence in the future. In both images, the Knight of Hope stood as proof that the backlands could be modernized and brought into the nation.

In the immediacy of the post-Vargas era, a wide range of groups openly celebrated the thirtieth anniversary. The Brazilian Newspaper Association held a public commemoration in Rio de Janeiro attended by a number of people whose presence would have until recently been unthinkable: along with establishment figures like General Felicíssimo Cardoso (a leading military ideologue), participants also included radicals such as Roberto Morena (who under Vargas had taken up exile in the Soviet Union) and Jorge Amado, Prestes's most famous supporter.[12] And, in São Paulo, General Miguel Costa—the less legendary coleader of the Prestes Column—hosted a commemoration to honor "the splendid acts of bravery and sacrifice that guided the path of that episode in our history, a decisive moment in the struggles of

FIGURES 9.3 AND 9.4. Images from commemorative issue of *Voz Operária*, October 29, 1954.

Viva XXX aniversário da COLUNA PRESTES!

NESTE NÚMERO:

A EPOPÉIA DA COLUNA — FAÇANHA DO NOSSO POVO (pág. central)

★

O BRAVO SIQUEIRA CAMPOS — FIEL COMPANHEIRO DE PRESTES (2.ª pág.)

★

"GENERAL PRESTES" — UMA CIDADE NA E. F. GOIÁS (4.ª pág.)

★

PRESTES, PATRIOTA SEM MÁCULA, IMAGEM DO CHEFE INCORRUPTÍVEL (5.ª pág.)

★

UM RAIO DE ESPERANÇA NAS TREVAS DO LATIFÚNDIO

★

O CAVALEIRO DA ESPERANÇA NÃO ABANDONA SEUS HOMENS

our people for democracy and progress."[13] As various groups maneuvered for power in the aftermath of Vargas's death, the mythic Knight of Hope—an intrepid horseman, a battle-tested explorer—was made to shine as a beacon for the country's future.

Artists added to the commemorations as well. In 1954, the Bahian writer Jacinta Passos wrote a poem called "A coluna" (The column). Over the course of 15 stanzas and 975 lines, Passos tells the story of the Prestes Column's march across Brazil. Passos opens her poem with the following:

Ó céus e terras, tremei
que a Coluna já partiu
neste ano de Vinte e Quatro
todo o brasil sacudiu
será Coluna de Fogo
que o viajante já viu?
Coluna de vento e areia
dos desertos desafio?
Ó céus e terras, tremei
que a Coluna já partiu.

. . . .

Através da terra imensa
abrindo caminho no chão,
seus cavalos, cavaleiros
e seu grande Capitão,
Coluna dos revoltosos
Coluna da decisão,
espinha dorsal no corpo
do Brasil, Insurreição.
Através da terra imensa
abrindo caminho no chão

Oh heavens and earth, have fear!
All set, the Column is near.
Twenty-Four is the year
All of Brazil quivers.
Is it the Column in flames
that the traveler blames?
Column of blowing sand,
a duel, from the hinterland?
Oh heavens and earth, have fear!

All set, the Column is near.

. . . .

Paving the way
through the vast land,
your horses, knights
and Captain valiant,
Column of revolt
Column of command,
the backbone
of Brazil, Rebellion.
Paving the way
through the vast land.[14]

For Passos, the column's passage was an epic feat in the true center of the country. Rather than a peripheral appendage, the interior is presented as the "backbone" of Brazil—a nod perhaps to Euclides da Cunha, who in *Os Sertões* famously described sertanejos as "the very core of our nationality, the bedrock of our race."[15] In the middle of the poem, as the rebels are preparing to cross into Bahia, Passos anthropomorphizes the region's topography. In a first-person exchange with the São Francisco River, Passos writes:

Ó São Francisco, barreira
entre o Oeste e o mar
tu vais servir ao Governo
para a Coluna cercar?!
Eu, nunca! Responde o rio
sou até capaz de secar
como outrora o Mar Vermelho
para a Coluna passer

Oh São Francisco, barricade
between the West and the sea
will you serve the State
trapping the Column, a siege?!
Me, never! The river accedes
I might even go dry
As once was the Red Sea
To let the Column pass by.[16]

Passos's personification of the São Francisco reflects a view of the interior not as passive or uncivilized, but as an agent of change. In Passos's telling, the column needed the interior's help, not the other way around. Here, it is not the sertanejo who comes to the rescue, but the actual geography of the interior itself. Given that the backlands had long been presented as a shadow protagonist in the column, it is not surprising that, in the cultural realm, artists like Passos took the narrative one step further and brought the interior to life. Compared to the stigmatized view of the backlands as a dangerous place, Passos offered a different perspective: while still relying on the imagery of the region's physicality, her poem reimagined the interior not as an adversary, but as an ally. Passos's own background adds important nuance for understanding the regional dimensions of the column's mythology. Although Passos was from Bahia, her life trajectory took her far from the northeastern sertão she wrote about: she grew up in the coastal capital of Salvador before moving to São Paulo and Rio de Janeiro in the late 1940s, where she joined the Brazilian Communist Party and became a journalist, poet, and left-wing activist. As such, despite a personal connection to the Northeast that most artists and commentators did not share, she nevertheless helped sustain the pattern of how the column's legacy was shaped primarily along the coast.

Views from the Interior: Cordel Literature

Capturing the perspective of the interior is an impossible task. Like all categories—geographic as well as social—there exists no single, authoritative voice. The condensed singularity of *the interior*, moreover, obfuscates the immeasurable range of experiences within what should more properly be referred to as *the interiors* (plural). And, given that the trope of a marginalized backlands is based on a real-world power imbalance, the weight of mainstream southern and coastal society has tended to overshadow the perspectives of the interior.

So far in this book, views from the interior regions have been shown through two main sources: newspapers from the time of the column's march and oral history interviews collected by journalists in the 1990s. As with any source, the news coverage and interviews were shaped by their context. Newspapers linked to powerful local oligarchs sought to turn popular opinion against the rebels, and journalists a half century later seemed partial to the more dramatic stories told by elderly Brazilians who had encountered the column in their youth. These sources suggest an enduring narrative of anger and mistrust in the wake of the column's violence. At least in the Northeast, one way to measure the life cycle of these memories—an approach that will highlight the various positive and negative attachments to the Prestes Column—is through cordel literature.

Literatura de cordel is a rhythmic style of poetry associated with Brazil's rural northeastern regions, where pamphlets (known as *folhetos*) are printed on both sides of large paper, then folded and strung up to be sold in markets (*cordel* means "twine"). Folhetos tend to have a woodcut illustration printed on the front and are written in six-line, rhyming stanzas. Traditionally, the poems have been sold in local markets, where the poets would read them aloud. As a highly performative medium, folhetos also appealed to people who could not read and may buy a story in order to have it read to them by literate family or friends. As Sarah Sarzynski has written, cordel literature almost defies categorization. The genre is undoubtedly connected to popular culture and the oral traditions of interior communities. But categorizing the genre—and its "authenticity"—is difficult. At the national level, cordel poems have often been romanticized as part of the "folk" culture of the impoverished Northeast, but it is also a misconception that the poems are a direct representation of a grassroots experience. The poems were often commissioned by rural and political elites, and the poets themselves did not always come from a working-class or peasant background. The question, then, is whether cordel poems are a way to challenge dominant culture, or an unwitting refraction of it. Drawing on recent scholarship about cordel literature specifically, and also theories of culture more broadly, Sarzynski recognizes "literatura de cordel as the dialectic space where both containment and resistance occur. . . . The political messages and struggles in the popular pamphlet poems illustrate how Northeasterners interpreted their world, fighting against the dominant culture while also being influenced by it."[17]

Cordel poems offer important insight into how Prestes and the column have been depicted locally. In previous chapters, they have often been represented together, where both Prestes (the man) and the column (the rebellion he led) were dealt with as part of the same larger symbol. Cordel literature, in contrast, helps elucidate how the two entities could have distinct legacies. Compared to the sizable body of poetry about Prestes, there has been a lack of folhetos about the column itself, suggesting that, in the Northeast, Prestes and the Prestes Column could be seen differently.

My research identified twenty-six folhetos relating either to Luís Carlos Prestes or to the Prestes Column—in addition to another dozen about the famed bandit Lampião, in which Prestes makes only a brief appearance.[18] Of the twenty-six poems, only four of them are about the Prestes Column itself, with the rest focusing on Prestes more generally. Of the four poems about the column, two focus on violent events of the rebellion—the massacre at Piancó and the battle at Crateús—and two can be categorized as "neutral." For the former, as will be shown, depictions of violence reflect a localized vision of the column as bandits. For the latter, the more neutral poems neither valorize nor chastise the column, but offer general descriptions of its passage.[19]

At first glance, it may seem puzzling why there are so many more cordel poems about Prestes than about the column. I propose four factors to help explain this imbalance. First, it is possible that more of these works exist than I was able to identify—though, even if that were the case, my analysis of over two dozen folhetos nonetheless offers a window into the localized meanings attached to both Prestes and the column. Second, cordels often focus on individual "hero" characters, making Prestes an easily invocable figure. Third, in the late 1940s and early 1950s, the Brazilian Communist Party organized rural campaigns through the creation of Peasant Leagues (Ligas Camponesas), which infused Prestes's already buoyant cult of personality with on-the-ground efforts to improve livelihoods in the countryside. These efforts included securing better wages, schools, health care, and drives for lower rents and access to credit.[20]

Local memory lore played a key role in these campaigns. As Sarzynski writes, "Rural social movement leaders realized that the most powerful strategy for gaining support for their political projects was to infuse the legends and historical symbols of the Northeast with new revolutionary meanings."[21] An example of this symbolic infusion was *Zé Brasil*, a 1947 book written by the famed children's author Monteiro Lobato, who had risen to prominence in the 1910s with his stories about Jeca Tatu, a fictional *caipira* (country bumpkin) from the interior of São Paulo. Compared to Jeca Tatu's depiction as a simple-minded yokel, Lobato's new character of Zé Brasil offered a far more positive vision of rural people, as Zé is shown to have a capacity to understand the fight for structural change in the countryside. The book is constructed as a dialogue between Zé and the author, and, when Zé appears to doubt the possibility of improving conditions for rural workers, he is told all about the legendary Luís Carlos Prestes. The book concludes with Zé proudly declaring: "Prestes! Prestes! That's why there are so many people who would die for him. I understand now. He is the only one who wants what's good for us."[22] The evolution of Lobato's characters, from Jeca Tatu to Zé Brasil, reflected a broader shift in perceptions about Brazil's interior, and the capacity of the heroic symbol of Prestes to be used to repurpose the stigma of rural backwardness toward one of rural potential.

Even after the PCB suffered a major internal split between 1956 and 1958, Prestes retained popular appeal in subsequent rural movements, such as those led by Francisco Julião in Pernambuco in the late 1950s and early 1960s—a period when organizers and writers began to reclaim rural archetypes like the *cangaceiro* bandit as a way to assert a national identity rooted in the struggles of the Brazilian people, *o povo*.[23] Decades later, Prestes remained a symbol of rural empowerment within Brazil's largest social movement, the Landless Workers Movement (MST), whose leaders cited Prestes as an inspiration on the same level as Che Guevara and José Martí.[24] In 2001, the MST named one of its land settlements in Sergipe after Luís Carlos Prestes. As such, even if Prestes had done very little to help rural communities during his actual march through the interior, his legacy was shaped more by perceptions of what he did afterward.

The fourth and final explanation for the relative lack of cordel poems about the Prestes Column relates to the same pattern evidenced in the newspapers of the 1920s and the interviews of the 1990s: violence committed by the tenente rebels. Of the few cordel folhetos I was able to locate about the column, half of them focused on violent episodes of the march across the Northeast. For example, to mark the eightieth anniversary of the column's passage through Paraíba, the poet Josealdo Rodrigues Leite wrote a cordel about the rebel massacre at Piancó, "Os mais violentos dias do Piancó" (The most violent days of Piancó). The text of the poem, which is accompanied by a graphic drawing of the massacre (fig. 9.5), includes the following lines, replete with a mythologized version of events that the rebel soldiers had cut off the testicles of Padre Aristides and stuffed them in his mouth:

O Padre foi sangrando
Pelo pescoço primeiro,
Foi capado como um porco
Por um facão ligeiro,
Em sua boca botou
Os culhões que arrancou
Foi um massacre verdadeiro

. . . .

Os outros viram a morte
Daquele bravo pastor
Também foram truciados,
Cada um com sua dor,
Seus corpos amontoados

Num barreiro jogados
Uma cena de terror.

The Father bled
First by the neck,
Castrated like a pig
With a knife, quick,
Stuck in his mouth
Balls that came out
True slaughter throughout.
. . . .
Others, death had seen
Of that Pastor, keen,
They too, slayed,
Each with their pain,
Their bodies piled
Thrown in a pit
A horror scene.[25]

FIGURE 9.5. Piancó massacre, drawn by Chico Jó, included in "Os mais violentos dias do Piancó," cordel written by Josealdo Rodrigues Leite, 2006. Courtesy of Biblioteca de Obras Raras Átila Almeida, Campina Grande, Paraíba.

In the decades since the column had ventured across the Northeast, the legend of the Knight of Hope had grown to such an extent that the popularity of Luís Carlos Prestes outpaced that of the column he had led. Prestes thus remained a symbol of unity and hope, even in the spaces where localized memories of his march remained contentious.

Cold War Visions

By the time that the global Cold War arrived in Brazil, the spaces of Brazil's interior had undergone dramatic changes, punctuated by the inauguration in April 1960 of Brasília as the new national capital. Although the capital's transfer from Rio de Janeiro to the Planalto Central had been stipulated in Brazil's 1891 Constitution, it did not actually happen until the presidency of Juscelino Kubitschek (1956–61). Incidentally—and in a telling reflection of the column's often ahistorical mythology—as final preparations were underway to inaugurate Brasília, the former tenente leader Miguel Costa would claim that the idea for an inland capital had occurred during the Prestes Column![26] Brasília represented both the culmination, and a refraction, of the "westward" efforts at state-building discussed in the previous chapter. In an interview with the American writer John dos Passos, conducted in the lead-up to Brasília, President Kubitschek said that, "during your pioneer days, you North Americans always had the Pacific Ocean for a goal to lure you on across the mountains. That's why you populated your part of the continent so quickly. Our way west has been barred by impenetrable forests and by the Andes. Brasília will constitute a goal, a place to head for on the high plateau. Building Brasília means . . . a movement of population into the fine farmlands of the interior."[27] As Frederico Freitas has written, not only did Brasília showcase how "Brazil's particular type of tropical modernity would be made concrete" but it also "served to introduce the idea of Planalto Central as a region where the country's future would be realized."[28] Even if much of the nation's financial and cultural power continued to rest in large urban areas along the coast, Brasília marked a watershed moment in Brazil's spatial history: the interior was now the political heart of the country.

The Cold War changed the calculus of what a backward interior could mean. In the aftermath of the Cuban Revolution, where peasants were seen to have helped overthrow a US-backed regime, the Latin American countryside became an increasingly polarized sphere. For Brazilians seeking to empower rural sectors, the early 1960s offered a new hope of transforming society. Brazil was governed by João Goulart, who had been the minister of labor under Vargas in the 1950s and then the vice president for two consecutive administrations. When President Jânio Quadros resigned in 1961, Goulart assumed the presidency, bringing a political tradition of *trabalhismo* (laborism) to Brazil's highest office. Among the various programs initiated by Goulart, arguably his most contentious of them related to the countryside. In 1963, he passed the Rural Laborer Statute, which regulated agricultural work, and by the following year he was preparing to pass comprehensive agrarian reform—a long-held goal of the Left and a long-reviled target of Brazil's landholding elite and their political allies. At a public rally in Rio de Janeiro on March 13, 1964, Goulart outlined a series of initiatives, including an agrarian reform bill that would fundamentally reorganize land tenure and agricultural production in Brazil.[29]

For Goulart's opponents, who already saw him as a dangerous subversive, his agrarian reform was the final straw. Two weeks later, on the night of March 31, the military staged a coup that overthrew Goulart and inaugurated a twenty-one-year dictatorship. Eager to enact its own vision for modernizing the countryside, as well as to avoid any peasant radicalization, the military regime passed its own rural legislation, the 1964 Land Statute, that expanded export-oriented agriculture while providing workers with a few scaled-down reforms.[30] The statute was one of many laws and repressive acts through which the dictatorship sought to consolidate its power. The dictatorship also relied on discursive strategies. As they had done in 1924 and 1930, military leaders again gave their actions the euphemistic title of "the Revolution of 1964." Yet, given the particular legacies of tenentismo, the army was careful to distance itself both from Vargas, whose position as a civilian leader had never sat well with many of Brazil's top military commanders, and from Prestes, the communist leader. Less than two months after seizing power, General Artur da Costa e Silva—the minister of war who would soon serve as the dictatorship's second appointed president—gave a lengthy interview to *O Estado de São Paulo* in which he linked the recent coup to the initial rise and successes of tenentismo:

> This Revolution, along with the common people [*sic*] and military men who participated, had as protagonists the survivors of a series of revolutions that had been polarizing, let's say, or rather building, on its original momentum since 1922. . . . In 1924, men such as Isidoro Dias Lopes, João Alberto, Nelson de Mello, Cordeiro de Farias and many others [led the way]. In 1930, the same ones, and also Góes Monteiro . . . all of them playing their part. . . . In 1930 we also won, but the political skills of the politicians who led this revolution made us uncomfortable . . . and

we suffered through a dictatorship until 1945. . . . We carry the long experience of all these movements. We are trained in revolution and this time they will not take from us the reins of revolution.[31]

General Costa e Silva could thus invoke the original tenentista rebellions without naming either Prestes or Vargas—an inversion of how the cordel poems elevated Prestes while ignoring tenentismo. With no hint of irony, Costa e Silva laments the dictatorship thrust upon the country during the Estado Novo and criticizes Vargas as a misguided civilian leader. His statement also shows that tenentismo still existed as an idea that could contextualize and justify military intervention. From its beginning, tenentismo had always lacked an overarching political ideology, and the enduring power of that vagueness allowed it to remain a potent symbol.

Four decades removed from the original tenentista movement, several of its leaders actively participated in the dictatorship of the 1960s. Juarez Távora was one of the three military leaders considered for the first postcoup presidency, though it went instead to General Humberto de Alencar Castelo Branco, who subsequently chose Távora to serve as the minister of transportation and public works. Távora had become one of the most influential former tenente leaders, and his nickname as the Viceroy of the North allowed him to use the symbolism of the interior for his own political purposes. When he ran for president in 1955, for example, he projected a military vision for bringing modernity into the backland. A campaign poster (fig. 9.6) depicts Távora at an army outpost in the jungle, contrasting the wild landscape in the background to the composed Távora, standing in profile with his face sternly looking forward—almost a mirror image to the commemoration of Prestes shown earlier in this chapter. Although Távora lost the election, this approach conditioned his work under the dictatorship. In his cabinet post, Távora oversaw a massive extension of Brazil's transit infrastructure, including the completion of the Rede Ferroviária Centro-Oeste (Mid-Western Railway) that linked the interior region of Goiânia with the coastal ports of Rio de Janeiro. Another detachment commander from the Prestes Column, Osvaldo Cordeiro de Farias, served in a similar capacity. In June 1964, only a few months after the coup, Cordeiro de Farias was appointed to lead the Special Ministry for the Coordination of Regional Organizations, which would soon be transformed into the Ministry of the Interior. Reflecting on this work, Cordeiro de Farias said that his motivation to modernize Brazil's interior came from his experience in the Prestes Column: "For two and a half years, I lived in contact with the suffering Brazil, with its people—who had no schools, no health care, no roads,

FIGURE 9.6. Poster, Juarez Távora's 1955 presidential campaign. Source: CPDOC: JT-07f. The caption reads "Juarez Távora: the veteran tenente"—literally, the white-haired tenente, suggesting age and experience.

no police, no justice, no anything—very poor and without hope. This image of our people and their problems has never left me. That was, and it still is today . . . the foundation of all my political conduct."[32] Across three different moments of military intervention (1922–27, 1930, and, 1964) spread out over four decades, the interior loomed as a proxy to explain the country's backwardness and a rationale to intervene in the political system.

Commemoration 2: A Sanitized Legacy

With the military again in power and conditioned by the anti-communist climate of the Cold War, it did not take long for the dictatorship to target the Knight of Hope. Luís Carlos Prestes was arrested several times in the early years of military rule, and, similarly to other leftist leaders and intellectuals, he eventually fled the country, taking up exile in February of 1971, first in Buenos Aires, then Paris, and finally settling in Moscow, forty years after he first arrived in the Soviet Union. While Prestes lived in exile, Brazil witnessed the most repressive period of military rule, the so-called years of lead (*anos de chumbo*) from 1969 to 1974 under General Emílio Médici that saw the highest rate of state-sponsored murder and torture. The end of this period was characterized by a new phase of dictatorship, where, under pressure from domestic and international opposition groups and human rights activists, General Ernesto Geisel oversaw a policy of *distensão* (political decompression) that sought to transition Brazil toward a "slow, gradual, and secure" return of civilian rule.[33] Although repression had officially waned, Brazil remained governed by a violent military regime. The commemoration of the column's fiftieth anniversary in 1974 thus posed a delicate set of challenges: how to celebrate a triumphant moment of national history—one that had been led by members of the military—without celebrating Prestes, the former tenente legend and current Communist Party icon.

The commemorations of 1974 took place in July, in line with the more mainstream legacy of tenentismo. Two commemorative newspaper issues reveal the flexibility of the column's mythology—its adaptability to shifting political contexts—as well as its continuity. Again, its symbolism served as a platform to discuss the development of Brazil's interior regions. The first example is the special inset of the *Jornal do Brasil*, whose headline proclaimed: "The Long March of the Liberals."[34] Here, the use of "liberals" is strategic: for most of the previous fifty years, the tenente rebels had been described not as liberals, but as revolutionaries. Yet, under military rule in the Cold War of the 1970s, to be a revolutionary—like Prestes, a communist—had taken on new meanings. As mentioned earlier, the military regime sought to appropriate the phrase for their own agenda, having branded their coup the previous decade as the Revolution of 1964. By downgrading the tenentes to the status of liberals, commemorations such as these walked the fine line of invoking the mythic glory of the column without stepping on the toes of the dictatorship's official narratives.

Throughout the *Jornal do Brasil* commemoration, references to Brazil's interior consistently signaled to readers the spatial and national implications of the long march. One of its articles, "1924—a Country Burdened by the Weight of the Past," offered a voyeuristic exposé of Brazil's profile in 1924: "The Prestes Column traveled through vast empty spaces . . . that reflected, in a physical sense, the social profile (*fisionomia social*) of Brazil at that time."[35] The *Jornal do Brasil* celebrated how the tenentes had marched deep into Brazil's soul, sounded the alarm of its backward realities, and, in doing so, set the nation on a path of modernity and progress. The dictatorship had a keen interest in presenting the backward interior as a relic of the past. As Anna Luiza Ozorio de Almeida notes, the 1970s was the "decade of colonization," during which the military regime embarked on massive development projects—particularly in the Amazon and northern regions—that included agricultural colonization, hydroelectric dams, and highway construction.[36] These projects represented the physical manifestation of the long-standing concept of *ufanismo*, a notion that Brazilian nationalism depended on opening up a supposedly uninhabited interior. If the interior of the 1920s had been an unmodern "empty space," then the interior of the 1970s, in the dictatorship's eyes, now stood ready to have its full potential unleashed.

The second commemorative example of 1974 is another newspaper supplement, from *O Cruzeiro*. With text written by the journalist Edmar Morel, the special issue opened with the headline "The Cannons of the Tenentes Woke Up Brazil."[37] After several pages of photographs and anecdotes—without ever mentioning Prestes by his full name—the paper included a large map of the expedition across the interior (fig. 9.7). Reflecting the same empty spaces concept from the *Jornal do Brasil*, the map had no lines or features to demarcate any of Brazil's territory; instead, the entire country was presented as a blank canvas on which the tenentes opened the path for a new nation. The only touch of flourish were the caricatures drawn in the upper left-hand corner, with palm trees, a parrot, and a snake. As Courtney Campbell and her colleagues have argued, although most spatial histories tend to concentrate on the evolution of borders and populated landscapes, it is also vital to "consider emptiness or 'nothingness' to be equal components in the fabric of real and imagined space, subject to, and created by, very similar sets of physical and discursive activities."[38] This emptiness also recalls Javier Uriarte's study of the "desertification" of the Latin American countryside, through which the incursion of armed state actors into rural and interior spaces transformed previously isolated voids into legible voids that could be incorporated into the nation-state.[39]

In the case of Brazil's interior, these projections of emptiness help to explain the appeal of the Prestes Column: its stature as a heroic march through landscapes that were simultaneously empty (of civilization) and full (of potential) provided a discursive template for imagining the country's future. This duality of emptiness is evident on the final page of *O Cruzeiro's* commemorative issue. Having celebrated the column across five full pages, Morel quotes at

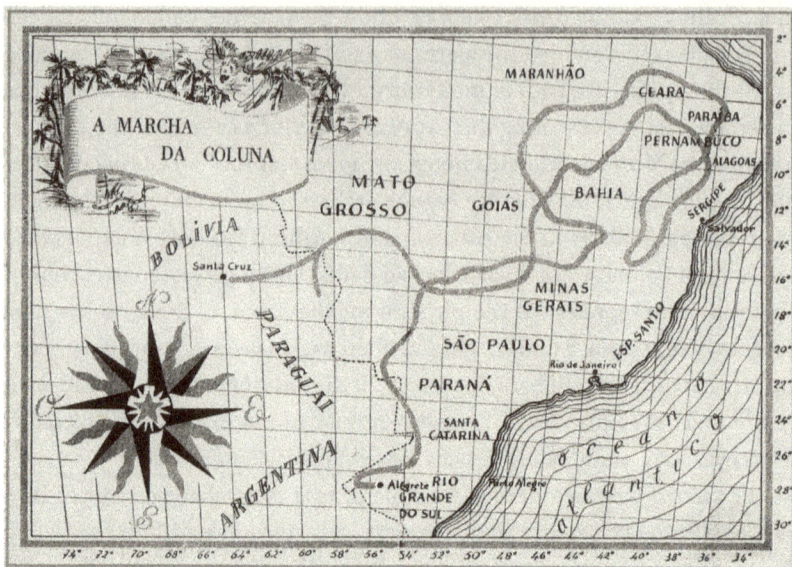

FIGURE 9.7. March of the column, *O Cruzeiro*, July 17, 1974, 81.

length from the same citation shown in the previous chapter from the memoir of Lourenço Moreira: the column "crossed hundreds of roaring rivers. It climbed endless mountains. It broke through impenetrable forests. It tore across wild canyons of *caatinga*. It crossed unimaginable stretches of wetlands. It galloped across the pampas of Rio Grande do Sul, the high plateaus of Minas Gerais and Bahia, in the wild expanse of the Northeast."[40] Here, the triumph was premised on the assertion that the column had experienced the full array of Brazil's landscapes, and, as a result, its leaders knew the true nature of the country. As it had a half century before, the symbolic Knight of Hope—even with Prestes made invisible by the dictatorship—continued to march steadily forward.

New Horizons and New Challenges

By the end of the 1970s, social movements and international solidarity campaigns successfully loosened the military's grip on power. The previous policy of distensão was replaced, in 1979, by a new set of democratization reforms known as *abertura*, the Portuguese word for "opening." The military would not officially step down for another six years—and, even then, the transition was heavily brokered to maintain the regime's influence and to preclude any legal trials against those who had committed murder, torture, and other abuses. As part of what historian James Green calls Brazil's "slow-motion return to democracy," the abertura reforms of 1979 did signal an important step in the return of political rights.[41] A key piece of abertura legislation was the Amnesty Law passed on October 20, 1979, which authorized exiles to return and enabled suspended politicians to regain their rights—though, as a compromise law, it also shielded agents of the regime from human rights prosecutions. Two months later, Luís Carlos Prestes came back to Brazil after eight years in Moscow. When he returned, he was met by a crowd of thousands at the Rio de Janeiro airport holding signs that, among other slogans, welcomed back the Knight of Hope. At one point the crowd chanted: "From North to South, from East to West, the people yell, Luís Carlos Prestes"—the rhyming scheme matching the name Prestes to the word for "West" (*oeste*).[42]

Within his own party, Prestes's arrival was far from a seamless homecoming. Having served as the PCB's secretary-general since 1943—and having fended off numerous challenges in order keep the party aligned with his vision—tensions had resurfaced during Prestes's exile in the Soviet Union. Upon his return to Brazil in late 1979, he felt that the Central Committee of the PCB had become too reformist, the same charge he had levied in the late 1950s. In an open letter, Prestes called on party militants to demand a new leadership committee, one that would keep the party from capitulating to reformist campaigns.[43] Unlike his earlier attempts, Prestes was no longer able to determine the party's direction. The following year, the PCB leadership voted to remove Prestes as its secretary-general. The rift lingered, and, in 1984, Prestes, at the age of eighty-six, was expelled from the Brazilian Communist Party.

As Prestes navigated his late-in-life conflict with the party that he had represented for much of the twentieth century, a final wave of cultural production signaled the enduring legend of the Prestes Column. It should be emphasized, however, that further works continued to appear over the following decades, including a 2014 children's book that follows a young boy named Jaguncinho, who, as part of the Prestes Column, encounters giant galloping fish, a village with ten-foot-tall Indigenous people, and other folkloric characters in the interior.[44] In the late 1970s and early 1980s, against the abertura backdrop of democratization, two northeastern writers wrote books that displayed the heroism of Prestes and the tenente rebels. Although sharing in the heroic narrative of noninterior writers such as Alfredo Varela, Jorge Amado, and Pablo Neruda, the books centered on the interior's contributions to the column, rather than the other way around. Both books offered fictionalized accounts of the column that sought to expose the realities of life in the Northeast—including poverty and the abuses of corrupt local leaders—while highlighting the region's contributions to national politics.

The first book was the 1979 novel *A coroa de areia* (The crown of sand), by Josué Montello, a writer from Maranhão—the northern state where the column had its "golden period" of relatively positive reception among locals. Montello's protagonist is João Maurício, a young law student who in the early 1920s travels from Maranhão to Rio de Janeiro. In the aftermath of the 1922 Copacabana revolt, João leads a protest in support of the rebels, for which the federal government imprisons and tortures him. João eventually gets out of jail, and in 1924 he joins the new tenente revolt and marches triumphantly with the Prestes Column all the way back to his native Maranhão. For Montello, it was not simply that the rebels had brought the light of freedom to Maranhão; it was that a man from Maranhão had helped bring them there: "You could say that those brave [soldiers] were not even real, crossing the immense desert plateau, surrounded by small glowing lights that turned on and off, on and off, illuminating a path through the surrounding shadows, all the while their heavy boots, caked with mud, were tamping down the earth."[45] In Montello's narrative, as it had been for a half century's worth of commentators, the Prestes Column softened the edges of a harsh interior—tamping down the earth, paving the way for an expanding modernity—and shone a light on the authentic heart of Brazil.

Three years later, a second northeastern novel told a similar story. Eulício Farias's 1982 book, *O dia em que a Coluna passou* (The day the column came), recounts the details of the massacre committed by Prestes's soldiers in the Paraíba town of Piancó. Unlike most local folklore about the violence at Piancó—illustrated previously in the cordel by Rodrigues Leite—the novel offered a decidedly pro-rebel account. Farias was actually from the Piancó valley, giving him a personal connection to the memory battles related to the 1926 massacre, and his home in the interior also sets him apart from Josúe Montello, who, although from Maranhão, came from the coastal capital city of São Luís. In Farias's novel, Padre Aristides is not a martyr, but a villain: the protagonist, Jonas, joins the column as a way to enact revenge against Aristides for having killed his father. The novel follows Jonas as he joins the Prestes Column and eventually takes part in the violence at Piancó. Farias tells his readers that although the column did commit violence in the interior, it was a necessary act against strongmen who had abused local communities for decades. Within the larger arc of the interior's history, the Prestes Column was just one node—however important—in a broader mythology about the struggle for justice in the backlands.

Commemoration 3: "Prestes Ends His March and Enters History"

On March 7, 1990, Luís Carlos Prestes died of cancer at the age of ninety-two. His passing occurred as Brazil was on the cusp of an important transition. Civilian rule had returned in 1985, yet only in late December 1989 was a president directly chosen by the populace, when Fernando Collor de Mello became Brazil's first democratically elected leader in almost thirty years. But Collor de Mello resigned two years later on the heels of a failed economic policy and a corruption scandal. When Prestes became ill in early March 1990, the spiraling collapse of Brazil's new civilian regime had not begun. Prestes was hospitalized in Rio de Janeiro on March 2, fell into a coma a few days later, and finally passed away on Wednesday, March 7. Collor de Mello was inaugurated as Brazil's president the following Thursday. With the twentieth century drawing to a close, the death of Prestes served as a platform to reflect on Brazil's past as well as its future.

The rally and funeral procession took place in Rio de Janeiro, and most media coverage of the events came from mainstream southwestern outlets. In discussing Prestes's death, newspapers presented the Knight of Hope as a mythologized symbol of national unity whose political currency still drew heavily on his exploits in Brazil's interior. Prestes had been a legendary figure for most of his life, and upon his death he was literally described as a myth. The front page of the *Jornal do Brasil* announced the death of the "Leader and the Myth," and *O Globo* ran an article titled "In the Life of 'The Knight of Hope,' a Brazilian Myth."[46] Prestes was placed squarely in Brazil's pantheon of heroes. In a refraction of the closing lines of Getúlio Vargas's suicide letter—"I leave life to enter history"—one headline declared that "Prestes Ends His March and Enters History."[47] Even in death, Prestes was heralded as a unifying force, with headlines such as "A Rare Unanimity: National Respect" and "At the Final Step, Political Truce."[48] The funeral procession in Rio de Janeiro received similar coverage. As seen in figure 9.8, Prestes's coffin was driven on the open bed of a truck, while crowds marched with it through downtown Rio. Newspapers gave particular attention to the opposition leaders in attendance: two of the pallbearers were Leonel Brizola and Luiz Inácio "Lula" da Silva, arguably the most important leftists during the dictatorship

O caixão de Prestes foi conduzido pelos bombeiros sob muitos aplausos

Rio presta a última homenagem a Prestes

FIGURE 9.8. Cover of *Tribuna da Imprensa*, March 10, 1990. The headline reads: "Rio Gives Prestes the Final Homage."

period and, in the case of Lula, the decades to come. Both men gave speeches at the funeral rally held in Rio de Janeiro's São João Batista cemetery, sharing that, in their final conversations with Prestes, the Knight of Hope had urged them to combine forces.[49] As he had been for much of the twentieth century, Prestes was a symbol of unity for those who envisioned a better future.

Almost every commemoration of Prestes opened with his origin story as the Knight of Hope, through which the fifteen-thousand-mile march across Brazil's interior gave birth to the mythic, unifying figure. As argued throughout this book, the legend of the column rested on a narrative that initially took root when the column crossed into exile, with journalists and politicians in Brazil cultivating a heroic tale that could help bring the rebels back home. In this framing, which became an origin story for both Prestes and modern Brazil, the Knight of Hope had awakened the dark and empty heart of Brazil, transforming rural communities into potential allies and bringing the promise of nationhood to new reaches of the country. As it had been sixty years earlier, the column was depicted as an otherworldly epic, and newspapers devoted lengthy sections to the lionized details of the expedition. The articles expounded on how far the column marched and how many battles it fought in such inhospitable lands. A large map helped readers visualize the journey into the interior and back again. In death, that journey had now come to an end. Fittingly, given the history of how he rose to fame, Luís Carlos Prestes was buried in Rio de Janeiro. The Knight of Hope, despite being forged in the discursive and spatial boundaries of Brazil's interior, was laid to rest exactly where his myth had always resonated most strongly: along the coast.

MEMORY BATTLES AT THE
TURN OF THE CENTURY

Luís Carlos Prestes's death in 1990 opened a new era in the legacy of the Prestes Column. With the Knight of Hope now deceased, a range of politicians, activists, artists, and writers grappled with how to honor a famous, if controversial, Brazilian. As a way to draw to a close this book's interior history of twentieth-century Brazil, this tenth and final chapter explores the memory battles that took place in the 1990s, focusing on three cases: books written about the column, monuments to Luís Carlos Prestes, and the drama that ensued when the family of a conservative tenente donated historical documents to an archive in Rio de Janeiro. A central thread in many of the debates about Prestes's legacy centered on an aspect of the column that had largely fallen out of mainstream discussions since the 1920s: the violent actions of rebel soldiers in the interior. The specter of banditry and violence had always factored into the symbolism of the column, yet in the aftermath of Prestes's death, discussions of rebel violence against interior communities became enmeshed with debates about the political legacy of the Knight of Hope and who—and which regions of the country—had the right to shape public memory.

By approaching the contested meanings of the column at the turn of the century, this chapter does more than simply provide contemporary evidence of the long-standing back-and-forth between proponents and detractors of the column; it also shows how engagement with the Prestes Column in the 1990s signaled a new way to think and write about Brazil's interior. In the context of democratization and a newly robust civil sector, reflections on the Prestes Column, and its passage through the supposedly untouched landscapes of a bygone era, became a way to lament the damage that modernizing projects had inflicted on the nation. At a time when long-held views about developmentalism were being challenged by emerging social critiques, the interior attained a new imaginative role. The "old" Brazil that the column had witnessed in the 1920s was no longer defined solely as a status to be overcome, but could additionally serve as a reminder of what might be possible if the modernizing campaigns of the prior century had never taken place. On the cusp of the twenty-first century, and with the tenente rebels now deceased, the memory battles of the 1990s became a flashpoint for how the symbolism of the column would transition into a new era of Brazilian politics. Old attachments endured, rivalries resurfaced, and, all the while, the interior continued to exist as a potent and adaptive symbol.

Three Journalists Go into the Interior

In the mid-1990s, three journalists helped to put the Prestes Column back in the public spotlight. As part of a common approach to "rediscover" the true history of the column, each of the three writers personally retraced parts or most of the column's route through the interior. The resulting publications were books by Eliane Brum (1994) and Domingos Meirelles (1995), and a ten-part series (1996) in the magazine *Manchete* from Luiz Carlos Prestes Jr., one of Prestes's children with his second wife, Maria. All three conducted interviews with some of the last surviving people in the interior who had interacted with the column, many of whom were in their eighties and nineties.

A useful comparison for understanding the pilgrimage-like retracing of the column's march again comes from Raymond Craib's cartographic history of Mexico. Following Mexico's loss of half its national territory in the 1848 war with the United States, the Mexican government commissioned a series of maps to show Hernán Cortés's route, three centuries earlier, from Veracruz to Mexico City—a symbolic if Eurocentric and violent origin story of the Mexican nation. Craib discusses the challenges of recreating geographic and social landscapes that were central to a process of nation-building: "If

Cortés's travels and travails were acts of national foundation, how could they be contingent and ambiguous? If the nation's roots were to be found in Cortés's route, how could it be anything other than a solid, firm line, boldly coursing across the center of the page?"[1] In this circular logic of space and nation, one should not have to work too hard to find the route, and those along the path should be fully aware of its existence. As such, the three journalists following in the footsteps of the Prestes Column sought to retrace not only the physical march of the tenentes but also its social geography: telling readers what remained the same from the period of the 1920s (proof of certain innate features of the Brazilian nation) and what had changed—a sign of potential threats to the "true" Brazil. Although armed with bylines and tape recorders rather than more traditional cartographic equipment, the three journalists confronted similar challenges of how to represent a spatial history whose literal route reverberated across almost the entire national territory.

The first of the three publications came from Eliane Brum, at the time a junior reporter at the Porto Alegre newspaper *Zero Hora* who has since become one of Brazil's most famous journalists and political commentators. Beginning in January 1993, Brum traveled for 44 days, interviewing 101 people in 50 cities across 15 states. Echoing the serialized coverage of the Prestes Column that was widely popular in the late 1920s, Brum's reporting first appeared in *Zero Hora* in early 1994 as a six-part series. The series proved so successful that, later that year, she published a lengthier version as a book, whose overall scope is stated in its title—*Coluna Prestes: O avesso da lenda* (Prestes Column: The other side of the legend). The book, in essence, is a long oral history of the violence committed by the rebels. In Brum's own assessment, she did not start out seeking evidence of tragedies in the interior, but, as she writes, "once we left Rio Grande do Sul behind, bitter memories began telling a different story, setting us on a darker path. In the villages of the Northeast, as abandoned as they were in the time of the rebellion, the mythical character of the column never showed up and the memories were still as raw as they were [seventy years earlier]."[2]

Media coverage of the book, while tapping into the trope of the interior as a dangerous backland, tended to applaud Brum for offering new perspectives on the dominant narrative. A book review in the *Jornal do Brasil*, for example, that ran under the headline "Journey through an Occult Brazil" compared sections of the book to Hollywood films about the atrocities of the Vietnam War: "Despite the much-celebrated image of Brazilians as 'peaceful creatures,' it is now known, through Eliane's work, that we are capable of the greatest savageries, similar to the situation of U.S. Marines in Vietnam."[3] For Brum, the legacies of the Prestes Column showed that, at the local level in the interior, the tenente rebellion had been a one-sided civil war. Brum's book offered the first major corrective to the heroic mythology of the column. But not everyone welcomed her reporting—most notably Anita Prestes, Luís Carlos Prestes's oldest child, who had been born in a Nazi prison and who would eventually earn a PhD in history and publish several books on the column. Anita Prestes called Brum an "irresponsible and biased" journalist who maligned "the memory of this important episode in our history."[4] Similar versions of this memory battle would continue throughout the decade.

A year after the release of Brum's account, the veteran journalist Domingos Meirelles published a book that returned to the traditional hero narrative. Meirelles titled his work *As noites das grandes fogueiras: Uma história da Coluna Prestes* (The nights of great fires: A history of the Prestes Column). If written, say, by someone with Eliane Brum's analysis, such a title might convey a counterheroic perspective, where the great fires could represent the destruction unleashed at certain moments of the rebel march. Instead, the title is a nostalgic reference to the *fogueira* (meaning "campfire" or "bonfire"), the traditional open pit barbecues that gaucho cowboys use to cook their meat. For Meirelles, the nightly meals shared by the tenentes—itself an exaggeration, given the column's chronic shortage of food—symbolized the bonds of rebel solidarity established in Brazil's interior: "The fires not only inspire ideas but they forge the connections that keep those ideas intertwined, as if they belonged to a common destiny. These conversations around the fire bring out insights and emotions that make those [sitting around the flames] prisoners of each other, handcuffed by the same dreams and passions. The nights spent around these great fires cements the nobility of affection that turns all those men into brothers."[5] The book follows a general narrative, where, in the inhospitable landscapes of Brazil's interior, the nightly fogueira ritual allowed the rebels to rise above their surroundings and reconnect with their true selves. Like that of Brum, Meirelles's book began as a newspaper exposé: in 1974, while working for São Paulo's *Jornal da Tarde*, Meirelles spent two months traveling around the country to prepare a report for the fiftieth anniversary of the tenente revolt of July 5, 1924. Over the next twenty years, while reporting for many of Brazil's leading newspapers, Meirelles worked on the book as a side project, periodically visiting archives to supplement the interviews he had collected. The resulting project received great acclaim. A year after its release, *As noites das grandes fogueiras* won the 1996 Jabuti Prize for the category of reporting, one of Brazil's highest literary honors.

The third and final work from this period was the ten-part exposé by Luiz Carlos Prestes Jr., a journalist at *Manchete* magazine. Compared to the previous two books, the coverage from Prestes Jr. was far more extensive in its engagement with local communities: whereas Eliane Brum and Domingos Meirelles had traveled the country for forty-four days and sixty days, respectively, Prestes Jr. trekked across the interior for ten months between February and December 1995. During his travels, Prestes Jr. also interviewed over three hundred people. The series was then published in early 1996 under the title "Nas trilhas da Coluna Prestes" (In the footsteps of the Prestes Column).[6] The platform of Prestes Jr.'s reporting shaped its contours: *Manchete* was one of Brazil's most popular weekly magazines, full of glossy photographs and covering topics from politics to pop culture—for the first installment of the Prestes Column series, the cover of that week's *Manchete* was the supermodel Naomi Campbell. Prestes Jr.'s reporting thus had a visual element that the other two books did not, as four photographers had accompanied him at different stages of the journey, taking over ten thousand pictures, dozens of which were printed, in full color, in the magazine. Most of these images were of the people and landscapes of the interior, providing readers with a glimpse of the elderly townspeople interviewed by Prestes Jr., as well as the mountains, deserts, forests, rivers, and other features that still stood as remnants of what the column had experienced. The symbolism of Prestes the son retracing the footsteps of Prestes the father was a key feature of the exposé.

As seen in figure 10.1, the series opened with side-by-side photos of the two men, the elder riding a mule in 1925 and the junior seventy years later, similarly bearded but with a camping backpack. The photo's caption explains that Prestes Jr. "retraces the steps of his father and discovers a new Brazilian reality"—a twist on the long-standing narrative of the column having discovered the interior. In total, Prestes Jr.'s *Manchete* series included over one hundred pages filled with photographs, travel descriptions, and lengthy interviews with locals. When the ten-part exposé concluded, the magazine ran a series of letters to the editor from appreciative readers, including one from a history teacher who used the reports in their classroom, and another from a reader who suggested that the series be made into a book.[7] Unlike Eliane Brum and Domingos Meirelles, Prestes Jr. did not end up turning his coverage into a book.

Across the three projects, the journalists shared a common approach of using interviews to try and unearth the "true" history of the Prestes Column. Given how few people from the original events were still alive, it is not surprising that the journalists ended up interviewing several of the same

28 NAS TRILHAS DA
COLUNA PRESTES:
DE PAI PARA FILHO

*Em lombo de mula, Luiz Carlos Prestes
lidera a Coluna na Picada Benjamin, Paraná,
em 1925. Setenta anos depois, Luiz Carlos
Prestes Filho (à direita, com o fotógrafo
Gustavo Stephan), refaz os caminhos do pai
e descobre uma nova realidade brasileira.*

FIGURE 10.1. Luís Carlos Prestes (*left*) and his son (*far right*), for the opening installment of the *Manchete* series "Nas trilhas da Coluna Prestes," January 13, 1996, 3.

townspeople. One such instance reveals the problems of how testimonies can be shaped to fit a particular narrative. In the Paraíba town of Piancó, both Brum and Prestes Jr. interviewed Joana Ferreira da Cruz, the daughter of Padre Aristides, whose throat had been slit by the rebels during the infamous Piancó massacre. Both journalists quote Ferreira da Cruz as telling a similar story, which, interestingly enough, revolved around Anita Prestes. Brum writes that Ferreira da Cruz, along with lamenting the brutality of the massacre, called the rebels liars: "The daughter of Prestes once said in an interview that my father was a cangaceiro. She lied. My father never killed anyone. . . . Prestes and his commanders who then became famous, they never had the courage to step foot here again."[8] In Prestes Jr.'s telling, Ferreira da Cruz provides more or less the same story, but with an entirely separate set of emotions: "Your sister, the historian, she came one time to the state capital (João Pessoa), to give a presentation about the rebels and she said that my father was a cangaceiro. Tell her that that's not true. I think that, even if just that gets clarified, part of Padre Aristides's reputation can be cleansed. . . . Brazil is so big and we shouldn't live with hatred. Seventy years have passed, we shouldn't have crime, or war, or anger."[9]

Without the transcripts of both interviews, there is no way of knowing whether Ferreira da Cruz told different versions of the story, or if the differing approaches or personalities of each journalist elicited different testimonies. But, based only on the printed texts, there is a clear divergence in how her experience was represented: for Brum, Ferreira da Cruz's statement was evidence of a seventy-year grievance, while, for Prestes Jr., the anger she felt at the negative effects on her father's reputation was softened by a personal effort to cultivate forgiveness. In both cases, Ferreira da Cruz wanted to contest the narrative of her father as a bandit. Yet while Brum presents her as a woman stuck in the endless traumas of life in Brazil's interior, Prestes Jr. instead shows a woman trying to move forward. In either portrayal, the original violence and pain is not called into question, but the difference is whether or not people in the interior are depicted as caught in an endless cycle of backland vengeance. Given the complexities of oral history as a source base, wherein multiple truths often coexist, the fact that Ferreira da Cruz offered two versions of the same story is less insightful than the meanings that can be distilled from how different journalists represented her.

The book by Domingos Meirelles provides additional insight into the use of oral sources. Whereas Brum and Prestes Jr. both prioritized the memories and details of people in the interior, Meirelles gave little space to local stories. Of the forty-seven interviews listed in his appendix, a majority were with former soldiers, politicians, and journalists. Only twenty-one so-called witnesses were local inhabitants, of whom only one was actually cited by name in the text of the book itself—the remaining twenty locals were only mentioned in footnotes. The lone in-text reference reflects the romanticized scope of Meirelles's book: he directly cites an interview that he conducted with a flute player named Possidônio Nunes de Queiroz, who remembered composing celebratory music to welcome the column upon its arrival in Oeiras, Piauí.[10] The only interior voice is thus used to reinforce the column's legacy as a triumph of liberation in the backlands.

The three publications also shared an interest in retracing the interior journey as a way to "rediscover" the old Brazil. For Meirelles, his research in the interior was in part an effort to reconnect with a simpler and more rugged Brazilian culture—the fogueira as a nostalgic relic of national virility. For Brum and Prestes Jr., the question of old Brazil related not to the contested legacy of whatever violence the rebels may have done to interior people, but, rather, to what the intervening seventy years of modernization had done to the backland. As shown in earlier chapters, government campaigns in the interior had pointed to its presumed backwardness as justification for contemporary efforts to develop the nation. Getúlio Vargas invoked old Brazil as a way to distance his regime from the First Republic, and the 1960s dictatorship sought to enact a technocratic form of developmentalism, with highways, dams, and modern agriculture in the backlands meant to signal the country's rise as a global power. In both cases, the label of old Brazil was a condition to be overcome through state-led modernization, and it was precisely the result of these development programs that so preoccupied the journalists. Particularly for Brum and Prestes Jr., who wrote in similarly declensionist tones, the disappearance of old Brazil was on stark display in the interior. In the mid-1990s, during the first decade of the return to civilian rule, Brum and Prestes Jr. reflected a backlash against the prevailing type of muscular modernity. If the Prestes Column had previously offered a template for governments to champion development in the backland, for the journalists and their readers, the interior now stood as a vestige of what had been lost.

In the preface to her book, Eliane Brum states that her original goal had been "to discover what the Brazil of Prestes looks like today."[11] To that end, one of her first research activities was to contact Anita Prestes. As recounted by Brum, Prestes received the phone call with sympathy, but said that "the Brazil that the column traversed doesn't exist anymore."[12] Undeterred, Brum continued with her plan to retrace the march.

While the central narrative of Brum's book is the story of rebel violence, a steady subplot concerns the fate of modernity in Brazil. Brum remarks on the destructive legacies of development projects in most regions that she visited, including the Itaipu Dam in the Paraná borderlands that flooded local towns and caused bad harvests for years afterward, the depressed state of Indigenous groups across the country whose lands had been encroached on by large-scale agriculture, and the brutal working conditions on charcoal estates in Minas Gerais. If her initial hope had been to discover the Brazil of old, her journey in the footsteps of the Prestes Column suggested that perhaps she agreed with Anita Prestes after all: maybe the Brazil of the 1920s no longer existed. But, whereas the column had helped amplify the perception that the interior still needed to be discovered, Brum's reporting in the backlands suggested that perhaps mainstream society had done *too much* discovering. Nearly a century's worth of development had exacerbated many problems in the interior.

Prestes Jr. made similar observations about the legacy of old Brazil, though he did so in a slightly more optimistic tone. Like Brum, his hope to find traces of an earlier era led to an awareness about the stark conditions in the interior. In the introduction to his ten-part exposé, readers were told that Prestes Jr. "did not find the Brazil that his father had dreamed of, but rather, in many regions, a nature destroyed."[13] The journalist thought that he would discover the "untouched lands" of old Brazil, but what he saw instead was "the development of the Brazilian interior, which rarely took into account the importance of environmental conservation and the maintenance of our cultural traditions." Toward the beginning of his journey, while traveling in Santa Catarina, Prestes Jr. met an old man named Luiz Vieira Fagundes who had been a soldier in the column. Vieira Fagundes recalled that during the rebellion he and the tenentes learned to appreciate Brazil's landscapes: "Nature used to be a barrier to be overcome. It took a while for it to really sink into your soul. . . . In the middle of the march, in the virgin forests, we discovered the value of the trees and the rivers."[14] For Prestes Jr.'s goal of writing about old Brazil, this quote offers a multivalent form of discovery: not only did the rebel march open Vieira Fagundes's eyes to the natural wonders of Brazil but the journalist's choice of quotation—that "nature used to be a barrier to be overcome"—also reflects the emerging environmentalism at the turn of the century. Like Brum, Prestes Jr. noted the destructive effects of large-scale development projects in the interior, though the son of the Knight of Hope pointed to the perseverance of local communities as proof that perhaps the backlands could still point the way forward. Having retraced almost the entire route that his father had taken seven decades prior, Prestes Jr. concluded that "in the column's wake, there still lives hope that Brazil can achieve a sustainable development."[15] Like his half-sister, Prestes Jr. also wanted his father's legacy to be a beacon of hope—though, rather than a strictly political legacy, he offered an environmental ethos as a new way for readers to find inspiration in Brazil's interior.

The Wayward Memorial: From Prestes in Rio to the Column in the Interior

What began as a proposal to honor Prestes in a posh area of Rio de Janeiro eventually materialized as a monument to the Prestes Column in Palmas, the interior capital city of the recently created state of Tocantins. Designed by Oscar Niemeyer—the famed architect of Brasília—and argued over in the pages of Brazil's major newspapers, the memorial became a highly visible example of the Knight of Hope's contested legacy.

In the aftermath of Prestes's death, supporters began pursuing commemoration projects. Many of these efforts took place in Rio de Janeiro, including renaming an avenue and a park after him.[16] By early 1992, a campaign emerged to do more than change the names on street signs or plaques: proponents wanted to construct an entire memorial complex, to be built in Barra da Tijuca, a wealthy suburb of Rio. Initially put forward by a city councilman from the Democratic Labor Party (PDT), the project received financial and political support from a wide range of groups. The memorial's building was planned by Niemeyer, its interior designed by the noted artist Carlos Scliar, and the exhibitions curated by the journalist Nelson Werneck Sodré. The project was also supported by the municipal secretary for public planning as well as the national secretary for culture, who pledged federal funding to cover one-third of the memorial's estimated cost of Cr$1.15 billion (US$300,000).[17] Niemeyer, who had been a close friend of Prestes and a fellow member of the Brazilian Communist Party, designed the memorial in his accustomed modernist style, with a concrete, elongated dome building comprised of two floors—a glass-enclosed exhibition hall on top, and an auditorium, an archive, and a set of offices below. From the main building, a circling ramp would take visitors up to the memorial's key feature: an elevated statue of Prestes.

Almost immediately, the project sparked controversy, with much of the drama revolving around where the memorial would be built. Barra da Tijuca is an affluent area of Rio de Janeiro, located on a stretch of beachfront property fifteen miles southwest of downtown—at the time, this area was effectively inaccessible to citizens of Rio who relied on public transit, as a metro would not reach Barra for two more decades. The plan called for constructing the memorial on five hundred square meters of the São Perpétuo Plaza, directly across from the Barra beach, and only a few minutes from the posh Itanhangá Golf Club. This location angered many who saw Prestes as a symbol of Brazil's popular classes. In a letter to O Globo, one person mocked the so-called experts (bambas) involved in the project: "Did it not occur to anyone that Barra da Tijuca, a bastion of the [upper] middle class, is the least suitable place to house this memorial? What does Luís Carlos Prestes have to do with a neighborhood of the Carioca bourgeoisie? It should be one of the plazas . . . where workers and their families actually walk through."[18] A similar letter compared the memorial controversy to the larger scandal unfolding in Brazil at that moment—the impeachment trial of President Fernando Collor—and vented in frustration that "people have enough of all this quixotic blah blah blah from these politicians who have only taken the country into chaos. I fully agree that the chosen location is not appropriate: Barra is for ocean, beaches, and relaxing. Luiz Carlos Prestes should be about land, the people, and work."[19] If Barra da Tijuca was deemed inappropriate for a memorial to the Knight of Hope, where might be a better option? That question would not get resolved for several more years.

Over the final months of 1992, when the nation's collective attention span became increasingly sucked into the unfolding impeachment of President Collor, the proposed memorial in Barra da Tijuca got pushed back until it dissolved all together. The initial opposition, from right- and left-wing commentators alike, achieved its goals, and the project was shelved. Not only was it unclear whether the memorial would be built in Barra da Tijuca but it also appeared possible that it might never get built at all.

A few years later, a fortuitous march through the interior revived the project. While retracing his father's footsteps for the *Manchete* exposé, Prestes Jr. was introduced to José Wilson Siqueira Campos, the governor of Tocantins. The state of Tocantins was Brazil's newest territory, formed in 1988 out of a northern portion of Goiás. In October 1925, the Prestes Column had stayed in the river town of Porto Nacional in what was then the state of Goiás. During his travels seventy years later, Prestes Jr. went to Porto Nacional and then visited Palmas, the state capital of Tocantins. While in Palmas, Prestes Jr. met with Governor Siqueira Campos, and, upon learning of the governor's personal admiration for the Knight of Hope, he suggested that his father's stalled memorial project be revived and brought to Tocantins.[20] Siqueira Campos—who claimed to be a distant cousin of Antônio Siqueira Campos, the Hero of Copacabana—had almost single-handedly led the movement to create Tocantins, and he saw a memorial as part of his larger goal to cultivate a creation myth for his newly created state. As observed by Patricia Orfila Barros dos Reis, a scholar of architecture in the region, it was clear that "the symbolic use of a memorial with no direct identity with the city of Palmas, or even with the contemporary history of Tocantins, belonged to his efforts of installing a myth in the popular imaginary."[21] But, given that Siqueira Campos was a right-wing politician who had been a fervent ally of the military dictatorship, the question remains why he would want to attach himself to the myth of Brazil's leading communist.

Rather than creating a memorial to Luís Carlos Prestes, as had originally been planned for Barra da Tijuca, the project was given a new name. In Tocantins, it became the Memorial to the Prestes Column. What was eventually inaugurated in 2001 (fig. 10.2) retained the exact layout and scope of the initial 1992 design. Yet the name switch subtly shifted of attention away from Prestes and toward the column. This imaginative adjustment, lacking any substantive change, reflected the column's enduring symbolism as a pliant beacon of nationhood.

Even a conservative governor could eagerly welcome an homage to Brazil's leading communist because the project could be used as a broader

FIGURE 10.2. Memorial to the Prestes Column, Palmas, Tocantins. Photo by author.

political tool—in this case, to give a newly created state an affected connection to national history. In this way, it was not dissimilar from the attempts
by Getúlio Vargas and his allies in the 1930s to disentangle the newly radical
Prestes from his role in the legendary march across the interior. As a person,
Prestes was a potential lightning rod of controversy, but as the Knight of
Hope he was an adaptive symbol of Brazil. For Siqueira Campos, at the head
of a new state located in central Brazil, the memorial was an opportunity to
reinforce the notion that Tocantins represented the true heart of the country.
As such, the project was given a pilgrimage into the interior. The statue of
Prestes, a bronze sculpture weighing four hundred kilograms and standing
nearly three meters tall, was built in Rio de Janeiro and then taken on a four-
thousand-mile journey in the back of a van.[22] Prestes's widow, Maria, accompanied the statue on its month-long excursion, which included stops at six
cities along the way to hold public commemorations with local leaders. At
each stop, Maria and the local officials ceremoniously wrapped the statue in
a Brazilian flag. When the statue arrived in Palmas, a front-page headline of
the *Jornal do Tocantins* triumphantly declared: "Prestes in the Heart of Brazil, Because Brazil Was His Heart."[23] Nearly a century after his initial journey,
the Knight of Hope went inland again.

Less than a decade removed from the creation of Tocantins, the memorial also showed the influence and creativity of interior regions. Not only had Tocantins' governor successfully led a project that had proved too troublesome for Rio de Janeiro but he also paired the Memorial to the Prestes Column with a second piece of public commemoration that installed an even more literal coastal presence in the interior. Built less than one hundred meters south of the column's memorial was a monument to the Copacabana revolt of 1922—the initial spark of the tenentista movement that begat the Prestes Column. The memorial showed eighteen soldiers atop a replica of the swirling black-and-white mosaics that famously adorn the pavements along Copacabana Beach (fig. 10.3).

With Prestes's bronze statue standing guard near a stairway linking the two memorials, the Copacabana monument imaginatively bridged the gap between Palmas and the Rio coastline over one thousand miles away. By transposing Brazil's most iconic beach into the backland, the distance between coast and interior gave way to a fused sense of space and nation. For longtime supporters of the memorial, its eventual location in Palmas showed that Brazil's interior could serve as a safety valve for coastal tension: with

FIGURE 10.3. Monument to the Eighteen of Copacabana, with the Memorial to the Prestes Column in the background. Palmas, Tocantins. Photo by author.

more available space and with fewer likely opponents, the backlands offered a physical refuge for a symbolic form of public commemoration. And, for Governor Siqueira Campos, the construction of these memorials showed how interior spaces and leaders could also assert their ability to shape the telling of national stories.

Drama in the Archives

A year after the bronze statue of Prestes arrived in Palmas, new drama emerged when a large cache of documents was donated to an archive in Rio de Janeiro. The material belonged to Juarez Távora, the commander in the Prestes Column who became a leading conservative politician in the middle decades of the twentieth century. Távora had passed away in 1975, though it was not until 1999 that his family donated his personal files to the Center for Research and Historical Documentation (CPDOC) at the Fundação Getúlio Vargas in Rio de Janeiro. The collection counted nearly 30,000 documents from throughout Távora's long career in politics, including 586 letters, maps, and reports from the Prestes Column. As shown in chapter 4, when the rebels passed through Távora's home state of Ceará in early 1926 the leadership decided to leave much of the column's archive-to-date at the Távora family home for safekeeping. It was for that reason that a key archive of the rebellion remained in Távora's possession.

To publicize the new archival holdings, CPDOC hosted an exhibition in March 1999, which focused largely on the nearly six hundred items relating to the Prestes Column. The most controversial were a set of documents that mentioned the violence committed by rebel soldiers. An article in *O Estado de São Paulo* called these items "the filet mignon of the archive." The newspaper gave excerpts from two of the most revealing documents. The first was a letter from an inhabitant of Formoso, Goiás, who wrote to the rebel leaders seeking compensation for the damage done by rebel troops, whom he accused of stealing his property and then setting his house on fire. The second was a report from Miguel Costa, who described his shock at seeing a town recently seized by the rebels: "I arrived here today, where complete anarchy reigns, installed by the inhumane looting . . . practiced here. Taking what is required for the troops . . . is a very different thing from practicing theft, arson and all the depredations that are found here."[24]

Media attention included a full range of opinions. On one side was Eliane Brum, who held up the archival findings as vindication of her book.[25] On another side was Anita Prestes, who had long championed the belief that any such criticism was an attack on her father.[26] In the aftermath of the exhibit at CPDOC, Anita Prestes stated that unfortunate excesses are a common feature in all wars: "It was an army at war, not a stroll in the woods. . . . Focusing on these excesses has the explicit and ideological goal of denigrating the figure of Prestes and that of the column's participants."[27] Others welcomed the newly released documents, including two noted historians. Décio Freitas, a former member of the PCB, wrote that, although Prestes never directly "authorized the disgraceful acts, [the documents] are proof of an unforgivable laxity," and Boris Fausto stated that "documentation about [this history] is sparse and the files of Juarez Távora may open an interesting vein."[28] A researcher at CPDOC named Regina da Luz Moreira linked the violence to the composition of the rebel forces, but with a key twist that seemed to absolve the "original" rebels for the violence, blaming it instead on people elsewhere in the interior: "Along the march, [the column] was joined by adventurers and people from local towns who were drawn to the myth of the column, but who, probably, had never even heard of President Artur Bernardes."[29] Such suggestions are implausible: not only did relatively few people join the column during its march but there is also no evidence of the violent soldiers' origins. Moreover, they reflect a larger theme of defining the backlands by its presumed violence and justifying any in-turn aggression that noninterior groups may have demonstrated.

The Távora archive was not the first time that similar documents had been made public. Nearly a decade earlier, and with no fanfare, the personal files of Lourenço Moreira Lima were donated by his family to the Edgard Leuenroth Archive at the State University of Campinas, an hour north of the city of São Paulo. The Leuenroth Archive—named in honor of a radical journalist and publisher—is one of Brazil's best collections of historical and media documents relating to left-wing politics and social movements. Moreira Lima's family gave his files to the archive in the 1980s, thus making available significant primary sources from the Prestes Column, including key documents that the rebels had not left with the Távora family in Ceará.[30] Compared to the somewhat oblique documents from the Távora archive (e.g., the letter from a local and Miguel Costa's observations about the conduct of the rebels), the Moreira Lima files contain explicit details of violence. Among the archive is the full record of thirty-one bulletins from the rebel high command, two of which discuss the punishments of unruly soldiers. In the first instance, two rebels were placed in confinement for having looted a farm in Mato Grosso, and the second, more egregious, example was that the rebel leadership executed four of its own soldiers by firing squad, one of whom had raped a woman in Goiás. As discussed in chapter 4, Moreira Lima omitted these incriminating details from his book; so did Anita Prestes. Even if these authors sought to protect certain aspects of the column's heroic aura, the archival record suggested otherwise. Yet the evidence at the Leuenroth Archive seems to have gone unnoticed. While the Távora files in the large CPDOC archive in Rio de Janeiro sparked controversy, Moreira Lima's far more explicit documents remained out of the public eye in a smaller archive. This relative obscurity persisted for three decades: as far as I can tell, I am the first person to publish the full details included in these files.

Another archive to Prestes and the column is currently in formation. Anita Prestes collected many documents from her father, and she always wanted to find a permanent home for the materials. As she told me during a Zoom video chat, she began corresponding in 2016 with archivists at the Federal University of São Carlos (UFSCar), and two years later an exhibit at the university's central library inaugurated the creation of the Prestes collection.[31] The preparation of the archive itself (e.g., preservation and cataloging) remains ongoing. At the present moment, the collection is still not available to the general public, though librarians can scan and share documents directly with interested scholars. I benefited from this process and was able to include many of the documents in this book.

When I learned that Anita Prestes had donated her collection to UFSCar, I became very excited. São Carlos is in the interior of São Paulo state, and my mind jumped to the possibility that perhaps Anita had chosen UFSCar as a way to bring her father's historical memory closer to where his legend had symbolically been born. That was not the case. As Anita told me, her decision was almost purely logistical. UFSCar had a well-developed center for preserving and curating historical documents, and it offered the space and personnel to receive the Prestes material. To the extent that any personal reasons nudged Anita Prestes toward UFSCar, it had nothing to do with the interior or the column. The family of Florestan Fernandes, one of Brazil's most influential sociologists and a friend of Luís Carlos Prestes, had donated his files to UFSCar. Anita Prestes liked the idea of having their archives under the same roof.[32]

At no conscious level, then, did the interior factor into Anita Prestes's decision. Given my own tendency to seek interior symbolism in everything, this was a useful reminder: not everything in the interior is *about* the interior. The goal remains to explore when and why particular meanings get invoked. This matters for a history of the Prestes Column and for any history of the people and spaces across the many interiors of Brazil.

In September 2021, only a few months after I first drafted this chapter on memory battles, I received a WhatsApp message from Luiz Carlos Prestes Jr. He wanted to let me know that a conservative councilwoman in Rio Grande do Sul had introduced legislation to change the name of a memorial in Prestes's hometown of Porto Alegre. Back in 1990, shortly after Prestes died, the city council of Porto Alegre approved a memorial project and set aside a plot of land along the Jacuí River, just south of the city's historical center. Progress was slow, though, unlike the proposed monument in Rio de Janeiro, the Porto Alegre project did remain in its original location: the groundbreaking ceremony took place in 1998, but it then took another 11 years for construction to actually begin, and the memorial did not open until 2017. Unlike in Palmas, the memorial retained its intended name and was called the Memorial Luiz Carlos Prestes.

The memorial had operated for several years without any sustained form of opposition, but, under the presidency of far-right president Jair Bolsonaro, it became a manufactured platform of ideological conflict. A right-wing councilwoman named Nádia Gerhard—who went by the name Comandante Nádia, having previously served as an army lieutenant-colonel—sought to strip the name of Prestes from the memorial. Claiming that a "historical correction" was necessary to remove the name of "a traitor to the nation," the councilwoman proposed renaming it as the "Memorial to the City of Porto Alegre."[33] Although she did not elaborate, the implication was that the contents of the museum would also change, with the life history of Prestes removed entirely.

It was precisely this threat of historical erasure that so worried Prestes's son. In his message to me, Prestes Jr. compared his father to Tiradentes, an eighteenth-century revolutionary leader of the Brazilian independence movement: "It took 100 years for Tiradentes to be recognized as a hero. While his enemies were still alive, they did everything they could to stop it. Tiradentes symbolized an uncomfortable truth about the shittyness of the Brazilian elite. It will take 200 years for the truth about Prestes to spread its light. Many of his enemies are still alive."[34] In the ongoing memory battles that shape politics and national identity in Brazil, with different sides locked in a battle to define history, public spaces of memorialization—and the names attached to them—seem likely to remain as polemical as ever.

Memory Sites in the Interior

Even while harboring a healthy criticism of the pilgrimage hagiography that has long dominated studies of the Prestes Column, I knew that I also had to travel through the interior. Because no witnesses to the march were still alive, and because I knew that simply retracing the column's footsteps would offer little in the way of new insight, I chose to organize my interior journey around a specific set of locations: memory sites. In his canonical study of *lieux de mémoire* (memory places), the French historian Pierre Nora argues that memory sites are "at once natural and artificial, simple and ambiguous, concrete and abstract, they are lieux—places, sites, causes."[1] For Nora and countless other scholars and writers, memory sites offer an important, if complex, window into the function of particular places within the collective memory of social groups as well as nations more broadly.

Rather than follow directly in the column's path, I charted an itinerary that linked a dozen monuments, tombstones, and museums that memorialized different aspects of the Prestes Column's march across the interior. The memory sites varied in size, from small roadside structures to a large building designed by Brazil's most famous architect. Half of the twelve sites were "pro-column" (championing a heroic view of the march), three sites were decidedly anti-column (built to honor those who had died fighting the rebels), and three were more neutral, wherein the passage of the column was presented mostly as a part of local history. The memory sites were physical proof of the themes discussed throughout this book, including the power dynamics of how local spaces in the interior could garner attention from wider audiences. Better-funded projects with connections to public figures in Rio de Janeiro tended to depict the column in triumphant terms, while the countermyth memorials were far smaller and existed outside of a mainstream spotlight.

Another key element was the interior's status as a refuge from coastal problems. Here, I was the one seeking refuge. I set off for a research trip in November and December of 2020, during one of the only early ebbs of the COVID-19 pandemic in Brazil—a relative term, of course, given the scores of people still dying every day. Knowing that population density was much lower outside of the major cities along the coast, I felt comfortable taking a trip across the interior. Mostly, I would be traveling by rental car, and, because I felt no need to retrace the column's exact steps, I also took several flights within the country to save time. Cities in the interior were by no means safe from the pandemic; nor was I immune from spreading the disease to them, were I to contract it along the way. But a research visit to the interior seemed feasible in a way that could not have happened in major coastal areas. And, although I did plan to visit a few archives along the way, my primary objective was not to read documents or interview people. Instead, I planned to observe the interior by visiting the dozen memory sites and watching the landscapes pass by my window as I drove, alone, for nearly two thousand miles. With a global pandemic making it difficult, and ethically dubious, to spend much time with individuals along the way, my focus was to visually experience the interior. Memory sites were a way to link my observations in the present with an understanding of how different communities have sought to commemorate their place in history.

Throughout my travels, I sought to remain as attuned as possible to why and how I moved through the spaces of the interior: Were my years of reading and reflection enough to see beyond my own coastal gaze? In the prism of perspectives on the interior, could I entirely shift my own vantage point? Probably not, but perhaps that was not the point. Rather than try to ignore or rationalize away the dominant narrative that preconditioned how I might interpret the interior, I hoped to find a balance between what I saw and my awareness of the tropes that filtered what I saw. Even if my inland travels were more self-aware than that of the tenente rebels a century earlier, I also wondered if I was not so different from them. Like the leaders of the column, my journey served my own (professional) purposes, and I similarly moved on after a few days at each stop—a byproduct, yes, of wanting to stay in motion during a pandemic, but also a reflection of a research agenda that at times required little more than parking in front of a statue and taking some pictures. As a historian in pursuit of memory sites, and with few planned conversations on my itinerary, my role was not always clear. Was I caught somewhere between being a traveler and a tourist, as reflected on by Ilan Stavans and Joshua Ellison in their fascinating work on travel writing?[2] Knowing that my book, despite its eventual Portuguese translation, was imagined largely for an Anglophone audience, would my analysis reproduce the same type of "imperial vision" that shaded colonial-era chronicles of Brazil's interior? With these questions at the front of my mind, I joined a long history of outsiders, motivated by a wide range of personal and financial reasons, who went into Brazil's interior looking for a story to tell.

* * *

Like most writers in the footsteps of the column, I began in Santo Ângelo, the town in Rio Grande do Sul where Luís Carlos Prestes led an uprising of gaúcho rebels on October 28, 1924. Although it was a bit clichéd to begin my travels here, I chose to start from what has become the symbolic birthplace of the Prestes Column.

After a twenty-two-hour series of flights from Europe to Brazil, I picked up my rental car in the state capital of Porto Alegre and drove six hours inland to Santo Ângelo. My main goal was to visit the Memorial da Coluna Prestes, which the municipal government had created in December 2004 by converting the town's old railroad station into a museum. The station had been where Prestes led his initial uprising, and the museum project was an effort to preserve the century-old building as a memory site for the town's most famous episode. In the months leading up to my travels, I had tried many times to contact the museum. Because of the pandemic, I was never able to get a firm answer about whether or not the museum was open. I went to Santo Ângelo all the same. In a twist of small-town good fortune, the woman in charge of my Airbnb used to work at the museum, and within twenty minutes of my arrival she had called someone who called someone who arranged a visit. The pandemic had indeed shuttered the museum, but, with the helpful nudge of my Airbnb host, the tourism office opened it just for me.

The next morning, I walked to the museum, a small building with a yellow façade and a brown-tiled roof (fig. E.1). I was greeted by a woman named

Aurora, who had very kindly opened the museum for me. Inside, I followed a sequence of displays and dioramas laid out in a half-dozen rooms. Most of the exhibits focused on the column, from the initial events in Santo Ângelo all the way through its termination in Bolivia. Having been unsure which aspects of the column's myth would be lionized—or potentially ignored—I was happily surprised to see a nearly floor-to-ceiling banner in homage of the "vivandeiras: revolutionary women." With images and descriptions of the vivandeiras, the banner proclaimed that, "amid the silence of history, the vivandeiras made history on the battlefields." I was equally surprised to see that the attic of the museum had been converted into an homage to another woman, one who had no direct connection with the column: Olga Benário. The area for Olga included the fake travel documents that she and Luís Carlos Prestes had used to sneak into Brazil, as well as the ID card of baby Anita Prestes, issued by Nazi authorities in Berlin and stamped with five swastikas. Although Olga has become a recognizable symbol in Brazil, her communist bona fides would seem to present a complicating factor for a small-town museum in southern Brazil. When I asked Aurora what she thought about the fact that Prestes eventually became a radical, she said that she was not a fan of communism and preferred not to talk about that side of his life. The visitor logbook echoed these sentiments—one entry declared that Brazil should "do away with Marxism." In large part because Luiz Carlos Prestes Jr. and his mother, Maria, had been active in creating the museum, the curation did not shy away from this history. In addition to the exhibit on Olga, several artifacts from Prestes's years as the PCB leader were on display.

By this point in my research, I had already spent many years thinking about the intertwined histories of Prestes and the column, but I was not entirely sure how much they would coexist at different locations across the country. At this first stop, at least, where Prestes's family had donated items and helped get the project off the ground, it was clear that a museum to the column would be about more than just the march. I was curious to see how this would continue along my travels.

Before leaving Santo Ângelo, I walked a mile along the main road leading into town. Six years prior to the creation of the museum, Santo Ângelo had inaugurated a different monument to the column: a forty-foot-tall concrete sculpture designed by Oscar Niemeyer. This was one of three replicas erected across Brazil, the other two being in Santa Helena in the state of Paraná, and Arraias in Tocantins. I would later learn that Prestes Jr. had also organized the creation of these three monuments—a continuation of his efforts to shepherd the Palmas memorial into existence. There are several interpretations

FIGURE E.1. Memorial to the Prestes Column, Santo Ângelo, Rio Grande do Sul. Photo by author.

of what the sculpture represents. It could be a lightning bolt meant to signal the column's liberating strike across the dormant lands of old Brazil; it could be a horse rearing back on its hind legs, a nod to the gaucho cowboys and the legendary Knight of Hope; or it could be a piece of vertical cartography, tracing the zigzagging march across the country. Niemeyer himself never publicly said what it represented. The plaque at the base of the monument states: "In tribute to the revolutionary march that began in Santo Ângelo, on October 28, 1924, and traveled twenty-five thousand kilometers across four-teen Brazilian states, leaving its heroic mark on the conscience of the nation." As such, a small town in the interior region of a southern borderland could hold itself aloft as the cradle of a foundational moment for modern Brazil.

From Santo Ângelo, I wound my way through the backroads of Rio Grande do Sul toward a monument to the battle at Ramada. This was the site of one of the bloodiest conflicts of the entire rebellion. But the monument was not for the rebels—it honored the nearly one hundred loyalist soldiers killed by Prestes's men. Ramada was the name of a nearby farm in the 1920s, and all I had as reference was the name of a crossing point somewhere nearby. The rural intersection, called Esquina Urma, was in the middle of a seemingly endless sea of soybean fields. Looking out at the fields extending in every direction—the legacy of another form of gaucho myth-making in the interior, the 1970s soy boom—I imagined that this was precisely the sort of landscape that the journalists of the 1990s would have lamented as a sign of "old" Brazil being destroyed by modern development. I walked to one of the few houses within eyeshot and talked to an older man sitting outside who gave me directions for the final mile. The monument consisted of four items in a large gravel plot: a white concrete tomb honoring the fallen soldiers, a metal lantern, a display sign with historical details (which had fallen to the ground, perhaps recently, perhaps long ago) and a statue of Jesus with open arms (fig. E.2). The mix of iconography made further sense when I read the inscription on the tomb: it had been inaugurated in October 1964. An homage to loyalist soldiers who had died fighting against Prestes thus served as a patriotic and pious counternarrative in the early phases of Brazil's new dictatorship.

My next stop was equally out of the way and also seemed to receive few visitors. In the northernmost region of Rio Grande do Sul, near the Uruguay River that forms the border with Santa Catarina, lays the town of Tenente Portela, named after the rebel leader Mário Portela Fagundes, who died in an ambush attack while drinking tea and waiting to cross the river. In 1999, to mark the centenary of Portela's birth, the town built a monument at the spot where he was killed. I drove from the namesake town to a small village called Pinheiro do Vale, and then five miles along dirt and stone roads. The monument had been constructed in collaboration with the local tourism office, which evidently hoped that the memory site would draw in nature enthusiasts: an "ecological trail" invited visitors through the jungle toward the Portela monument. Two decades after its creation, the nature path was almost entirely overgrown. A few littered beer cans were the only evidence of use. After ten minutes of walking, I arrived at the memorial site. On an embankment just above a small inlet of the Uruguay River, a tombstone lay next to two rows of small white crosses, representing Portela and the other rebels killed. The white crosses and the tan bricks surrounding the monument stood out against the dense green of the surrounding forest canopy.

A four-hour drive due north took me to Dionísio Cerqueira, a Santa Catarina city known mostly as a customs depot along the Argentine border. I had come to meet Mauro Prado, a high school history teacher who had previously served as a local *vereador* (councilman). I learned about Mauro on Facebook, where I stumbled upon a video he had recorded in 2020 as part of his reelection campaign. In it, Mauro spoke to viewers from an old cemetery just outside of town that consisted of a century-old wooden cross making the

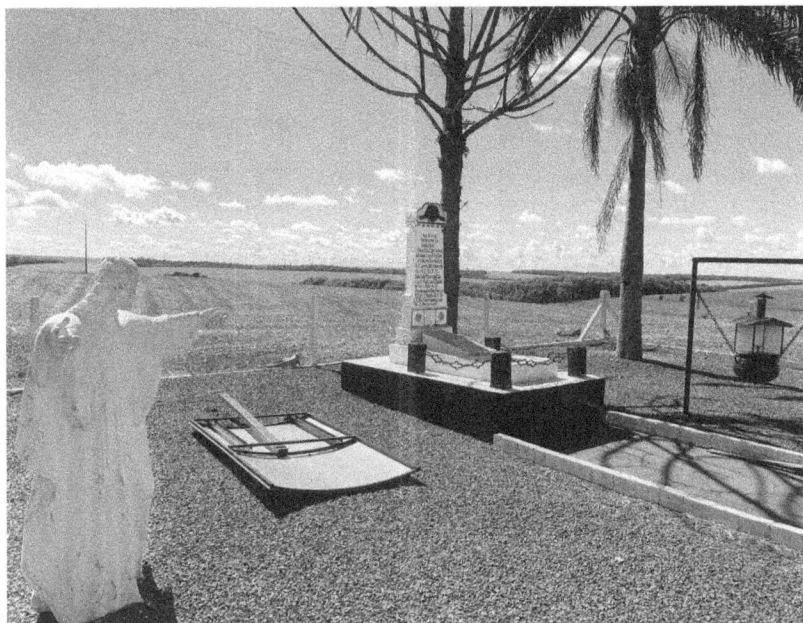

FIGURE E.2. Memorial to loyalist soldiers, near Esquina Urma, Rio Grande do Sul. Photo by author.

graves of government soldiers killed by the rebels (fig. E.3). Mauro met me one morning outside my hotel, and I followed him in my car to the cemetery. There he explained that he had been part of a local effort in 2011 to protect the area by building a concrete wall to keep out cows from an adjacent farm. A decade later, the area was still in need of renovations—the commemorative plaques had all but faded and the front gate hung precariously on rusted hinges. Mauro was proud of the work they had done, but knew that the cemetery required more attention. Similar to the pitch from his campaign video, he told me that it could be an important tourism site for the city, and he wanted to build a small museum that would include detailed signs, historical artifacts, and a glass enclosure to preserve the wooden cross. Mauro's failed reelection bid complicated his planned renovation project. However, he told me that he would continue to seek funding.

From Dionísio Cerqueira I continued north into Paraná, veering east around the Iguaçu National Park and following the Paraná River toward Foz do Iguaçu. En route, I drove past the city of Santa Helena and turned left onto the Prestes Column Highway, a stretch of road that led me a short distance toward the Ipanema River. There, at a spot where Prestes's troops had evaded

FIGURE E.3. Screenshot of Facebook video posted by Mauro Prado, October 21, 2020.

enemy forces by setting a bridge on fire, a series of concrete monuments had been erected to honor the rebels. Both the memorial and the renamed highway were part of the memory initiatives led by Luiz Carlos Prestes Jr. As he had in Santo Ângelo, Prestes Jr. arranged the construction of an Oscar Niemeyer monument—the same vertical statue that was either a horse, or lightning, or a map. Across from the Niemeyer piece, several concrete posts were laid out in a semicircle, and an information board was nestled among a grove of trees, though whatever text had initially been inscribed was no longer visible. What was legible, however, were a series of names carved into the concrete posts. Far from being homages to anyone related to the Prestes Column, the names appeared to be of young couples: *David and Cristina, Marco and Elaine, Karine and Daniel*. Probably not what Prestes Jr. and Niemeyer had in mind, but at least people were visiting.

After nearly two weeks tacking fairly closely to the column's march, I then jumped forward quite a bit. The next memory site on my itinerary was over one thousand miles away, in Mato Grosso. This required going to Foz do Iguaçu and flying to the Mato Grosso capital of Cuiabá, where I rented another car and drove to Barra do Bugres, a small town on the Paraguay River. This was where the column fought one of its final battles before ending the rebellion in Bolivia. Nearly seventy years later, in 1995, the town constructed a memorial to "Fifteen Martyrs" who had died defending the town against the rebel passage (fig. E.4). The centerpiece of the memorial is a forty-foot metal statue of a Mato Grosso fighter, with hat, poncho, and rifle aimed over the Paraguay River, ready to defend the town. A plaque lay just behind the statue, on an elevated concrete platform. But, to read the inscription honoring the fifteen fallen locals, I had to move aside an old plastic bag, partially filled with liquid, that had seemingly calcified onto the metal engraving. Along with listing the fifteen names, the plaque also provided commentary on how they died: "At first light on November 20, 1926, from the other side of the river, where they had arrived during the night, the rebels unleashed a surprise attack against the defenders of this peaceful village." Here, in local memory lore, there was no question as to who the real bandits had been.

Four days and three connecting flights later, I arrived in Palmas, the capital of Tocantins. As discussed in the previous chapter, neither the city of Palmas nor the state of Tocantins existed at the time of the Prestes Column, yet in the 1990s it became an unexpected center of tenente memorialization. Eager to tether his new state to a piece of symbolic national history, Governor José Wilson Siqueira Campos had, with the initial nudging of Prestes's oldest son, overseen the construction of two monuments in the city center, just a stone's throw from the governor's palace. The first was the Memorial to the Prestes Column, a slightly changed title from the original memorial to Luís Carlos Prestes that had been planned for a posh area of Rio de Janeiro. The second was the Monument to the Eighteen of Copacabana, complete with a replica of the stone pavement that rings the famous beach. Accompanying me on my visit to the memorials was Patricia Orfila Barros, an architecture professor whose work I had come across in preparation for the trip, and a young art student named Saulo, who worked at the museum. I saw the large statue of Prestes that had traveled up from Rio de Janeiro in 1998, as well as the display of artifacts and reproduced documents in the museum's large gallery space. Because the museum had undergone few changes from the initially planned memorial to Prestes, it retained a large focus on Prestes's life. Behind the display of Prestes memorabilia, for example, a wall-sized photo shows him shaking hands with Fidel Castro. The three of us spent a fun afternoon together, as thunderclouds slowly gathered on the summer horizon. Between the two of them, Patricia and Saulo plied me with more anecdotes than I could have hoped for. While I already knew a bit about Governor

FIGURE E.4. Monument to the Fifteen Martyrs, Barra do Bugres, Mato Grosso, built in 1995. Photo by author.

Siqueira Campos's personal motivations to build the monuments, I had no idea that it veered into a vanity project. For the monument to the Copacabana soldiers, the governor had the lead figure made in his likeness, with the bronze face of the flag-wielding leader made to resemble that of Tocantin's larger-than-life governor (fig. E.5). A good reminder that monuments are not only about the subject they explicitly memorialize; they are also part of the legacy of those who get them built.

It was while staying in Palmas that I made what I would hope was my only questionable decision. My planned itinerary for Tocantins included seeing the second horse-lightning-map sculpture designed by Oscar Niemeyer. As in Santa Helena, Luiz Carlos Prestes Jr. had helped to orchestrate the renaming of a state highway, and the plan was to take the Rodovia Coluna Prestes south of Palmas to the town of Arraias, where the Niemeyer sculpture stood along the side of the road. The only problem was that Arraias was a five-hour drive away. I have no doubt that traveling across southern Tocantins would have been enriching, but after almost a month on the road I felt pretty unenthused about a ten-hour trip to see the same sculpture I had already seen elsewhere. Knowing that I was scheduled to visit the third sculpture later in

FIGURE E.5. Monument to the Eighteen of Copacabana, Palmas, Tocantins. Photo by author.

the month, and with an eye toward trying to maintain my stamina for the long drive across the Northeast, I opted to skip Arraias.

After my stay in Palmas, which did not exist at the time of the column, I went to a city that the rebels had indeed passed through. Nestled on the southern bank of the Tocantins River, the town of Porto Nacional has a special place in the lore of the Prestes Column. It was where, in what at the time belonged to the state of Goiás, the column spent two weeks in late 1925. As mentioned throughout this book, a picture taken of the rebel high command in front of the Porto Nacional convent—with a bearded Prestes sitting in the front row—became arguably the march's most famous image. With the help of Patricia Orfila Barros, the architecture professor in Palmas, I arranged to visit the town's history museum, a small two-story rowhouse a few blocks from the river. Luzinete, an older woman who runs the museum, showed me through each of the museum's four main exhibit rooms, which included items dating back several hundred years. In a back corner on the second floor, a large poster board offered a few paragraphs about the column's passage through Porto Nacional, displaying a large print of the iconic photo in front of the convent. Although the sign included a direct quotation from the memoir of Father Audrin, it gave only a positive description of the column's passage through town. Absent was any mention of Audrin's frustration that the rebels had overstayed their welcome. As I quoted in chapter 3, Audrin's initial enthusiasm at the column's arrival soon dissolved, and he later declared that "the title of 'the Undefeated Column' is inaccurate, I prefer, if you will, the 'Column of Death.'" As one aspect of the museum's larger presentation of local history, it opted for a less complex narrative about the rebels' time in Porto Nacional. I asked Luzinete about the column, and she said that she wished the original convent building was still around, so that people could recreate the famous photo.

From Tocantins, I drove farther into the Northeast. My first stop was in Carolina, Maranhão, where the town's history museum was far more developed than in Porto Nacional. Though small in size, Carolina benefited from its proximity to the Chapada das Meses National Park, which in nonpandemic times attracts a steady amount of tourism. In the center of one of the museum's main rooms was the original printing press that the rebels had used to print the eighth issue of *O Libertador*, a copy of which was displayed prominently. This was the first full copy of any issue of the rebel bulletin that I had yet to find.

Almost a week later, after making my way across Piauí, I arrived at Crateus in the state of Ceará. This town had two memory sites to the column. The first was a cemetery where two rebel soldiers were buried. Like the "ecological trail" in Tenente Portela, this monument had been envisioned as a mixed-use tourism and leisure park. The welcome sign stated "Municipal Natural Monument—the Cavaliers of Hope." The sign, however, had seen far better days. The bottom right corner seemed to have suffered fire damage, and dozens of small holes suggested that it had been used as target practice. The second site was in much better shape. In the center of town, near the old rail station, was the third and final Niemeyer sculpture, which had been inaugurated in 2004. At the time of my visit in late December, the town's Christmas decorations were still up in the plaza (fig. E.6). I sat at a sidewalk café across the street from the sculpture, and, with an açaí in hand, I observed the winter wonderland, with a Santa Claus, nutcrackers, snowmen, and a polar bear all keeping watch over the Prestes Column.

The last two sites of my travels veered away from a triumphal portrayal of the column and showed local views of the rebels as violent invaders. I

FIGURE E.6. Monument in Crateus, Ceará. Photo by author.

was almost one thousand miles from Bahia, where the column unleashed its most intense wave of violence, but monuments to those killed by the rebels still dotted the northeastern landscape. In the municipality of Custódia, in the state of Pernambuco, a small memorial had been built along the side of the highway in honor of state police who had died fighting the Prestes Column. I had learned about this monument from a blog written by a local writer named Paulo, and we exchanged emails to help me determine its precise location. Paulo told me that it was about ten kilometers outside the small town of Sítio dos Nunes, but that it had no signage or directions. I sent Paulo screenshots from Google Earth, asking if this or that intersection was where I should look for the roadside memorial. Even with Paulo's approximate suggestions, it took me a while to find the site. The monument is some five feet tall and situated down an embankment; I drove past it twice before I finally saw it (fig. E.7). Paulo told me that local police had cleaned up the area only a few months prior, picking up garbage and trimming the bushes to make it more visible. I left my car on the highway shoulder and walked down to the monument. A stone plaque read: "A tribute from the Pernambuco military police to the memory of the heroes who fell here in the line of duty on February 14, 1926. Fighting against the Prestes Column." No names were included,

FIGURE E.7. Monument to police killed by the Prestes Column, near Sítio dos Nunes, Pernambuco. Photo by author.

just a simple statement on a white rectangular statue with a metal cross on top, hoping to catch the eye of passing motorists.

I continued driving north, heading to Piancó in the state of Paraíba, the site of the column's most infamous attack: the killing of Padre Aristides and twelve other locals who had defended the town. Given how centrally the Martyrs of Piancó featured in cultural lore, I assumed that the town would have made a bigger deal of the memorial site. But, as far as I could tell, except for the monument itself, there was no way to know what had taken place. No signs pointed potential visitors to the site, and, if it were not for the fact that its location was georeferenced on Google Maps, I would not have easily found it. The monument itself seemed camouflaged: images online showed a small plaza ringed by a concrete wall, with large lettering that stated "Monument to the Martyrs of Piancó," but, when I arrived, the words had been painted over. The gate to the plaza, moreover, was locked. Looking through, I saw two cats lounging on an overgrown stone pathway leading to a white obelisk inside, where a metal plaque listed the names and professions of the thirteen people killed. At a hotel that evening, I looked up images of the plaque, having been unable to travel the final fifty feet to see the monument firsthand. It was not clear how long the plaza had been shuttered—at least since the start of the pandemic and, given that the sign had been painted over, perhaps even longer.

The next week I arrived in Bahia. There were no more memory sites on my list, but I had a few days to kill before flying out of Brazil. Even though Bahia had no monuments related to the column, I wanted to see what had so transfixed the rebels and scores of others whose writings had helped make it one of the most symbolic regions of the country. I knew that my interest in Bahia was a bit at odds with my arguments about the need to demythologize certain regions, but I was drawn to it all the same. My first stop in Bahia had nothing to do with the Prestes Column: on my southwestwardly drive across the state, I stopped in Canudos to visit the history museum built on the site of the millenarian settlement that the federal army had destroyed in 1897. I wanted to see how Canudos, ever-memorialized in the writings of Euclides da Cunha, had been curated as a memory site for the contemporary public. Especially on the heels of seeing a handful of small monuments to the column, I was struck by the scale of the Canudos museum, particularly its open-air design, in which glass-encased displays sprung from the ground, sprinkled among the ruins of old stone buildings left over from the war. Perhaps due to the pandemic, I was the only person there during my visit.

From Canudos I drove to Lençóis, the old seat of the Matos family who had made such a dogged pursuit of the column. Lençóis has since become a tourist center in the Chapada Plateau, with boutique hotels catering to travelers wanting to swim in turquoise grottos and hike along the quartzite ridges. After nearly two months on the road, and with no specific research itinerary, I spent my days strolling along Lençóis's cobblestone streets and enjoying as much outdoor dining as possible before returning to Europe's pandemic winter. With my flight beckoning from Salvador back to Scotland, I then made my way to the coast.

My final twenty-four hours in Brazil provided several insights into the relative boundaries, both geographic and social, between interior and coast. With the luxuries of a rental car and paved roads—amenities that Prestes did not have a century earlier—it only took me six hours to drive from one of Brazil's most emblematic interiors to the Atlantic coastline. Yes, a hundred years' worth of technological progress had bridged the physical distance between coast and interior, but the perception of a dichotomous landscape still remained. When I checked into my hotel that evening, I chatted with the concierge about my long drive across the interior. He seemed rather shocked at my choice of travel destination, and he wanted reassurance about how I would spend my final hours in Brazil: "Before your flight tomorrow, you're going to the beach, no?"

INTRODUCTION

1. "O XXX Aniversário da Coluna Prestes," *Nosso Povo*, 1954; included in "Coleção Luiz Carlos Prestes," Biblioteca Comunitária, Universidade Federal de São Carlos, Brazil.
2. In this paragraph I draw on a coauthored essay with my colleague Frederico Freitas, "Introduction," in Blanc and Freitas, *The Interior: Rethinking Brazilian History from the Inside*, edited volume in progress.
3. Lima, *Um sertão chamado Brasil.*
4. Grandin, *End of the Myth*, 116.
5. Salvador, *História do Brasil*, 5.
6. Pratt, *Imperial Eyes*, 3.
7. Winichakul, *Siam Mapped.*
8. "A quelque chose malheur est bon," *Gazeta de Noticias*, January 13, 1927, 2.
9. Craib, *Cartographic Mexico*, 5.
10. The term *ufanismo* was popularized by Afonso Celso's 1900 book, *Porque me ufano do meu paiz*. For a recent analysis of ufanismo, particularly as it relates to culture and geography in the twentieth century, see Brandt, "Brazilian Scene."
11. As quoted in Iorio, "Cordeiro de Farias."
12. Amado, *O Cavaleiro da Esperança*, 91.
13. "A torva figura que ameaçou asphixiar o paiz," *A Manhã*, July 5, 1927, 15.
14. Nunes, *Cannibal Democracy*, 24.
15. Uriarte, *Desertmakers*. Esther Breithoff makes a similar argument about war and "conflict landscapes" in her book *Conflict, Heritage and World-Making*.
16. As quoted in Brum, *Coluna Prestes: O avesso da lenda*, 91.
17. Miguel Costa, untitled essay, n.d. Arquivo Edgard Leuenroth, Campinas (hereafter AEL), ser. Miguel Costa (hereafter MC), folder 56. This document

was issued in 1962 by Costa's son, Miguel Jr., three years after the elder's death. As such, it is not possible to know the exact year when the essay was written.

18. "Luiz Carlos Prestes," *Correio da Manhã*, 16 December 1927, 2.
19. Morel, *A marcha da liberdade*, 60.
20. Blake, *Vigorous Core of Our Nationality*, 14.
21. Miguel Costa, untitled essay, n.d., AEL.
22. Wainberg, *Império de palavras*, 42.
23. Conde, *Foundational Films*, esp. 131–55.
24. Morais, *Chatô*, 105.
25. Guimarães Rosa, *Grande Sertão*, 3.
26. Guimarães Rosa, *Grande Sertão*, 82.
27. For a discussion of the motif of the Prestes Column in *Grande Sertão: Veredas*, see Mozzer, "Presença da Coluna Prestes."
28. Nielson, "Unmappable Sertão," 10.
29. Bacellar, "São Paulo and Its Interior," in Blanc and Freitas, *The Interior*.
30. For example, "Livros à venda," *Diário do Rio de Janeiro*, July 20, 1822, 2; and the speech from Sr. Hollanda Cavalcante, reproduced in the *Annaes do Parlamento Brasileiro*, May 6, 1829, 13.
31. Though originally a pejorative name—a status that persists to today— *sertanejo* would also be reappropriated by northeastern intellectuals and cultural leaders in the early decades of the twentieth century, as a way to strengthen a regional identity. For more, see Albuquerque, *Invention of the Brazilian Northeast*.
32. Morel, *A marcha da liberdade*, 74.
33. Her publications include *Coluna Prestes*; *Luiz Carlos Prestes*; and *Viver é tomar partido*.
34. An exception is Diacon, "Searching for the Lost Army."
35. Macaulay, *Prestes Column*.
36. Examples include Meirelles, *As noites das grandes fogueiras*; and Morel, *A marcha da liberdade*.
37. An exception is Menezes, *Coluna Prestes*, written by a retired army colonel whose main objective is to unmask the myth of the Prestes Column as a triumphant and patriotic example of military brilliance.
38. In a telling example that shows the blending of mythology and research, a book from 2009 retraced the steps of three writers who, in 1988, had themselves retraced the steps of the rebellion's entire fifteen-thousand-mile journey. Amaral, *Expedição sagarana*.
39. The twenty-plus regional books include Otaviano, *Coluna Prestes na Paraíba*; Bandeira, *A Coluna Prestes na Bahia*; and Castro, *A Coluna Prestes no Piauí*.
40. Love, *Rio Grande do Sul*; Wirth, *Minas Gerais in the Brazilian Federation*; Levine: *Pernambuco in the Brazilian Federation*.
41. Gebara, *História regional*; Silva, *A república em migalhas*; Albuquerque, *Invention of the Brazilian Northeast*.

42. Weinstein, *Color of Modernity*; Blake, *Vigorous Core of Our Nationality*; Woodard, *Place in Politics*; Sarzynski, *Revolution in the Terra do Sol*; Campbell, *Region Out of Place*.
43. A useful analysis of language and modern-day mythology comes from the literary theorist and semiotician Roland Barthes, *Mythologies*. For a Brazil-specific reflection on myths and nationhood, see Viotti da Costa, *Brazilian Empire*.
44. Among the large body of work, a recent book of note is Thomas, Fowler, and Johnson, *Silence of the Archive*.
45. Chasteen, *Heroes on Horseback*, 133.

CHAPTER 1. REBELLION AND THE BACKLANDS

1. Cunha, *Rebellion in the Backlands*, 444.
2. Levine, *Vale of Tears*, 4.
3. A useful historiographic essay on *Os Sertões* is Oliveira, "Euclides da Cunha, Os Sertões e a invenção de um Brasil profundo." A recent book that offers a fresh analysis of representations of the Canudos War is Johnson, *Sentencing Canudos*.
4. Levine, *Vale of Tears*, 24.
5. Lima, "Century of Nonfiction Solitude," 164.
6. A classic book on this subject is Torres, *O positivismo no Brasil*.
7. For more on Brazilian literary journalism, see Coutinho and Passos, "Voices in War Time."
8. Cunha, *Rebellion in the Backlands*, 89–90.
9. Cunha, *Rebellion in the Backlands*, 223.
10. For more on the army during this period, see McCann, *Soldiers of the Pátria*.
11. See Love, *Revolt of the Whip*.
12. McCann, *Soldiers of the Pátria*, 222.
13. McCann, *Soldiers of the Pátria*, 226.
14. Weinstein, *Color of Modernity*.
15. Borges, *Tenentismo e revolução brasileira*, 20.
16. Forjaz, *Tenentismo e política*, 24.
17. Fausto, *História geral da civilização Brasileira*, vol. 3, 17.
18. For contemporary accounts of the São Paulo revolt, see, for example, Americano, *A lição dos factos*, and Neto, *A Revolta de 1924*.

CHAPTER 2. THE ACCIDENTAL MARCH

1. Luís Carlos Prestes, interview, *La Nación*, December 28, 1941, in Alexander, "Brazilian 'Tenentismo,'" 231.
2. For more on the 1923 fighting in Rio Grande do Sul, see Antonacci, RS.
3. Landucci, *Cenas e episódios*, 29.
4. For more on Rondon, see Diacon, *Stringing Together a Nation*.

5. Juarez Távora to Luís Carlos Prestes, Artigas, October 12, 1924, AEL, files of Lourenço Moreira Lima (LML) series "Cartas," no. 20, 103–7.

6. Macaulay, *Prestes Column*, 44; Ferreira, *A marcha da Columna Prestes*, 20–23.

7. As quoted in "Na trilha da Coluna Prestes," *Manchete*, January 13, 1996, 32.

8. Ferreira, *A marcha da Columna Prestes*, 20–23; Macaulay, *Prestes Column*, 55–56.

9. Woodard, *Place in Politics*, 138. During their westward retreat in early August, the paulista rebels published two issues of a short leaflet, also titled *O Libertador*, in the São Paulo town of Assis.

10. Carneiro, "Imprensa irreverente," 27.

11. *O Libertador*, included in the University of California, Los Angeles, Special Collections, Juarez Távora series.

12. João Francisco to Joaquim de Assis Brasil and Isidoro Dias Lopes, January 14, 1925, Centro de Pesquisa e Documentação de História Contemporânea do Brasil–Fundação Getúlio Vargas (hereafter CPDOC), JF c 1925.01.14.

13. Estimates on troop numbers from Lins de Barros, *Memórias*, 66–67; and Moreira Lima, *A Coluna Prestes*, 595.

14. Prestes, *A Coluna Prestes*, 142–49.

15. João Francisco to Luís Carlos Prestes, January 25, 1925, reproduced in Moreira Lima, *A Coluna Prestes*, 534–53.

16. Luís Carlos Prestes to Antônio Siqueira Campos, Porto Feliz, January 26, 1925, CPDOC, SVM c 1925.01.26.

17. Lins de Barros, *Memórias*, 67.

18. S. Dias Ferreira to Luís Carlos Prestes, January 14, 1925, reproduced in Ferreira, *A marcha da Columna Prestes*, 101–3.

19. The three subsequent quotations come, respectively, from Brum, *Coluna Prestes*, 21, 50, and 24.

20. Ferreira, *A marcha da Columna Prestes*, 93.

21. Quoted in Prestes, *A Coluna Prestes*, 153.

22. Details from letter from Luís Carlos Prestes to Antônio Siqueira Campos, Porto Feliz, January 26, 1925, CPDOC, SVM c 1925.01.26; and Osvaldo Cordeiro de Farias, report on the rebel march from São Luis to Porto Mendes, reproduced in Moreira Lima, *A Coluna Prestes*, 594–99.

23. Moreira Lima, *A Coluna Prestes*, 130.

24. Hahner, *Emancipating the Female Sex*; Roth, *Miscarriage of Justice*.

25. *A Capital*, February 6, 1925, 1, Arquivo Público do Estado de Mato Grosso, newspaper archive, series 01–8, folder 024.

26. Osvaldo Cordeiro de Farias to Luís Carlos Prestes, n.d., in CPDOC, SVM c 1924–1927.00.00–11; Moreira Lima, *A Coluna Prestes*, 109, 597; Lins de Barros, *Memórias*, 75.

27. Luís Carlos Prestes to Isidoro Dias Lopes, exact date unknown, though, based on details in the letter, most likely around February 8, 1925; CPDOC, SVM c 1924–1927.00.00–24.

28. Miguel Costa to Isidoro Dias Lopes, Santa Cruz, Paraná, February 8, 1925, CPDOC, JT dpf 1924.05.10 I-23.

29. Lins de Barros, *Memórias*, 74.
30. Rubem Silveira call to Luís Carlos Prestes, Barração, March 18, 1925, AEL, LML, series "Ligações," CL 265.P3 387.
31. As reproduced in Carvalho, "Vivendo a verdadeira vida," 147.
32. Luís Carlos Prestes to Isidoro Dias Lopes, exact date unknown, though, based on details in the letter, most likely around February 8, 1925; CPDOC, SVM C 1924–1927.00.00–24.
33. Isidoro Dias Lopes to Luís Carlos Prestes, Foz do Iguaçu, February 25, 1925, CPDOC, JT dpf 1924.05.10 I-26. The *real* was Brazil's currency from the colonial period all the way until 1942; historical exchange rates calculated from "Statistical Tables, Exchange Value of the Milreis in US Dollars, 1831–1930," included in Duncan, *Public and Private Operation of Railways in Brazil*, 183.
34. As cited in Teixeira, "Coluna Prestes," 40.
35. Sodré, *História da imprensa no Brasil*, 419.
36. Morais, *Chatô*, 103.
37. The *O Jornal* series was titled "A Atlântida no sertão brasileiro?" and ran in May and June 1925.
38. Edwin V. Morgan, US consular note no. 2387, Rio de Janeiro, April 28, 1925, USNA, Brazil 1910–29, microfilm 832.00—505.
39. Teixeira, "Coluna Prestes," 12.
40. William F. Hoffman, US consular note no. 36, Porto Alegre, November 8, 1924, USNA, Brazil 1910–29, microfilm 832.00—470.
41. Woodard, *Place in Politics*, 137–38.
42. Examples include "A rebelião no sul," *O Paiz*, March 11, 1925, 2; "Sensacionaes revelações de um desiludido," *Correio Paulistano*, March 12, 1925; and "Os rebeldes em acção, a pilhagem no Rio Grande do Sul," *A Noticia*, November 17, 1924.
43. "'Knock Out!,'" *Gazeta de Noticias*, March 24, 1925, 1.
44. Osvaldo Cordeiro de Farias, Report on the rebel march from São Luis to Porto Mendes, reproduced in Moreira Lima, *A Coluna Prestes*, 594–99; and Prestes, *Luiz Carlos Prestes*, 68–69.
45. Cabanas, *A Columna da Morte*, 328–29.
46. Tabajara de Oliveira, *1924*, 134.
47. Details on the meeting from Tabajara de Oliveira, *1924*, 134–35; Moreira Lima, *A Coluna Prestes*, 113–18; and Távora, *Guisa de depoimento*, 12–13.
48. Bulletin no. 1, rebel high command, Santa Helena, April 14, 1925, reproduced in Moreira Lima, *A Coluna Prestes*, 540–44.
49. Details from bulletins nos. 4–8, rebel high command, produced, respectively, April 17, 19, 24, 26, and 27, all included in AEL, LML, series "Boletins." Examples of pro-government media include "Telegrammas," *Jornal de Recife*, April 19, 1925, 2.
50. Moreira Lima, *A Coluna Prestes*, 119–21.
51. Moreira Lima, *A Coluna Prestes*, 122.
52. Exact estimates vary. A US consular report provides a likely exaggerated number of "2,400 men, a couple thousand animals and considerable artillery,"

while the rebels placed the number closer to 1,200. US Consular note no. 1525, Asunción, Paraguay, May 29, 1926, USNA, Brazil 1910–29, microfilm 832.00— 517; Ferreira, *A marcha da Columna Prestes*, 127.

53. Statement from rebel high command to Paraguayan detachment in Alto Paraná, Porto Mendes, April 26, 1925, Arquivo Público Mineiro (hereafter APM), Belo Horizonte, included in series Artur Bernerdes (AB), folder PV- Cx.07, doc.131.

54. For more on Mate Laranjeira, particularly the history of its workers, see Ar- ruda, *Frutos da terra*.

55. Cabanas, *A Columna da Morte*, 245.

56. Draft of unpublished autobiography by Juarez Távora, included in the Univer- sity of California, Los Angeles, Special Collections, Juarez Távora series; and Macaulay, *Prestes Column*, 99.

57. Receipt for rebel purchases, Campanario, Mato Grosso, 1925, CPDOC, JT dpf 1924.05.10 IV-105, and bulletin no. 10, rebel high command, Ponta Porã, Mato Grosso, May 14, 1925, CPDOC, JT dpf 1924.05.10 III-40.

58. Moreira Lima, *A Coluna Prestes*, 130.

59. Bulletin no. 5, rebel high command, Santa Helena, Paraná, April 19, 1925, AEL, LML, series "Boletins," 414–15; Prestes, *Luiz Carlos Prestes*, 180.

60. Bulletin no. 9, May 3, 1925, Fazenda Jacarei, Mato Grosso. AEL, LML, series "Boletins," 426–29.

CHAPTER 3. BANDEIRANTES OF FREEDOM

1. Bulletin no. 9, May 3, 1925, Fazenda Jacarei, Mato Grosso, AEL, LML, Série III Coluna, Subsérie Boletins, 426–29.

2. The classic work on bandeirantes is Taunay, *Historia geral das bandeiras paulistas*. More recent work includes Monteiro, *Negros da terra;* and the 2005 special issue of *Americas* edited by A. J. R. Russell-Wood.

3. The trend was led by historian Afonso d'Escragnolle Taunay and supported by civic institutions such as the newly formed Historical and Geographic In- stitute of São Paulo and the Paulista Museum. Weinstein, *Color of Modernity*, 37–40.

4. Teixeira, "Letra e o mito," 38.

5. Moreira Lima, *A Coluna Prestes*, 136.

6. Lins de Barros, *Memórias*, 89.

7. "Political situation in São Paulo," American consulate letter no. 239, May 23, 1925, USNA, Brazil 1910–29, microfilm 832.00—511.

8. Klinger, *Narrativas autobiográficas*, 17–22; bulletin 10, rebel high command, May 14, 1925 in Ponta Porã, AEL, LML, Série III Coluna, Subsérie Boletins no. 10 430–36.

9. Lins de Barros, *Memórias*, 91–92

10. "Ao povo brasileiro," May 30, 1925, CPDOC, JT dpf 1924.05.10 III-55.

11. Examples, respectively, are from Isidoro Dias Lopes, "Ao povo de São Paulo," July 28, 1924, CPDOC AAP 24.07.28; "Ao povo de Santo Ângelo," October 29, 1924, CPDOC SVM C 1924–1927.00.00–10; and "Manifesto ao povo das Fronteiras do Sul," October 16, 1924, APM, series AB, folder PV-Cx.07, doc.131.

12. Unnamed local resident to rebel leaders, Campo Limpo, June 16, 1925, CPDOC, JT dpf 1924.05.10 III-70.

13. Moreira Lima, *A Coluna Prestes*, 137.

14. Unnamed local resident to rebel leaders, Campo Limpo, June 16, 1925, CPDOC, JT dpf 1924.05.10 III-70.

15. As quoted in Alves de Oliveira, "Representações da passagem," 147.

16. Military police investigation, Municipality of Campo Grande, Mato Grosso, May 29, 1925. CPDOC, JT dpf 1924.05.10 III-53.

17. Report from Lourenço Moreira Lima, June 8, 1925, CPDOC, JT dpf 1924.05.10 III-62.

18. Unless otherwise noted, the remaining details in this paragraph are from Moreira Lima, *A Coluna Prestes*, 147–48.

19. Brum, *Coluna Prestes*, 58–59.

20. For a larger analysis of women in the Column, see Carvalho, "Mulheres na marcha da Coluna Prestes."

21. Moreira Lima, *A Coluna Prestes*, 131.

22. Silva, *Farrapos de nossa história*, 76.

23. Landucci, *Cenas e episódios*, 167–68.

24. There is a rich body of scholarship on cangaço; for an overview, see Wiesebron, "Historiografia do cangaço." For a recent analysis of gender and cangaço, see Pereira and Rêses "Mulheres e violência no cangaço."

25. Moreira Lima, *A Coluna Prestes*, 132.

26. Lins de Barros, *Memórias*, 172.

27. Moreira Lima, *A Coluna Prestes*, 130.

28. As quoted in "Na trilha da Coluna Prestes," *Manchete*, February 3, 1996, 38.

29. Macaulay, *Prestes Column*, 112.

30. Moreira Lima, *A Coluna Prestes*, 149–50.

31. Bulletin no. 14, rebel high command, Fazenda Cilada, Mato Grosso, June 10, 1925, AEL, LML, Série III Coluna, Subsérie Boletins no. 14 450–52.

32. Moreira Lima, *A Coluna Prestes*, 553.

33. Prestes, *A Coluna Prestes*, 428.

34. For more on Brazil's census during this period, see Loveman, "Race to Progress."

35. Nearly a century later, the Malaquias settlement at Santa Tereza would persevere as one of only two dozen quilombolas (officially recognized Afrodescendent communities) in the state. Presently, Santa Tereza is recognized largely for its annual religious festival, the Festa do Divino Espirito Santo.

36. Moreira Lima, *Marchas e combates*, 154.

37. As quoted in Brum, *Coluna Prestes*, 62.

38. "1a Divisão do Exercito Libertador em Operações no Nordeste do Brasil," June 15, 1925, CPDOC, JT dpf 1924.05.10 III-68.
39. Miguel Costa to Batista Luzardo, Rio Bonito, Goiás, July 5, 1925, CPDOC, JT dpf 1924.05.10 III-89.
40. Moreira Lima, *A Coluna Prestes*, 155.
41. Macaulay, *Prestes Column*, 122–23.
42. As recounted in Brum, *Coluna Prestes*, 63–64.
43. The town of Rio Bonito has since changed its name to Caiapônia. Moreira Lima, *A Coluna Prestes*, 168–69.
44. Miguel Costa to Batista Luzardo, Rio Bonito, Goiás, July 5, 1925, CPDOC, JT dpf 1924.05.10 III-89.
45. Prestes, *A Coluna Prestes*, 362.
46. Bulletin of the rebel high command. CPDOC, JT dpf 1924.05.10 III-94. Although the statement does not have a date, its mention of the one-year anniversary suggests that it was the materials dispatched with Ataíde da Silva.
47. Radio call from Djalma Dutra to Luís Carlos Prestes, Margem de São Domingos, July 17, 1925, AEL, LML, Série III Coluna, Subsérie Ligações, CL 16.P2 189–90.
48. Bulletin 16, Command of the Revolutionary Forces, Fazenda Aguas Brancas, Goiás, August 7, 1925, AEL, LML, Série III Coluna, Subsérie Boletins, 456–68.
49. Moreira Lima, *A Coluna Prestes*, 555–59.
50. Moreira Lima, *A Coluna Prestes*, 181.
51. Morais, *Chatô*, 106.
52. "A revolução invencível," *Folha do Povo*, August 19, 1925, 2.
53. Moreira Lima, *A Coluna Prestes*, 182–87.
54. Luís Carlos Prestes to João Alberto Lins de Barros, August 22, 1925, reproduced in Moreira Lima, *A Coluna Prestes*, 565.
55. Moreira Lima, *A Coluna Prestes*, 184.
56. Ferreira, *A marcha da Columna Prestes*, 264–65.
57. As quoted in Brum, *Coluna Prestes*, 100.
58. "A situação do paiz," *O Combate*, September 23, 1925, 1.
59. Lins de Barros, *Memórias*, 126–27.
60. Copy of letter to Isidoro and Luzardo in Moreira Lima, *A Coluna Prestes*, 190–93.
61. Moreira Lima, *A Coluna Prestes*, 187.
62. Women of Arraias (Maranhão) to the rebel leaders, September 22, 1925. Written by a local scribe named Manuel Segunato, the letter was signed by forty-two women. CPDOC, JT dpf 1924.05.10 IV-12.
63. A local exception to the maintenance of these gender norms occurred two decades later, in the so-called Revolta de Dona Noca in 1951, when a woman from the interior of Maranhão named Joanna da Rocha Santos (known as Dona Noca) led a contingent of over ten thousand men to march on the state capital in protest of what she claimed was a fraudulent election for governor.
64. Women of Arraias (Maranhão) to the rebel leaders, September 22, 1925, CPDOC, jt dpf 1924.05.10 iv-12.

CHAPTER 4. COMPETING VISIONS OF THE SERTÃO

1. João Ayres Joca to rebel leaders, Porto Nacional, Goiás, October 14, 1925, CPDOC, JT dpf 1924.05.10 IV-23.
2. Audrin, *Entre sertanejos e Indios*, 251–52.
3. Audrin, *Entre sertanejos e Indios*, 252–53.
4. Ferreira, *A marcha da Columna Prestes*, 149.
5. Moreira Lima, *A Coluna Prestes*, 198.
6. *O Libertador*, no. 7, October 20, 1925, Porto Nacional, Goiás, APM, series AB, folder PV-Cx.07, doc. 215.
7. Moreira Lima, *A Coluna Prestes*, 199.
8. As quoted in Brum, *Coluna Prestes*, 78.
9. José M. Audrin to Miguel Costa, Porto Nacional, October 21, 1925, CPDOC, JT dpf 1924.05.10 IV-31.
10. Audrin, *Entre sertanejos e Indios*, 260–61.
11. Miguel Costa to Tarquinio Lopes Filho, October 23, 1925, CPDOC, JT dpf 1924.05.10 IV-35.
12. "Bemvindos sejam!," *Folho do Povo* (Maranhão), October 26, 1925, APM, series AB, folder PV-Cx.07, doc. 174.
13. Landucci, *Cenas e episódios*, 85.
14. Both Moreira Lima and Ferreira use the same terms to identify the group, *Chavantes* or *Javahés*. However, as Audrin points out in his memoir, because the two tribes mentioned above were living farther away in the Araguaia valley at this time, it is more likely that the group in question was the Xerentes (*Entre sertanejos e Indios*, 181–86).
15. "Na trilha da Coluna Prestes," *Manchete*, March 16, 1996, 63.
16. Moreira Lima, *A Coluna Prestes*, 200.
17. Unless otherwise noted, all details from Carolina are from Moreira Lima, *A Coluna Prestes*, 206–8.
18. As quoted in Brum, *Coluna Prestes: O avesso da lenda*, 81.
19. Moreira Lima, *A Coluna Prestes*, 206.
20. "A entrada das Forças Revolucionarias nesta cidade," *A Mocidade*, November 28, 1925, 1; as reproduced in Prestes, *A Coluna Prestes*, 227.
21. "Festa da bandeira," text of speech from Oswaldo Cordeiro de Farias, Carolina, November 19, 1925, CPDOC, JT dpf 1924.05.10 IV-47.
22. Moreira Lima, *A Coluna Prestes*, 205.
23. Lins de Barros, *Memórias*, 152.
24. Moreira Lima, *A Coluna Prestes*, 182.
25. Moreira Lima, *A Coluna Prestes*, 202–3.
26. Moreira Lima, *A Coluna Prestes*, 203.
27. Moreira Lima, *A Coluna Prestes*, 205.
28. Radio call from Juarez Távora to Luís Carlos Prestes, Riachão, Maranhão, November 26, 1925, AEL, LML, Série III Coluna, Subsérie Ligações, CL 96.P2 258–59. The town of Riachão has since been renamed Monsenhor Hipólito.
29. Cunha, *Os revolucionários do sul*, 38.

30. Logbook of João Gomes, November 1925. Arquivo Histórico do Exército (hereafter AHEx), Série: Revoluções internas, Sub-Séries: Revoltas tenentista, Forças em operações no Norte da Republica, 1924/1925/1926, I-14, 06, 5303.
31. Luís Carlos Prestes to Miguel Costa, Nova Iorque, December 12, 1925, CPDOC, JT dpf 1924.05.10 IV-87.
32. Moreira Lima, *A Coluna Prestes*, 218.
33. When a new state of Tocantins was created in 1988, the city of Palmas became a second inland northern capital.
34. Moreira Lima, *A Coluna Prestes*, 221, 275.
35. Mathias Olímpio de Melo, "Ao povo piauhyense," December 5, 1925, reproduced in governor's address to State Assembly of Piauí, June 1, 1926, http://www.crl.edu/pt-br/brazil/presidential (accessed July 14, 2018), 24.
36. Josias Carneiro Leão to Luís Carlos Prestes, Natal, Piauí, January 5, 1926, CPDOC, JT dpf 1924.05.10 V-9.
37. Luís Carlos Prestes and Miguel Costa to Josias Leão, Natal, Piauí, January 5, 1926, CPDOC, JT dpf 1924.05.10 V-12.
38. For an incisive summary of the 1926 Recife conference, see Campbell, *Region Out of Place*, 46–53.
39. Albuquerque, *Invention of the Brazilian Northeast*, 42.
40. Freyre, *Manifesto Regionalista*, 67.
41. In the coming years, the antiestablishment goals of both groups would lead to an allyship between northeasterners and gaúcho forces in their fight against the café-com-leite political system of the Old Republic.
42. Embassy note no. 4, from Mr. Ramsey, Rio de Janeiro, January 7, 1926, Series 371, Folder A, doc. 517/516/6, British National Archives, Foreign Office (hereafter FO), Kew, London.
43. Luís Carlos Prestes and Miguel Costa to Isidoro Dias Lopes, Prata, Piauí, January 8, 1926. CPDOC, JT dpf 1924.05.10 V-14.
44. Lins de Barros, *Memórias*, 144.
45. "A invasão do Estado pelas hordas rebeldes," *O Nordeste*, January 14, 1926. The archive of *O Nordeste* is held at the Biblioteca Pública Estadual do Ceará (BECE) in Fortaleza, Ceará.
46. Moreira Lima, *A Coluna Prestes*, 241.
47. "Ecos da incursão dos rebeldes," *O Nordeste*, February 17, 1926.
48. "O tufão revolucionario no Ceará," *O Nordeste*, February 19, 1926; "A acção devastadora dos rebeldes," *O Nordeste*, February 4, 1926.
49. "O Ceará limpo de rebeldes," *O Nordeste*, February 12, 1926.
50. For details of the looting of São Miguel, see Nonato, *Os revoltosos*, 79–131.
51. This statement, and that of the governor of Paraíba that follows, are reproduced from Nathaniel P. Davis, "Notes on Revolutionary Activities in the Pernambuco Consular District," February 10, 1926, USNA, Brazil 1910–29, microfilm 832.00—559.
52. Macaulay, *Prestes Column*, 205–6.
53. Otaviano, *A Coluna Prestes na Paraíba*, 110–12, 145.

54. Otaviano, *A Coluna Prestes na Paraíba*, 112, 115–16, 121; Moreira Lima, *A Coluna Prestes*, 255–58; Ferreira, *A marcha da Columna Prestes*, 179–80; Landucci, *Cenas e episódios*, 114.

55. Moreira Lima, *A Coluna Prestes*, 258.

56. Moreira Lima, *A Coluna Prestes*, 257–58; Otaviano, *A Coluna Prestes na Paraíba*, 117–23, 139–40; Diario do Congresso Nacional, July 20, 1926, 1435; Ferreira, *A marcha da Columna Prestes*, 180–81; Landucci, *Cenas e episódios*, 114–15.

57. Otaviano, *A Coluna Prestes na Paraíba*, 144–45.

58. Otaviano, *A Coluna Prestes na Paraíba*, 145.

59. "A carnificina em Piancó," *O Norte*, February 14, 1926.

60. "Os Furores da rebeldia," *O Rebate*, February 27, 1926.

61. "O tufão revolucionario no Nordeste," *O Nordeste*, February 21, 1926.

62. Amado, *O Cavaleiro da Esperança*, 116.

63. Schumaher and Brazil, *Dicionário mulheres do Brasil*, 590–91.

64. Carvalho, "Vivendo a verdadeira vida," 160.

65. A classic work on Padre Cícero is Della Cava, *Miracle at Joaseiro*. For more analysis of folk Catholicism, see Pessar, *From Fanatics to Folk*.

66. Cícero Romão Batista to Luís Carlos Prestes, February 20, 1926; reproduced in Prestes, *A Coluna Prestes*, 450–51.

67. Neto, *Padre Cícero*, 464.

68. For more on the meeting between Cícero and Lampião, see Neto, *Padre Cícero*, 463–82.

69. For example, "Alliado ao padre Cicero, o bandido 'Lampeão' luta pela causa da maioria da Camara," *Correio da Manhã*, May 27, 1926, 5.

70. As cited in Teixeira, "A Coluna Prestes," 131.

71. As cited in Morais, *Châto*, 106.

72. Barros, *Década 20 em Pernambuco*, 119–26.

73. General Mariante, report to minister of war, February 1926, AHEx, Acervo Góes Monteiro caixeta 4a, caderno 1.

74. Landucci, *Cenas e episódios*, 119–20.

75. Moreira Lima, *A Coluna Prestes*, 274, 613.

CHAPTER 5. BANDEIRANTES IN BAHIA

1. Pratt, *Imperial Eyes*.

2. Landucci, *Cenas e episódios*, 128.

3. Pang, *Coronelismo e oligarquias*, 20.

4. Pang, "Revolt of the Bahian Coronéis," 6.

5. Moreira Lima, *A Coluna Prestes*, 274.

6. Landucci, *Cenas e episódios*, 126.

7. Moreira Lima, *A Coluna Prestes*, 276–77.

8. Various sources provide statistics on troop sizes in Bahia, including Moreira Lima, *A Coluna Prestes*, 293; Howard Donovan, consular note from Salvador,

Bahia, April 17, 1926, USNA, 832.00—575; and Álvaro Mariante, "Histórico dos acontecimentos desde a passagem do Rio São Francisco pelos rebeldes," AHEx, Acervo Góes Monteiro caixeta 4a, caderno 12, 19.

9. Lins de Barros, *Memórias*, 149.

10. As quoted in Brum, *Coluna Prestes*, 89.

11. Moreira Lima, *A Coluna Prestes*, 182; Lins de Barros, *Memórias*, 152.

12. As quoted in Prestes, *A Coluna Prestes*, 231.

13. Prestes, *Luiz Carlos Prestes*, 90.

14. Moreira Lima, *A Coluna Prestes*, 369.

15. Ferreira, *A marcha da Columna Prestes*, 188.

16. Cunha, *Rebellion in the Backlands*, 30.

17. Landucci, *Cenas e episódios*, 127.

18. Álvaro Mariante, "Histórico dos acontecimentos desde a passagem do Rio São Francisco pelos rebeldes," AHEx, Acervo Góes Monteiro caixeta 4a, caderno 12, 4–5.

19. Álvaro Mariante, "Histórico dos acontecimentos desde a passagem do Rio São Francisco pelos rebeldes," AHEx, Acervo Góes Monteiro caixeta 4a, caderno 12, 4–5. For more on the influence of the French Military Mission, see Diacon, "Searching for a Lost Army," 427.

20. Álvaro Mariante to Fernando Setembrino de Carvalho, Pirapora, Minas Gerais, May 19, 1926; reproduced in Prestes, *A Coluna Prestes*, 452–60.

21. "O sertão assolado pelos bandos revolucionarios," *Correio do Bonfim*, March 21, 1926.

22. "A bravura do Sertanejo Bahiano," *Diario Oficial* (Bahia), April 1926, APM, series AB, folder PV-Cx.07, doc.177.

23. "Uma pagina romanesca da revolta," *Diário da Bahia*, March 25, 1926; "O momento no nordeste," *O Paladino*," April 4, 1926.

24. "Uma pagina romanesca da revolta," *Diário da Bahia*, March 25, 1926.

25. As cited in Carvalho, "Vivendo a verdadeira vida," 174.

26. Álvaro Mariante, "Ordens, instruções e informações recebidas do Comandante das FONR," February 1926, AHEx, Series Góes Monteiro, box 4a, folder 4, annex no. 7, 10.

27. "Descripção dos factores occoridos até a travessia da Via Férrea em Santa Luzia," March 15, 1926, AHEx, Acervo Góes Monteiro caixeta 4, caderno 16, 14.

28. "A bella generala e a piedosa enfermeira," *Diário de Noticias*, April 16, 1926.

29. "Recursos e modos de agir dos rebeldes," AHEx, Acervo Góes Monteiro caixeta 4, caderno 17, 2.

30. "O sertão assolado pelos bandos revolucionarios," *Correio do Bonfim*, March 21, 1926.

31. Howard Donovan, "Movementes of Rebel Troops in the State of Bahia," April 8, 1926, USNA, 832.00—571; Moreira Lima, *A Coluna Prestes*, 283; Ferreira, *A marcha da Columna Prestes*, 188.

32. Moreira Lima, *A Coluna Prestes*, 284.

33. Moreira Lima, *A Coluna Prestes*, 346.

34. An insightful history of Horácio and the Matos family is Chagas, *O chefe*.
35. For more on the federal intervention of 1920, see Pang, "Revolt of the Bahian Coronéis."
36. Moraes, *Jagunços e heróis*, 153.
37. "Descripção dos factores occoridos até a travessia da Via Férrea em Santa Luzia," March 15, 1926, AHEx, Acervo Góes Monteiro caixeta 4, caderno 16. 5.
38. "Operações—Methodo e medidas adoptadas—Execução," June 14, 1926, Pirapora, AHEx, Acervo Góes Monteiro caixeta 4, caderno 25.
39. "Movements of Revolutionary Troops in the State of Bahia," April 17, 1926, USNA, Brazil 1910–29, microfilm 832.00–575.
40. Copy included in "Movements of Revolutionary Troops in the State of Bahia," April 17, 1926, USNA, 832.00–575.
41. Howard Donovan, "Movements of Rebel Troops in the State of Bahia," April 8, 1926, USNA, 832.00–571.
42. Army reports on hospitals and health situation, March 15, 1926, AHEx, folder 5278, doc. 173.
43. Dr. A. Cajaty, Health Service report, March 1926, AHEx, Acervo Góes Monteiro caixeta 4, caderno 24.
44. Álvaro Mariante, communications logbook with minister of war, February 26–27, March 1926, AHEx, Acervo Góes Monteiro caixeta 4a, caderno 1, 35.
45. Army report, March 15, 1926, AHEx, Acervo Góes Monteiro caixeta 4, caderno 16.
46. Lins de Barros, *Memórias*, 150.
47. "A devastação e os crimes praticados pelos rebeldes," May 1, 1926, AHEx, Acervo Góes Monteiro caixeta 4, caderno 34, 4.
48. "Até a loucura!," *Diário da Noticias*, April 22, 1926.
49. "A corrida da morte," *O Sertão*, April 11, 1926.
50. Landucci, *Cenas e episódios*, 129.
51. Descriptions of the three towns come from Moreira Lima, *A Coluna Prestes*, 299–304.
52. A detailed account of this event can be found in Moraes, *Jagunços e heróis*, 154.
53. Moreira Lima, *A Coluna Prestes*, 300.
54. Amado, *O Cavaleiro da Esperança*, 112.
55. Moreira Lima, *A Coluna Prestes*, 305–6.
56. Diacon, "Searching for the Lost Army," 435.
57. Moreira Lima, *A Coluna Prestes*, 306.
58. Lins de Barros, *Memórias*, 154–55.
59. Prisoner interrogations, Salvador, April 19, 1926, AHEx, Série: Revoluções internas, Sub-Série: Coluna Prestes, Forças em operações no Norte da Republica, 1925/1926. I-14.02 5269
60. A few of the remaining prisoners were actually loyalist fighters whom the tenente rebels had previously captured in battle.

61. Landucci, *Cenas e episódios*, 130.
62. "Em torno do futuro governo," *O Nordeste*, April 14, 1926.
63. Senado Federal, *Anais do Senado*, book 1, 1926, 14, https://www.senado.leg .br/publicacoes/anais/pdf/Anais_Republica/1926/1926%20Livro%201.pdf (accessed August 8, 2018).
64. Batista Luzardo speech to Câmara dos Deputados, May 25, 1926; included in Câmara dos Deputados, *Perfis Parlamentares* 22, 132–50.
65. "O Segundo Discurso do Sr. Batista Luzardo," *O Jornal*, May 27, 1926, 1.
66. "A columna da morte através dos sertões brasileiros," *O Paiz*, July 3, 1926, 1.
67. Moreira Lima, *A Coluna Prestes*, 343.
68. Landucci, *Cenas e episódios*, 139.
69. Details of the four battles come from army telegram logbook, May–June 1926, AHEx, Acervo Góes Monteiro caixeta 5, pasta 2, caderno 2; and Moreira Lima, *A Coluna Prestes*, 334–42. Details of sexual violence come from "A devastação e os crimes praticados pelos rebeldes," May 1, 1926, AHEx, Acervo Góes Monteiro caixeta 4, caderno 34, 4.
70. As quoted in Bandeira, *A Coluna Prestes na Bahia*, 124.
71. Brum, *Coluna Prestes: O Avesso da lenda*, 126.
72. Brum, *Coluna Prestes: O Avesso da lenda*, 143.
73. "A devastação e os crimes praticados pelos rebeldes," May 1, 1926, AHEx, Acervo Góes Monteiro caixeta 4, caderno 34, 4.
74. Moreira Lima, *A Coluna Prestes*, 335.
75. "Activities of Rebel Troops in the State of Bahia," June 1, 1926, USNA, Brazil 1910–29, microfilm 832.00–581.
76. As quoted in Bandeira, *A Coluna Prestes na Bahia*, 71, 90.
77. Granja's acts and his letter are summarized in "Activities of Rebel Troops in the State of Bahia," June 1, 1926, USNA, Brazil 1910–29, microfilm 832.00–581.
78. "Rebeldes e legalistas no nordeste bahiano," unnamed Bahia newspaper, April 17, 1926, APM, series AB, folder PV-Cx.07, doc. 177.
79. Letter reproduced in Moreira Lima, *A Coluna Prestes*, 630.
80. "Recursos e modos de agir dos rebeldes," 1926, AHEx, Acervo Góes Monteiro caixeta 4, caderno 17, 2.
81. Álvaro Mariante, orders and instruction logbook, February 1926, AHEx, Acervo Góes Monteiro caixeta 4a, caderno 4, 19.
82. "A columna da morte," *Gazeta de Noticias*," July 6, 1926, 1.
83. Moreira Lima, *A Coluna Prestes*, 346, 349.
84. Lins de Barros, *Memórias*, 155–57.
85. Moreira Lima, *A Coluna Prestes*, 367.
86. Moreira Lima, *A Coluna Prestes*, 368.
87. Moreira Lima, *A Coluna Prestes*, 369; Ferreira, *A marcha da Columna Prestes*, 198.
88. Rebel high command, bulletin no. 23, Rodelas, Bahia, July 2, 1926, AEL, LML, Série III Coluna, Subsérie Boletins no. 23 511–521.

89. Moreira Lima, *A Coluna Prestes*, 371; Landucci, *Cenas e episódios*, 129.
90. The other bulletin in Bahia was rebel high command, bulletin no. 232, Baixa do Coxo, Bahia, February 28, 1926, AEL, LML, Série III Coluna, Subsérie Boletins no. 22 500–510.
91. Macaulay, *Prestes Column*, 225.
92. Moreira Lima, *A Coluna Prestes*, 369.

CHAPTER 6. MAPPING A MYTH

1. "A Columna Prestes através do Brasil," *A Noite*, July 3, 1926, 1.
2. "Episodios da coluna Prestes," *O Jornal*, August 29, 1926, 1.
3. Wainberg, *Império de palavras*, 166–67.
4. I am grateful to a peer reviewer on this manuscript for help in formulating the idea of cartographic picaresque.
5. "A marcha da columna Prestes," *O Dia*, July 9, 1926, 1.
6. "A columna Prestes através do Brasil," *A Gazeta*, three issues on August 24, August 25, and September 6, 1926; "A columna Prestes através do Brasil," *O Estado do Paraná*, five issues published between July 9 and September 5.
7. "Prohibida a publicação das reportagens sobre a columna Prestes," *O Dia*, September 10, 1926, 8.
8. "A marcha da columna Prestes e os seus commentadores," *A Gazeta*, August 27, 1926, 1.
9. "A columna Prestes," *Gazeta de Noticias*, August 25, 1926, 1.
10. Bulletin no. 24, rebel high commands, Barra da Estiva, July 31, 1926, AEL, LML, Série III Coluna, Subsérie Boletins no. 24 522–528; Moreira Lima, *A Coluna Prestes*, 371–73.
11. "Promoções na columna Prestes," *A Gazeta*, September 3, 1926, 1.
12. Moreira Lima, *A Coluna Prestes*, 397.
13. Army radio log, month of July 1926, 27, AHEx, Acervo Góes Monteiro caixeta 5, pasta 2b caderno 3.
14. Of the 3,600 fighters chasing down the column during this period, less than a third belonged to the patriotic battalions. Telegram logbook, August–December 1926, 171, AHEx, Acervo Góes Monteiro caixeta 4a, caderno 2.
15. "A columna Prestes—o sr. Batista Luzardo pronunciou mais um discurso," *Correio da Manhã*, August 25, 1926, 2.
16. "A pacificação," *O Jornal*, October 19, 1926, 2.
17. "O problema do cangaço," *A Gazeta*, February 3, 1927, 1.
18. Macaulay, *Prestes Column*, 228
19. Prestes, *Luiz Carlos Prestes*, 94; Moreira Lima, *A Coluna Prestes*, 412–27.
20. Moreira Lima, *A Coluna Prestes*, 449.
21. Lins de Barros, *Memórias*, 165–69.
22. As quoted in "Na trilha da Coluna Prestes," *Manchete*, February 10, 1996, 59.
23. Luís Carlos Prestes, "Liberdade ou morte—titulo de dominio," CPDOC, JT 1924.05.10, IV-118. Although the document includes three names as

signatories (Miguel Costa, Luís Carlos Prestes, and Juarez Távora), the letter was in Prestes's handwriting; Távora, moreover, was still in jail at this point. There is no date attached, though, because Prestes is identified as "General"— his promotion had come in January 1926—and as it mentions their current location in Mato Grosso, the document could only have been written between October 1926 and January 1927.

24. For more on the history of agrarian reform movements, see Welch, *Seed Was Planted*.
25. B. Alston, "Political Situation in Brazil," November 16, 1926, FO, London, series 371, folder A, doc. 6614/516/6.
26. Leôncia Correia, "Pela harmonia da familia brasileira," *O Dia*, November 18, 1926, 2.
27. "A quelque chose malheur est bon," *Gazeta de Noticias*, January 13, 1927, 2.
28. Campbell, Giovine, and Keating, *Empty Spaces*, 1.
29. B. Alston, Foreign Office annual report on Brazil for 1926, April 26, 1926, NA, FO 371, A 2932/2932/6.
30. Decree no. 19.395, of November 8, 1930, published in *Diário Oficial da União*, Section 1, November11, 1930, 206–21. For more, see Schneider, *Amnesty in Brazil*.
31. Moreira Lima, *A Coluna Prestes*, 486.
32. "A Columna Prestes em Matto Grosso," *A Capital*, n.d., 4; included in Arquivo Público do Estado de Mato Grosso, Cuiabá, newspaper archive, series 01–8, folder 024.
33. Ferreira, *A marcha da Columna Prestes*, 225.
34. C. R. Cameron, US consular note no. 7, São Paulo, January 31, 1927, USNA, Brazil 1910–29, microfilm 832.00—616.
35. "O movimento revolucionário," *A Manhã*, January 13, 1927, 1.
36. "O movimento revolucionário," *A Manhã*, January 20, 1927, 1.
37. "Prestes, maior do que Annibal!," *Gazeta de Noticias*, January 19, 1927, 1.
38. "Homens e coisas da revolução brasileira," *A Manhã*, January 4, 1927, 5.
39. Guimarães, *O Índio Afonso*, 9. For analysis of this novella and other interior-set novels of the nineteenth century, see Sá, "Romantic Sertões."
40. Ferreira, *A marcha da Columna Prestes*, 232.
41. Lins de Barros, *Memórias*, 187.
42. Landucci, *Cenas e episódios*, 183.
43. "Movimento revolucionario," *A Manhã*, January 28, 1927, 2.
44. Moreira Lima, *A Coluna Prestes*, 497–99.
45. Moreira Lima, *A Coluna Prestes*, 499.
46. Prestes, *A Coluna Prestes*, 313.
47. Moreira Lima, *A Coluna Prestes*, 497–99.
48. Major Carmona Rodó, Miguel Costa, and Luís Carlos Prestes, joint declaration on terms of surrender, February 4, 1927; reproduced in Landucci, *Cenas e episódios*, 188–89.
49. "A revolução caminha para o triumpho final," *Folha do Povo*, February 3, 1927, 1.

1. League of Nations, *Dispute between Bolivia and Paraguay*, 17.
2. Prestes, *Luiz Carlos Prestes*, 102.
3. Carvalho, "Vivendo a verdadeira vida," 138.
4. Lins de Barros, *Memórias*, 194.
5. "Um quadro do inferno verde," *O Jornal*, May 21, 1927, 1.
6. "O inferno verde," *O Jornal*, May 21, 1927, 2.
7. "A torva figura que ameaçou asphixiar o paiz," *A Manhã*, July 5, 1927, 15.
8. "Sursam corda!," *Correio da Manhã*, February 11, 1927, 4.
9. "Tópicos & Noticias," *Correio da Manhã*, February 25, 1927, 4.
10. For example, "Ouvindo e falando a Luiz Carlos Prestes," *O Jornal*, March 17, 1927, 1.
11. "Conversando com as mulheres da Columna Prestes," *O Jornal*, July 10, 1927, 6.
12. "A mae de Prestes," *O Jornal*, 16 March 1927, 2.
13. "Ouvindo e falando a Luiz Carlos Prestes," *O Jornal*, March 10–23, 1927.
14. Morais, *Chatô*, 128.
15. "Ouvindo e falando a Luiz Carlos Prestes," *O Jornal*, March 17, 1927, 1.
16. "Ouvindo e falando a Luiz Carlos Prestes," *O Jornal*, March 11, 1927, 1.
17. "Conversando com Luiz Carlos Prestes," *O Jornal*, June 28–July 29, 1927.
18. "Um 'raid' journalistico de doze mil kilometros," *O Jornal*, June 6–14, 1927.
19. "Um 'raid' journalistico de doze mil kilometros," *O Jornal*, June 8, 1927.
20. Conde, *Foundational Films*, 95.
21. "Conversando com as mulheres da Columna Prestes," *O Jornal*, July 10, 1927, 6.
22. "Contra as incoherencias de nossa descentralização politica," *O Jornal*, May 29–July 17, 1927; "A cavalgada indomita," *O Jornal*, June 17, 1927, 3.
23. Figure compiled from "Em prol dos soldados da columna Prestes," *O Jornal*, November 22, 1927, 4; and "Subscripção em favor dos revolucionarios," *A Gazeta*, April 29, 1927, 8.
24. Morais, *Chatô*, 118.
25. "Em prol dos soldados da Columna Prestes," *O Jornal*, March 17, 1927, 2.
26. "Pro-Prestes," *O Dia*, June 1, 1927, 1; "Pelos bravos da columna Prestes," *O Dia*, June 12, 1927, 7; "A columna Prestes e a mocidade academica," *O Jornal*, May 24, 1927, 2.
27. "Edificante exemplo de gratidão dos chefes da 'Columna Prestes,'" *A Esquerda*, August 9, 1928, 3.
28. Reis, *Luís Carlos Prestes*, 110.
29. Speech reproduced in "O 5 de julho no desterro de la Gaiba," *Correio da Manhã*, July 22, 1927, 5.
30. "Os dois 5 de julho," *Vanguarda*, July 5, 1927.
31. "Luiz Carlos Prestes," *Correio da Manhã*, December 16, 1927, 2.
32. Amado, *O Cavaleiro da Esperança*, 98, 127.
33. The letter, originally written on May 25, 1927, was reproduced, with contextualizing details, in "Uma Carta escripta em 1927 por Luiz Carlos Prestes," *Correia da Manha*, February 1929, 5, 1.

34. For the early history of the Party, see Pereira, *Formação do PCB*.
35. Reis, *Luís Carlos Prestes*, 114–15.
36. Open letter from the PCB leadership, January 5, 1927; as reproduced in Pereira, *Formação do PCB*, 116–20.
37. Pereira, *Formação do PCB*, 125.
38. Pereira, *Formação do PCB*, 132.
39. Pereira, *Formação do PCB*, 131.
40. Information on Prestes in Buenos Aires from Prestes, *Luiz Carlos Prestes*, 105–6.
41. Prestes, "Como cheguei ao comunismo," 7.
42. Prestes, "Como cheguei ao comunismo," 4–7.
43. "Luiz Carlos Prestes fala ao 'Diário Nacional,'" *Diário Nacional*, April 19, 1928, 1.
44. "Prestes, o homem do Brasil," *A Cultura*, August 13, 1929.
45. For example, "Voto de consciencia," *Correio da Manhã*, January 16, 1929, 7; and "O Rio Grande Homenageando Prestes," *A Manhã*, December 30, 1928, 3.
46. "O movimento Democratico-Libertador no Norte do Paiz," *Diário Nacional*, June 14, 1928, 3.
47. "Mais uma candidatura a presidência da republica," *A Manhã*, April 5, 1929, 3.
48. Aranha, *A viagem maravilhosa*, 82.
49. For context and a critical analysis of the book, see DeStafney, "Dialectic of the Marvelous."
50. For more analysis, see Almeida, "Leituras de 'Jantando um defunto.'"
51. Minas, *Jantando um defunto*, 5.
52. Printed in *A Gazeta*, October 4, 1926, 2.
53. Printed in *O Jornal*, March 11, 1928, 9.
54. Printed in *O Jornal*, June 21, 1931, 22.
55. "Imperativos do momento politico," *A Manhã*, April 26, 1929, 3.
56. Quotations in the paragraph from program of the PCB Third Party Congress, February 12, 1929, AEL, IC, no. 3, 537–574.
57. Bausbam, *Uma vida em seis tempos*, 69.
58. As reproduced in Moraes and Viana, *Prestes*, 44.
59. Williams, *Culture Wars in Brazil*, 4.
60. Moraes and Viana, *Prestes*, 47–49.
61. Luiz Carlos Prestes, "Como cheguei ao comunismo," 7.
62. "Os dois Prestes," *Correio da Manhã*, March 9, 1930, 4.
63. "O capitão Luiz Carlos Prestes define a sua atitude actual," *Diário da Noite* (Rio de Janeiro), May 29, 1930, 1.
64. "A nova directriz do Commandante Prestes," *Diário Carioca*, May 29, 1930, 1.
65. Open letter opposing Prestes, October 1930, CPDOC, series PEB c 1930.10.00–8 microfilm 390–91; "O marechal Isidoro Dias Lopes discorda do commandante Luis Carlos Prestes," *Diário Carioca*, June 4, 1930, 12.
66. "Ainda o manifesto Prestes," *Diário Carioca*, June 4, 1930, 12.
67. "As novas ideas de Luiz Carlos Prestes e o problema brasileiro," *Diário Carioca*, June 19, 1930, 1.

68. Juarez Távora to Luís Carlos Prestes, 1930 [n.d.]; included in Juarez Távora series, Special Collections, University of California, Los Angeles.

69. Letter from Juarez Távora to Luís Carlos Prestes, June 25, 1930; included in Juarez Távora series, Special Collections, University of California, Los Angeles.

70. "Ainda o manifesto do comandante Luiz Carlos Prestes," *O Jornal*, June 11, 1930, 3.

71. Moraes and Viana, *Prestes*, 51.

72. "A réplica dos comunistas ao sr. Luiz Carlos Prestes," *Diário de Noticias*, September 2, 1930, 1.

73. Getúlio Vargas manifesto, October 4, 1930; reproduced in Silva, *Revolução traída*, 430–33.

74. William Seeds, Foreign Office annual report on Brazil, 1930, written February 23, 1931, FO, London, series 371, folder A, doc. 1849/1849/6.

75. Love, *Rio Grande do Sul and Brazilian Regionalism*, 242.

76. Holanda, *Raízes do Brasil*, 171.

77. Among the vast historiography on the Revolution of 1930, a good primer is Fausto, *A revolução de 1930*.

78. "Os bravos de uma grande epopéa," *Diário Carioca*, October 25, 1930, special issue, 1.

79. "Uma photographia que já se tornou historica," *Correio da Manhã*, October 25, 1930, 3.

80. Getúlio Vargas, speech on November 3, 1930; reproduced in Vargas, *Discursos, mensagens e manifestos*, 11–20.

81. "Um revolucionário histórico," *O Jornal*, December 30, 1930, 2.

82. "Vencemos," lyrics by Henriques de Casaes, music by Octavio Dutra, November 12, 1930; published in Porto Alegre, CPDOC FC tp 1929.09.04 31.

CHAPTER 8. POLITICAL CONFLICT AND THE SPATIAL
LEGACIES OF TENENTISMO

1. For example, Costa and Goes, *Sob a metralha*; Americano, *A lição dos factos*; Assis, *Nas barrancas do Alto-Paraná*; Neto, *A Revolta de 1924*; Tavora, *Guisa de depoimento*; Cunha, *No paiz das Amazonas*; Leite, *Dias de pavor*; Soares, *Justiça*; Duarte, *Agora nos!*; Figueiredo, *1924*; Marcigaglia, *Férias de Julho*; and Noronha, *Narrando a verdade*.

2. Távora, *Guisa de depoimento*; Cabanas, *A Columna da Morte*; Ferreira, *A marcha da Columna Prestes*; Gama, *Columna Prestes*.

3. Moreira Lima, *Marchas e combates*, ix.

4. "Marchas e combates," *A Manhã*, November 15, 1928, 2.

5. For example, the book was referenced as "in preparation" in "Miguel Costa, no livro de um desaffecto," *A Manhã*, September 19, 1929, 4.

6. Jorge Amado, preface to Moreira Lima, *Marchas e combates*, 9; the remaining two citations from Morel, *A marcha da liberdade*, 20–21.

7. For example, "Na trilha da Coluna Prestes," *Manchete*, March 9, 1996, 59 and 61.
8. Moreira Lima, *Marchas e combates*, vol. 1, xv.
9. Moreira Lima, *Marchas e combates*, 139.
10. Moreira Lima, *Marchas e combates*, 239–40.
11. Moreira Lima, *Marchas e combates*, vol. 2, 362.
12. Moreira Lima, *Marchas e combates*, vol. 2, 371.
13. Dutra, *O ardil totalitário*, 154.
14. Vargas, speech on November 3, 1930; reproduced in Vargas, *Discursos, mensagens e manifestos*, 19.
15. Decree no. 19.770, passed in March 1931, "Regula a sindicalização das classes patronaes e operarias e dá outras providências," http://www.planalto.gov.br/ccivil_03/decreto/Antigos/D19770.htm (accessed October 28, 2020).
16. For example, "De pé, os mortos!," *O Jornal*, July 10, 1931, 6.
17. Rosalina Coelho Lisboa, Rio de Janeiro, July 5, 1931, CPDOC, RCL 1931.07.07.
18. Prestes, *Luiz Carlos Prestes*, 135.
19. Decree no. 19.395, November 8, 1930. The law also automatically incorporated the rebels into the army. Because Prestes refused the amnesty and stayed in exile, technically he became an army deserter; after his 1936 arrest, the Vargas regime, among other crimes, charged him with desertion stemming back to 1930.
20. Details about Prestes in Uruguay come from Prestes, *Luiz Carlos Prestes*, 13–39.
21. "Carta Aberta," March 12, 1931; reproduced in Bastos, *Prestes e a revolução social*, 220–31.
22. Unless otherwise noted, details on Prestes's time in the Soviet Union from Prestes, *Luiz Carlos Prestes*, 140–62.
23. Reis, *Luís Carlos Prestes*, 172–73.
24. Dulles, *Vargas of Brazil*, 83.
25. Clube 3 de Outubro, "Esboço do Programa Revolucionário de Reconstrução Política e Social do Brasil," February 1932; as cited in Welch, "Vargas and the Reorganization of Rural Life," 6.
26. Weinstein, *Color of Modernity*, 74.
27. Skidmore, *Politics in Brazil*, 14.
28. Neto, "O socialismo tenentista."
29. Moreira Lima, *Marchas e combates*, 1934, ix.
30. "A História da Columna Prestes," *O Radical*, April 17 to October 19, 1935.
31. "A columna Prestes," *O Radical*, August 22, 1935, 6.
32. French, *Brazilian Workers' ABC*, 62–63.
33. Reis, *Luís Carlos Prestes*, 175–76.
34. Reis, *Luís Carlos Prestes*, 175.
35. "A bandeira da columna Prestes em um comicio da A.N.L.," *Diário da Noite*, May 28, 1935, 5; "Um comicio hoje, á noite, em Nictheroy," *Diário da Noite*, June 1, 1935, 2.
36. Flyer for ANL rally, June 2, 1935. AEL, IC, no. 8, 23.
37. Bezerra, *Memórias*, 234.
38. "O manifesto do sr. Luiz Carlos Prestes," *O Jornal*, July 6, 1935, 11.

39. "O Cavalleiro da Lua," *O Jornal*, July 6, 1935, 2.

40. As cited in Morais, *Chatô*, 252.

41. Reis provides a good overview on the debates—both political at the time and historiographic since—about Prestes's manifesto (*Luís Carlos Prestes*, 177–78).

42. Skidmore, *Politics in Brazil*, 22.

43. For more on the union strikes after July, see French, *Brazilian Workers' ABC*, 64–65.

44. "Orientação Communista da A.N. Libertadora," *Diário Carioca*, September 21, 1935, 3; "Um documento esmagador, *O Jornal*, September 21, 1935, 5.

45. Bezerra, *Memórias*, 238–46.

46. For a more detailed account of the uprisings, particularly the actions of Prestes, see Prestes, *Luíz Carlos Prestes*, 173–84; and Reis, *Luís Carlos Prestes*, 181–88.

47. Camargo and Góes, *Meio século de combate*, 220–25.

48. Details in this paragraph are from Skidmore, *Politics in Brazil*, 23.

49. Reis, *Luís Carlos Prestes*, 196–97.

50. "A prisão de Luiz Carlos Prestes," *O Jornal*, June 6, 1936, 1.

51. "Depõe Harry Berger," *A Noite*, June 6, 1936, 26.

52. Plínio Salgado, *A Offensiva*, March 15, 1936, as reproduced in Salgado, *O drama de um héroi*, 16.

53. "O depoimento de Luiz Carlos Prestes," *A Noite*, September 9, 1937, 1.

54. For an insightful biography, see Morais, *Olga*.

55. Skidmore, *Politics in Brazil*, 24–29.

56. "A sentença," *A Noite*, September 9, 1937, 1. The other defendants received lower sentences, ranging from three to thirteen years.

57. Skidmore, *Politics in Brazil*, 37.

58. A recent biography of Müller suggests that although torture happened within the police ranks under Müller's command, there is no archival evidence to implicate him personally. Rose, *O homem mais perigoso do País*.

59. Welch, "Vargas and the Reorganization of Rural Life," 7.

60. For a contemporary account, see Escobar, *A marcha para o Oéste*. These interior spaces, of course, were not empty, having been occupied for thousands of years by Indigenous groups, and more recently by runaway enslaved people, migrants, and other categories of interior populations. For more on the adverse effects of this policy on Indigenous groups in particular, see Garfield, *Indigenous Struggle at the Heart of Brazil*, 28–33.

61. Maia, "Fronteiras e state-building periférico."

62. Wolfe, *Autos and Progress*, 104.

63. Craib, *Cartographic Mexico*, 9.

64. As quoted in Lenharo, *Sacralização da política*, 56.

65. Travassos, *Projeção continental do Brasil*. The book's most influential edition was republished in 1938.

66. A good overview of Travassos's geopolitical vision is Albuquerque, "80 Anos da projeção continental do Brasil."

67. Ricardo, *Marcha para o Oeste*.

68. For more, see Evans and Dutra e Silva, "Crossing the Green Line."

69. For more on Turner's frontier thesis, see Grandin, *End of the Myth*, 113–31.

70. Prestes's extensive correspondence from jail has been published as a trilogy, edited by his daughter, Anita, and his sister, Lygia: Prestes and Prestes, *Anos tormentosos*.

71. Luís Carlos Prestes, interview, *La Nación*, December 28, 1941; cited in Alexander, "Brazilian 'Tenentismo,'" 231.

72. Ramos, "Jorge Amado e o Partido Comunista."

73. For the reception and dissemination of the book, see Gaudêncio, "O Cavaleiro da Esperança."

74. Amado, *O Cavaleiro da Esperança*, 91.

75. Amado, *O Cavaleiro da Esperança*, 94.

76. Amado, *O Cavaleiro da Esperança*, 90.

77. "Como Prestes reconquistou a liberdade," *O Globo*, April 19, 1945, 1.

78. It is difficult to say precisely when the book was published, but it was already evident in newspapers by July; for example, an advertisement for the book ran in the July 29, 1945, issue of *Tribuna Popular*.

79. Moreira Lima, *A Coluna Prestes*, 5.

80. Carvalho, *Memórias*.

81. "Estilos à procura de idéias," *Jornal do Brasil*, March 10, 1954, 5.

82. "Luiz Carlos Prestes opina sobre a situação no mundo, na América e no Brasil," *O Globo*, March 15, 1945, 1.

83. Santana, "Re-imagining the Cavalier of Hope," 120.

84. For a study of Vargas's suicide note, see Rogers, "I Choose This Means.'"

CHAPTER 9. VISIONS OF THE FUTURE

1. For example, Hall, *Representation*.

2. The 1952 film was titled *Las aguas bajan turbias*, directed by and starring Hugo del Carril. Compared to the original novel, the film reimagined the workers not as yerba pickers, but as factory union workers, a reflection of Peronism's influence on the politics of the era.

3. Mateu, "Encuentros y desencuentros entre dos grandes obras."

4. Varela, *El río oscuro*, 291.

5. Rodrigues, "O tempo e o vento."

6. Souza, "A Coluna Prestes em discursos," 157.

7. Pablo Neruda, "Dura Elogia," 1940; reproduced in Maior, *Luiz Carlos Prestes na poesia*, 112–17.

8. Martins Fontes, "O camarada lendário," *Imprensa Popular*, October 29, 1954, special issue, 4.

9. Most notably, Prestes published the August Manifesto of 1950 that, along with the expropriation of latifundios, called for the use of mass violence "inevitable and necessary." For more on these shifts, see Vinhas, *O Partidão*, 129.

10. Chilcote, *Brazilian Communist Party*, 63.
11. "O XXX Aniversário da Coluna Prestes," *Nosso Povo*, 1954; included in "Coleção Luiz Carlos Prestes," Biblioteca Comunitária, University of São Carlos, Brazil.
12. "30° aniversário da columna Prestes," *O Dia*, October 29, 1954, 5.
13. "Homenagem de São Paulo ao 30° aniversário da Coluna Invicta"; included in AEL, series Miguel Costa (MC), folder 57.
14. Jacinto Passos, "Coluna"; reproduced in Amado, *Jacinta Passos, coração militante*, 163–209. Translation courtesy of Laiz Ferguson.
15. Cunha, *Rebellion in the Backlands*, 464.
16. Passos, "Coluna"; reproduced in Amado, *Jacinta Passos*, 179. Translation courtesy of Laiz Ferguson.
17. Sarzynski, "Reading the Cold War," 130.
18. Research conducted at the Biblioteca de Obras Raras Átila Almeida, Universidade Estadual da Paraíba (Campina Grande, PB); Fundação Casa Rui Barbosa (Rio de Janeiro, RJ); and cordels reproduced in Maior, *Luiz Carlos Prestes na poesia* and Amado, *O Cavaleiro da Esperança*.
19. The two cordels that discuss the violence are "Os mais violentos dias do Piancó" (2006) and "A besta fera e o disco voador: a passagem da Coluna Prestes por Crateús" (no date attributed, but, given its location in the archive, a reasonable estimate places them in the late 1990s or early 2000s). The "neutral" cordels are Adolfo Mariano's 1940 "ABC da Revolução," Adolfo Mariano, 1940 (partially reproduced in Bastos, *Prestes e a revolução social*, 183) and "Os Revoltosos no Nordeste," by Francisco das Chagas Batista, n.d., but, given that Batista died in 1930, it is reasonable to place its date in the late 1920s, after the column's exile in 1927. Reproduced in Maior, *Luiz Carlos Prestes na poesia*, 277.
20. Welch, "Camponeses," 129.
21. Sarzynski, *Revolution in the Terra do Sol*, 5.
22. Lobato, *Zé Brasil*, 21.
23. In the early 1960s, Prestes and Julião briefly collaborated on rural organization drives. The 1958 split in the PCB was triggered by the reactions among the party leadership to a conflict in Moscow, when Nikita Khrushchev delivered his "secret speech" denouncing Stalinism. Prestes sided with the Stalinist line, the fallout from which led many of the expelled members to form a new party in 1962, the Maoist-leaning Partido Comunista do Brasil (PC do B, Communist Party of Brazil). For analysis of the reclaiming of the cangaceiro, see Sarzynski, *Revolution in the Terra do Sul*, 65–111.
24. Stilde and Fernandes, *Brava gente*, 63.
25. Josealdo Rodrigues Leite, "Os mais violentos dias do Piancó: Vida e morte do Padre Aristides, 80 anos da passagem da Coluna Prestes," 2006; translation courtesy of Laiz Ferguson.
26. Miguel Costa, untitled essay, n.d. AEL, 16.
27. As cited in Brandt, "Brazilian Scene," 14–15.
28. Freitas, "Charting the Planalto Central," unpublished book chapter.
29. Welch, "Keeping Communism Down on the Farm," 36.

30. Blanc, *Before the Flood*, 217.
31. "Integra da entrevista do gen. Costa e Silva," *O Estado de São Paulo*, May 28, 1964, 7–8.
32. As quoted in Iorio, "Cordeiro de Farias."
33. For the period of distensão, see Moreira Alves, *State and Opposition in Military Brazil*, 133–53.
34. "A longa marcha dos liberais," *Jornal do Brasil*, July 7, 1974, 1.
35. "1924—um país sob o peso do passado," *Jornal do Brasil*, July 7, 1974, 2.
36. Ozorio de Almeida, *Colonization of the Amazon*, 1–29.
37. "A epopéia dos 36.000 km," *O Cruzeiro*, July 7, 1974, 76.
38. Campbell, Giovine, and Keating, *Empty Spaces*, 4.
39. Uriarte, *Desertmakers*.
40. "A chance dos revolucionários," *O Cruzeiro*, July 7, 1974, 82.
41. Green, *We Cannot Remain Silent*, 321.
42. "Prestes afirma que não há democracia sem os comunistas," *Jornal do Brasil*, October 21, 1979, 3.
43. "Carta aos comunistas"; reproduced in Reis, *Luís Carlos Prestes*, 434.
44. The 2014 children's book is *Jaguncinho* by Flávia Portela. Other examples include a hit song in 1994 by the Brazilian singer Taiguara titled "O Cavaleiro da Esperança" and a 2006 young adult historical fiction novel by the journalist Thales Guaracy, *Amor e Tempestade*.
45. Montello, *A coroa de areia*, 109.
46. "Rio enterra Prestes com honras ao líder e ao mito," *Jornal do Brasil*, March 8, 1990, 1; "Na vida do 'Cavaleiro da Esperança,' um mito brasileiro," *O Globo*, March 8, 1990, 12.
47. "Prestes encerra marcha e vira História," *Correio Braziliense*, March 8, 1990, 8.
48. "Uma rara unanimidade: o respeito nacional," *Correio Braziliense*, March 8, 1990, 9; "No último passeio, acordos políticos," *Tribuna da Imprensa*, March 9, 1990, 3.
49. "Adeus, Luiz Carlos Prestes," *Tribuna da Imprensa*, March 10, 1990, 3.

CHAPTER 10. MEMORY BATTLES AT THE TURN OF THE CENTURY

1. Craib, *Cartographic Mexico*, 48.
2. Brum, *Coluna Prestes*, 6.
3. "Viagem por um Brasil oculto," *Jornal do Brasil*, February 11, 1995, 5.
4. Prestes, "Uma estratégia da direita."
5. Meirelles, *As noites das grandes fogueiras*, 546.
6. Luís Carlos Prestes Filho, "Nas trilhas da Coluna Prestes," *Manchete*, January 13–March 30, 1996.
7. "Viva Prestes," letters to the editor, *Manchete*, April 20, 1996, 58.
8. Brum, *Coluna Prestes*, 106.
9. Prestes Filho, "Nas trilhas da Coluna Prestes," *Manchete*, March 23, 1996, 70.
10. Meirelles, *As noites das grandes fogueiras*, 570.

11. Brum, *Coluna Prestes*, 6.
12. Brum, *Coluna Prestes*, 5.
13. Prestes Filho, "Nas trilhas da Coluna Prestes," *Manchete*, December 16, 1995, 24.
14. Prestes Filho, "Nas trilhas da Coluna Prestes," *Manchete*, January 20, 1996, 34.
15. Prestes Filho, "Nas trilhas da Coluna Prestes," *Manchete*, December 16, 1995, 24.
16. Via Parque was changed to Avenida Senador Luiz Carlos Prestes. "Prestes é nome de rua no Rio," *Jornal do Brasil*, May 20, 1992, 2; and Projeto de Lei no. 1367/91, proposal made by Rio de Janeiro councilman Emir Amed, to rename the Radial Sul Plaza to the Plaza Luiz Carlos Prestes.
17. Details on the planned memorial from "Memorial de Prestes," *Jornal do Brasil*, July 10, 1992, and "Um memorial para o 'Cavaleiro'" *Tribuna da Imprensa*, July 18, 1992.
18. "Prestes," *O Globo*, July 23, 1992.
19. "Prestes," letter to the editor of *O Globo*, n.d., included in Arquivo Nacional–Rio de Janeiro, Series LC, file 0102, doc. 2, 2.
20. Luiz Carlos Prestes Filho, interview with author, September 7, 2021.
21. Reis, *Modernidades tardias no cerrado*, 123.
22. "Cavaleiro de bronze," *Manchete*, November 15, 1997, 96; "Cem anos de uma esperança," *Jornal do Brasil*, November 2, 1997, 3.
23. "Prestes no coração do Brasil, porque o Brasil foi o seu coração," *Jornal do Tocantins*, November 23, 1997.
24. "A outra face da Coluna Prestes," *O Estado de São Paulo*, April 11, 1999, 4.
25. "Face violenta da Coluna Prestes," *Diário Catarinense*, May 30, 1999.
26. Prestes, "Uma estratégia da direita."
27. "A outra face da Coluna Prestes."
28. Quotes, respectively, from "Coluna Prestes revisitada," *Zero Hora*, June 13, 1999, 23; and "A outra face da Coluna Prestes."
29. "A outra face da Coluna Prestes."
30. The archive's catalog guide for the Moreira Lima files does not offer a more specific date of donation; the entry says only that it occurred in the 1980s.
31. Anita Prestes, interview with author, November 28, 2020.
32. Anita Prestes, interview with author, November 28, 2020.
33. "Contra o 'comunismo,' vereadora do DEM propõe mudar nome do Memorial Prestes," Sul21, September 24, 2021, https://sul21.com.br/noticias/cultura/2021/09/contra-o-comunismo-vereadora-do-dem-propoe-mudar-nome-do-memorial-prestes/.
34. Luiz Carlos Prestes Filho, WhatsApp exchange with author, September 27, 2021.

EPILOGUE

1. Nora, *Realms of Memory*, 14.
2. Stavans and Ellison, *Reclaiming Travel*.

ARCHIVES

Arquivo Edgard Leuenroth, Campinas, Brazil (AEL)
Arquivo Histórico do Exército, Rio de Janeiro, Brazil (AHEx)
Arquivo Nacional, Rio de Janeiro, Brazil
Arquivo Público do Estado de Mato Grosso, Cuiabá, Brazil
Arquivo Público Mineiro, Belo Horizonte, Brazil (APM)
Biblioteca Comunitária, Universidade Federal de São Carlos, Brazil
Biblioteca de Obras Raras Átila Almeida, Universidade Estadual da Paraíba,
    Campina Grande, Brazil
Biblioteca Pública Estadual do Ceará (BECE), Fortaleza, Ceará, Brazil
British National Archives, London, United Kingdom (FO)
Centro de Pesquisa e Documentação de História Contemporânea do Brasil–
    Fundação Getúlio Vargas, Rio de Janeiro, Brazil (CPDOC-FGV)
Fundação Casa Rui Barbosa, Rio de Janeiro, Brazil
United States National Archives, College Park, USA (USNA)
University of California, Los Angeles, Special Collections

DIGITAL ARCHIVES

Hemeroteca Digital, Biblioteca Nacional. https://bndigital.bn.gov.br/hemeroteca
    -digital/
Russian State Archive of Socio-Political History (RGASPI), http://sovdoc
    .rusarchives.ru/

NEWSPAPERS

Asterisks denote newspapers accessed online through the Biblioteca Nacional's
    Hemeroteca Digital

A Capital (Cuiabá)
A Cultura
A Esquerda
A Gazeta *
A Manhã *
A Mocidade
Annaes do Parlamento Brasileiro
A Noite *
A Noticia
A Pátria
Careta
Correio Braziliense *
Correio da Manhã *
Correio do Bonfim
Correio Paulistano
Diário Carioca *
Diário da Bahia
Diário da Manhã *
Diário da Noite (Rio de Janeiro) *
Diário de Noticias *
Diário do Rio de Janeiro
Diário Nacional *
Diário Oficial (Bahia)
Diário Oficial da União
Fifó
Folha do Povo *
Gazeta de Noticias *
Imprensa Popular *
Jornal de Recife *
Jornal do Brasil *
Jornal do Tocantins
La Nación (Chile)
Manchete *
O Combate *
O Cruzeiro
O Dia *
O Estado de São Paulo *
O Estado do Paraná
O Globo
O Jornal *
O Nordeste
O Norte
O Paiz *
O Paladino

O Radical *
O Rebate
O Sertão
Revista do Globo
Tribuna da Imprensa *
Tribuna Popular *
Vanguarda
Voz Operária
Zero Hora

INTERVIEWS

Anita Prestes, November, 28, 2020. Zoom.

SECONDARY SOURCES

Albuquerque, Durval Muniz de., Jr., trans. *The Invention of the Brazilian North-east.* Durham, NC: Duke University Press, [1999] 2014.

Albuquerque, E. S. de. "80 Anos da projeção continental do Brasil, de Mário Travassos." *Revista Do Departamento De Geografia* 29 (2015): 59–78.

Alexander, Robert J. "Brazilian 'Tenentismo.'" *Hispanic American Historical Review* 36, no. 2 (1956): 229–42.

Almeida, Leandro Antonio de. "Leituras de 'Jantando um defunto.'" *Revista de História* 155, no. 2 (2006): 261–82.

Alves de Oliveira, Alex. "Representações da passagem da Coluna Prestes no sertão cearense." Master's thesis, Universidade Estadual do Ceará, 2011.

Amado, Janaína. *Jacinta Passos, coração militante: Obra completa: Poesia e prosa, biografia, fortuna crítica.* Salvador: Editora EDUFBA, 2010.

Amado, Jorge. *O Cavaleiro da Esperança.* Lisbon: Publicações Europa-América, [1942] 1979.

Amaral, Renata Xavier B. *Expedição sagarana: História e memória nas trilhas da Coluna Prestes.* Campinas: Editora Unicamp, 2009.

Americano, Jorge. *A lição dos factos.* São Paulo: Livraria Academica Saraiva, 1924.

Anderson, Benedict. *Imagined Communities: Reflections on the Origin and Spread of Nationalism.* London: Verso, 1991.

Antonacci, Maria Antonieta. *RS: As oposições e a Revolução de 1923.* Porto Alegre: Mercado Aberto, 1981.

Aranhã, Graça, *A viagem maravilhosa.* Rio de Janeiro: Livraria Garnier, 1929.

Arruda, Gilmar. *Frutos da terra: Os trabalhadores da Matte-Laranjeira.* Londrina: Editora UEL, 1997.

Artal, Andreu Mayayo, Alberto Pellegrini, and Antonio Segura Mas, eds. *Centenary of the Russian Revolution (1917–2017).* Newcastle upon Tyne: Cambridge Scholars, 2019.

Assis, Dilermando Candido de. *Nas barrancas do Alto-Paraná; fragmentos históricos da Revolução de 1924*. Rio de Janeiro: Paulo, Pongetti, 1926.

Audrin, José M. *Entre sertanejos e Indios do Norte: O bispo-missionário Dom Domingos Carrérot*. Rio de Janeiro: Edições Púgil, 1946.

Bacellar, Carlos. "São Paulo and its Interior in the Eighteenth and Nineteenth Centuries." In *The Interior: Rethinking Brazilian History from the Inside*, edited by Jacob Blanc and Frederico Freitas. Austin: University of Texas Press, under contract.

Bandeira, Renato Luís. *A Coluna Prestes na Bahia: Trilhas, combates e desafios*. Salvador: self-published, 2013.

Barthes, Roland. *Mythologies*. New York: [1957] Noonday, 1972.

Barros, Souza. *A década 20 em Pernambuco: Uma interpretação*. Rio de Janeiro: Gráfica Editora Acadêmica, 1972.

Basbaum, Leonicio. *Uma vida em seis tempos: Memórias*. São Paulo: Editora Alfa-Omega, 1978.

Bastos, Abguar. *Prestes e a revolução social*. São Paulo: Editora Hucitec, [1946] 1988.

Bell, Duncan S. A. "Mythscapes: Memory, Mythology, and National Identity." *British Journal of Sociology* 54 no. 1 (2003): 63–81.

Bezerra, Gregório. *Memórias, Vol. 1, 1900–1945*. Rio de Janeiro: Editora Civilização Brasileira, 1979.

Blake, Stanley. *The Vigorous Core of Our Nationality: Race and Regional Identity in Northeastern Brazil*. Pittsburgh, PA: University of Pittsburgh Press, 2011.

Blanc, Jacob. *Before the Flood: Itaipu and the Visibility of Rural Brazil*. Durham, NC: Duke University Press, 2019.

Blanc, Jacob, and Frederico Freitas, eds. *The Interior: Rethinking Brazilian History from the Inside*. Austin: University of Texas Press, under contract.

Borges, Vavy Pacheco. *Tenentismo e revolução brasileira*. São Paulo: Editora Brasiliense, 1992.

Brandt, Samuel T. "The Brazilian Scene: David Lowenthal, John Dos Passos, and the Importance of 'Scene' and Brazil to Geographic Inquiry." *Geographical Review* 113, no. 2 (2021): 1–20.

Breithoff, Esther. *Conflict, Heritage, and World-Making in the Chaco: War at the End of the Worlds?* London: UCL Press, 2020.

Brum, Eliane. *Coluna Prestes: O avesso da lenda*. Porto Alegre: Artes e Ofícios, 1994.

Cabanas, João. *A Columna da Morte Sob o Commando do Tenente Cabanas*. Rio de Janeiro: Almeida and Torres, 1928.

Câmara dos Deputados. *Perfis Parlamentares: Batista Lusardo*. Brasília: Câmara dos Deputados, 1983.

Camargo, Aspásia, and Walder de Góes. *Meio século de combate: Diálogo com Cordeiro de Farias*. Rio de Janeiro: Nova Fronteira, 1981.

Campbell, Courtney J. *Region Out of Place: The Brazilian Northeast and the World, 1924–1968*. Pittsburgh, PA: University of Pittsburgh Press, 2022.

Campbell, Courtney J., Allegra Giovine, and Jennifer Keating. *Empty Spaces: Perspectives on Emptiness in Modern History.* London: University of London Press, 2019.

Carneiro, Maria Luiza Tucci. "Imprensa irreverente, tipos subversivos." In *A imprensa confiscada pelo DEOPS, 1924–1954*, org. Maria Luiza Tucci Carneiro and Boris Kosso, 19–61. São Paulo: Atelié Editorial / Imprensa Oficial do Estado de São Paulo, 2003.

Carvalho, Fernando Setembrino de. *Memórias: Dados para a história do Brasil.* Rio de Janeiro: n.p., 1950.

Carvalho, Maria Meire de. "Mulheres na marcha da Coluna Prestes: Histórias que não nos contaram." *OPSIS: Catalão* 15, no. 5 (2015): 356–69.

Carvalho, Maria Meire de. "Vivendo a verdadeira vida: Vivandeira, mulheres em outras frentes de combates." PhD diss., Universidade de Brasília, 2008.

Castro, Chico. *A Coluna Prestes no Piauí: A República do Vintém.* Brasília: Senado Federal, 2007.

Celso, Afonson. *Porque me ufano do meu paiz.* Rio de Janeiro: Livraria Garnier, 1900.

Chagas, Américo. *O chefe: Horácio de Matos.* São Paulo: Bisordi, 1961.

Chasteen, John Charles. *Heroes on Horseback: A Life and Times of the Last Gaucho Caudillos.* Albuquerque: University of New Mexico Press, 1995.

Chatterjee, Partha. *Nationalist Thought and the Colonial World: A Derivative Discourse?* London: Zed Books, 1986.

Chilcote, Ronald H. *The Brazilian Communist Party: Conflict and Integration, 1922–1927.* New York: Oxford University Press, 1974.

Conde, Maite. *Foundational Films: Early Cinema and Modernity in Brazil.* Berkeley: University of California Press, 2018.

Costa, Cyro, and Eurico de Goes. *Sob a metralha: Historico da revolta em São Paulo.* São Paulo: Monteiro Lobato, 1924.

Coutinho, Manuel João, and Mateus Yuri Passos. "Voices in War Times: Tracing the Roots of Lusophone Literary Journalism." *Literary Journalism Studies* 12, no. 1 (2020): 43–63.

Craib, Raymond. *Cartographic Mexico: A History of State Fixations and Fugitive Landscapes.* Durham, NC: Duke University Press, 2004.

Cunha, Euclides da. *Rebellion in the Backlands [Os Sertões].* Chicago: University of Chicago Press, [1944] 2012.

Cunha, Hygino. *Os revolucionários do sul através dos sertões nordestinos do Brasil.* Teresina: Officinas de O Piauhy, 1926.

Cunha, Themistocles. *No paiz das Amazonas; a revolta de 23 de Julho.* Bahia: Livraria Catalina, 1925.

Della Cava, Ralph. *Miracle at Joaseiro.* New York: Columbia University Press, 1970.

DeStafney, John Watford. "The Dialectic of the Marvelous: Graça Aranha's Fictional Philosophizing." Master's thesis, University of Texas at Austin, 2011.

Diacon, Todd. "Searching for the Lost Army: Recovering the History of the Federal Army's Pursuit of the Prestes Column in Brazil, 1924–1927." *Americas* 54, no. 3 (1998): 409–36.

Diacon, Todd. *Stringing Together a Nation: Cândido Mariano da Silva Rondon and the Construction of a Modern Brazil, 1906–1930*. Durham, NC: Duke University Press, 2004.

Duarte, Paulo. *Agora nos! Crónica da revolução paulista com os perfis de alguns heroes da retaguarda*. São Paulo: n.p., 1927.

Dulles, John W. F. *Vargas of Brazil: A Political Biography*. Austin: University of Texas Press, 1967.

Duncan, Julian Smith. *Public and Private Operation of Railways in Brazil*. New York: Columbia University Press, 1932.

Dutra, Eliana de Freitas. *O ardil totalitário: Imaginário político no Brasil dos anos 30*. 2nd ed. Rio de Janeiro: Editora UFRJ, 2012.

Escobar, Ildefonso. *A marcha para o Oéste: Couto de Magalhães e Getúlio Vargas*. Rio de Janeiro: A Noite, 1941.

Evans, Sterling, and Sandro Dutra e Silva. "Crossing the Green Line: Frontier, Environment, and the Role of Bandeirantes in the Conquering of Brazilian Territory." *Fronteiras* 6, no. 1 (2017): 120–42.

Farias, Eulício Farias de. *O dia em que a Coluna passou*. Rio de Janeiro: Editora Cátadra, 1982.

Fausto, Boris. *História geral da civilização Brasileira. III: O Brasil republicano. Estrutura de poder e economia (1889–1930)*. 4th ed. São Paulo: Difel, 1985.

Fausto, Boris. *A revolução de 1930: Historiografia e historia*. São Paulo: Companhia das Letras, 1997.

Ferreira, S. Dias. *A marcha da Columna Prestes*. Pelotas: Livraria do Globo, 1928.

Figueiredo, Antonio dos Santos. *1924: Episodios da revolução de S. Paulo*. Porto: n.p., 1924.

Freitas, Frederico, "Charting the Planalto Central: The Quest for a New Capital and the Opening of the Brazilian Interior in the 1890s." In *The Interior: Rethinking Brazilian History from the Inside*, edited by Jacob Blanc and Frederico Freitas. Austin: University of Texas Press, under contract.

Foucault, Michel. "Orders of Discourse." *Social Science Information* 10, no. 2 (1971): 7–30.

Forjaz, Maria Cecília Spina. *Tenentismo e política: Tenentes e camadas médias urbanas na crise da Primeira República*. São Paulo: Paz e Terra, 1987.

French, John. *The Brazilian Workers' ABC: Class Conflict and Alliances in Modern São Paulo*. Chapel Hill: University of North Carolina Press, 1992.

Freyre, Gilberto. *Manifesto Regionalista*. 4th ed. Recife: IJNPS-MEC, 1967.

Gama, A. B. *Columna Prestes: 2 anos de revolução*. Salvador: Officinas Gráphicas de Fonseca Filho, 1928.

Garfield, Seth. *Indigenous Struggle at the Heart of Brazil: State Policy, Frontier Expansion, and the Xavante Indians 1937–1988*. Durham, NC: Duke University Press, 2001.

Garfield, Seth. *In Search of the Amazon: Brazil, the United States, and the Nature of a Region*. Durham, NC: Duke University Press, 2013.

Gaudêncio, Bruno Rafael de Albuquerque, "O Cavaleiro da Esperança: Jorge Amado, o romance biográfico e os círculos intelectuais comunistas dos anos 1940." In *Proceedings of the II Encontro Nacional de História Política*, vol. 1, 1–15. João Pessoa, 2017.

Gebara, Ademir. *História regional: Uma discussão*. Campinas: Editora UNICAMP, 1987.

Gonçalves, Leandro Pereira, and Odilon Caldeira Neto. *O fascismo em camisas verdes: Do integralismo ao neointegralismo*. Rio de Janeiro: FGV Editora, 2020.

Grandin, Greg. *The End of the Myth: From the Frontier to the Border Wall in the Mind of America*. New York: Metropolitan, 2019.

Green, James. *We Cannot Remain Silent: Opposition to the Brazilian Military Dictatorship in the United States*. Durham, NC: Duke University Press, 2010.

Guaracy, Thales. *Amor e tempestade*. Rio de Janeiro: Objetiva, 2009.

Guimarães, Bernardo. *O Índio Afonso*. Rio de Janeiro: H. Garnier, 1873.

Guimarães Rosa, João. *Grande Sertão: Veredas*. Rio de Janeiro: Nova Fronteira, [1956] 1986.

Hahner, June Edith. *Emancipating the Female Sex: The Struggle for Women's Rights in Brazil, 1850–1940*. Durham, NC: Duke University Press, 1990.

Hall, Stuart, ed. *Representation: Cultural Representations and Signifying Practices*. London: SAGE, 1997.

Haurélio, Marco, *Breve história da literatura de cordel*. São Paulo: Claridade, 2010.

Hobsbawm, Eric, and Terrence Ranger, eds. *The Invention of Tradition*. New York: Cambridge University Press, 1983.

Holanda, Sérgio Buarque de. *Raízes do Brasil*. São Paulo: Companhia das Letras, [1936] 1995.

Iorio, Gustavo Soares. "Cordeiro de Farias e a modernização do território Brasileiro por via autoritária: A gênese do Ministério do Interior (1964–1966)." *Terra Brasilis*, no. 6 (2015). Accessed May 3, 2023. https://journals.openedition .org/terrabrasilis/1638.

Jeiffets, Víctor, and Lazar Jeifets. *América Latina en la Internacional Comunista, 1919–1943*. Buenos Aires: Consejo Latinoamericano de Ciencias Sociales, 2017.

Johnson, Adriana Michéle Campos. *Sentencing Canudos: Subalternity in the Backlands of Brazil*. Pittsburgh, PA: University of Pittsburgh Press, 2010.

Klinger, Bertoldo. *Narrativas autobiográficas: 360 léguas de campanha, em 3 mezes*. Rio de Janeiro: Empresa Gráfica "O Cruzeiro" SA, 1949.

Landucci, Italo. *Cenas e episódios da Coluna Prestes*. 2nd ed. São Paulo: Editora Brasiliense, [1947] 1952.

League of Nations. *Dispute between Bolivia and Paraguay: Report of the Chaco Commission*. Geneva: League of Nations, 1934.

Leite, Aureliano. *Dias de pavor: Figuras e scenas da revolta de S. Paulo*. São Paulo: Monteiro Lobato, 1924.

Lenharo, Almir. *Sacralização da política*. Campinas: Papirus, 1986.

Levine, Robert M. *Pernambuco in the Brazilian Federation, 1889–1937*. Stanford, CA: Stanford University Press, 1978.

Levine, Robert M. *Vale of Tears: Revisiting the Canudos Massacre in Northeastern Brazil, 1893–1897*. Berkeley: University of California Press, 1995.

Lima, Edvaldo Pereira. "A Century of Nonfiction Solitude: A Survey of Brazilian Literary Journalism." In *Literary Journalism across the Globe: Journalistic Traditions and Transnational Influences*, edited by John Bak and Bill Reynolds, 162–83. Amherst: University of Massachusetts Press, 2011.

Lima, Nísia Trindade. *Um sertão chamado Brasil: Intelectuais e representação geográfica da identidade nacional*. Rio de Janeiro: IUPERJ, 1998.

Lins de Barros, Joao Alberto. *Memórias de um revolucionário*. Rio de Janeiro: Editora Civilização Brasileira, 1954.

Lobato, Monteiro. *Zé Brasil*. Rio de Janeiro: Vitória, [1947] 1950.

Love, Joseph. *The Revolt of the Whip*. Stanford, CA: Stanford University Press, 2012.

Love, Joseph. *Rio Grande do Sul and Brazilian Regionalism, 1882–1930*. Stanford, CA: Stanford University Press, 1971.

Loveman, Mara. "The Race to Progress: Census Taking and Nation Making in Brazil (1870–1920)." *Hispanic American Historical Review* 89, no. 3 (August 2009): 435–70.

Macaulay, Neill. *The Prestes Column: Revolution in Brazil*. New York: F. Watts, 1974.

Maia, João Marcelo Ehlert. "Fronteiras e state-building periférico: O caso da Fundação Brasil Central." *Vária História* 35, no. 69 (2019): 895–919.

Maior, Laércio Souto. *Luiz Carlos Prestes na poesia: Contendo estudo da saga prestista, antologia poética, iconografia e cartas*. Curitiba: Travessa dos Editores, 2006.

Mancing, Howard. "The Picaresque Novel: A Protean Form." *College Literature* 6, no. 3 (1979): 182–204.

Marcigaglia, Luiz. *Férias de Julho: Aspectos da revolução militar de 1924 ao redor do Lyceu Salesiano de S. Paulo*. São Paulo: Escolas Profissionaes do Lyceu Coração de Jesus, 1924.

Martins, José de Souza. *O poder do atraso: Ensaios de sociologia da história lenta*. São Paulo: Hucitec, 1994.

Mateu, Christina. "Encuentros y desencuentros entre dos grandes obras: El río Oscuroy Las aguas bajan turbias (Argentina, 1943/1952)." *Nuevo Mundo Mundos Nuevos* (July 11, 2012): n11. https://journals.openedition.org/nuevomundo/63148#tocfrom1n1.

Mawe, John. *Travels in the Interior of Brazil, Particularly in the Gold and Diamond Districts of That Country*. London: Longman, Hurst, Reed, Orme, and Brown, 1812.

McCann, Frank. *Soliders of the Pátria: A History of the Brazilian Army, 1889–1936*. Stanford, CA: Stanford University Press, 2004.

Meirelles, Domingos. *As noites das grandes fogueiras: Uma história da Coluna Prestes*. Rio de Janeiro: Record, 2008.

Meinig, D. W. "The Continuous Shaping of America: A Prospectus for Geographers and Historians." *American Historical Review* 83, no. 5 (1978): 1186–205.

Menezes, Adalberto Guimarães. *Coluna Prestes: Desmascarando um embuste.* Belo Horizonte: 3i Editora, 2018.

Metcalf, Alida C. *Family and Frontier in Colonial Brazil: Santana de Parnaíba, 1580–1822.* Austin: University of Texas Press, 2005.

Minas, João de. *Jantando um defunto: A mais horripilante e verdadeira descripção dos crimes da revolução.* Rio de Janeiro: Editora Alpha, 1929.

Monteiro, John Manuel. *Negros da terra: Índios e bandeirantes nas origens de São Paulo.* São Paulo: Companhia das Letras, 1994.

Montello, Josué. *A coroa de areia.* Rio de Janeiro: José Lympio, 1979.

Moraes, Dênis de, and Francisco Viana. *Prestes: Lutas e autocríticas.* Rio de Janeiro: Mauad, [1982] 1996.

Moraes, Walfrido. *Jagunços e heróis: A civilização do diamante nas lavras da Bahia.* Brasilia: Câmara dos Deputados, 1984.

Morais, Fernando. *Chatô.* Sebo Digital, 1994.

Morais, Fernando. *Olga.* São Paulo: Alfa-Omega, 1985.

Moreira Alves, Maria Helena. *State and Opposition in Military Brazil.* Austin: University of Texas Press, 1988.

Moreira Lima, Lourenço. *A Coluna Prestes: Marchas e combates.* 2nd ed. São Paulo: Editora Brasiliense, 1945.

Moreira Lima, Lourenço. *Marchas e combates: A Columna invicta e a Revolução de Outubro.* Pelotas: Livraria do Globo, 1931.

Moreira Lima, Lourenço. *Marchas e combates: A Columna invicta e a Revolução de Outubro.* São Paulo: Legião Civica 5 de Julho, 1934.

Morel, Edmar. *A marcha da liberdade: A vida do reporter da Coluna Prestes.* Petrópolis: Vozes, 1987.

Mozzer, Marcelo Luiz Cesar. "Presença da Coluna Prestes nas veredas do Grande sertão." *Contexto,* no. 15 (2009): 246–59.

Neto, Adalberto Coutinho de Araújo. "O socialismo tenentista: Trajetória, experiência e propostas de políticas públicas e econômicas dos socialistas tenentistas no Estado de São Paulo na década de 1930." PhD diss., Universidade de São Paulo, 2012.

Neto, Elias Chaves. *A Revolta de 1924.* São Paulo: O. de Almeida Filho, 1924.

Neto, Lira. *Padre Cícero: Poder, fé e guerra no sertão.* São Paulo: Companhia das Letras, 2009.

Nielson, Rex P. "The Unmappable Sertão." *Portuguese Studies* 30, no. 1 (2014): 5–20.

Nonato, Raimundo. *Os revoltosos em Sao Miguel: 1926.* Rio de Janeiro: Sebo Vermelho, 1966.

Nora, Pierre. *Realms of Memory: The Construction of the French Past. 1: Conflicts and Divisions.* Edited by Lawrence D. Kritzman. Translated by Arthur Goldhammer. New York: Columbia University Press, 1996.

Noronha, Abilio de. *Narrando a verdade.* São Paulo: Monteiro Lobato, 1924.

Nunes, Zita. *Cannibal Democracy: Race and Representation in the Literature of the Americas.* Minneapolis: University of Minnesota Press, 2008.

Oliveira, Ricardo de. "Euclides da Cunha, Os Sertões e a invenção de um Brasil profundo." *Revista Brasileira de História* 22 (2002): 511–37.

Otaviano, Manuel. *A Coluna Prestes na Paraíba: Os Mártires de Piancó*. João Pessoa: Acauã, 1979.

Ozorio de Almeida, Anna Luiza. *The Colonization of the Amazon*. Austin: University of Texas Press, 1992.

Pang, Eul-Soo. *Coronelismo e oligarquias, 1889–1934: A Bahia na primeira República Brasileira, 1889–1934*. Rio de Janeiro: Civilização Brasileira, 1979.

Pang, Eul-Soo. "The Revolt of the Bahian Coronéis and the Federal Intervention of 1920." *Luso-Brazilian Review* 8, no. 2 (1971): 3–25.

Pereira, Astrojildo. *Formacão do PCB: (Partido Comunista Brasileiro): 1922–1928*. Lisboa: Prelo, 1976.

Pereira, Maria Carreiro Chaves, and Erlando Silva Rêses. "Mulheres e violência no cangaço: Breve história de vida de Maria Bonita e Dadá." *Linguagem: Estudos e Pesquisas* 25, no. 1 (2021): 61–70.

Pessar, Patricia R. *From Fanatics to Folk: Brazilian Millenarianism and Popular Culture*. Durham, NC: Duke University Press, 2004.

Pratt, Mary Louise *Imperial Eyes: Travel Writing and Transculturalation*. 2nd ed. New York: Routledge, [1992] 2008.

Prestes, Anita. *A Coluna Prestes*. São Paulo: Brasiliense, 1990.

Prestes, Anita. *Luiz Carlos Prestes: Um comunista brasileiro*. São Paulo: Boitempo Editorial, 2015.

Prestes, Anita. "Uma estratégia da direita: Acabar com os 'mitos' da esquerda." *Cultura Vozes* 91, no. 4 (May 19, 2010): 51–62.

Prestes, Anita. *Viver é tomar partido: Memórias*. São Paulo: Boitempo, 2019.

Prestes, Anita, and Lygia Prestes. *Anos tormentosos: Luiz Carlos Prestes, correspondência da prisão, 1936–1945*. São Paulo: Paz e Terra, 2000.

Prestes, Luís Carlos. "Como cheguei ao comunismo." *Problema da Paz e do Socialismo*, no. 1 (1973): 1–13.

Ramos, Tânia Regina Oliveira, "Jorge Amado e o Partido Comunista: Papéis avulsos (1941–1942)." *Anuário de Literatura* 19, no. 1 (2014), 111–20.

Reis, Daniel Aarão. *Luís Carlos Prestes: Um revolucionário entre dois mundos*. São Paulo: Companhia das Letras, 2014.

Reis, Patrícia Orfila Barros dos. *Modernidades tardias no cerrado: Arquitetura e urbanismo na formação de Palmas*. Florianópolis: Insular, 2018.

Ricardo, Cassiano. *Marcha para o Oeste: A influência da bandeira na formação social e política do Brasil [March to the West: The influence of the Bandeiras in the social and political formation of Brazil]*. Rio de Janeiro: Livraria José Olympio, 1940.

Rodrigues, Mara Cristina de Matos. "O tempo e o vento: Lietratura, história e desmitificação." *Métis: História y Cultura* 5, no. 9 (2006): 289–312.

Rogers, Thomas D. "'I Choose This Means to Be with You Always': Getúlio Vargas's *Carta Testemunha*." In *Vargas and Brazil: New Perspectives*, edited by Jens R. Hentschke, 227–55. New York: Palgrave Macmillan, 2006.

Rose, R. S. *O homem mais perigoso do País: Biografia de Filinto Müller, o temido chefe da polícia da ditadura Vargas*. Rio de Janeiro: Editora Civilização Brasileira, 2017.

Russell-Wood, A. J. R. "New Directions in Bandeirismo Studies in Colonial Brazil." *Americas* 61, no. 3 (2005): 353–71.

Roth, Cassia. *A Miscarriage of Justice: Women's Reproductive Lives and the Law in Early Twentieth-Century Brazil*. Stanford, CA: Stanford University Press, 2020.

Sá, Lucia. "The Romantic Sertões." In *The Interior: Rethinking Brazilian History from the Inside*, edited by Jacob Blanc and Frederico Freitas. Austin: University of Texas Press, under contract.

Saint-Hilaire, Auguste de. *Voyages dans les provinces de Rio de Janeiro et de Minas Gerais*. Vol. 1 of *Voyages dans l'intérieur du Brésil*. Paris: Grimbert et Doerz, 1830.

Salgado, Plínio. *O drama de um herói*. São Paulo: Casa de Plínio Salgado, 1990.

Salvador, Vicente do. *História do Brasil, 1500–1627*. 5th ed. São Paulo: Edições Melhoramentos, [1627] 1965.

Santana, Marco Aurélio. "Re-imagining the Cavalier of Hope: The Brazilian Communist Party and the Images of Luiz Carlos Prestes." *Twentieth Century Communism*, no. 1 (2009): 110–27.

Sarzynski, Sarah. "Reading the Cold War from the Margins: Literatura de Cordel as a Historical Prism." *Americas* 75, no. 1 (2019): 127–53.

Sarzynski, Sarah. *Revolution in the Terra do Sol: The Cold War in Brazil*. Stanford, CA: Stanford University Press, 2018.

Schneider, Ann M. *Amnesty in Brazil: Recompense after Repression, 1895–2010*. Pittsburgh, PA: University of Pittsburgh Press, 2021.

Schumaher, Schuma, and Érico Vital Brazil. *Dicionário mulheres do Brasil: De 1500 até a atualidade*. Rio de Janeiro: Jorge Zahar, 2001.

Schwartz, Joan M., and Terry Cook. "Archives, Records, and Power: The Making of Modern Memory." *Archival Science* 2, no. 1 (2002): 1–19.

Silva, Hélio. *1926, a grande marcha*. Rio de Janeiro: Civilização Brasileira, [1965] 1972.

Silva, Hélio. *1930: A revolução traída*. Rio de Janeiro: Civilização Brasileira, [1966] 1972.

Silva, João. *Farrapos de nossa história: Marcha da Coluna Prestes do Extremo Sul às cabeceiras do Rio Apa*. São Luiz Gonzaga: São Nicolau, 1959.

Silva, Marco Antonio. *A república em migalhas: História regional e local*. São Paulo: Marco Zero, 1990.

Skidmore, Thomas E. *Politics in Brazil, 1930–1964: An Experiment in Democracy*. New York: Oxford University Press, [1969] 1973.

Soares, José Carlos de Macedo. *Justiça: A revolta militar em São Paulo*. São Paulo: Livraria Universal, 1924.

Souza, José Augusto de. "A Coluna Prestes em discursos." Master's thesis, Universidade Federal do Paraná, 2005.

Sodré, Nelson Werneck. *A Coluna Prestes: Análise e depoimentos*. Rio de Janeiro: Civilização Brasileira, 1978.

Sodré, Nelson Werneck. *História da imprensa no Brasil*. Civilização Brasileira, [1966] 2011.

Stavans, Ilan, and Joshua Ellison. *Reclaiming Travel*. Durham, NC: Duke University Press, 2015.

Stoler, Ann Laura. *Along the Archival Grain: Epistemic Anxieties and Colonial Common Sense*. Princeton, NJ: Princeton University Press, 2009.

Stilde, João Pedro, and Bernardo Mançano Fernandes. *Brava gente: A trajetória do MST e a luta pela terra no Brasil*. 2nd ed. São Paulo: Expressão Popular, 2012.

Tabajara de Oliveira, Nelson. *1924: A revolução de Isidoro*, São Paulo: Nacional, 1956.

Taunay, Affonso d'Escragnolle. *História geral das bandeiras paulistas*. São Paulo: Heitor L. Canton, 1930.

Távora, Juarez. *Á guisa de depoimento sobre a revolução Brasileira de 1924*. São Paulo: Ed. O Combate, 1927.

Távora, Juarez. *Uma vida e muitas lutas: Memórias*. Vol. 1—*Da planície à borda do altiplano*. Rio de Janeiro: José Olympio Editora, 1973.

Teixeira, Ana Lúcia. "A letra e o mito: Contribuições de Pau Brasil para a consagração bandeirante nos anos de 1920." *Revista Brasileira de Ciências Sociais* 29 no. 86 (2014): 29–44.

Teixeira, Eduardo Perez. "A Coluna Prestes vista por *O Paíz* e o *Correio da Manha* (1924–1927)." Master's thesis, Universidade de Brasília, 2018.

Thomas, David, Simon Fowler, and Valerie Johnson. *The Silence of the Archive*. London: Facet Publishing, 2017.

Torres, João Camillo de Oliveira. *O positivismo no Brasil*. Rio de Janeiro: Editora Vozes, 1957.

Travassos, Mário. *Projeção continental do Brasil*. São Paulo: Companhia Editora Nacional, 1935.

Turner, Frederick Jackson. *The Significance of the Frontier in American History*. Alexandria, VA: Alexander Street, [1893] 2008.

Uriarte, Javier. *The Desertmakers: Travel, War, and the State in Latin America*. New York: Routledge, 2020.

Varela, Alfredo. *El río oscuro*. Buenos Aires: Hyspamerica, [1943] 1985.

Vargas, Getúlio. *Discursos, mensagens e manifestos, 1930–1934*. Rio de Janeiro: Imprensa Nacional, 1935.

Veríssimo, Érico. *O arquipélago*. São Paulo: Companhia das Letras, [1962] 2004.

Vinhas, Moisés. *O Partidão: A luta por um partido de massas, 1922–1974*. São Paulo: Hucitec, 1982.

Viotti da Costa, Emília. *The Brazilian Empire: Myths and Histories*. Chicago: University of Chicago Press, 1985.

Waack, William. *Camaradas: Nos arquivos de Moscou, a história secreta da revolução brasileira de 1935*. São Paulo: Companhia das Letras, 2004.

Wainberg, Jacques Alkalai. *Império de palavras*. Porto Alegre: EDIPUCRS, 2003.

Weinstein, Barbara. *The Color of Modernity: São Paulo and the Making of Race and Nation in Brazil*. Durham, NC: Duke University Press, 2015.

Welch, Cliff. "Camponeses: Brazil's Peasant Movement in Historical Perspective (1946–2004)." *Latin American Perspectives* 36, no. 4 (2009): 126–55.

Welch, Cliff. "Keeping Communism Down on the Farm: The Brazilian Rural Labor Movement during the Cold War." *Latin American Perspectives* 33, no. 3 (2006): 28–50.

Welch, Cliff. *The Seed Was Planted: The São Paulo Roots of Brazil's Rural Labor Movement, 1924–1964*. University Park: Penn State University Press, 1999.

Welch, Cliff. "Vargas and the Reorganization of Rural Life in Brazil (1930–1945)." *Revista Brasileira de História* 36, no. 71 (January–April 2016): 1–25.

Wiesebron, Marianne L. "Historiografia do cangaço e estado atual da pesquisa sobre banditismo em nível nacional (Brasil) e internacional." *Ciência y Trópico* 24 (1996): 417–44.

Williams, Daryle. *Culture Wars in Brazil: The First Vargas Regime, 1930–1945*. Durham, NC: Duke University Press, 2001.

Winichakul, Thongchai. *Siam Mapped: A History of the Geo-body of a Nation*. Honolulu: University of Hawai'i Press, 1997.

Wirth, John D. *Minas Gerais in the Brazilian Federation, 1889–1937*. Stanford, CA: Stanford University Press, 1977.

Wolfe, Joel. *Autos and Progress: The Brazilian Search for Modernity*. New York: Oxford University Press, 2010.

Woodard, James P. *A Place in Politics: São Paulo, Brazil, from Seigneurial Republicanism to Regionalist Revolt*. Durham, NC: Duke University Press, 2009.

Page numbers followed by *f* refer to figures, and those followed by *m* refer to maps.

Prestes, Leocádia, 135, 175, 188–89, 191

Prestes, Luís Carlos: attitude toward violence, 270n9; Brazilian Communist Party (PCB) and, 145, 151, 182, 211; commemoration of, 185, 191–95, 208, 224–29, 232, 236, 241; communist politics of, 183–84, 271n23; cult of personality of, 135–37; cultural production regarding, 147–48, 186, 187–88, 189–91, 200–202; death of, 213–14, 214f, 215, 216; discipline by, 65, 119; documents of, 231; exile in Argentina, 207–8; exile in Bolivia, 129, 132, 136f; formation of the Prestes Column and, 1, 31, 36–37, 47–48, 115–16; gaúcho uprising (1924) and, 33–34, 35, 46; Getúlio Vargas and, 161–62, 164–65, 182–84; imprisonment under Vargas regime, 174, 175–76, 178–79, 180; interior communities and, 95–96; leadership of, 41, 60, 62, 64, 66, 74, 89; legacy of, 19, 180–81, 205–6, 220; military strategy of, 67, 79, 82, 104, 121; mythology of, 38, 123, 130–31, 142, 177; newspaper coverage of, 88, 125, 146, 173f; photos of, 83f, 243; political evolution of, 143–44, 150–51, 152–53, 165–66, 172–73; political strategy of, 71–72, 73; political vision of, 33, 80, 122; rebel violence and, 108–9, 230; refusal of amnesty by, 268n19; return to Brazil, 167, 169, 170; support for, 139–40; symbolism of, 149, 171, 204; "war of movement" strategy of, 43, 97–98, 101. See also Knight of Hope

Prestes Column, the: archival documentation regarding, 16; naming of, 114–16; origins of, 31; photo of leadership of, 72f; political platform of, 68, 81–82; prevailing narrative of, 6; route of, 9, 40m, 54m, 71m; scale of, 128–29; scholarship regarding, 14–15, 18, 233

Prestes Column highway, 239, 240

Prestes, Luiz Carlos, Jr., 217, 221–24, 221f, 226, 232, 236, 240, 242

print media. See newspapers

Projeção continental do Brasil, 177

propaganda, 56, 93, 106

provisions, 55–56, 62–63, 78, 94, 99–100, 102, 108, 121–22

public opinion, 83, 118, 120, 139, 185, 199–200

Quadros, Jânio, 205

quilombos, 3, 255n35

race, 9–10, 27, 28–29, 60–61, 110–11, 159

racial democracy, 10

racialization: of the Bolivian backlands, 132–33; the environment and, 106; of the interior, 9–10, 28–29, 143; of interior communities, 108; mythologization and, 79, 87; nationalism and, 158; newspapers and, 110–11; violence and, 95; women and, 58–59

Raízes do Brasil, 157

Ramada, battle at, 239f

Ramada, Rio Grande do Sul, 237–38, 239f

rape: committed against rebel women, 104; committed by rebels, 8, 57, 78, 93, 108, 119; documentation of, 230–31; omission of, 17, 65–66

Realengo Military Academy, 33

rebels: accusations of banditry against, 79–80, 83; archival sources regarding, 105; commemorations of, 208–9; in cordel literature, 186; *coronéis* and, 62, 91–93; discipline among, 65, 119, 230–31; exile to Bolivia of, 118, 127–29, 132–33, 134f, 144–45; images of, 28f, 128f, 141f; Indigenous peoples and, 75; interior communities and, 8–9, 50, 51–52, 76–77; narrative of liberation by, 6–7, 53, 61, 73, 84, 95, 106; as picaresque protagonists, 116; political trajectory of, 2; public opinion regarding, 107; racialization of, 110–11, 111f; sexualization of, 98. See also paulista rebels; violence, of rebels

Recife, Pernambuco, 80, 81, 82, 89, 100

recruitment, 70, 74–75, 94, 95

Rede Ferroviária Centro-Oeste, 206

regionalism, 15–16

Reis, Daniel Aarão, 144, 170

Reis, Patricia Orfila Barros dos, 226, 241, 243

reportagens, 45

Revista do Globo, 156

Revolt of the Whip, 27

www.ingramcontent.com/pod-product-compliance
Lightning Source LLC
Chambersburg PA
CBHW020829270326
41928CB00006B/461